Slow Cities

Conquering our Speed Addiction for Health and Sustainability

Slow Cities

Conquering our Speed Addiction for Health and Sustainability

Paul Tranter

Rodney Tolley

ELSEVIER

Elsevier
Radarweg 29, PO Box 211, 1000 AE Amsterdam, Netherlands
The Boulevard, Langford Lane, Kidlington, Oxford OX5 1GB, United Kingdom
50 Hampshire Street, 5th Floor, Cambridge, MA 02139, United States

Library of Congress Cataloging-in-Publication Data
A catalog record for this book is available from the Library of Congress

British Library Cataloguing-in-Publication Data
A catalogue record for this book is available from the British Library

ISBN: 978-0-12-815316-1

For information on all Elsevier publications
visit our website at https://www.elsevier.com/books-and-journals

Publisher: Joe Hayton
Acquisitions Editor: Brian Romer
Editorial Project Manager: Aleksandra Packowska
Production Project Manager: Punithavathy Govindaradjane
Designer: Vicky Pearson

Typeset by Thomson Digital

This book is
dedicated to our children,
Ben, Joel, Nick,
Rebecca and Sarah,
who have the opportunity
to help create a healthier,
slower world.

Contents

Foreword

Readers of 'Slow Cities' are embarking on a fascinating journey of discovery and adventure. You will, of course, learn a lot of information you had not known about before. But equally important, you will be delving into a realm of new and exciting ideas, insights and perspectives. This book goes far beyond any existing book about transport, travel behaviour or cities. It reveals how the speed of urban transport systems affects individual and societal health, well-being and happiness and the sustainability of our environments and economies. The wisdom imparted by this book is superior to a mere statistical analysis of transport, as it is deeper, more meaningful, more comprehensive, more thought-provoking and even mind-expanding. Indeed, for me, reading this book was also a kind of spiritual experience. Many of the ideas discussed get at the very essence and meaning of life, both for individuals and society.

In the spirit of this book, I read it slowly, no more than one chapter per day, savouring every paragraph and every new insight. I hope you will do the same. This is not a book to skim through quickly, as there are many ideas that require slowing down, pausing and thinking about before proceeding further. Indeed, by slowly reading this book, by paying full attention to the ideas being presented, and giving myself time to consider them, I found myself delving into the here and now, the present moment and pondering each new idea and its relevance to my own life, my community and the transport research I conduct.

As the authors Paul Tranter and Rodney Tolley brilliantly explain, there are many reasons to slow down our cities: improved traffic safety; more daily physical activity from walking and cycling; less noise, air pollution, energy consumption and greenhouse gas emissions; time savings from not having to earn the money necessary to buy, own, operate, park, and maintain a car; and economic benefits for individuals, businesses and cities. Perhaps most important, however, slowing down our cities would make them more liveable, more interesting, more people-oriented. Our cities would become places that would foster natural social interactions, especially in residential neighbourhoods, where streets could function as extended front yards, places where children could safely play, adults could comfortably linger to talk with their neighbours and everyone could enjoy the safe public spaces that neighbourhood streets should be.

The authors convincingly document the many reasons to slow down our cities, but equally important, they examine in practical detail the many ways to do this, and that's the really good news in this book. Even in the notoriously car-oriented metropolitan areas of the United States, roughly a quarter of all trips are a mile or shorter, and a third of trips are two miles or less. Those distances are feasible for most people to cover by walking or cycling. Key prerequisites, however, are expanding, improving, and connecting walking and cycling facilities, while at the same time slowing down cars and reducing car traffic in residential neighbourhoods. Those measures are not just a theoretical possibility.

Most European cities have already extensively traffic-calmed their residential neighbourhood streets via 30 km/h speed limits and a range of physical road modifications such as speed bumps and humps, narrowed streets, raised intersections and artificial dead-ends for cars with convenient pass-throughs for pedestrians and cyclists. Traffic calming started in the Netherlands in the 1980s and has now become the norm in Europe. Policies necessary to slow down cities take time but have great promise and eventually produce the intended results. Most of Western Europe's largest and most important cities have implemented an integrated package of pro-walk, pro-bike, pro-public transport and car-restrictive policies over the past three decades, resulting in impressive reductions in the car's share of total daily trips.

Even in New York City, facilities for walking and cycling have been vastly improved over the past two decades, while the general speed limit for all roads except highways has been reduced to 25 mph (40 km/h). Similar to Western European cities, New York now has a car mode share of daily trips of only 32 per cent compared to 62 per cent of trips by some combination of walking, cycling and public transport. In short, the city slowing measures examined in this book are not only possible, but have actually been implemented with great success, even in car-oriented countries like the US. That should give readers confidence that the wide range of city-slowing measures they will read about in this book are achievable, realistic and happening already in cities around the world.

Slow cities start on the individual level with you, the reader. Each person can start slowing down right now and enjoy the benefits of doing so. Try setting aside some time each day for a walk or a short bike ride, even if just around the neighbourhood. Consider setting aside some time once a week for a longer walk or bike ride on a nearby off-road greenway or trail as well as 15 or 30 minutes a day as quiet time, when you do nothing at all. Try being fully present in the moment and appreciating who you are and where you are, and the gift of life itself. Place a limit on your use of mobile phones, computers and other digital devices. Perhaps you could set aside certain times of the day or days of the week (e.g. the weekend) when you de-connect from the internet and enjoy the freedom from the cyber-noise we are subjected to almost constantly when we use such digital devices. As reported in this life-changing book, more and more people are already slowing down, and they report feelings of deep peace, contentment and true joy. It is certainly worth a try, and it costs nothing. Indeed, it will save you both time and money.

And now settle comfortably into an easy chair to slowly savour the new information, insights, wisdom and perspectives offered by this irresistible book.

John Pucher
Professor Emeritus, Rutgers University

Preface

The principal reasons for writing this book were our increasing concerns about the collective societal addiction to speed in the city and the conviction that conquering this addiction and developing 'slow cities' would provide tremendous benefits for health. One of the original ideas for our book title was 'Slowing the city: inoculating against the hurry virus', which given the 2020 global coronavirus crisis, would have been prescient. COVID-19 arrived as we were editing the final proofs, and consequently we have included an 'Afterword' that explains the critical relevance of 'slow cities' in a world affected by a pandemic.

We begin the book by outlining how speed came to have such a dominant impact on the way we plan, design and operate cities, even though the supposed advantages of speed are largely illusory when they are carefully assessed: indeed, instead of providing advantages, speed steals our time, our money and our health. In Part 2 of the book, we explain how a focus on speed in city transport undermines human, environmental and economic health, whilst Part 3 outlines the policies, strategies, tactics and behavioural interventions that can be employed to create healthier 'slow cities'. By 'slowing the city' we mean both reducing the speed of existing motorised transport as well as encouraging a mode shift to the supposedly 'slower' modes of walking, cycling and public transport.

The ideas in this book come from multiple sources of material and every effort has been made to acknowledge them precisely. However, sins of omission and commission are inevitable, so we offer sincere apologies to anyone that we have embarrassed by failing to acknowledge them or by doing so inaccurately.

We are enormously grateful to many people for their support and encouragement during the long gestation period of this book. We are especially indebted to Mario Alves, Matt Burke, Mark Cramer, Tim Gill, Annie Matan and Ray Vaughan for their careful and invaluable reviews of early drafts of the book and to family members, Kathy McGoldrick, Sarah Roach and Nick Tranter for their perceptive observations. Generous friends and colleagues, including Paul Fraser, Peter Lumb, Murray May, Warwick Pattinson and Ben Rossiter, provided helpful feedback and ideas, and John Pucher crafted a thoughtful foreword to the book. Others too numerous to mention here (many name-checked in Section 1.6) have provided valued inspiration, stimulation and encouragement over many years of correspondence and enjoyable creative encounters. We would also like to thank the thousands of students and conference delegates, who over the last few decades have been open to new ways of thinking about sustainable transport and have helped to shape the ideas that eventually crystallised into this book.

We also acknowledge the support and encouragement from staff at Elsevier: Ali Afzal-Khan, Ashwathi Aravindakshan, Punitha Govindaradjane, Aleksandra Packowska, Brian Romer and Sabrina Webber.

We are thankful for the generosity of several people and organisations who provided photographs for us to use in the book: Andrea Cook, Mark Cramer, Sybil Derrible, Elliot Fishman, Hackney Council (London), Matthias Heskamp, London Play, The National Association of City Transportation Officials (NACTO), Juliana O'Rourke, Nick Tranter, Suzanne Tranter and the Western Sydney Regional Organisation of Councils. Particular thanks are due to Carlos Felipe Pardo, for his insights into the problems created by speed and the value of slow cities, his enthusiastic support for the ideas in this book and for his photographs of slow mobility from around the world. We also greatly appreciate the support of Jeff Kenworthy, Todd Litman, Rob Methorst, Claudio Olivares Medina, Jeff Steinacker and the Victorian Department of Environment, Land, Water and Planning, for help in creating or sourcing diagrams, and Rodney Garnett for his editing of the front cover image.

Last, but by no means least, we would like to express our sincere gratitude to Kathy McGoldrick and Suzanne Tranter for their patience, support and understanding, as well as their gentle reminders to us to 'slow down'.

Paul Tranter
Canberra, Australia

Rodney Tolley
Ellicottville, New York
April 2020

Part I

Speed

Chapter 1

Introduction: changing cultures of speed

'There is more to life than simply increasing its speed'.

Mahatma Gandhi

Abstract

This chapter outlines the widespread acceptance of speed as a positive aspect of urban transport during the 20th century, along with a growing recognition in recent decades that speed may not provide the advantages that have long been assumed. In 21st century urban planning, no longer are higher speeds always seen as the main objective. New goals are increasingly recognised as being more important: accessibility, liveability, economic vitality, child-friendliness, sustainability and health. The concept of 'health' in this book applies to human health, as well as economic health and environmental health. We explain how all of these types of health can be enhanced using the simple strategy of slowing city transport. A brief history of increases in transport speed is followed by a discussion of the evolution of the culture of speed in modern societies, to a level that can be compared to an addiction. An important aspect of the culture of speed is the story of motordom, the grouping of automobile clubs, car dealers and car manufacturers that began in the United States in the 1920s. A concerted campaign by motordom comprehensively dismissed the public's negative views on speed. We then outline how, from the 1980s onwards, new thinking began to emerge about motorised city transport, in which the value of slowing it down became more widely discussed. We provide examples of various slow movements that have emerged since the 1980s. While some citizens and policy-makers may question (or even ridicule) the idea of slow movements, we reflect on where the 'fast movement' has taken us over the last 100 years. This chapter concludes with a preview of the chapters and parts of the book.

1.1 Introduction: a faster route to health

From the mid-1920s, after the motor car became the dominant transport mode in many cities, few people questioned whether speed was good or bad. They simply assumed that faster was always going to be better. City transport policy in the 20th century became concerned mainly with faster roads and increased parking for growing numbers of cars. The (supposedly) 'slower' modes of walking and cycling were denigrated as 'old fashioned' and were ignored in policy-making.

Slow Cities. http://dx.doi.org/10.1016/B978-0-12-815316-1.00001-0

Over the last few decades, there has been a discernible change in city transport policy. Many policy-makers, planners, politicians and members of the public are reassessing the way they think about the role of cities. Their focus is moving away from the singular goal of promoting speed to new goals: accessibility, liveability, economic vitality, child-friendliness, sustainability and health. Increasing numbers of decision-makers are embracing the concept of 'slow cities' (see Box 1.1), which can help achieve all these goals.

BOX 1.1 What do we mean by 'slow cities'?

In a society that values speed, 'slow' can be associated with pejorative synonyms such as lethargic, idle, indolent and slothful. We are not advocating cities that have these characteristics. Instead, we are thinking of the meaning of 'slow' in the sense of 'lower speed', which elicits synonyms such as 'calm', 'careful', 'cautious', 'deliberate', 'leisurely', 'relaxed', 'measured', 'peaceful' and 'unhurried'. Our belief is that a city described in that way would have vibrant communities, living healthy and sustainable lives. Slowness in this sense is associated with several characteristics that are highly appreciated by people seeking a better quality of life, as explained in books such as *In Praise of Slow* (Honoré, 2004).

As this chapter outlines, 'slow cities' reflect the outcomes of two synergistic strategies: reducing the speed of motorised travel on the one hand and encouraging much greater use of walking, cycling and public transport on the other hand. The first of these strategies has already been implemented in large areas of many cities throughout the world, for example by implementing 30 km/h (or 20 mph) zones. Reducing motorised traffic speed supports efforts to increase walking, cycling and public transport in multiple ways, not least being the impact that lower speeds have on making streets safer and more pleasant for vulnerable road users. Six images that serve to illustrate these strategies are as follows (see Fig. 1.1):

a. Nelson, New Zealand: A residential area reduces traffic speeds through lower posted speed limits and re-design as a shared space, with visual and physical encouragement provided by a raised entrance gateway.

b. Stoke-on-Trent, United Kingdom: Unsigned traffic calming using a raised speed table at a junction, with psychological calming elements provided by different coloured and textured surfaces.

c. Bowden, Adelaide, Australia: A model of a planned low-speed development, incorporating healthy land-use elements designed to deter fast car movement and support active travel, such as high densities, short blocks, cut throughs for people on foot and bicycle, shade and easy access to recreation and play space.

d. Cambridge, MA, United States: Reducing traffic speeds by lowering the number and width of travel lanes, and re-allocating space in the roadway corridor in order to widen footways and add protected 'Copenhagen style' bicycle lanes.

e. Calle Madero, Mexico City: Many cities have slowed central areas by pedestrianising streets. The results are usually popular and economically successful, but their reconstruction frequently encounters opposition, especially from traders mistakenly fearing loss of business. After a long fight, Calle Madero was pedestrianised in 2010 and is now the second most economically successful street in Latin America. However, it should be stressed that a pedestrianised CBD does not make a 'slow city' if speeds are not reduced across the whole urban area.

f. Houten, The Netherlands: While many places have some elements of city slowing, few have pursued them as systematically as this small city near Utrecht. Here, all of the approaches deployed in images A–E have been used (and many others besides) in an attempt to harness their synergistic benefits. This image shows the result that can be achieved when land-use planning, traffic management, infrastructure provision and promotion of the connections between public transport, cycling and walking are combined into a comprehensive policy.

FIGURE 1.1 Images referred to in Box 1.1: (A) Nelson, New Zealand; (B) Stoke-on-Trent, United Kingdom; (C) Bowden, Adelaide, Australia; (D) Cambridge, MA, United States; (E) Calle Madero, Mexico City; and (F) Houten, The Netherlands. *(Credit: All photos by Rodney Tolley)*

Many of the arguments about slowing city transport systems already have strong appeal with audiences that have experienced the benefits of slowing down or living in areas where walking and cycling are safe, enjoyable and convenient. However, while there are encouraging signs of a change in transport planning paradigms, the culture of speed is still dominant amongst many city transport experts and policy-makers, including transport planners and modellers. Transport plans continue to use performance metrics where faster motor car speeds are the fundamental criterion for success (Proffitt, Bartholomew, Ewing, & Miller, 2019). The professional training of many transport planners and modellers has often involved learning how to use decision-making tools that supposedly demonstrate the benefits of speed, for example in saving time. These benefits are often illusory.

This book is written for an audience of planners, policy-makers, students and concerned citizens who have an interest in creating healthier places to live, work and play. We focus on the relationship between speed and health. Almost everyone sees an improvement in health as a worthwhile goal. Lists of the most important things that people value in their lives and their communities invariably include the topic of health. Any strategy that aims to promote health is likely to be widely welcomed by policy-makers, planners, traffic engineers, politicians and members of the public. A similar welcome is likely for any strategy to reduce a harmful addiction: in Chapter 2, we make the case that cities are currently addicted to speed and in Chapters 8–10 we outline approaches to conquering that addiction.

In our analysis of health, we adopt a broad view that recognises the separate but related dimensions of human, economic and environmental health. When thinking about health, people likely immediately consider the health of individuals: their physical, mental and emotional health. In addition, we also examine environmental health, which is critical for the other dimensions of health. If we examine environmental health at the global scale (e.g. ecological diversity and climate health), then we can include 'planetary health' in our analyses (Capon, Talley, & Horton, 2018). Finally, we consider economic health, which can be applied at different spatial scales: households (e.g. lower transport bills), neighbourhoods and businesses (e.g. higher retail turnover) and cities (e.g. lower infrastructure costs). We explain how all three types of health can be improved through the simple strategy of 'slowing the city'. Throughout the book, when we use the term 'slowing the city' we are referring to the slowing of transport, rather than the slowing of the pace of life or any other type of slowing.

'Slowing city transport' as discussed here refers to slowing the speed of motorised vehicles, as well as encouraging the use of (supposedly) slower active modes: walking, cycling and public transport. These active modes are also the healthiest and most sustainable modes (Giles-Corti et al., 2016; Pucher & Buehler, 2017; Pucher, Buehler, Bassett, & Dannenberg, 2010). We include public transport as an 'active' mode because it usually involves some walking or cycling before or after a bus, tram or train trip. We recognise that not all public transport is 'slow'. In many cities trains have higher speeds than cars, and the global average ratio of metro/suburban rail speed to road speed has been steadily increasing over the last few decades (Newman, Kenworthy, & Glazebrook, 2013).

While we see public transport as an important part of 'slow cities', our main focus, particularly in Part 3 of the book (on strategies), is on walking and cycling. As we explain in more detail in Chapter 9, if the walking environment can be made more attractive, this increases the acceptable walking distances to public transport, and this can have a significant positive impact on its viability. We are also aware of the other side of this particular coin—that walking and cycling levels at trip ends can be increased by interventions in infrastructure, equipment and operational procedures that make public transport more attractive and increase patronage. However, discussion of how this might be achieved would necessarily be lengthy and would divert attention away from the core issues in 'slow cities'. We support the approach of encouraging a mode shift to public transport, as this will help to promote the use of the 'slower' modes of walking and cycling: walking and cycling trips become more important as motorised transport becomes less orientated to cars.

Using examples from North, Central and South America, Europe, Asia, Africa and Australasia, the book explores the paradox that slowing city transport can save time and simultaneously improve the health of individuals, communities, cities, economies and the planet. 'Slow cities' may, indeed, provide a faster route to health and sustainability.

Our focus is on transport 'within' the city. We acknowledge that trends in inter-city transport, especially via air travel, also have concerning impacts on health and sustainability. However, rather than attempting a discussion of the slowing of aviation, we see this as the subject for a whole new book. The issues surrounding air travel are complex and sometimes different from the transport issues we examine in this book. For example, while demand management is now an accepted practice in city transport planning (see Chapter 10), it has as yet seen little application in aviation (Ryerson & Woodburn, 2014). Air travel also involves infrastructure that is often outside the control of urban and regional planners. Yet, the concept of slowing transport can, and we believe should, be applied to aviation. Not only could there be a slowing in the speeds of long-distance travel (e.g. through increased use of airships for cargo) there could also be a reduction in the total volume of air travel. A slowing of long-distance travel would be a more effective strategy for sustainability than efficiency improvements and new fuels in air travel (Higham & Hopkins, 2016). Other researchers have begun to address the importance of reducing the amount of air travel, and have shown how this could be achieved, even in Australia, a nation heavily dependent on aviation for international travel (Young, Markham, Higham, & Jenkins, 2017). However, our focus is on the importance of slowing city transport and how this can be achieved.

Our emphasis on transport does not mean that we discount the value of other types of slowing. Indeed, we would argue that many aspects of our economy and society would likely benefit from slowing. In Section 1.8, we outline various slow movements that recognise the benefits of a slower approach to life, including slow parenting, slow sex, slow medicine, slow gardening, the Cittaslow slow cities movement, slow travel and slow thinking. Aspects of many of these are relevant to our discussion of slowing city transport.

1.2 Holistic perspectives on slowing city transport

For over two centuries there have been significant increases in the speed and distance of travel, both within cities and between them. There is a growing awareness that faster transport increases the level of energy use and carbon in travel. There is much less awareness that increasing speed often has perverse impacts on the goal of making cities more efficient. As we explain in Chapter 4, instead of reducing the time devoted to transport, increasing speed can actually increase it. One of the reasons for this is that as the speed of transport increases, the costs associated with transport also increase: 'speed is not free' (Thackara, 2006, p. 31). When we factor in the time required to earn the money to pay for these costs, we can calculate the 'effective speed' of any mode of transport (Tranter, 2012). Effective speed considers not only the time spent moving, but also the total time costs of transport. Because the costs of faster modes (e.g. motor cars) are significantly higher than the costs of walking, cycling and public transport, the effective speeds of the 'faster' modes can be very low. The concept of effective speed helps individuals, policy-makers and planners to think differently about speed and the ways that transport systems are designed in cities.

Understanding the value of slowing the city requires a holistic assessment of the impact of speed on the daily behaviours and life choices of individuals and households, as well as the interaction between transport and land use, particularly the density of housing and the distribution of shops, services and schools. The impact of policies designed to increase the speed of travel within cities is much greater than transport planners sometimes appreciate. Speed has impacts on health, happiness, social interaction, wealth, property values, pollution, liveability and environmental quality. If our aim is to improve cities in all these dimensions, one important strategy may provide much of the solution: 'slowing the city', which includes slowing the speed of cars.

It is important to realise that any gains for health provided by slowing the speed of cars may be undermined by countervailing forces. Even if the speeds of motor cars can be significantly reduced, a continuing rise in the use of motor vehicles, encouraged by continued road building, would have multiple negative health impacts, which have been the subject of a wide body of research starting in the 1970s and growing in momentum (Davis, 1994). These negative impacts include road deaths, pollution, inactivity, obesity, noise, community severance and the health impacts of the climate crisis. Consequently, an important part of the strategy of 'slowing the city' is the transfer of mobility from private motor vehicles to 'slower' modes, particularly walking and cycling, and also public transport.

It is important not to conflate two connected ideas, those of challenging car-centric planning and this book's specific focus on reducing the 'speed' of motorised traffic in the city. Clearly, speed reduction requires tackling car-centric planning, but it needs much more besides. We use a health lens to focus on the benefits of a simultaneous application of the twin strategies of slowing the speed of existing vehicle traffic, and changing the modal split towards the 'slower' modes. Though both head towards the same goal, they are synergistic because it is not possible to significantly increase the use of the 'slower' modes unless existing and planned motorised traffic is also slowed.

The strategy of slowing the city will likely be increasingly relevant in future cities. Medium- and long-term changes in transport are likely to involve technologies such as on-demand autonomous electric vehicles, perhaps owned by fleets rather than individuals. There is a danger that an excessive focus on technological solutions to transport problems may simply promote the assumption that high-speed motor car transport should be the goal, 'if only cars can be designed and operated differently'. We explain why a widespread introduction of new technologies should be used in ways that slow the city, rather than speed it up. We also explain how many of the problems created by high-speed city transport are unlikely to be solved by technology.

As well as looking to the future, it is important to understand the history of speed and slowness in society and in cities. There are two strands to consider here. First, we discuss the adoption of new technologies that led to increased speed of travel. Second, and perhaps more importantly, we examine the evolution of the culture of speed in modern societies.

1.3 Increasing speed: technological advances throughout history

As civilisation developed, humans invented new means to increase their speed of travel, including animal-powered devices (from around 5,000 BCE), and the wheel, or more precisely, the wheel and axle system, invented around 3,500 BCE. While there were advances in the speed of travel over water, on land the speed of travel using wheeled carts and animal power varied little until the introduction of the railway. Though some wheeled carts could travel faster than others (e.g. chariots and stagecoaches designed for speed), the difference between the speed of human travel (walking) and animal assisted transport in cities was only a few km/h.

Until the early 1800s, the speed of travel (and hence the distance travelled) was limited to walking (5 km/h) and horse riding (10 km/h) speeds. The arrival of the steam-powered railway in the 19th century, along with the use of fossil fuels, changed the speed of travel in an unprecedented way. Railways increased speeds to over 40 km/h, and, as they developed, to over 100, then over 300 km/h with high-speed rail. While railways were initially used for travel between cities, they came into use for urban travel soon after. The world's first underground rail line opened in London in 1863. The railway transformed the speed of travel, yet the technology that did the most to promote speed in city transport was the motor car.

From an early stage in motor car development, car design and marketing focussed on speed. 'Of the multitude of development paths, the royal road to the speed machine was taken: large high performance vehicles, and later, small, spirited cars became the models of automotive design' (Sachs, 1992, p. 132). Car racing not only made speed exciting for the masses, but it also decisively influenced the early and ongoing technical development of the motor car. However, as Sachs explains, this path did not have to be the one chosen. Indeed, early in the development of the motor car industry, Karl Benz (in contrast to Daimler Mercedes) attempted to choose another path, one that focussed on safety and comfort rather than speed. His attempts proved futile, and he (along with other opponents of the trend towards speed) could not stem the growing expectations for higher top speeds and quick acceleration as the main priorities in motor car design.

The expectations of motorists about the speeds that their cars should be able to achieve continue to climb. Since their introduction into city transport, the speed potential of cars has increased enormously thanks to the application of technology, often developed in the motor racing industry. Car manufacturers continue to market their cars on the basis of speeds that could never be legally achieved in most nations, now over 200 mph (320 km/h) for some cars. Such high performance from modern cars is unnecessary for practical purposes. In most nations, there are few roads where speeds over 70 mph (or 110 km/h) are legal. Modern cars 'with their powerful engines, their streamlined bodies, and their high-speed suspension systems … are as suited to the delays of city traffic as a chainsaw is for cutting butter' (Sachs, 1992, p. 124).

As explained in Chapters 2 and 3, the quest for higher motorised speed began to dominate transport planning in cities from the mid-1920s. It was assumed that increasing speed in urban transport would produce positive results for cities, the economy and society. However, the efficacy of speed in city transport should not be taken as given (Taylor, 2014).

A central concept in transport analysis is that time should be saved. This was seen as particularly important for any transport task. Transport planning orthodoxy saw travel as a 'derived' demand—derived from the need to participate in activities at an alternative location, meaning that time spent travelling was 'wasted time'. There is often no acknowledgement that time spent travelling may have an intrinsic utility (Mokhtarian & Salomon, 2001), or, as we demonstrate in Chapter 4, that time is rarely saved by increasing speed (Metz, 2008). The belief in time saving was a central component of transport decision-making from the 1920s. The appraisal of transport proposals continues to be dominated by the (usually unjustified) expectation of user benefits resulting from travel time savings, which promotes continuing pressure to increase the speed of traffic (Banister, 2011).

The distances travelled by city dwellers increased as transport became faster. Until around 1860, when walking was the main mode of transport with travel speeds of around 5 km/h (3 mph), daily travel distances were less than 1 km (0.6 miles) per person per day. There was a slow increase in speed until the 1960s, when daily travel distance had increased to 10 km (6 miles). However, by 2000, this had increased to 50 km (or about 30 miles) (Banister, 2011). Banister asked where this exponential increase might end, or whether there are no limits to the distance that could be travelled.

1.4 The growing cultural obsession with speed and time saving

Cities have not always been associated with speed. Medieval cities in Europe were seen as much as 'places of rest, worship and periodic festivity as they were of motion' (Latham & McCormack, 2008). With the arrival of industrialism and capitalism, cities became a more powerful force in economy and society, and they also became places where speed was seen as advantageous. One of the first markers of this speed was the rapid expansion of railways across North America and Europe in the 19th century. Railways were instrumental in changing the way people thought about the relation between society and space, and also about the value and meaning of time. The advent of the railway initiated a concern with timetabling, which led to urban social and working life being increasingly scheduled (Urry, 2007). Railways made the notion of 'clock time' the dominant way of understanding time (Fig. 1.2). This meant precise timing of work and leisure activities, and the view of time as a resource that could be saved, consumed, organised and monitored, and used as 'productively' as possible. This required the clear separation of personal time from work time and 'a regimentation of the movement of goods and people, both of which were deemed dependent on centralised transport planning and the engineering of circulation (hence Le Corbusier's metaphor of city as machine)' (Hubbard & Lilley, 2004, p. 276). The concern with timetabling increased with every new transport system that was adopted (Urry, 2007).

Before the advent of the railways, speed was not of great concern to people. With railways came the idea that speed is valuable, and that faster trains are better than slower trains. Once this was accepted, it was also assumed that new railways (or any transport infrastructure) were justified if trips became faster, and that higher speeds aided economic competitiveness. This was also based on the assumptions that time spent travelling is wasted time and that faster speeds would save time.

At first the speed of the railway was alien to people, generating fears (of derailment or collisions), yet this speed soon became a societal reality that was taken

FIGURE 1.2 Clock time is still important for railways. Swiss train station clocks are models of simplicity and elegance admired the world over: clock and meeting point at Zurich main station, Switzerland. *(Credit: Joachim Kohler Bremen—Own work, CC BY-SA 4.0, https://commons.wikimedia.org/w/index.php?curid=60254453)*

for granted. The growth of the railway and its transformative power on societal attitudes to speed and progress was intertwined with the growth of capitalism. By 1900 speed was equated with modernism and vitalism (Trentmann, 2016). Ironically, the 20th century, which began with promises of time saving and abundant leisure, ended with anxieties about time pressure and a time famine, leading to a global disquiet about the speed of life (Trentmann, 2016) and the growth of the various 'slow movements' outlined in Section 1.8.

Modern Western cities evolved in a cultural context of a growing acceptance of speed and a culture of individualism. Because the dominant cultural belief about speed was that 'faster is always better', when people attempted to use speed to their own advantage, there seemed little choice for others but to continue to increase their own speed. This culture of speed affected all aspects of the city, not least our transport systems.

How did our society develop an obsession with speed and time saving in motorised city transport? Was it an expression of mass preference? Was it the product of a natural Darwinian evolution by technological selection, where the fitter motor car drove slower modes to extinction (Norton, 2007)? Was it because humans are hard-wired to want to go faster and faster? Or are there other explanations of how our cities, particularly in modern Western societies, came to be dominated by the quest to increase the speed of travel? As we explain later, the likely explanation is that our attitudes to speed in the city were manipulated by powerful interest groups.

Western societies have developed a mythology that speed is always good. Yet as this book demonstrates, speed does not give us the advantages that many people (including planners and policy-makers) believe it does. In many cases, increasing speed achieves exactly the opposite of what we expect. Instead of saving time, it can consume our time. More importantly, it can undermine our health—the health of individuals, communities, cities, nations, economies and the planet. To understand why the mythology of the benefits of speed has become so dominant, it is important to examine the little-known history of the growth in the acceptance of speed in city transport, dating from early in the 20th century.

This culture of speed did not simply develop due to some inexorable logic. Speed in city transport did not come to be dominant because it has innate advantages for cities or for society. Modern Western cities could have evolved differently, without an obsessive focus on speed in motor cars. The story that a 'love affair with the automobile' was the reason the motor car became so dominant so quickly was also part of the mythology of the acceptance of speed. The 'love affair' metaphor first appeared during a 1961 episode of a television programme titled the DuPont Show of the Week (sponsored by DuPont, which then owned almost a quarter share of General Motors). The love affair story was a carefully crafted strategy developed as a response to protests about road construction in New York. It helped to promote two ideas that became embedded in American society for decades afterwards: that Americans are bound to cars by something more than need, and that anyone who challenges that bond must, by inference, be anti-American (Badger, 2015). It was not a concept that evolved naturally in the 1920s when cars began to occupy city streets in large numbers.

Even after the invention of motor cars and their appearance on city streets, it seemed at first as though civic leaders and the general public were going to prevent the development of a culture of speed in the city. Different social values were dominant in cities in the first two decades of the 20th century. The freedom and safety of people walking and cycling, and the acceptance of the street as a public space, were regarded as more important than speed.

In the United States, as motor cars increased in number, so too did the number of people killed by cars. Between 1920 and 1928, road crash fatalities doubled to 26,000 per year. The initial response to this slaughter was an outcry:

from the public, in cartoons, editorials and letters to the editor in major newspapers, from chambers of commerce, and from police, judges and juries. Common law defended the right of people on foot to use the street: under the common law tradition, which both the United States and Canada inherited, the street is a public space for all, to be used by any persons as long as they do not endanger or obstruct other users. Speed limits averaging 10 mph (16 km/h) in US cities in 1910 were set. These would have limited cars to pre-motor age speeds, thus negating a perceived advantage of motor cars in cities (Norton, 2007).

Even the Model T Ford was originally envisaged as a farmer's car to connect the farmer to the market; its popularity was expected to wane as the United States urbanised (Flink, 1990). In cities, people already had more efficient, inexpensive and convenient forms of transport in walking, cycling, streetcars and commuter railways. While people in rural areas welcomed the speed provided by the motor car, 'Cars met with particular hostility in densely settled cities, where people living in crowded tenements used the streets for games, socialising, buying and selling, and other activities that had nothing to do with transportation. In this environment, the appearance of an automobile represented a threat to an accustomed way of life, while at the same time posed a very real safety hazard' (Volti, 2004, p. 18).

The powerful individuals who made up the motoring lobby at first tried to accommodate the dominant view of the street as a place for people, encouraging drivers to slow down so that the public did not resent the motor car. But they soon learned that they needed to respond to the negative public and official views about speed in the city, which would undermine the sale of cars and the expansion of the motoring industry. They recognised that speed could be marketed as an advantage that the motor car had over other modes, and it was speed that made cars most attractive to potential buyers. But how could the motoring lobby respond to the outcry against speed?

The most important step in the response to the outcry against speed was to become an organised and united group. Once the groups supporting the motor car became organised, any opposition to speed was effectively and forcibly suppressed. Even though speed was a critical factor undermining road safety, the economic forces of the automobile industry comprehensively dismissed the public's negative views on speed. This was 'one of the biggest shifts in the status quo that ever occurred in history … and it affords some lessons that can be useful' (Norton, 2015).

1.5 Motordom—constructing a culture of speed in the city

The organisations that eventually became known as motordom in the United States—automobile clubs, car dealers and car manufacturers—were not a coherent group at first. At the Hoover National Conference on Street and Highway Safety in 1924 (convened by Herbert Hoover, the then US Secretary of Commerce and later the US President) they met, became organised and developed a common strategy (Norton, 2011). They coined the term 'motordom' to describe the grouping of these organisations. As well as becoming an organised group, motordom recognised a common enemy—those who opposed speed in the city. To be successful, motordom needed funding, which they realised could be had from the motorists themselves through gasoline taxes. These taxes were astutely seen by motordom as a way of paying for roads and streets to solve traffic problems. By 1925, all but four US states were taxing gasoline.

Understanding the history of motordom, and how it changed the mental infrastructure of speed in the city, is critical to the arguments here. This book shows how proponents of slowing city transport can learn lessons from the tactics and successes of motordom. The arguments in this section are based largely on the research of Peter Norton, author of *Fighting Traffic: The Dawn of the Motor Age in the American City* (2011). Similar accounts of the rapid acceptance of speed in the city can be found in Canada and other nations (Davies, 1987). Almost 100 years ago, motordom used creative ways to challenge dominant notions about speed in the city. If motordom could so comprehensively transform how society envisioned speed in the city, it is also possible that in the 21st century, a culture of slowing city transport can occupy centre stage in the minds of the public, planners, other professionals and politicians.

The challenge for motordom in the 1920s was immense. The speed provided by motor cars in city streets was creating unprecedented carnage in road crashes (mainly cars killing people walking). Children aged 5–14 were the most vulnerable group: there was a 94 per cent increase in child fatalities for the period from 1913–17 to 1918–22 (Zelizer, 1994, p. 38). Instead of motor cars, the public wanted improvements in public transport (McShane, 1995). Public hostility towards speeding cars in cities was strong and growing in the early 1920s. A major threat to the future of the motor car as a faster mode of transport was the many calls for technological solutions to the dangers caused by speed, including equipping cars with governors (devices designed to limit car speeds).

This speed governor idea emerged as a real proposal in Cincinnati in 1923, when over 40,000 people (more than 10 per cent of the city population) signed petitions for the introduction of a local ordinance requiring that cars be fitted with speed governors limiting them to 25 mph. If this was passed into law, it would reinforce the view that motorists' speed was the road safety problem. It would also deprive motorists of what they regarded as their chief advantage over other modes. 'Terrified city automotive interests organized a massive and well-funded "vote no" campaign, and on election day, voters crushed the plan' (Norton, 2007, p. 339). This was one of many inventive, intensive and ultimately successful public relations campaigns conducted by motordom.

As motor cars grew in number, another problem emerged: congestion was becoming an issue, not just for the motorists, but also for all other street users, including the streetcars. Motordom had to devise an alternative narrative to explain why motor cars and speed were not the problem, and the real causes of all the problems were to be found elsewhere.

As Peter Norton explains, motordom had to change the stories about the past, and the visions we have of the future. The dominant story we now have of the early 20th century is that we constructed cities for cars because that was what we preferred. In this dominant story, which many people now believe, the approval of the speed provided by cars was due to mass preference; it was a product of natural evolution. In reality, people then were saying that they preferred to have streets for people, not motor cars. The vision for the future promoted by motordom involved notions of modern, new, faster cities and a 'new age'—'the motor age'. Peter Norton explains that when you are told 'it's a new age', that implies that the ways we have been doing things are now open to question and outdated (Snyder, 2014).

There were several components to this re-imagining of the problems of city transport in the era of speed. The whole mind-set about the city, the street and speed needed to be changed. First, the blame had to be shifted from cars to 'reckless drivers', and more importantly to 'reckless pedestrians'. The blame (for both road crashes and for congestion) had to be shifted from cars themselves to the space provided for cars. To support these shifts in blame, licensing of drivers, road safety 'education' (particularly for children) and the application of civil engineering to complement traffic engineering were all employed.

Another strategy employed by motordom was to reframe the way in which road fatalities were reported and recorded. In the early days of the motor car, accounts of traffic deaths were framed by opponents of speed in terms of outrage against automobile killings as individual tragedies, such as the death of a child, or by comparing the total number of automobile deaths annually with deaths in the first World War. The response of motordom to this perspective on road crash fatalities was to promote a new way to frame the problem—in fatalities per mile travelled (Vardi, 2014). This would show that as car travel increased, the fatality 'rate' lowered, suggesting that the road safety policies adopted by authorities were having a positive effect.

Motordom also realised that cars could not compete with other modes for the efficient use of space, or the efficient movement of large numbers of people. Motordom did, however, make a claim that cars provided freedom (e.g. from fixed tracks and from timetables), offering the prized convenience of seamless door-to-door movement. In combination with strategies to switch attention from cars as the cause of congestion and road crashes, motordom reframed the conception of motor cars as the mobility mode that promoted 'freedom', a concept with considerable nationalistic appeal in the United States.

The idea that motor cars were killing people was a particular problem that had to be dealt with. One strategy was to move the blame to people, and away from the motor car. (This strategy has parallels with the gun lobby argument that 'guns don't kill people, people do'.) By focussing on people as drivers, motordom lobbied governments to introduce licensing for motor car drivers. They developed a story that reckless drivers were the problem, not cars themselves. By arguing that these reckless drivers would lose their driving licences, keeping them off the streets, this deflected blame from the motor car itself.

FIGURE 1.3 People crossing the street at Fifth Avenue and Broadway, New York, 1910, before the concept of jaywalking was invented. *(Reproduced from Library of Congress, Prints & Photographs Division [LC-DIG-ggbain-15110], https://www.loc.gov/pictures/item/2014695084/)*

Motordom was also successful in separating recklessness from speed. In addition to reckless drivers, slow street users (people walking or cycling) could be cast as reckless. Hence, motordom developed the idea of training children to stay off the streets and to insist that people walking take responsibility for their own safety (i.e. to not be reckless).

To keep people on foot 'in their place', cities across the United States began to regulate where people walking could cross streets. Before the 1920s, people could (and did) cross streets wherever they chose (see Fig. 1.3). During the 1920s, crosswalk lines began to be marked on streets. These were routinely ignored at first. When the motoring lobby promoted the idea that people walking on streets without regard for cars were reckless and irresponsible, they also invented a new term to ridicule such people—'jaywalker'. In the United States in the early 20th century the term 'jay' was a term of derision and condescension, referring to a rural 'hick', regarded by city dwellers as stupid or naïve. Such persons were unaccustomed to the pace of a city.

Laws to guide the behaviours of people walking were introduced in cities throughout the United States: jaywalking was legally outlawed in Los Angeles and Washington by 1923, with signs indicating 'Jay Walking Prohibited by Order—Police Department'. The Automobile Club of Southern California paid for the signs in Los Angeles. Anti-jaywalking laws became the norm in US cities by the 1930s. However, rather than legal rules and signs, ridicule was seen as a more powerful socialising force to restrict the behaviour of people on foot.

The term 'jaywalking' gained acceptance during the 1920s and a massive shaming campaign prompted a radical shift in public attitudes to the use of streets, largely due to a concerted effort from members of motordom. Motordom employed the volunteer services of the Boy Scout movement, all over North America, to hand out cards to jaywalkers (similar to propaganda pamphlets). These cards had messages such as 'For safety's sake, cross here, not here, not this way … Quit Jay Walking'. In some cities clowns were used to depict jaywalkers as ignorant rural folk, behaving in pre-motor age ways. Newspaper coverage of road crashes changed from most articles blaming the driver in 1923, to most blaming jaywalkers in 1924 (Norton, 2011). Ridiculing jaywalking became a prominent feature of traffic safety campaigns in North America. However, in the early 20th century the strategy of restricting walking behaviour in cities was also becoming commonplace in other countries, as Box 1.2 illustrates.

An important component of gaining public (and legal) acceptance of speed in cities was the way in which the meaning of 'traffic safety' was formulated by motordom. The National Automobile Chamber of Commerce formed a 'Safety Committee', which soon became the leading national institution for traffic safety. The committee argued that to achieve high levels of safety required the education of all road users, but particularly pedestrians, and even more so, child pedestrians. The American Automobile Association (AAA) and local automobile clubs took over all school safety patrols in the 1920s. Under this new control, these school safety patrols operated in a way that supported the freedom of motorists to speed, rather than promoting a child-friendly urban environment, where children's independent mobility is valued. Previously, when the patrols were run by local safety councils, cars would be stopped so that children could cross safely. In contrast, the AAA-operated patrols made the children wait till there were no cars before they were allowed to cross the street.

BOX 1.2 The Little Golden Calf.

As the following quote from a satirical Russian novel indicates, cities in Russia also imposed grave restrictions on the freedom to walk, dating from at least the 1930s.

'When everything was finished, when our beloved planet assumed a fairly habitable look, motorists appeared on the scene. One should note that the automobile itself was invented by pedestrians but somehow the motorists forgot that very quickly. Gentle and intelligent pedestrians began to get squashed. Streets, created by pedestrians, were usurped by motorists. Roadways were widened to double their former size, sidewalks narrowed to tape width and pedestrians began to cower in fear against the walls of buildings. In a large city, pedestrians lead a life of martyrdom. A kind of transportation ghetto was set up for them. They are allowed to cross streets only at intersections, that is precisely in those places where traffic is heaviest and where the hair by which a pedestrian's life usually hangs is most easily broken … and if, on occasion, a pedestrian succeeds in escaping from under the silver nose of an automobile, he is promptly fined for violating the traffic law' (Ilf & Petrov, 1932).

FIGURE 1.4 One False Move: a UK road safety poster from the 1980s. *(Credit: Public Domain, https://commons.wikimedia.org/w/index.php?curid=7376762)*

The AAA became the leader in the provision of school safety information. It supplied this free to public schools, and the materials instructed children on how to stay safe on the streets. For example, the AAA provided a colouring-in book for children, with one picture of traffic in a street having the words 'The street is for autos' constantly visible in the middle of the page as children coloured in. Safety campaigns promoted streets as places for cars in other nations as well, and these continued well into the 20th century. A famous road 'safety' campaign in the United Kingdom depicted a pair of child's feet on the kerb, with the slogan 'One false move and you're dead' (see Fig. 1.4). As Brent Toderian tweeted, 'Fear-based messages like this were about reducing pedestrian deaths by reducing pedestrians' (Toderian, 2014). But it was not just in schools that motordom influenced road safety. The car maker Studebaker provided a grant of $10,000 to Harvard University in 1926, to set up the Albert Russel Erskine Bureau for Street Traffic Research, which remained active through much of the 1930s.

The Erskine Bureau quickly developed a reputation as the only recognised organisation for traffic expertise. Its graduates were highly regarded, particularly in comparison to engineers from other institutions. With the help of the Erskine Bureau, motordom could argue with authority that the way to promote road safety and relieve congestion was to re-engineer and re-build cites, rather than limiting the speed of cars and promoting the inherently safer modes of walking, cycling and public transport.

The next challenge for the motoring lobby was dealing with the negative perception that cars created congestion on city streets. Motordom set about convincing the world that congestion was not due to an excess of cars, but was caused by a lack of space in the streets. This lack of space could be remedied by civil engineers, working with traffic engineers. The civil engineering argument was also applied to traffic safety. Road crashes were attributed to 'dangerous failures in road design—failures which highway engineers, with enough money, could fix' (Norton, 2011, p. 246). As one road safety 'expert' argued, cars had the '"right to speed" and the real problem is that "the road is too slow for the car"' (Norton, 2011, p. 247). Ultimately, highway engineers devised a solution that would not only allow, but also require, high speeds: building 'safe urban highways' that were designed for speeds of 50 or 60 mph (Norton, 2011, p. 235).

Streets were redefined as places where people walking, particularly children, did not belong. This redefinition is now an accepted practice in cities around the world. 'Safety education' enabled the reduction of child injuries without slowing cars. Motordom proved to be so powerful in spreading its arguments that it even 'used persistent casualties to argue for more accommodation' in cities for cars (Norton, 2011, p. 174). Motordom continued to push the view that cars were not the main road safety problem in the 1930s. In 1936, the AAA announced a comprehensive education program for greater safety on streets. In a published textbook on driver safety it explained 'most of the people killed by motorcars are pedestrians, and the majority of these fatal accidents have been caused by the pedestrian himself' (Norton, 2011, p. 247). Putting the blame onto jaywalkers continued, as indicated by a poster from 1937, seen in Fig. 1.5).

An important concept in understanding the impact of motordom is the exercise of power. Motordom exercised enormous power: through the gasoline taxes used for road construction; through direct political links with the Commerce Department; and through its well-funded education and propaganda campaigns. Drivers were part of this exercise of power to promote speed 'every time they travelled at speed in streets, resorting to the horn instead of the brake to proceed' (Norton, 2011, p. 259). This power, exercised by motorists, forced people walking and cycling from the street.

FIGURE 1.5 Don't Jay Walk poster from 1937. *(Credit: Isadore Posoff, Wikipedia Commons, Public Domain, https://commons.wikimedia.org/w/index.php?curid=6646707)*

While motordom was exercising this power to promote speed, opponents to the invasion of streets by speeding motor cars attempted to organise themselves, for example into local safety councils. Yet, the opponents lacked the funding of motordom and were unable to develop their own institutions. The electric street railways, which provided effective public transport in the early 20th century, also attempted to prevent the dominance of the culture of speed. However, motor car interest groups, notably General Motors, contributed to the demise of these street railways by acquiring them, and then scrapping them and substituting them with buses (Norton, 2011). By the late 1920s street railways were not able to provide effective opposition to the speed of the motor car.

The story of motordom provides important lessons for this book. It shows how the supporters of speed used tactics involving a construction of the meaning of transport that changed the culture of cities in ways that undermined health in multiple and powerful ways. The story of motordom also illustrates the importance, in any attempt to change culture, of adopting a 'coherent rhetorical stance' (Norton, 2011, p. 258). Using a careful analysis of the research on city transport and health, this book shows how to respond to the rhetoric and mythology created by motordom. While some of the ideas behind the advantages of slower city transport date back to the 19th century (and even earlier), a groundswell of ideas about transport that recognised the value of the (supposedly) slow modes began to develop from the 1970s. In the following section, we outline some key ideas that are part of this groundswell, and show how this new thinking is becoming mainstream.

1.6 New thinking, new thinkers

The motordom perspective started to come under increasing pressure from the 1970s onwards, in a global context of emerging challenges to established social, economic and environmental conditions. These include, but are by no means limited to: the oil crises beginning in the 1970s; the rise of the sustainability movement (Brundtland, 1987); awareness of pollution in general (and of air pollution and global heating in particular); and growing assertiveness of inner-city populations over injustices such as segregation, 'urban renewal' and freeway construction and blight.

As far as city transport issues are concerned, at first this pressure came from a small number of thinkers and activists, and this grew into a new wave of thinking that is now becoming much more accepted. This progression is now advanced and widespread: indeed, much of this book is illustrated with examples of policy, strategy, tactics and community action which have resulted from—and continue to extend—this changed emphasis on 'slower' forms of movement in cities. The shift took place in many countries and cities across the world, with thought leadership progressively extended from researchers, practitioners and politicians in different cities at varying rates. At times advances in particular cities were stalled by politics, but each new high-tide mark in thinking and action became the baseline for the next round of innovation elsewhere. The overall tide of slower movement cultures has risen across the world and provides much of the underpinning of the approach taken in this book.

It is valuable here to illustrate this growing repudiation of the motordom perspective and the increasing recognition of the centrality of slower movement to healthy cities and lives. Although advances have been spectacular across all of the 'slower' modes, the focus here is on walking, where the most extensive transformation of thinking has taken place. A brief review of leading research themes from the 1980s onwards will help place the new way of thinking in perspective.

Signs of changing thinking in walking research in the 1980s were arguably first discernible in the United Kingdom, influenced by many researchers, but three individuals in particular. John Roberts was the founder of TEST (Transport & Environment Studies) and one of the pioneers of sustainable transport planning and a mentor to many. Amongst over 150 publications were *Quality Streets*

(1988), *User Friendly Cities* (1989) and *Travel Sickness* (1992) (Roberts, 1989; Roberts, Cleary, Hamilton, & Hannah, 1992; TEST, 1988). Much of Roberts' writing is now available in recent issues of the journal *World Transport Policy and Practice*.

A second key thought leader was Mayer Hillman, known particularly for his work on cycling and health and as a trenchant critic of inadequate policy on climate change, but also for his seminal works on walking, such as *Walking is Transport* (Hillman & Whalley, 1979). With John Adams and John Whitelegg he published the frequently cited *One False Move: A Study of Children's Independent Mobility* that linked the recent reduction in child casualties on British roads with the loss of freedom that children have experienced because of the increase in traffic. Third, John Whitelegg is founder and editor of the journal of *World Transport Policy & Practice*. His papers and speaking appearances have inspired a generation of young researchers as have his many books, including *Transport for a Sustainable Society* (1993), *Critical Mass* (1997) and *Mobility: A New Urban Design and Transport Planning Philosophy for a Sustainable Future* (Whitelegg, 1993, 1997, 2016).

By the 1990s there was a clear growth of a research paradigm on sustainable transport—and later, on walking—involving researchers such as Jan Gehl from Denmark; Carmen Hass-Klau, Helmut Holzapfel and Rolf and Heiner Monheim from Germany; Robert Cervero, John Fruin, Allan Jacobs, Rich Untermann, Anne Vernez Moudon and Holly Whyte from the United States; David Engwicht, Jeff Kenworthy and Peter Newman from Australia; and John Adams, David Banister, Phil Goodwin, Tim Pharoah and Rodney Tolley from the United Kingdom. The latter edited *The Greening of Urban Transport: Planning for Walking and Cycling in Western Cities* in 1990, followed by two further editions in 1997 and 2003 (Tolley, 1990, 1997, 2003) and founded CAST (Centre for Alternative and Sustainable Transport) in 1996, which was the first research institute wholly focussed on walking and cycling. CAST was the lead convenor of the UK's inaugural Local Authority Walking Group and of the 1997 UK National Walking Conference, both of which were probably the first of their kind.

It is interesting to trace the development of approaches to walking research in the 20 years since these gatherings. Amongst the main conclusions from the 1997 UK conference were:

- Walking is not an index of deprivation but of sustainability of life;
- 'Transport' is not just 'motorised vehicles': walking also is transport;
- Promoting walking is not a bolt-on extra: it is fundamental to reducing traffic;
- Walking is healthy physiologically, psychologically, environmentally; and
- A good walking environment is a good economic environment.

From a current perspective, these seem basic first principles, but they certainly were not seen in that light by many practitioners and politicians at the time.

FIGURE 1.6 In 2015, nine Western Sydney councils signed the Walk21 International Charter for Walking, joining more than 500 councils around the world in a commitment to encourage more everyday walking. *(Credit: Western Sydney Regional Organisation of Councils (WSROC))*

Indeed, the conclusions stirringly reported 'We are at a crossroads, a point in history where these key issues are now being recognized'.

Built on these foundations, the year 2000 was a significant one for the expansion of walking research and promotion. First, the UK government commissioned research in order to provide a judgemental forecast of the future of walking throughout Europe during the first decade of the 21st century. The Delphi study that resulted questioned 'experts' from across Europe (Tolley, Bickerstaff, & Lumsdon, 2003) and analysed the rich and thick source of comments provided by them. These included 'How can the myth that "cars save time" be challenged?' and 'What messages and communication media will convince councils that they cannot have more walking without less car travel?'

Second, a partnership of the UK's leading walking policy-makers, researchers, campaigners and practitioners organised an international conference on walking, in London in February 2000 (Walk21, 2000). Stimulated by the London Walking Forum's (2000) publication *Walking: Making it Happen*, the resulting Walk21 organisation—the name referring to 'Walking in the 21st Century' or 'Walking coming of age'—has since become an international organisation supporting and promoting walking. Its objectives include disseminating knowledge; showcasing cities with good walking policies; integrating walking into transport, land-use planning, health and other relevant policy sectors; and involving stakeholders from political, professional and public arenas. The Walk21 Conference Series, The International Charter for Walking (see Fig. 1.6 and Chapter 9) and The Global Walk21 Network are some of the delivery mechanisms that have resulted.

At the London Walk21 conference, there was much focus on the need for research, resources and communication. A key conclusion was that '"Talking the talk" is a necessary precondition to knowledge and understanding, and indeed to raising awareness of these issues amongst those who do not even conceptualise walking as a form of transport at all. In the past, walking—disadvantaged by its very ubiquity—has been an unexplored byway of research'. As Jan Gehl's (2000) opening address noted, 'There is much more to walking than walking'. Another conclusion, reflecting concerns of delegates at the time, was that 'We have to encourage a paradigm shift in the way that policy-makers think about walking: meeting travel demands for walkers is a pre-requisite for global sustainability' (Walk21, 2000).

The Walk21 conference has been held in a different city every year since 2000, and its conclusions are contemporary indicators of the concerns of walking research at the time. To take just 5-year snapshots, Walk21 in Zurich 2005 was titled 'Everyday Walking Culture' and the themes focussed on such issues as 'How can we establish a walking culture and create a positive image of walking?' (Walk21, 2005). By 2010 in the Hague, there was a focus on public spaces as economic assets and the word 'sojourning' began to be widely used to reflect the value of 'parked pedestrians' to urban life. The conference also called for better measurement and data and for us to 'measure walking and value happiness—it's a universal currency' (Walk21, 2010). By 2015, Walk 21 was in Vienna, one of the most walkable and liveable cities in the world where the focus had moved on from Gehl's 'necessary activities' to 'optional' and 'social' activities in the city (Gehl, 2010)—in other words to comfort, attractiveness and quality of walking environments. Clearly, the earlier foci of walking research—individual road user behaviour and infrastructure provisions—have been augmented over time by more sophisticated concerns. These include: the needs of people living in the city; ideological issues, such as the myths and perceptions of individuals, planners and politicians; and the role of institutions in fields such as regulation, finance and data.

The extraordinary upsurge of walking research has by no means solved all of the pressing issues that walking faces—as this book testifies—but each stage in the evolution of thinking has raised the bar and increased the sophistication of the debate. That is also cause and consequence of increasingly intense practical interventions by all levels of government, communities and the burgeoning numbers of NGOs and advocacy movements. Individual thought leaders have been critical to advancing the walking agenda—and although it is invidious to mention just a few names from a burgeoning list of inspirational researchers, writers and speakers—it is reasonable to name-check (apart from those already mentioned) Mario Alves, Eric Britton, Werner Brög, Ralph Buehler, Matt Burke, Nick Cavill, Mark Fenton, Larry Frank, Billie Giles-Corti, Dario Hildalgo, Sonia Lavadinho, Matt Lerner, Todd Litman, Dinesh Mohan, Ian Napier, Enrique and Gil Peñalosa, John Pucher, Janette Sadiq-Khan, Daniel Sauter, Jeff Speck, Bronwen Thornton, Geetam Tiwari, Ellen Vanderslice, Celia Wade-Brown and

Jim Walker. The point is emphasised by noting that the Delphi study cited earlier struggled to find more than 100 'walking experts' in Europe in 2000 across fields of research, practice, advocacy, policy and planning, whereas it is evident now from a cursory scrutiny of publications, conferences, webinars, blogs and posts in the fields of urban and transport planning, urban design, health engineering and many more—that there is a huge reservoir across the world of understanding and expertise in walking. Indeed, a Google search of 'promoting walking' now produces over 70,000 results. It is no exaggeration to say that in little more than two decades, walking has gone from periphery to mainstream in the debate on the future liveability of cities.

1.7 The growing momentum towards 'slower' city transport

The focus on walking is part of a wider trend towards supporting a 'slowing' of city transport. There are signs that the societal obsession with speed is slowing. This is evident in city transport systems, where there is a growing realisation that low-speed environments have advantages. As Carlos Pardo (2017) suggests, policy-makers and planners are searching for 'different measures or policies that will reduce speeds and increase liveability and even increase efficiency'. Throughout this book we describe many of these policies. Here we provide three examples from different parts of the world: lower motorised traffic speeds, first appearing in European cities; freeway removal; and the concept of Ciclovía.

First, European cities have shown the way in reducing the speed of motorised traffic in cities. Since the first 30 km/h speed limit was introduced in the small German town of Buxtehude in 1983, the idea of lower speeds, particularly in residential streets, has spread across Europe and to many other parts of the globe. In Switzerland, 30 km/h zones have been allowed by law since 1989, and were first established in 1991 in Zurich. Graz, Austria, was the first city to introduce a city-wide 30 km/h limit on all roads apart from main arterials, in 1992 (see Fig. 1.7). In the United Kingdom, more than 13 million people live in 20 mph zones, which are publicised using the slogan '20's Plenty for Us'. In the United States, 20 mph 'neighbourhood slow zones' are being trialled in New York and Philadelphia, and Portland, Oregon, has installed thousands of 20 mph speed signs in residential streets (Small, 2019). The road safety benefits of lower speeds are clearly demonstrable, and there are other benefits as well, including lower pollution levels, increased active transport, higher property values and increased levels of children's independent mobility.

A second, dramatic, example of slowing city transport by the removal of a high-speed road comes from South Korea. In Seoul in 2003 the Cheonggyecheon expressway that carried 168,000 cars per day was demolished, uncovering a section of the historic Cheonggyecheon stream, creating both ecological and recreational opportunities along a 9 km corridor in the city centre. The

FIGURE 1.7 Streets in central Graz, Austria, where a 30 km/h speed limit applies to more than 75 per cent of the road system. There are no speed limit signs here, as everyone knows what the default speed limit is. *(Credit: Rodney Tolley)*

expressway, built in the 1950s, had been regarded as a success shortly after its construction, covering an eyesore of polluted water and symbolising the successful industrialisation and modernisation of South Korea. However, by the 1990s, the expressway was seen as destroying downtown Seoul with traffic and pollution. Taking down the expressway was widely regarded as political suicide that would create traffic chaos. Yet, traffic chaos did not eventuate, partly due to improved public transport, and the expressway was replaced with a green river park that gave the residents of Seoul a place to walk, sit and enjoy an unpolluted environment (see Fig. 1.8). Property values near the corridor increased by 300 per cent. Fish, insects and bird species have thrived in and around the stream. The urban heat island effect was also diminished (Rao, 2011). More than a dozen expressways have been demolished in Seoul since 2003, and public transport continues to be strengthened.

The third example is the global spread of Ciclovía—the practice of closing streets to cars at weekends and opening them to walkers, people on bikes, rollerbladers, jugglers, dancers and life in general. Ciclovía began in Bogotá in 1974 and is now in place in hundreds of cities across the world including Ottawa, La Paz, Paris and many cities in countries as diverse as India and Mexico, sometimes under different names such as Open Streets, Sunday Bikedays and Car-free Streets (see Fig. 1.9). Today, 120 km of Bogotá streets are closed every Sunday, when

FIGURE 1.8 The green river park and reclaimed Cheonggyecheon stream in Seoul, South Korea, after removal of the Cheonggyecheon expressway. *(Credit: Sybil Derrible)*

FIGURE 1.9 People of all ages on bicycles and skates, enjoying the Sunday morning Ciclovía in Mexico City. Even the dog gets an outing, if not exercise. *(Credit: Rodney Tolley)*

people participate in Ciclovía. Almost a million of the 10 million inhabitants join this remarkable festival of active movement in public space (Begg, 2013).

All of these examples are accompanied by a broader societal reaction against the culture of speed, manifested in new social movements to promote slowness. We turn now to a brief discussion of these developments.

1.8 The rise of slow movements

Increasing numbers of people are recognising the value of a slower pace of life, and the costs of living life at high speed. A powerful explanation of the problems of a life built around speed and the benefits of a slower pace is provided in a Western Australian Road Safety advertisement, created with the input of Carl Honoré, author of *In Praise of Slow*. Box 1.3 provides extracts from the text of this advertisement.

The first slow movement began in Italy as the Slow Food movement in the 1980s, and several other slow organisations have emerged since then. In Norway in 1999, Geir Berthelsen created *The World Institute of Slowness*, which outlined a vision for a 'slow planet', and the need to teach the world about the value of slowness. Similarly, in Austria, *The Society for the Deceleration of Time* was founded in 1990. One of its imaginative strategies for slowing people's walking

BOX 1.3 Enjoy the ride.

If life's a race, where's the finish? And who are we competing with?

Is there a prize for first place? Or do we just reach the end a little quicker?

We're only just skimming the surface of life. Humans just aren't designed to go that fast. Sooner or later we crash. To cope with this speeding life our bodies release chemicals that activate our adrenal glands, increase our heart rate and raise our blood pressure. These responses cause us to grind our teeth, sleep poorly, crave fatty and sugary food, get headaches, feel stressed, get sick more often and lose our sex drive. And in the long term we're in the fast lane to heart disease, sexual dysfunction, allergies, diabetes, depression, anxiety, muscular pain and a load of other stuff with names too long to remember.

But when we slow down, we discover that life has a natural pace. And it's good. We slide into a groove that's always been there. Life becomes richer, more pleasurable and more fulfilling.

We may do fewer things, but what we do we do well. We breathe. When was the last time you actually took time to breathe? Not just the shallow ticking over of your respiratory system. To really breathe. Taking a long slow breath in to its comfortable conclusion. And letting it all out, and doing it again, and again and again until you're flooded with calm. Imagine life lived in this zone. So why haven't we slowed down before? If you're worried life will overtake you, you're wrong. Life is where you are and what you're doing right now, and now, and now.

Source: Transcribed from the Western Australian Road Safety Advertisement—Enjoy the Ride (Road Safety Council WA Australia, 2011).

behaviour was similar to one of the motordom tactics. In town centres, people seen rushing were stopped and given a symbolic fine—a toy tortoise that they were asked to steer for 50 slow yards before they were permitted to continue (Trentmann, 2016). Other creative disruptions by this society include placing hundreds of deck chairs for a collective siesta and presenting red cards to people who damage the quality of life with mindless acceleration (redolent of motordom's jaywalking pamphlets) (Liebmann, 2015).

The slow philosophy has been applied to almost every aspect of life (Honoré, 2004, pp. 216–217). There is slow gardening (where gardeners take their time and follow seasonal rhythms), slow medicine (taking time to evaluate a patient carefully), slow design and slow fashion (where objects are designed to last and made from sustainably-sourced materials), slow travel, slow science, slow living, slow sex, slow parenting, slow cities (Cittaslow) and slow thinking. There is also slow politics (Agacinski, 2003), which recognises that the survival of democracy depends on citizens' commitment to claim time for the 'proper conduct of debates essential for democratic life' (Jaffe, 2014, p. 9). For the purposes of this book, two types of slow movements are particularly important: slow cities and slow thinking.

The slow cities movement (known as Cittaslow when founded in Italy) favours local and traditional cultures and a relaxed pace of life (Knox, 2005). When the principles of Cittaslow slow cities are adopted at a shallow level, strategies such as flexitime and telework can reduce peak transport demand. At a deeper level, slow cities promote a less frenetic pace of life, where it becomes the social norm to live life at a pace appropriate to human well-being. While full membership of Cittaslow is open only to towns or cities with less than 50,000 people, slow city principles can be applied in any city. Cittaslow's charter encourages the promotion of technologies that improve the quality of the environment and the urban fabric. More specifically, it promotes values and practices such as greater areas of green space and vibrant public spaces, reducing noise, air and light pollution, and improving public transport and opportunities for walking and cycling. The emphasis is on people, not speed.

The concept of 'slow thinking' is explained in Daniel Kahneman's *Thinking, Fast and Slow*. A key theme in the book is human irrationality and cognitive bias. One example of such bias is the 'planning fallacy': the tendency of humans to overestimate benefits and underestimate costs (Kahneman, 2011). The history of transport modelling (see Chapter 3) suggests that this cognitive bias has affected city transport systems (in largely negative ways). Kahneman identifies two broad types of thinking: 'System 1' is fast, instinctive and emotional; 'System 2' is slower, more deliberative and more logical. Fast thinking dominates the way people think in modern societies, where people rely on swiftness to make decisions. In fast thinking, automatic responses can dictate our thoughts, feelings and behaviour. The problem with fast thinking is that it often leads to incorrect conclusions.

The relevance of slow and fast thinking to city transport is that many people react with positive emotion to the idea of fast travel, simply accepting unchallenged norms, and they may find it difficult to think rationally about an emotional topic. While thinking fast leads us to believe that speed saves us time, thinking slow allows us to question this belief, and to consider whether slowing transport may be a more effective strategy if saving time (and promoting wealth and health) is our goal. Whilst everybody can benefit from using the thinking slow approach, it will be most useful for those who can lead change towards creating healthier cities: planners, politicians and policy-makers. As we explain in Chapter 10, these leaders will be pivotal in creating future 'slow cities'.

1.9 Conclusion

In order to create healthier places to live, work, learn, shop and play, we need to rethink the widely held assumption that faster is always better in city transport, and recognise that speed can destroy place. 'Slowing city transport' is a necessary (but not the only) step towards creating healthy places. For city residents to truly experience a place, they must move slowly, or, indeed, 'stay in place'.

While the cultural obsession with speed may prompt some to question, or even ridicule the 'slow movement', it is worth considering where the 'fast movement' has taken us over the last 100 years. Transport systems based on the 'faster is always better' motto have created a damaging and costly legacy:

- 1.35 million road deaths globally each year (World Health Organization, 2020);
- a huge burden of maintaining road infrastructure (the United States needs to spend over $4 trillion by 2025 to repair roads, bridges and other infrastructure) (Thompson & Matousek, 2019);
- deaths from air pollution from cars—more Americans die from car pollution than from crashes (Caiazzo, Ashok, Waitz, Yim, & Barrett, 2013);
- surging obesity rates—across nations vehicle use (annual vehicle miles travelled) correlates approximately 99 per cent with annual obesity rates (Jacobson, King, & Yuan, 2011);
- growing levels of road rage (Møller & Haustein, 2018);
- huge and growing demands for energy—transport uses more than two-thirds of the world's oil production (Chicca, Vale, & Vale, 2018); and
- a climate emergency—transport is a major (and growing) contributor to increasing greenhouse gases.

We recognise that changing the current status quo, where speed is automatically assumed to be beneficial, will not be achieved with old thinking. It is important that planners, policy-makers and urban residents open their minds to ideas that may at first appear counter-intuitive, or which at least challenge the status quo of the last century, which is leading us to disaster in terms of personal, economic and planetary health. Despite a growing awareness of the importance of 'slowing' city transport, there is a huge inertia in transport infrastructure towards maintaining the speed of travel, both within and between cities. Combined with this is a set of ingrained cultures of thinking, training and political and public attitudes that need to be reversed urgently.

The challenge of overturning 100 years of transport policy aimed at promoting speed could be regarded as what has been defined as a 'wicked problem': one that is difficult to solve because of complex and changing requirements. This wicked problem involves multiple stakeholders with diverse views, influenced by personal values, which in turn are often moulded to suit the vested interests of powerful groups. Many individuals feel trapped into a dependency on high-speed modes, as everyone else is using them, and they react with hostility to any suggestion that the brakes be applied to urban transport.

One strategy that can be useful in approaching this wicked problem involves focussing on the concept of child-friendly cities. This concept came to international prominence in 1996, when UNICEF launched its Child Friendly Cities Initiative, which aimed to 'put children first' in making cities liveable places for all (UNICEF, 2009). Since then the concept has been applied by several organisations and researchers as a way to promote children's rights in cities throughout the world (ARUP, 2017). As we explain in more detail in Chapter 11, a focus on children's well-being can help lift discussions about transport and speed above narrow self-interest, encouraging more collective decision-making. Importantly for this book, the goals of 'slowing city transport' and 'creating child-friendly cities' are closely aligned. The child-friendly transport modes are the 'slower', active modes of walking, cycling and public transport. And there is a growing urgency to move towards these modes.

The urban road transport systems of many cities are now approaching peak capacity. In many nations, there is a discernible shift in policy focus away from planning solely for the speed of motorised traffic towards greater consideration of road safety and the reliability of the transport system. In transport planning and traffic engineering, the emphasis has started to move away from maximising speed to reducing the speed of motorised traffic, recognising that the minimal benefits of speed (especially in residential streets or busy commercial centres) are far outweighed by the disadvantages. These disadvantages can be measured in traffic crashes, reduced physical activity, the loss of children's independent mobility and, perhaps most notably, the impact of higher speeds on the spreading out of the city, forcing people to travel longer distances to dispersed land uses and requiring significantly more road space and energy consumption. The way in which increased speed leads to increased distance travelled (rather than time saved) is discussed in detail in Section 3.4.2.

In the same way that motordom claimed that the motor age was a new age, almost 100 years ago, supporters of more healthy, sustainable and 'slower' city transport can justifiably make the case that the 'motor age' is itself now outdated, outmoded and ready to be superseded by a smarter approach, one that recognises that speed can steal our time, money and health. Even though the motoring lobby continues trying to push back progress towards 'slowing' the city, the advantages of 'slower' transport and the disadvantages of speed in the city are now much more widely understood. We show how new environmental, economic, social and political pressures are emerging to increasingly challenge the dominance of speed. Cities throughout the world are learning that speed is not the magic solution that motordom promised, and are moving towards new, healthier, more child-friendly and 'slower' forms of transport.

1.10 Preview of the book

The book is divided into three parts: Speed, Health and Strategies. In the first part—Speed—we examine and critique the standard arguments about the benefits of speed, for individuals and for the economy and society (Chapters 2 and 3). In Chapter 4, we resolve a paradox, that 'slowing' city transport will not only improve our health, but will also 'save time'. The second part—Health—focusses on the explanation of the ways in which health is promoted through 'slower' travel. The most obvious way in which 'slower' transport benefits health is in terms of human health (physical, mental and emotional) (Chapter 5). In addition, we demonstrate how both environmental health (Chapter 6) and economic health (Chapter 7) will benefit from a 'slower' city.

The third part of the book—Strategies—provides a game plan for implementing the ideas in the book to create 'slower', healthier cities. Chapter 8 examines the importance of reducing the speed of motorised traffic as an alternative to policies that have sought to adapt the city and its citizens to speed. Different approaches to achieve this reduction in speed are discussed. Chapter 9 focusses on planning, in particular the rearranging of land uses to shorten trips. It also stresses the importance of ensuring that zoning ordinances and regulations are not biased in favour of high-speed transport. Chapter 10 examines the behaviours, values and cultures that need to be changed to effectively slow city transport. Importantly, we argue here that it is not only the transport behaviours of urban citizens that need to be changed, but also that a fundamental change in the prevailing transport paradigm is required.

The concluding chapter asks whether our collective addiction to speed is, in fact, a central issue in our inadequate response to the global threats facing humanity. Realising the immense difficulty of overcoming these challenges, we show how a child-friendly focus for city planning can provide a potentially fruitful way to navigate the complex issues surrounding the societal dependency on fast modes of transport. We note that slower cities are child-friendly cities and that child-friendly cities must be slower cities, and that both are healthier for everyone, yet until recently speed was seen as a 'goal' by city authorities. This begs the question of why we don't think about speed as a problem rather than as a solution. In an attempt to do just that, based on the research for this book and the arguments presented in the first ten chapters, we conclude with a proposal for a ten-point Manifesto for 21st Century Slow Cities (Tranter & Tolley, 2020). In response to the devastating impact of COVID-19, the final chapter is followed by an Afterword, which emphasises the importance of 'slow cities' in a world affected by a global pandemic.

References

Agacinski, S. (2003). *Time passing: Modernity and nostalgia* (J. Gladding, Trans.). New York: Columbia University Press.

ARUP. (2017). *Cities alive, designing for urban childhoods*. London: ARUP. Available from: https://www.arup.com/-/media/arup/files/publications/u/cities_alivedesigning_for_urban_childhoods.pdf.

Badger, E. (2015). The myth of the American love affair with cars. *The Washington Post*. Available from: https://www.washingtonpost.com/news/wonk/wp/2015/01/27/debunking-the-myth-of-the-american-love-affair-with-cars/.

Banister, D. (2011). The trilogy of distance, speed and time. *Journal of Transport Geography, 19*(4), 950–959.

Begg, D. (2013). *World class? London's transport: Progress and future challenges*. London: Transport Times. Available from: https://www.transporttimes.co.uk/reports.php.

Brundtland, G.H. (1987). *Report of the World Commission on Environment and Development: Our common future*. Available from: https://sustainabledevelopment.un.org/content/documents/5987our-common-future.pdf.

Caiazzo, F., Ashok, A., Waitz, I. A., Yim, S. H., & Barrett, S. R. J. A. E. (2013). Air pollution and early deaths in the United States. Part I: Quantifying the impact of major sectors in 2005. *Atmospheric Environment, 79*, 198–208.

Capon, A. G., Talley, N. J., & Horton, R. C. (2018). Planetary health: What is it and what should doctors do? *Medical Journal of Australia, 208*(7), 296–297.

Chicca, F., Vale, B., & Vale, R. (2018). *Everyday lifestyles and sustainability: The environmental impact of doing the same things differently*. New York: Routledge.

Davies, S. J. (1987). *Ontario and the Automobile, 1900-1930: Aspects of Technological Integration*. Doctor of Philosophy. McMaster University. Available from: https://macsphere.mcmaster.ca/bitstream/11375/11901/1/fulltext.pdf.

Davis, A. (1994). The speed and mobility culture: The sacrifice of health and quality of life. *Traffic Engineering and Control, 35*(10), 568–572.

Flink, J. J. (1990). *The automobile age*. Cambridge, MA: MIT Press.

Gehl, J. (2010). *Cities for people*. Washington, DC: Island Press.

Giles-Corti, B., Vernez-Moudon, A., Reis, R., Turrell, G., Dannenberg, A. L., Badland, H., et al. (2016). City planning and population health: A global challenge. *The Lancet, 388*(10062), 2912–2924.

Higham, J., & Hopkins, D. (2016). Low carbon mobility: Urgent futures and radical transitions. In D. Hopkins, & J. Higham (Eds.), *Low carbon mobility transitions* (pp. 266–276). Goodfellow: Oxford.

Hillman, M., & Whalley, A. (1979). *Walking is transport*. London: Policy Studies Institute.

Honoré, C. (2004). *In Praise of Slow: How a worldwide movement is challenging the cult of speed*. London: Orion.

Hubbard, P., & Lilley, K. (2004). Pacemaking the modern city: The urban politics of speed and slowness. *Environment and Planning D: Society and Space, 22*(2), 273–294.

Ilf, L., & Petrov, E. (1932). *The little golden calf*. New York: Farrar and Rinehart.

Jacobson, S. H., King, D. M., & Yuan, R. (2011). A note on the relationship between obesity and driving. *Transport Policy, 18*(5), 772–776.

Jaffe, I. (2014). *Slow movies: Countering the cinema of action*. New York: Columbia University Press.

Kahneman, D. (2011). *Thinking, fast and slow*. New York: Farrar, Straus and Giroux.

Knox, P. L. (2005). Creating ordinary places: Slow cities in a fast world. *Journal of Urban Design, 10*(1), 1–11.

Latham, A., & McCormack, D. (2008). Speed and slowness. In T. Hall, P. Hubbard, & J. R. Short (Eds.), *The SAGE companion to the city* (pp. 301–317). London: Sage.

Liebmann, M. (2015). Society for the Deceleration of Time - Verein zur Verzögerung der Zeit. *Zeitpolitisches Magazin*, 12(26), 15–16. Available from: http://www.zeitpolitik.de/pdfs/zpm_26_0715.pdf.

McShane, C. (1995). *Down the asphalt path: The automobile and American City*. New York: Columbia University Press.

Metz, D. (2008). The myth of travel time saving. *Transport Reviews, 28*(3), 321–336.

Mokhtarian, P. L., & Salomon, I. (2001). How derived is the demand for travel? Some conceptual and measurement considerations. *Transportation Research Part A: Policy and Practice, 35*(8), 695–719.

Møller, M., & Haustein, S. (2018). Road anger expression—changes over time and attributed reasons. *Accident Analysis & Prevention, 119*, 29–36.

Newman, P., Kenworthy, J., & Glazebrook, G. (2013). Peak car use and the rise of global rail: Why this is happening and what it means for large and small cities. *Journal of Transportation Technologies, 3*(4), 272–287.

Norton, P. D. (2007). Street rivals: Jaywalking and the invention of the motor age street. *Technology and Culture, 48*(2), 331–359.

Norton, P. D. (2011). *Fighting traffic: The dawn of the motor age in the American City*. Cambridge, MA: MIT Press.

Norton, P. D. (2015). What can post-carbon mobility design learn from the rise of Motordom? Youtube video. Available from: https://www.youtube.com/watch?v=5W1Esz9S1pY.

Pardo, C. (2017). Reducing speeds for better mobility and quality of life. *UN Habitat*. Available from: https://new.unhabitat.org/reducing-speeds-for-better-mobility-and-quality-of-life-carlosfelipe-pardo.

Proffitt, D. G., Bartholomew, K., Ewing, R., & Miller, H. J. (2019). Accessibility planning in American metropolitan areas: Are we there yet? *Urban Studies, 56*(1), 167–192.

Pucher, J., & Buehler, R. (2017). Cycling towards a more sustainable transport future. *Transport Reviews, 37*(6), 689–694.

Pucher, J., Buehler, R., Bassett, D., & Dannenberg, A. (2010). Walking and cycling to health: A comparative analysis of city, state, and international data. *American Journal of Public Health, 100*(10), 1986–1992.

Rao, K. (2011). Seoul tears down an urban highway and the city can breathe again. *Grist*. Available from: https://grist.org/infrastructure/2011-04-04-seoul-korea-tears-down-an-urban-highway-life-goes-on/.

Road Safety Council WA Australia. (2011). Speed: Enjoy the ride. *Road Safety Advertisement*. Available from: https://www.rsc.wa.gov.au/Campaigns/Speed.

Roberts, J. (1989). *User-friendly cities: What Britain can learn from mainland Europe*. Oxford: Transport Studies Unit, Oxford University.

Roberts, J., Cleary, J., Hamilton, K., & Hannah, J. (1992). *Travel sickness: The need for a sustainable transport policy for Britain*. London: Lawrence & Wishart.

Ryerson, M. S., & Woodburn, A. (2014). Build airport capacity or manage flight demand? How regional planners can lead american aviation into a new frontier of demand management. *Journal of the American Planning Association, 80*(2), 138–152.

Sachs, W. (1992). *For love of the automobile: Looking back into the history of our desires*. Berkeley, CA: University of California Press.

Small, A. (2019). Why speed kills cities. *Citylab*. Available from: https://www.citylab.com/transportation/2019/08/low-speed-limit-vehicle-safety-crash-data-traffic-congestion/588412/.

Snyder, T. (2014). Q&A with Peter Norton: History is on the side of vision zero. *Streetsblog USA*. Available from: https://usa.streetsblog.org/2014/10/16/qa-with-peter-norton-history-is-on-the-side-of-vision-zero/.

Taylor, M. C. (2014). *Speed limits: Where time went and why we have so little left*. New Haven, CA/London: Yale University Press.

TEST. (1988). *Quality streets: How traditional urban centres benefit from traffic calming*. Technical Report 75. London: Transport & Environment Studies.

Thackara, J. (2006). *In the bubble: Designing in a complex world*. Cambridge, MA: MIT Press.

Thompson, C., & Matousek, M. (2019). America's infrastructure is decaying—here's a look at how terrible things have gotten. *Business Insider*. Available from: https://www.businessinsider.com/asce-gives-us-infrastructure-a-d-2017-3/?r=AU&IR=T.

Toderian, B. (2014). Fear-based messages like this were about reducing pedestrian deaths by reducing pedestrians. Available from: https://twitter.com/BrentToderian/status/474938012166389760.

Tolley, R. (1990). *The greening of urban transport: Planning for walking and cycling in Western cities*. London: Belhaven Press.

Tolley, R. (1997). *The greening of urban transport: Planning for walking and cycling in Western cities* (2nd ed.). London: John Wiley & Sons.

Tolley, R. (Ed.). (2003). *Sustainable transport: Planning for walking and cycling in urban environments*. Abingdon: Woodhead Publishing.

Tolley, R., Bickerstaff, K., & Lumsdon, L. (2003). Social and cultural influences on the future of walking. In R. Tolley (Ed.), *Sustainable transport: Planning for walking and cycling in urban environments* (pp. 238–251). Cambridge: Woodhead Publishing.

Tranter, P. (2012). Effective speed: Cycling because it's faster. In J. Pucher, & R. Buehler (Eds.), *City cycling* (pp. 57–74). Cambridge, MA: MIT Press.

Tranter, P., & Tolley, R. (2020). Manifesto for 21st Century Slow Cities. Available from https://slowcitiesmanifesto.com/.

Trentmann, F. (2016). *Empire of things: How we became a world of consumers, from the fifteenth century to the twenty-first*. London: Allen Lane.

UNICEF. (2009). *Child friendly cities. Fact Sheet*. Available from: https://www.unicef.de/blob/23350/110a3c40ae4874fd9cc452653821ff58/fact-sheet--child-friendly-cities--data.pdf.

Urry, J. (2007). *Mobilities*. Cambridge, MA: Polity Press.

Vardi, I. (2014). Quantifying accidents: Cars, statistics, and unintended consequences in the construction of social problems over time. *Qualitative Sociology*, *37*(3), 345–367.

Volti, R. (2004). *Cars and culture: The life story of a technology*. Baltimore, MD: The John Hopkins University Press.

Walk21. (2000). Walk21-I: London, England. Available from: https://www.walk21.com/london.

Walk21. (2005). Walk21-VI: Zurich, Switzerland: Everyday walking culture. Available from: https://www.walk21.com/zurich.

Walk21. (2010). Walk21-XI: The Hague, The Netherlands. Available from: https://www.walk21.com/the-hague.

Whitelegg, J. (1993). *Transport for a sustainable future: The case for Europe*. London: Belhaven Press.

Whitelegg, J. (1997). *Critical mass: Transport environment and society in the twenty-first century*. London: Pluto Press.

Whitelegg, J. (2016). *Mobility: A new urban design and transport planning philosophy for a sustainable future*. Shropshire, UK: Straw Barnes Press.

World Health Organization. (2020). Road traffic injuries. Available from: https://www.who.int/news-room/fact-sheets/detail/road-traffic-injuries.

Young, M., Markham, F., Higham, J., & Jenkins, J. (2017). Life in a post-flying Australia, and why it might actually be ok. *The Conversation*. Available from: https://theconversation.com/life-in-a-post-flying-australia-and-why-it-might-actually-be-ok-70388.

Zelizer, V. A. (1994). *Pricing the priceless child: The changing social value of children*. Princeton, NJ: Princeton University Press.

Chapter 2

The benefits of speed for individuals: real or illusory?

'The hurrier I go, the behinder I get'.

A popular aphorism, commonly misattributed to the White Rabbit in Alice in Wonderland

Abstract

In modern societies, speed has become such a central part of life that its value is largely accepted without question: there is rarely any serious reflection about alternatives to constant acceleration. The chapter outlines several of the conventional arguments about why speed is of value for individuals and households, and then shows how a careful assessment of these arguments reveals that speed is not always as beneficial as we assume. The claimed advantages of faster transport include saving time and allowing wider access to facilities and activities. Yet whilst these claims may seem logical, they are highly questionable, and we explain why this is the case. Whilst in theory, increasing speeds might improve many aspects of the lives of individuals, when speeds increase, the city also changes in response and there are a range of costs for individuals and households. Increased speed often results in increased travel distances, and a loss of time, money and health.

2.1 Introduction

Many urban residents, conditioned by a lifetime of exposure to positive messages about speed, might be hesitant to believe that 'slowing city transport' is a sensible strategy, or that slowing their own movement in the city might have benefits. Over the last century, throughout most of the world, speed became such a central part of urban life that its value was largely accepted without question. This chapter examines the strength of the belief in the positive value of speed for individuals. We outline the conventional and (till recently) dominant arguments and values regarding speed that have influenced human behaviour in cities. We then show how a careful assessment of these arguments reveals flaws: speed is not always as beneficial or as valued as we might think. The arguments about the advantages of speed become less convincing when a holistic perspective is taken, and they lose much of their appeal when the various costs of speed are considered alongside any claimed advantages. In this chapter we

Slow Cities. http://dx.doi.org/10.1016/B978-0-12-815316-1.00002-2

demonstrate how speed often results in a reduction in quality of life, a loss of meaning and a loss of time, money and health.

2.2 A long history of valuing speed

Throughout human history speed has been valued and associated with success. Higher speed provided many advantages, even for hunter-gatherers. Speed was an advantage in flight/fight responses, and humans evolved to enable running at reasonable speed with exceptional endurance. This long-distance running speed enabled pre-historic humans to be successful hunters. Speed had a functional value for human life and survival.

In ancient Greek Olympic games, speed was lauded for its own sake and also had a pragmatic value in some events. One was a race over two to four stades by athletes in armour (a stade was the length of the stadium—192 m). This event was valuable training for the speed and stamina Greek men required in their military service (The Perseus Project, 2017). The speed of travel at sea also came to be highly valued by the Greeks in naval warfare, where speed was required for ramming enemy galleys. The need for speed led to longer and larger ships (which allowed more oars and hence more speed). When the growing ship lengths led to structural weakness, the solution was a second or third row of oarsmen. Trireme galleys (also used by the Phoenicians and the Romans) were the dominant warships of the Mediterranean from the 7th to 4th centuries BCE. However, apart from the invention of the wheel and axle system and advances in sailing techniques, there were few significant advances in the speed of human travel until industrialisation and the use of fossil fuels to propel vehicles. With the use of fossil fuels, speeds far exceeding human or animal running speed became available to large numbers of people.

There is a long history of speed being celebrated in competitions, from the Greek Olympics to the modern Olympics, from children's 'billy cart' races to motor racing events. However, in these events speed was only experienced by the competitors and for everyone else was just a spectacle. The experience of speed by large numbers of people became possible in the 20th century using the new technology of the motor car. As the first modern Olympic games were being staged, the first mass-produced cars were going into production and as the age of the motor car emerged, speed became a major goal in transport policy and vehicle design. 'The "need for speed" in contrast to the need for mobility, has dominated the development of motor vehicles and road transport systems' (Redshaw, 2008, p. 158). Yet, as more and more people are realising, such a focus may create more problems than solutions in cities.

2.3 Problems with seeing speed as 'valuable'

Speed is not always celebrated or associated with success. Throughout the centuries wise people from every tradition have understood the value of slowness, and sometimes stillness, as an important factor in their lives. In modern societies, with a culture of hurrying and constant pressure to be productive, with emails, cell phones and twittering and instant everything, we forget that many things can only be done slowly.

Ralston Saul identifies problems in the assumption that speed is valuable in society. He accepts that speed and efficiency may have value in a limited administrative sense for the delivery of services, yet he argues that speed is not a useful indication of the nature of human civilization: ‘Any animal can rush around a corral four times a day. Only a human being can consciously oblige himself to go slowly in order to consider whether he is doing the right thing, doing it the right way, or ought in fact to be doing something else’ (Saul, 2013, p. 259).

When people consider what they really value, speed is rarely near the top of their lists. ‘People want to live in environments which secure and promote their health’ (World Health Organization, 2008, p. 64). For most people quality of life is more about health, political stability, family relationships and community life, autonomy and job security. Yet these aspects of quality of life are often marginalised when speed dominates urban life. In contrast, not only is health valued by individuals, research clearly demonstrates the positive impact of human health on labour productivity, and hence economic health (Well, 2007).

Since the start of the industrial era people have been told (and usually accepted) that travel will always get faster and this will improve lives for everyone. Yet, people seem to have become blind to the dis-benefits of speed. Whilst the negative environmental impacts are likely the most obvious (see Chapter 6), there are other impacts on our lives that are sometimes overlooked. The lives of modern city dwellers are now so hurried that they deprive themselves of the joy and wonder of living in the moment, and instead see the next task as always being more important than the present (Whitelegg, 1993). The lives of many city dwellers have likely become even more harried in the last few decades: even leisure time has become more rushed, partly due to the ‘increasing habit of multitasking with digital devices’ (Wajcman, 2015, p. 5).

Whilst it has been argued that speed allows travellers to experience more of what is real, there is an irony in this experience: ‘the faster we go, the less we truly see’ (Bertman, 1998, p. 107). Travelling at speed means that we are insulated from the organic detail of the environment we move through. Space is not experienced as real place, but as ‘a disembodied medium through which we move’ (Bertman, 1998, p. 106). We may see more, but we observe and appreciate less. When we travel at speed, we become stressed by any impediment, such as a traffic jam, which occurs precisely because of society’s quest for speed.

Even in modern societies, we can ask: do we need speed all the time? Just because there are advantages in speed in some circumstances, does this mean that everything we do has to be done as quickly as possible? Does it really make sense that ‘increasing speed’ is the first objective of major city transport plans? (See Section 3.4.1 for more discussion of these plans.)

Speed is not always beneficial, and in many instances, 'slower' transport provides advantages. Individuals who move slowly are able to feel more connected to both the natural environment and the people in their community. More individuals are seeking ways to slow down their lives, and this includes slowing down the way they move through their cities: ' ... it's clear that more and more Americans desperately want to slow down' (Walljasper, 1997). A growing number of people are 'downshifting'—cutting back work hours to spend more time doing the things that they want to do and leading a less hurried life (Hamilton, 2003). Although speed has been seen as a way to help us achieve mastery over our environment, ironically more and more people want to slow their lives down because they feel they have lost control. There is growing awareness that faster may not always be better, and that there may be negative psychological consequences of being addicted to speed. For many residents in modern Western cities 'it seems that the faster we go, the farther we fall behind. Not only in the literal sense of not getting done what we set out to do, but at a deeper level too' (Andrews & Urbanska, 2009, p. 182).

As the German environmental researcher Wolfgang Sachs explains, when we live in a fast-paced world, we can devote more energy to arriving and departing than into experiencing life itself: '... our obsession with constant motion virtually guarantees that we miss the very experience to which we are rushing' (Maser, 1999, p. 44). The American economic and social theorist, Jeremy Rifkin, makes similar points. He suggests that as the pace of life continues to accelerate, people lose touch with the biological rhythms of the planet.

Maser (1999) makes the important observation that 'slowness is not in opposition to speed, but rather is the middle path between fast and inert' (Maser, 1999, p. 45). It is also important to realise that the 'slowing down' we advocate in this book does not mean that people can never go fast, or that we should remove the ability to experience speed or to enjoy going fast. We recognise that there is a time and a place for speed. People can experience the thrill of fast action in sporting activity or on the dance floor. However, many people recognise that they would like to spend more time going slowly, giving themselves time to connect with their world, and to escape the pressure to constantly go faster. This can be achieved each day simply by choosing 'slower' modes of movement in the city.

'Slower' modes of transport such as walking have been seen as providing a way 'to allow one to engage in a kind of mobile contemplation, a slow but thorough immersion in the rhythms of everyday life' (Latham & McCormack, 2008, p. 313). Walking can provide these benefits even 'alongside faster ways of being in the city' (Latham & McCormack, 2008, p. 313). However, the mode shares of walking and cycling are influenced by the speed of motorised traffic. Lower motorised speeds encourage more walking and cycling. Research in the United Kingdom identified increases in active travel of between 12 per cent and 25 per cent in traffic-calmed 20 mph zones in Bristol (Jones & Brunt, 2017).

Whilst speed may appear to provide advantages for all, in reality it advantages only a small percentage of the city population. Everybody must adapt

FIGURE 2.1 School students waiting on a narrow median strip for a break in traffic on a busy arterial road in Adelaide, Australia. *(Credit: Rodney Tolley)*

to an urban environment where speed is privileged for some. People walking, people riding bicycles, children and the elderly all have their freedoms curtailed when high speeds dominate cities (see Fig. 2.1). When the objective is to get to destinations as fast as possible, people become less patient, less aware of their surroundings, and less joyful. Even animals have been forced to adapt to high-speed cities. Research on urban wildlife has uncovered some of the mysteries of urban adaptation. For example, coyotes in Chicago have learnt to avoid areas with high-speed traffic (Bisceglio, 2018). The nocturnal singing of European robins has also been affected by dramatic increases in levels of ambient noise from busy city transport networks. These highly territorial birds reduce acoustic interference by singing at night rather than during the day (Fuller, Warren, & Gaston, 2007) and when birds sing at night instead of sleeping, this can alter behavioural patterns in urban species (Parris & McCauley, 2019).

As discussed in Chapter 5, a transport system that privileges speed leads to inequities in access, as well as unequal exposure to the negative impacts of transport: 'speed creates a hierarchy which privileges an elite who enjoy the power it confers at the expense of others who live life in the "slow lane"' (Northcott, 2008, p. 216). Speed in modern cities depends on an energy system that draws fossil fuels (particularly oil) from regions where local inhabitants reap few of the 'benefits' of speed and suffer deleterious consequences, including being forced from their homes and land, and having their access to clean water disrupted by mining and drilling operations. Even if city transport systems transition to more sustainable energy sources, this will not address other inequities associated with high-speed transport. For example, speed leads to an inequitable distribution of road crashes: people in the lowest income areas of cities, or the lowest income nations, have the highest fatality rates (Northcott, 2008).

Other examples of such inequitable consequences can be seen in cities in the Global South, where a small number of people 'benefit' from the speed of their cars whilst contributing to congestion and slower movement for all of those who do not have access to cars. Although walking, and to a lesser extent cycling, are ideal transport modes in dense cities in the Global South, these modes are now being compromised by increasing numbers of private vehicles (Fig. 2.2). This is particularly evident in large Chinese cities, where car ownership has grown rapidly over the last two decades. By 2017, China had almost as many vehicles as the total human population of the United States. Ten of the 25 most congested cities in the world are found in mainland China, and six major Chinese cities have more than three million registered cars (Zheng, 2017). Similarly, India's car numbers are growing so rapidly that it is expected to surpass Japan's position as the third largest car market by 2020. This is producing chronic gridlock in Delhi and many other Indian cities (Hayakawa, 2018). Smaller nations in the

FIGURE 2.2 Kampala, Uganda, a city where an increasing quest for speed leads to inequities in access as well as unequal exposure to the negative impacts of transport. The sign behind the pole reads: 'Scratch for a car, win a car a week'. *(Credit: Carlos Felipe Pardo, https://www.flickr.com/photos/carlosfpardo/15539977639/in/album-72157648746803917/)*

Global South are also experiencing growing traffic congestion, from both cars and motorcycles (Fig. 2.3).

Modern societies have reached a state in which speed has become so entrenched in our lives that there is rarely any serious reflection about alternatives to constant acceleration. The 'ecstasy' of speed described by Kundera (1996)—'Speed is the form of ecstasy the technical revolution has bestowed on man'—leads to detachment, or obliviousness to the violent effects of speed on the people who have been killed by speed. 'Speed involves a kind of moral perversion which is indicated in the extent to which danger to life and limb from fast cars forms part of the appeal of cars' (Northcott, 2008, p. 221). For many motorists, there is something to the thrill of speed that provides a feeling of 'being on the edge', on the precipice of losing control. This ethical distortion that comes from the cultural adulation of speed is not limited to young drivers infatuated with street racing. There is a widespread cultural obsession with speed, powerfully promoted in car advertisements that depict cars moving at high speed, often through empty city streets with no apparent traffic congestion or speed limits. These advertisements have helped promote a desire within many motorists to travel like bullets, zinging through space without friction. Road rage is often triggered by frustration at being impeded from that frictionless dream.

FIGURE 2.3 Traffic congestion in Ho Chi Minh City, Vietnam. *(Credit: Rodney Tolley)*

The impact of advertising on road safety is recognised in many nations. In the United Kingdom, for example, the Advertising Standards Authority (ASA) has stipulated restrictions on what can be depicted in car advertisements, including particular guidelines on images and incitements to speed. Under their rules for motoring advertisements, Rule 20.4 states:

> *'Motoring advertisements must not refer to speed in a way that might condone or encourage dangerous, competitive, inconsiderate or irresponsible driving or motorcycling ... Speed or acceleration claims must not be the main selling message of an advertisement' (Advertising Standards Authority, 2019).*

One advertisement that was banned in the United Kingdom for encouraging fast driving featured words written in red and brief clips of cars in a backdrop of a salt plain. As the ad progresses words appear more rapidly on the screen, such as 'You can surprise yourself. Suddenly you find you can go faster than you thought ... Keep pushing and get to better faster'. The ASA explained that 'While the ad did not include realistic depictions of the vehicles being driven in a dangerous manner, we considered, when taken altogether, the fast changing on-screen text, references to "pushing yourself" and "going faster", the scenes of the cars, sound effects and accompanying sound track was likely to leave viewers with the impression that speed was the central message of the ad' (Oakes, 2015). The fact that these regulations exist indicates the desire of motordom to sell speed and bodily pleasure, rather than simply a means of transport.

Speed's ability to distort values about the importance of human life is part of the reason that Amish communities have resisted technological devices that promote speed. The Amish realise that increasing their speed of travel, particularly through the use of cars, would lead to increases in distances travelled, which would then lead to a breakdown of the close-knit communities that are central to Amish society. Bans on the use of cars also reflect the control of individualism, and the promotion of the virtues of family, community, humility and self-denial. By adopting lifestyles and farming methods that refuse to be dominated by speed, the Amish have become more successful farmers: many Amish farms have thrived at the same time their speed-obsessed neighbours have gone into bankruptcy (Berry, 1996). By adopting an approach that rejected speed and excessive mobility, the Amish have become one of America's most economically successful farming groups, as well as maintaining the ecology of their farming landscapes (Northcott, 2008).

2.4 Speed, excitement and bodily pleasure

People in modern Western societies exhibit a fascination with speed. Promoted by relentless advertising, government sponsorship and Hollywood action films, the dominant view is that fast cars, fast athletes and fast results are highly desired. In this section we explore this human fascination with speed and the excitement associated with it, before (in the following section) examining some of the physiological and psychological sources of this fascination.

In modern societies many people find the speed enabled by technological inventions such as the motor car to be thrilling. Humans have been conditioned for over a century to regard speed and the sensations associated with it as enjoyable, even exhilarating. When mass production of cars became established, a 'new avalanche of pop culture worked hard in advance to ensure that speed's customers had established a desire for speed's pleasures' (Duffy, 2009, p. 108). The popularity of roller-coasters and dodgem cars in amusement parks stimulated our desire for speed, or perhaps our quest for excitement. This exhilaration has been linked to the 'neuronic stimulation provided by the sensation of speed' (Diekstra & Kroon, 1997). For drivers, the central nervous system is stimulated by 'the sensation of speed, the sound of the car, the rhythm of the wheels and the continually changing lights and colours' inducing a kind of narcotic effect, which is similar to the addictive response of more conventional drugs ... 'this addiction to speed among some drivers is excellently expressed in the term "speedaholics"' (Diekstra & Kroon, 1997, p. 154). Conquering this addiction is, of course, the focus of this book.

The development of new technological innovations in transport in the late 19th and early 20th centuries, particularly the motor car, provided large numbers of people with a new and exciting experience: moving at what appeared to be great speed, and being able to control that movement (Duffy, 2009). Until the motor car became widely available, the focus on speed in modernity had become onerous, with its emphasis on Taylorist efficiency, clocks and schedules. With the development of Fordist production, time was required to be used as efficiently and productively as possible, which required the strict control of work time and the careful planning of the movement of goods and people, which in turn depended on centralised transport planning (Hubbard & Lilley, 2004, p. 276)

Whilst the car was mass-produced with boring assembly line labour in the Fordist factories of the 20th century, it also allowed workers (even the assembly line workers) to experience the excitement of speed in their own cars. With the motor car, speed 'was repackaged as a sensation and a pleasure to be put at the disposal of the individual consumer' (Duffy, 2009, p. 5). Duffy explains how the motor car promised experiences at a heightened level of intensity, giving drivers new and personal power, both over the sensation of speed, and over its effect on others—'most starkly, after the first car crash, the power of life or death' (Duffy, 2009, p. 5).

In many nations the motor car promised to provide the speed, freedom, mobility, privacy and pleasure that Americans, in particular, seemed to desire (Throgmorton & Eckstein, 2000). Car advertising played a crucial role in promoting concepts such as driving pleasure, as well as other 'benefits' of speed, including facilitating the escape to the country (Goulden, Ryley, & Dingwall, 2014, p. 144). Along with facilitating this bodily pleasure, the motor car also made new demands on the behaviour of its drivers. They had to develop new powers of alertness, sensory perception and response times, and new ways of seeing the spaces they travelled through at speed. The motor car enlivened drivers whilst allowing them higher speeds. For many individuals (particularly young males) the speed of cars was linked with not only freedom, but with excitement and self-esteem, and as a way to gain social kudos (Redshaw, 2008).

As the industrial era developed, many technologies enabled society and economies to operate at higher speeds. The private motor car, however, was a critical technology. It not only provided for faster travel, it was associated with bodily pleasure and the individual human control of speed: 'when under personal control, speed proved especially exhilarating' (Jakle & Sculle, 2008, p. 217). Drivers 'were given a sense of excitement, a thrill, which was unprecedented' (Duffy, 2009, p. 6). The motor car promised, through a new technology, the experience of space at a new and higher level of intensity.

2.5 The elusive excitement of speed

The apparent human preference for speed over slowness can be linked to the process of human evolution, where for many thousands of years before human civilisation developed, speed provided evolutionary advantages, including the ability to catch prey in hunting or to escape from predators. However, this evolutionary advantage is not helpful in modern societies when considering city transport. On the contrary when pleasure is associated with driving fast, and when car manufacturers promote cars as vehicles of freedom that provide the excitement of speed, this contributes to high road crash rates. In recent decades governments are questioning their support of speed, and 'more emphasis is being given to other factors … such as the impact of urban speeds, especially on children' (Redshaw, 2008, p. 67). As Redshaw suggests, calls for lowering of speed limits (e.g. on the Great Ocean Road in Victoria, Australia, which is a favoured road for drivers and motorcyclists seeking the thrill of speeding around bends) may indicate 'road safety overtaking thrill and speed discourses for the first time since the 1920s' (Redshaw, 2008, p. 68).

Researchers studying the innate preference for speed have identified biological stimuli that help explain this. When we experience speed the immediate biological reaction in the human body is the release of adrenaline, causing an increase in blood pressure, as well as body temperature and heart rate (Tiwari, 2015). Both men and women experience these reactions when driving a fast car, but the reactions are much stronger in males. Additionally, the experience of speed also triggers the release of monoamine oxidase, a regulator in our brains linked with dispensing dopamine into our bodies. Dopamine is a neurotransmitter, the brain's feel-good chemical (Park, 2008). Dopamine is responsible for the 'high' humans feel when they experience something daring or risky such as sky diving or driving fast. Another factor is that as a driver, making your vehicle go faster can be ego-boosting, which can also be habit-forming (Tiwari, 2015). All of these factors contribute to a craving for speed amongst many drivers, particularly men.

Is speed as good as we think it is? A problem for individuals seeking a 'high' via speed in modern cities is that city driving is often associated with traffic congestion, where there are limited opportunities for experiencing the thrill of speed (Fig. 2.4). This can lead to frustration, and a more desperate, almost addictive search for more thrills, which has negative consequences for road safety. The adrenalin rush from the speed on a roller coaster or vertical free-fall rides (such as the Giant Drop in Australia's Gold Coast Dreamworld, with its 135 km/h fall from 119 metres) has proven popular with thrill seekers. Such excitement, however, is rarely experienced in city traffic. Whilst the bodily pleasure associated with speed can help explain our fascination with theme park rides (or with illegal street racing), it is rarely relevant to commuting, where the bodily experience is often more about the tension created by being stuck in traffic.

'Speed has been an issue that has been fought over since the advent of motor vehicles and has mostly favoured the demands of the motor vehicle lobby' (Redshaw, 2008, p. 137). However, the pleasure and freedom promised by speed in the motor car was steadily eroded as the car has become more widely available. The very first cars likely did provide an experience of excitement from the skilful control of the car. Yet as cars began to dominate city transport systems, driving as a pleasurable experience or as a demonstration of freedom transformed

FIGURE 2.4 The occupants of the cars experience the frustration of being stuck in traffic in Vancouver, Canada, whilst the man on the bicycle speeds past them. *(Credit: Paul Tranter)*

into a more and more controlled 'mechanical activity of driving within the confines of white lines, speed limits and the constraints of traffic' (Redshaw, 2008, p. xii), partly due to efforts by governments to make roads safer. The reality of driving as a controlled activity, devoid of freedom and pleasure, was identified at least as early as the mid 20th century, when the philosopher Max Horkheimer identified a paradox in the supposed 'freedom' provided by the car:

> *'There are speed limits, warnings to drive slowly, to stop, to stay within certain lanes ... We must keep our eyes on the road and be ready at each instant to react with the right motion. Our spontaneity has been replaced by a frame of mind which compels us to discard every emotion or idea that might impair our alertness to the impersonal demands assailing us' (Horkheimer, 1947, p. 69).*

Reflecting on this quotation, one researcher suggested that it is 'no wonder some of us are keen to get the machine to take over driving and let us do something more interesting' (Redshaw, 2008, p. xii). Since Horkheimer made his telling observation over 70 years ago, driving has become more managed by signs, traffic signal lights and lines, and driving is more and more likely to be in congested traffic: the average New York driver spends 91 hours in traffic jams each year (the same as in Moscow), but in Los Angeles the figure is even higher at 102 hours (McCarthy, 2018).

Autonomous vehicles (discussed in detail in Chapter 8) will likely take away the thrill of speed (and controlling that speed) for individuals in motor cars, and may replace this with other excitements, such as that derived from watching videos whilst being transported through the city. There will also be a reduction of awareness of the environments being travelled through, as there will be no need to even look out of car windows, yet another example of how the quality of the lived experience and the interaction with the city can be eroded by modes which promote speed.

Whilst speed may not have delivered on the promise by Huxley (1931, p. 227) when he proclaimed 'Speed, it seems to me, provides the one genuinely modern pleasure', it was widely assumed that speed would provide advantages for all individuals when city transport systems were designed to maximise the speed of movement. The following section outlines the advantages that many individuals assume they gain from faster transport.

2.6 Claimed advantages of faster transport for individuals and households

As we explain in the following chapter, transport planners see speed as positive, most importantly because they assume it is associated with time savings. There is a considerable literature in economics on the valuation of time, including travel time. From early in the development of transport planning, planners and economists argued that motorists valued higher-speed travel as this allowed them to spend less time travelling and more time in other activities.

City residents also expected other advantages in faster transport, besides simply 'saving time'.

In cities that are dominated by private motor car transport, speed is believed to allow city residents to engage in a wider range of activities. Access to the speed of cars is thought to provide choice in social, recreational, sporting and shopping activities, as well as in employment locations and opportunities, and in choice of schools and residential location. The speed provided by the motor car allows parents to drive their children to many stimulating activities that would not be available if they had to rely on 'slower' modes (in low-density, car dominated cities). Higher-speed travel in cities designed for the car allows parents to choose the 'best' schools, even if they are many kilometres away from their residence.

Higher transport speed allows residents to live in suburban or even rural locations, whilst still being able to access distant shops, friends, relatives, schools, services and workplaces. It provides opportunities to travel out of the city for visits to rural areas. Faster transport gives employers a wider pool of potential employees, and has facilitated the development of large supermarkets and big-box stores, both of which provide a variety of consumer goods at lower prices than smaller corner stores or local department stores. High-speed transport in cars also allows consumers to transport large quantities of food and other goods in a single trip. It is also believed that higher-speed transport assists individual households in emergencies, providing for more rapid responses by police, fire and ambulance services.

2.7 Do individuals and households really benefit from faster transport?

All of the arguments in the earlier section, whilst seemingly sound, are highly questionable. Many of them have a starting point of a city designed around high-speed travel in private motor cars. If cities designed for other modes are examined, then higher densities of shops, schools and services mean that high speeds are not needed for individuals to access all the activities and things that they need: accessibility is provided through proximity. Let us examine each of the arguments above in turn.

First, does driving faster save your time? The short answer is 'no'—or not much. This question is addressed in more detail in Chapter 4. Many drivers, particularly young drivers, believe that if they are running late, driving faster will get them to their destination on time (Redshaw, 2008, p. 134). However, in urban areas, very little time is saved by driving faster. Many factors contribute to travel time apart from driving speed, including congestion and traffic control signals.

Does speed really allow residents to engage in a wider range of activities, and if so, is this really an advantage? In a low-density city, without access to the speeds provided by private motor cars, the access to activities is indeed low. But this low level of access is largely a function of the lack of local shops, schools and services, which have been replaced by more distant (and larger) shops, super-schools and services. Data from Melbourne, Australia show that the number of accessible land uses (e.g. business, industrial, parks) within 800 metres of a person's home declined dramatically from 1951 to 2005, a period of significant growth in car ownership. In 1951 over 70 per cent of the city was within 800 metres of five or more land uses, but by 2005, this had fallen to just over 40 per cent (Kelly et al., 2012). The access to different land uses fell as new suburbs were built. For new Melbourne suburbs built between 1971 and 2005, only 9 per cent of the area was within 800 metres of five or more land uses, and for the newest suburbs (established between 2001 and 2005) this had fallen to 4 per cent. The result is that people have to travel further to access the destinations they need. Low-density housing can leave residents isolated, reliant on motor car speeds to access shops and services (Fig. 2.5).

Similar trends are evident in other nations. In the three decades after 1980, 'when a model of urban development was encouraged in the UK that promoted private car use over public transport' the distance travelled for essential journeys (school, shops and work) increased by up to 40 per cent (Thorne, Filmer-Sankey, & Alexander, 2009, p. 20). In cities where 'slower' modes are dominant (e.g. Amsterdam, Copenhagen and Freiburg) there is a much denser provision of

FIGURE 2.5 Single family low-density sprawl, served with wide, fast roads in Toronto, Canada. *(Credit: Rodney Tolley)*

FIGURE 2.6 Local shops accessible on foot and by bicycle and tram in the sustainable model district of Vauban, in Freiburg, Germany. *(Credit: Elliot Fishman)*

services and shops, meaning that access to these is not dependent on high-speed transport (see Fig. 2.6).

Many parents in low-density cities see the speed enabled by cars as beneficial in providing their children with access to stimulating activities such as sport, music lessons, maths tutoring or visiting their friends. However, there are significant costs in providing this transport, including the time demands on parents. A recent Australian study found that nearly two-thirds of parents and carers spend eight hours each week driving their children to school and other activities (Allianz Australia, 2018). In more child-friendly cities designed for safer travel on foot, bicycle or using public transport, children are able to access many activities themselves, freeing parents from their chauffeuring roles (as is the case in many European cities).

High-speed travel also allows parents to make choices about the 'best' schools, even if that involves long journeys each day. However, apart from the extra time, financial cost, environmental impact, and the stress involved in these long journeys (for parents and children), there is the cost of a loss of children's valuable playful and social experiences, including opportunities for them to interact with adults (see Fig. 2.7). Children in cars may see more (if they bother to look out of the windows), but they learn less, and they are deprived of close personal contact with their neighbourhood and community. They miss out on the joy and wonder of walking and cycling around their neighbourhood

FIGURE 2.7 Cycling across generations in Houten, The Netherlands. *(Credit: Rodney Tolley)*

(O'Brien, 2003). (See Chapter 11 for more discussion of the value of the child-friendly modes of walking, cycling and public transport.)

Many parents compete with each other to provide their children with the best opportunity of being successful adults in a consumerist world, believing that a more expensive school education will give children an advantage. Experts question the value of this strategy: a society that allows children to walk and cycle to school, sport and their friends' houses is likely to lead to the development of more resilient, happier children who can also concentrate better at school (Goodyear, 2013; Stevenson, 2017).

High-speed transport does allow more people to live in low-density or rural locations. Yet, the reality of living in such locations may not always be positive. Isolation and the constant pressure to drive everywhere mean that living in low-density suburbs or rural locations, whilst seemingly appealing, creates family stresses that do not exist in more walkable neighbourhoods (Montgomery, 2013) (See Box 2.1).

Whilst escaping the city to visit the countryside is made easier with the speed of motor cars, excursions to the country, hiking, beaches, mountains or a swimming hole should not be the 'property' of car owners. Ideally, public transport should connect inner city walkers and cyclists to the joys of nature. Currently, even those public transport systems that do reach beyond city limits, often do so mainly for peri-urban commuters and have limited service on week-

BOX 2.1 How high-speed cities can lead to loneliness.

Loneliness is a major health problem in modern cities. The science behind this is clear: when people feel lonely, they have higher levels of norepinephrine in their blood. This chemical helps protect us in life-threatening situations, but also reduces our immune defence systems and makes us more vulnerable to infection. People with strong social networks involving daily face-to-face contacts with a wide range of people get sick less often, and when they do get sick it is not as serious, and they live longer, healthier lives: they have a stronger 'social immune system' protecting their physical as well as their mental health (Crowhurst, 2019).

The relevance of this to 'slow cities' is that high-speed transport systems have facilitated the growth of sprawling, anonymous suburbs where few people meet other people walking or cycling to local shops, schools or services. Such suburbs 'encourage social isolation and loneliness and do not easily support vibrant community life' (Baum, 2018, p. 100). Even in central city areas, in many cities decades of freeway building have promoted a culture of speed over people, where getting to places faster is seen as more important than making places for people. There is a growing body of research demonstrating the impacts of transport and land use systems designed for cars and speed on loneliness, lack of contact with neighbours, and reduced sense of community, as houses turn their backs on the street (see Fig. 2.8) and people drive into their houses without even getting out of their cars,

FIGURE 2.8 Housing facades without front doors and dominated by garages and stark concrete driveways, discouraging social interaction with passers-by: Lethbridge, Alberta, Canada. *(Credit: Rodney Tolley)*

(Continued)

BOX 2.1 How high-speed cities can lead to loneliness. ***(Cont.)***

often using remote-controlled garage doors. Using the 'slow' modes, and planning for walking, cycling and public transport, helps to combat loneliness.

Whilst there is an assumption amongst many modern city residents that getting to more friends (social connectedness) is facilitated by speed, the reverse is the case. People living on streets with heavy traffic have fewer friends and acquaintances than people living on quiet streets (see Section 5.4.3), and are also more likely to be ill (Hart & Parkhurst, 2011). As we explained in Section 2.7, speed leads to a spreading out of land uses and people, which damages connectedness. Research clearly identifies commuting as a corrosive force on social ties: in Switzerland, for every extra six miles of commuting, friends are 1.39 miles further away, and 'an extra 1.46 miles apart from *each other*' (Montgomery, 2013, p. 58).

When the health of people rather than speed becomes the focus of urban planning, strong communities can develop, and loneliness is reduced. One successful urban planning project is credited to female city planners in Vienna, Austria (see Section 5.4.4), where the Frauen-Werk-Stadt precinct was developed in 1993. Here, housing was built as close as possible to schools, public transport and shops and services. Walking was encouraged through wider sidewalks, well-lit pathways, and attractive public parks. 'The United Nations touts Frauen-Werk-Stadt as one of the best housing projects for gender equity in the world' (Rao, 2018). The housing promoted stronger community, connection and safety, not through fences and gates (which are oppressive and isolating) but through encouraging passive surveillance. Spaces that might have been seen simply as movement corridors were 're-imagined as "social spaces": appealing courtyards, wide staircases, and covered walkways designed for interaction' (Rao, 2018). These are features of the type of 'slow city' that this book promotes, and they promote all types of health (see Chapters 5, 6 and 7).

ends. If high-quality public transport to rural areas around the city is provided (as is the case now in areas surrounding Zurich for example, and as formerly available a century ago in many cities in the United States and elsewhere), then the supposed advantage of car speed is largely negated. Also, when city residents rely on 'escaping' the city, authorities may be less inclined to provide access to nature within the city. What is needed is already occurring in many cities, where carefully nurtured green spaces allow residents to enjoy the benefits of being in natural spaces within the city. For example, in Curitiba, Brazil almost 20 per cent of the city is parkland, whilst in Berlin, Tiergarten Park provides access to nature in a 210 hectare (520 acre) public park close to the city centre (see Fig. 2.9).

Employers may seem to benefit from having potential employees with access to high-speed private transport. But there are disbenefits with this as well. Parking often has to be provided at employers' expense, and (as discussed in Chapter 5) employees who have long commutes to work are likely to have more sick days, or have children who have more illness, requiring more days off

FIGURE 2.9 Enjoying access to nature in Tiergarten Park within a 10-minute bicycle ride of the centre of Berlin, Germany. *(Credit: glasseyes view, https://www.flickr.com/photos/axelhartmann/184675511)*

work. Because car travel timing is unpredictable, there are likely to be more late arrivals or workers arriving stressed from their daily commute. In low-speed cities, where the active modes of transport are supported, employers have access to a wide range of employees who can get to work more reliably on foot or by bicycle—and in a more positive frame of mind (see Chapter 5).

When considering the journey to work, the 'reliability', rather than the speed, of transport is regarded as being vital by employees and businesses. David Banister (2008, p. 74) makes the important point that people are more concerned with how long it will take to travel to work 'with a reasonable degree of certainty … the key policy objective now becomes that of reasonable travel time, rather than travel time minimisation'. This is the reasoning behind 'smart motorways' in the United Kingdom and other nations, where reducing speed limits from 70 mph to a lower limit increases throughput. It replaces high speeds (on some days) with more predictable journey times on most days. When transport planners make higher speed their priority, commuters do not know when they set off for work whether this would be a 'good' day in terms of congestion or a 'bad' day, so they always have to assume that it will be a 'bad' day and allow extra time for the trip. Reducing speed limits increases predictability and therefore reduces average journey time—another example of the 'slow paradox' that we will discuss in Chapter 4.

Employees who believe they are benefiting from high-speed transport are also not fully considering their predicament in terms of financial indebtedness. The development of capitalist societies was linked to the speed of the car through low-density suburbs, which compelled longer commutes to employment. This meant that employees were committed to borrowing to pay for cars, which became an important aspect of consumer culture, where the survival of the system required high levels of personal and national debt. 'Borrowing from the future can work while interest rates are low and there is confidence in sustained income, but it is risky economics and puts consumers in the hands of the finance industry' (Dant, 2018). In many Western nations, including the United States, United Kingdom and Australia, a new generation of employees, already in debt from student loans, high housing costs and intermittent employment, are postponing both buying cars and learning to drive. In the United Kingdom, numbers of new car registrations are declining, and fears of a collapse in the used car market leave the car industry exposed (Dant, 2018).

There is little doubt that high-speed transport has supported the growth of large out-of-town shopping centres, often providing lower cost goods than smaller shops closer to people's homes. Yet there are costs associated with this. Large corporations come to dominate the retail market, meaning that local employment is often decimated. The term Walmartization has been used to describe the combined negative impacts on people and the environment (Atcheson, 2011): '... the chain store business model, and WalMart in particular, has destroyed local Main Street economies all over America, as well as the networks of social relations that went with these economies, in which local business owners employed local people and had to take responsibility for how they treated them' (Kunstler, 2013). Kunstler describes the desolation of traditional downtowns, as well as the loss of local business owners as community leaders, and the transformation of landscapes into parking lots and big-box stores (Fig. 2.10). As more people drive to these stores, streets become more dangerous places for walking, cycling and for children. And when people drive to large grocery stores, this encourages purchases of greater quantities of processed and high-energy food and drinks, which can be transported easily by car. This has been shown to be linked to high obesity and overweight problems in many nations (Roberts & Edwards, 2010).

The final claimed advantage for individuals of faster transport discussed earlier relates to the response times by emergency services. It may seem logical that fast roads will lead to rapid response times, but this is not the case. Faster roads mean that the density of housing and provision of emergency service stations is reduced. Research clearly shows that low-density (high-speed) environments lead to longer response times. A Japanese study found that living in a low-density area was associated with longer ambulance call-response intervals, and low survival rates for out-of-hospital cardiac arrest (Yasunaga et al., 2011). A US study produced similar findings: sprawl was found to be associated with

FIGURE 2.10 Walmart and Sam's Club (retail warehouses) located on the outskirts of Chino, California, in a car-dependent location backing on to a multi-lane highway. *(Credit: Walmart, https://www.flickr.com/photos/walmartcorporate/5249869745)*

longer emergency medical service (EMS) response time and hence a higher chance of delay in ambulance arrival after motor-vehicle crashes in the United States. 'The results of this study suggest that promotion of community design and development that follows smart-growth principles and regulates urban sprawl may improve EMS performance and reliability' (Trowbridge, Gurka, & O'connor, 2009, p. 428). As Chapter 5 stresses, it seems that speed is bad for our health in more ways than many realise.

2.8 Conclusion

Faster car travel has changed the lives of individuals in cities around the world. In particular it has changed the pace of life, so that people can now expect to travel further and faster each day. Whilst the impact of these changes has often been assumed to be positive for individuals, the supposed advantages of speed turn out to be illusory, limited to certain groups, or come at a cost—often negating any advantages. Faster travel was assumed to bring new experiences of space and time to city life, bringing freedom of movement and the pleasure of speed. Yet a holistic perspective shows how speed creates other impacts that destroy the advantages that speed itself was supposed to create.

If city transport could be made faster, without changing any other aspects of the city and without adding to the cost of transport, then perhaps speed would confer the advantages it has been assumed to provide. However, whenever speeds are increased, this changes the city in various ways: reducing the density, safety, economic viability and liveability of the city. As we explain in Chapters 5 to 7, faster transport in the city has a range of significant negative impacts on human, environmental and economic health. In contrast, slowing city transport enhances all aspects of city life.

Higher speeds change the city in ways that cancel out the expected benefits of speed, through: sprawl; closure of shops, schools and services; emasculation of public transport; and increased road danger. In cities designed for the speeds of the car, the car may be the only choice for those who wish to maintain the advantages that speed appears to provide. However, for many individuals, more speed brings less freedom (to choose other modes of transport) and the increased discomforts and human costs of both congestion and sprawl. Speed negatively impacts the lives of those who wish (or are forced) to move slowly, including children walking to school, people on bicycles and elderly people trying to cross roads. The daily routines of these individuals are 'merely obstacles to the high speed traffic that cuts mercilessly through slower-moving pathways and dwellings' (Sheller & Urry, 2000, p. 744). The construction of city transport systems that maximise the speed of car travel devastated many inner-city neighbourhoods, as homes, shops and schools were demolished to make way for new roads, 'though this was of little concern to those who glided by on the highways in the comfort of their cars' (Redshaw, 2008, p. 31).

The speed provided by the car also 'coerces almost everyone to juggle tiny fragments of time in order to put together complex, fragile and contingent patterns of social life, especially within the city' (Sheller & Urry, 2000, p. 744). The world many city residents live in is 'hectic, fast-paced, fractured, hurried' (Babauta, 2010). This juggling or multi-tasking whilst moving—sending texts, reading, sipping coffee, eating, shaving and applying make-up—is linked to what has been labelled the 'virus of hurry' (Honoré, 2013) whereby individuals are constantly trying to do more in less time, to be more productive, appearing busy to others, always rushing on to the next task and never feeling that they have enough time to do the things that they want to do (Tranter, 2014). Paradoxically, as explained in Chapter 4, designing a city around 'slower' modes of transport reduces time pressures and saves time for everyone, whilst promoting health and sustainability.

Whilst this chapter has demonstrated that the benefits of speed for individuals are at best highly questionable, and more likely illusory, the benefits for economy and society must still be examined. Is it possible that whilst individuals may not benefit from speed (as was widely assumed), transport systems that promote speed may provide advantages for cities (or nations) in terms of economic development? The following chapter addresses this question.

References

Advertising Standards Authority. (2019). 20 Motoring BCAP Code. *ASA UK*. Available from: https://www.asa.org.uk/type/broadcast/code_section/20.html.

Allianz Australia. (2018). Aussie parents add full work day to their week driving kids about, reveals survey. Available from: https://www.allianz.com.au/media/news/2018/aussie-parents-add-full-work-day-to-their-week-driving-kids-about.

Andrews, C., & Urbanska, W. (2009). *Less is more: Embracing simplicity for a healthy planet, a caring economy and lasting happiness*. Gabriola Island, BC: New Society Publishers.

Atcheson, J. (2011). The Walmartization of America redux: How the relentless drive for cheap stuff undermines our economy, bankrupts our soul, and pillages the planet. *Common Dreams*. Available from: https://www.commondreams.org/views/2011/12/16/walmartization-america-redux-how-relentless-drive-cheap-stuff-undermines-our.

Babauta, L. (2010). *Focus: A simplicity manifesto in the age of distraction*. Available from: https://focusmanifesto.s3.amazonaws.com/FocusFree.pdf.

Banister, D. (2008). The sustainable mobility paradigm. *Transport Policy, 15*(2), 73–80.

Baum, F. (2018). *Governing for health: Advancing health and equity through policy and advocacy*. New York: Oxford University Press, USA.

Berry, W. (1996). *The Unsettling of America* (3rd ed.). San Francisco: Sierra Club Books.

Bertman, S. (1998). *Hyperculture: The human cost of speed*. Westport: Praeger Publishers.

Bisceglio, P. (2018). Are cities making animals smarter. *The Atlantic*. Available from: https://www.theatlantic.com/science/archive/2018/08/cities-animal-intelligence-fishing-cats/567538/

Crowhurst, S. H. (2019). Loneliness is life threatening: We can design cities to foster community. *International Making ities Livable*. Available from: https://www.livablecities.org/blog/loneliness-life-threatening-we-can-design-cities-foster-community.

Dant, T. (2018). What would a post-car world look like? *RSA Journal*. Available from: https://medium.com/rsa-journal/what-would-a-post-car-world-look-like-cd8e31d8ffca.

Diekstra, R., & Kroon, M. (1997). Cars and behaviour: Psychological barriers to car restraint and sustainable urban transport. In R. Tolley (Ed.), *The greening of urban transport: Planning for walking and cycling in Western cities* (2nd ed., pp. 147–157). Chichester: Wiley and Sons.

Duffy, E. (2009). *The speed handbook: Velocity, pleasure, modernism*. Durham: Duke University Press.

Fuller, R. A., Warren, P. H., & Gaston, K. J. (2007). Daytime noise predicts nocturnal singing in urban robins. *Biology Letters, 3*(4), 368–370.

Goodyear, S. (2013). The link between kids who walk or bike to school and concentration. *City Lab*. Available from: https://www.citylab.com/transportation/2013/02/kids-who-walk-or-bike-school-concentrate-better-study-shows/4585/.

Goulden, M., Ryley, T., & Dingwall, R. (2014). Beyond 'predict and provide': UK transport, the growth paradigm and climate change. *Transport Policy, 32*, 139–147.

Hamilton, C. (2003). Downshifting in Britain: A sea-change in the pursuit of happiness. The Australia Institute Discussion Paper No. 58. 42p. Available from: https://www.tai.org.au/sites/default/files/DP58_8.pdf.

Hart, J., & Parkhurst, G. (2011). Driven to excess: Impacts of motor vehicles on the quality of life of residents of three streets in Bristol UK. *World Transport Policy & Practice, 17*(2), 12–30.

Hayakawa, A. (2018). India zooms past Germany as fourth-largest auto market. *Nikkei Asian Review*. Available from: https://asia.nikkei.com/Business/Automobiles/India-zooms-past-Germany-as-fourth-largest-auto-market2.

Honoré, C. (2013). *The slow fix: Solve problems, work smarter and live better in a fast world*. New York: HarperCollins.

Horkheimer, M. (1947). *Eclipse of Reason*. New York: Continuum.

Hubbard, P., & Lilley, K. (2004). Pacemaking the modern city: The urban politics of speed and slowness. *Environment and Planning D: Society and Space*, *22*(2), 273–294.

Huxley, A. (1931). Wanted, a new pleasure. In *Music at Night and Other Essays*, (pp. 221–229). New York: Doubleday Doran. Available from: https://archive.org/details/in.ernet.dli.2015.166397/page/n4/mode/2up.

Jakle, J. A., & Sculle, K. A. (2008). *Motoring: The highway experience in America*. Athens, Georgia: University of Georgia Press.

Jones, S. J., & Brunt, H. (2017). Twenty miles per hour speed limits: A sustainable solution to public health problems in Wales. *Journal of Epidemiology and Community Health*, *71*(7), 699–706.

Kelly, J. F., Breadon, P., Mares, P., Ginnivan, L., Jackson, P., Gregson, J., et al. (2012). *Tomorrow's suburbs*. Melbourne: Grattan Institute.

Kundera, M. (1996). *Slowness* (L. Asher, Trans.). London and Boston: Faber and Faber.

Kunstler, J. H. (2013). James Howard Kunstler: Walmart and the corn-pone Nazis. Available from: http://redgreenandblue.org/2013/03/04/james-howard-kunstler-walmart-and-the-corn-pone-nazis/.

Latham, A., & McCormack, D. (2008). Speed and slowness. In T. Hall, P. Hubbard, & J. R. Short (Eds.), *The SAGE companion to the city* (pp. 301–317). London: Sage.

Maser, C. (1999). *Vision and leadership in sustainable development*. Boston: Lewis Publishers.

McCarthy, N. (2018). The cities where U.S. drivers spend the most time stuck in traffic. *Forbes*. Available from: https://www.forbes.com/sites/niallmccarthy/2018/02/08/the-cities-where-u-s-drivers-spend-the-most-time-stuck-in-traffic-infographic/#381f5f2316d8.

Montgomery, C. (2013). *Happy city: Transforming our lives through urban design*. New York: Penguin Random House.

Northcott, M. (2008). The desire for speed and the rhythm of the earth. In S. Bergmann, & T. Sager (Eds.), *The ethics of mobilities: Rethinking place, exclusion, freedom and environment* (pp. 215–232). Aldershot: Ashgate.

O'Brien, C. (2003). Transportation that's actually good for the soul. *National Center for Bicycling and Walking (NCBW) Forum (Canada), 54*, 1–13. Available from: http://www.bikewalk.org/pdfs/forumarch0104transportation.pdf.

Oakes, O. (2015). Honda 'speed-reading' ad banned for encouraging fast driving. *Campaign*. Available from: https://www.campaignlive.co.uk/article/honda-speed-reading-ad-banned-encouraging-fast-driving/1360614.

Park, A. (2008). Why we take risks – it's the dopamine. *Time Magazine*. Available from: http://content.time.com/time/health/article/0,8599,1869106,00.html.

Parris, K., & McCauley, R. (2019). Noise pollution and the environment. *Australian Academy of Science*. Available from: https://www.science.org.au/curious/earth-environment/noise-pollution-and-environment.

Rao, A. (2018). Our cities are designed for loneliness. *Vice Magazine*. Available from: https://www.vice.com/en_us/article/kzvzpv/our-cities-are-designed-for-loneliness-v25n4.

Redshaw, S. (2008). *In the company of cars: Driving as a social and cultural practice*. Hampshire: Ashgate.

Roberts, I., & Edwards, P. (2010). *The energy glut: The politics of fatness in an overheating world*. London: Zed Books.

Saul, J. R. (2013). *Voltaire's bastards: The dictatorship of reason in the West*. New York: Simon and Schuster.

Sheller, M., & Urry, J. (2000). The city and the car. *International Journal of Urban and Regional Research*, *24*(4), 737–757.

Stevenson, B. (2017). Children's independence: A conceptual argument for connecting the conduct of everyday life and learning in Finland. *Children's Geographies*, *15*(4), 439–451.

The Perseus Project. (2017). Ancient Olympic events: Running. Available from: http://www.perseus.tufts.edu/Olympics/running.html.

Thorne, R., Filmer-Sankey, W., & Alexander, A. (2009). Transportation. In A. Ritchie, & R. Thomas (Eds.), *Sustainable urban design: An environmental approach* (2nd ed., pp. 21–30). Taylor and Francis: London.

Throgmorton, J. A., & Eckstein, B. (2000). *Desire lines: The Chicago area transportation study and the paradox of self in post-war America. Literary and Visual Representations of Three American Cities, 1870s to 1930, A project web site of the 3 Cities Project of the Universities of Nottingham and Birmingham, United Kingdom.* Available from: https://ir.uiowa.edu/cgi/viewcontent.cgi?article=1007&context=urban_pubs.

Tiwari, A. (2015). Why do we feel so thrilled by speed? *Science, ABC*. Available from: https://www.scienceabc.com/pure-sciences/why-do-we-feel-so-thrilled-by-speed.html.

Tranter, P. (2014). Active travel: A cure for the hurry virus. *Journal of Occupational Science*, *21*(1), 65–76.

Trowbridge, M. J., Gurka, M. J., & O'connor, R. E. (2009). Urban sprawl and delayed ambulance arrival in the US. *American Journal of Preventive Medicine*, *37*(5), 428–432.

Wajcman, J. (2015). *Pressed for time: The acceleration of life in digital capitalism*. Chicago: University of Chicago Press.

Walljasper, J. (1997). The speed trap: Why it's so hard to slow down—and why we can't wait any longer. *Utne Reader.* Available from: https://www.utne.com/mind-and-body/the-speed-trap-aesthetic-of-slowness.

Well, D. N. (2007). Accounting for the effect of health on economic growth. *The Quarterly Journal of Economics*, *122*(3), 1265–1306.

Whitelegg, J. (1993). Time Pollution. *The Ecologist*, *23*(4), 131–134.

World Health Organization. (2008). *The world health report 2008: Primary health care: now more than ever* (9241563737). Available from: https://www.who.int/whr/2008/en/.

Yasunaga, H., Miyata, H., Horiguchi, H., Tanabe, S., Akahane, M., Ogawa, T., et al. (2011). Population density, call-response interval, and survival of out-of-hospital cardiac arrest. *International Journal of Health Geographics*, *10*(1), 26.

Zheng, S. (2017). China now has over 300 million vehicles ... that's almost America's total population. *South China Morning Post*. Available from: https://www.scmp.com/news/china/economy/article/2088876/chinas-more-300-million-vehicles-drive-pollution-congestion.

Chapter 3

The benefits of speed for economy and society: challenging the dominant narrative

'America is all about speed. Hot, nasty, badass speed'.

From the 2006 movie *Talladega Nights*

Abstract

The dominant narrative in modern Western 20th century cities was one that equated speed with social progress and economic growth. This chapter outlines the standard arguments regarding the 'benefits' of speed for economy and society. These include: the role of speed in supporting capitalist society and economic growth; the way in which speed became central to visions of the 'modern city;' and the idea (clearly evident in transport models) that increasing the speed of transport would save time, and hence improve productivity. Each of these arguments is shown to be open to challenge. A new narrative about cities is emerging, where liveable, healthy and sustainable environments are supported by a move towards slower city transport.

3.1 Introduction

If a dominant narrative about city transport and speed in the 20th century could be identified, it would likely be 'the story of speed as the begetter of progress according to the model of regulated technological economic growth' (Tomlinson, 2007, p. 64). In modern Western societies, people have been told, and largely accepted, a story about what is valuable and what represents 'progress' in city life. We have been told that in a capitalist society, increasing the speed of travel will boost economic growth, which will lead to increased prosperity for everyone. We have been told that an enterprising vision of a modern city necessitates large-scale transport engineering in the form of high-speed roads. Transport modelling experts tell us that higher speeds on these new roads will save time for everyone, hence creating a more productive society and contributing to economic growth, so that the whole cycle of progress is reinforced. 'An

Slow Cities. http://dx.doi.org/10.1016/B978-0-12-815316-1.00003-4

essential attribute of our contemporary model of progress (in which consumption substitutes for quality of life or personal contentment) is that the faster you can do something, the better it must be' (Porritt, 2005, p. 44).

This narrative is giving way to a new story, in which:

- the notion of progress through economic growth is increasingly being questioned;
- new visions of the modern city based on creating more liveable, healthier and sustainable places are emerging; and
- basic assumptions in transport modelling (e.g. that faster is better) are shown to be flawed.

In the previous chapter we explained how the assumptions about the benefits of speed for individuals are largely illusory. This chapter examines the claimed benefits of speed in the wider context of the economy and society. These claimed benefits are now being questioned in light of new understandings of sustainability. The (till now) conventional beliefs that 'speed is good' and 'faster is always better' are becoming outmoded, replaced by a more thorough appreciation of the complex impacts of speed. Even if we were to accept parts of the dominant narrative (e.g. that economic growth should be promoted), a close inspection reveals that slowing city transport can provide economic advantages for the host city and region (see Chapter 7). In this chapter we examine several components of this dominant narrative, discovering in each case that speed does not necessarily provide the assumed benefits to economy and society.

3.2 Speed, industrialism and capitalism

3.2.1 Is speed good for capitalism and economic growth?

The accepted story about the value of speed is clearly demonstrated in terms of the link between speed and capitalism. Speed was a desire that suited capitalism and was fostered by capitalism 'in every mass-cultural genre from car advertisements to car chase films' (Duffy, 2009, p. 35). The speed provided to the masses by the motor car helped to promote the growth of capitalism and the development of industry in the United States that made it the world's foremost industrial nation in the 20th century. High-speed individualised transport was central to the operation and development of the 'auto-mobile industrial complex' (Sweezy, 2000). This provided the foundation for strong economic growth in several ways. For example, the motor car industry itself included huge companies that were amongst the most profitable of the world's largest industries. The road construction industry and associated transport planning and modelling agencies generated economic activity. In addition, widespread access to the speed of mass-produced cars promoted the growth of suburbs, which were effective catalysts for boosting consumer purchases, which in turn created economic growth. Low-density suburban living increased demand for consumer goods such as lawnmowers, furniture (including outdoor furniture), carpets and curtains, and cars (Eliot Hurst, 1981).

In modern societies where economic growth is prized, anything that promotes faster growth fits well with dominant economic ideology. Faster transport is linked with growth in GDP and economic growth generally. Slow speed caused by traffic congestion is seen as more than simply inconvenient; 'it is widely believed to impose a real cost to the economy of a city, a region or a nation' (Low & Odgers, 2012, p. 190). Frequent reference to this view has been used to support the arguments for the injection of funding into transport infrastructure, particularly roads, even though the evidence that such funding boosts economic growth is not clear (Banister & Berechman, 2003).

Central to capitalism is the operation of the means of production for profit. The faster goods and services can be produced (and sold), the greater the profit. As Benjamin Franklin famously argued, 'time is money'. Applying this maxim to society, a seemingly logical deduction is that faster is better, as time (and money) can be saved. 'Faster is seen to be better, as it achieves more in a given time frame. High-speed is viewed as less time consuming and therefore less costly and thus more efficient and profit creating or enhancing' (Harris, Lewis, & Adam, 2004, p. 6). This reasoning has been applied to the speed of travel, and also to the speed of production and of consumption. 'Greater speed means more goods and services can be produced, transported and sold, and bought in a given period of time' (Homer-Dixon, 2006, p. 113).

The more rapidly individuals can consume products, the more effective is capitalist society. Thus it was widely assumed that 'capitalist growth demands faster movement' (Duffy, 2009, p. 57). Increasing the speed of urban transport was seen to be effective in boosting consumption. As Lefebvre explained: 'speed ... gets to be capitalism's good: people will work, and goods will move, faster and faster' (Duffy, 2009, p. 35).

3.2.2 Downsides of capitalism and economic growth supported by speed

In this section we examine two arguments that involve economic growth: first, whether it can be achieved in the long term by increasing speed; and second, even if it is achieved, whether this economic growth is ecologically sustainable.

While the speed of the motor car did provide a boost for capitalism and economic growth initially, this emphasis on speed created vulnerabilities in capitalist societies. Key aspects of the 'auto-mobile industrial complex' described earlier—the motor car industry, the road construction industry and the growth of suburbs—made the US economy susceptible to collapse when faced with challenges such as high global oil prices and the impacts of hurricanes Rita and Katrina on US oil refining capacity in the years leading to the global financial crisis of 2007–09.

The motor car industry in the United States came close to collapse in 2009. The number of workers employed in car and parts manufacturing in April 2006 was over one million. By June 2009, that had fallen by 43 per cent to 624,000 (Amadeo, 2018). The largest US car makers were saved only by an injection of almost US$80 billion from a federal bailout. Many US taxpayers were not impressed that three CEOs from these car manufacturing companies flew to Washington in their corporate jets to ask for a bailout, and were further dismayed to hear reports that more than $10 billion of those bailout funds may not be repaid (Hathaway, 2015). Supporting a capitalist system based on speed suited capitalist governments and the owners of private capital, but not necessarily all citizens of capitalist societies.

The effect of the road construction industry on economic growth also needs to be carefully considered. Proponents of the construction of high-speed roads invariably point out that this provides a boost to jobs and GDP, but they rarely discuss whether more jobs and GDP growth could be achieved by alternative investment approaches. Indeed, Lloyd Wright, Senior Transport Specialist at the Asian Development Bank, estimates that for the price of one road overpass in the Global South, you could have around 400,000 bicycles, about 800 km of quality footpaths or 80 years of weekly car free events. He concludes that 'Walkability is not a financial issue, walkability is not a technical issue, but walkability IS a political issue' (Wright, 2019).

Negative long-term economic implications of road building become evident as high-speed roads deteriorate. City road infrastructure generates a huge maintenance and repair bill, yet politicians are often reluctant to commit the necessary funds. This reluctance has been referred to as the 'tyranny of the ribbon' (Jaffe, 2015), where politicians view valuable opportunities in ribbon cutting ceremonies for major new road building projects. However, these same politicians see little value in being associated with stale maintenance of a predecessor's old road project. This has resulted in a huge and increasing backlog of maintenance projects for America's roads.

In 2015 an estimated US$45 billion per year was required to keep US roads in good repair, yet only $16.5 billion was spent on maintenance (Jaffe, 2015). The American Society of Civil Engineers produces a *Report Card for America's Infrastructure* every four years. The 2017 report assigned a grade (similar to a school report card) based on the condition of infrastructure and the investment 'needed for improvement'. For the 'Roads' category, the grade was 'D'. The report noted that 21 per cent of the nation's highways had poor surface condition, costing US motorists over $120 billion in additional vehicle repairs and operating costs. The highway system had been underfunded for decades, creating a $836 billion backlog of highway and bridge repair needs (American Society of Civil Engineers, 2017):

> *'we need to use all the available road money each year to fix our roads, and then some, to prevent them from falling into a state of disrepair that endangers public safety. And the more roads we build, the more we need to one day fix. And yet we build.*

We build without seeming to appreciate that every mile of fresh new road will one day become a mile of crumbling old road that needs additional attention' (Jaffe, 2015).

The cost–benefit analyses that justified building massive city freeways over the last 50 years failed to take into account that within about 50 years (or less) much of this infrastructure would reach its 'use-by' date and would need to be rebuilt, so that future generations would have to pay for the life-expired freeways. Cities are realising that 'investing in freeways is a bad business decision' (Garfield, 2018).

As we explain later, many cities are now deciding that the most effective strategy (for economic as well as environmental and social reasons) is to demolish high-speed urban expressways rather than repair them. And it is not only the high-speed roads that have become problematic. So too are the suburbs that are accessed by these roads.

The suburbs that seemed an ideal way to promote consumer spending and economic growth were also the areas most susceptible to the mortgage crisis created by the global financial collapse of 2007–09. This recession was precipitated by the failure of an eight trillion-dollar housing bubble, which led to huge declines in consumer spending. Many residents in the outer suburbs could not afford the cost of fuel to get from their dormitory suburbs to work, or even to the nearest shops, schools or services. The high-speed car-based transport systems that enabled the construction of these suburbs made their residents vulnerable to financial ruin.

In contrast to what many might expect, slowing city transport may lead to an economic boost for cities that adopt the 'slower' modes (as detailed in Chapter 7), or for those sections of the city that promote the 'slow city' ideals that we advocate here. For example, city neighbourhoods that are transformed into more walkable areas experience higher rates of growth in real estate value, as well as improved retail performance.

There is also growing recognition that promoting speed- and car-dominated cities does not work for the 'knowledge economy' (see Chapter 7) in which growth is related to the quantity, quality and accessibility of information and intellectual capabilities, rather than on physical inputs or natural resources (Powell & Snellman, 2004). Even some neoliberal urban economists who collectively once resisted land use and transport planning policies that supported urbanity and 'slow cities' (density, public transport investment, walkability improvements and bicycle infrastructure) have now joined the urbanist camp. They realise that walkability adds value, and that the creativity that develops in cities requires face-to-face interaction, not rapid mobility. This is evident in *Triumph of the City* by Edward Glaeser (2011). While Glaeser presents some standard neoliberal arguments in his criticism of government regulation, he also is an advocate of Jane Jacobs' ideas for concentrating creativity—and human capital—in cities (see Section 3.3.2). He decries the massive government road subsidies that promoted urban sprawl during the 20th century.

FIGURE 3.1 Abandoned housing and commercial buildings in Detroit, USA. Evidence of Detroit's economic decline has been seen for many years, though there are recent signs of revival in some districts. *(Credit: Rodney Tolley)*

Cities that have attractive, walkable central areas are far more successful in attracting the 'creative class'—college educated 25–34-year olds. This group is now credited with the ability to confer benefits upon a host city, such as new ideas and high-tech industry. In contrast, cities where the majority of the workforce is employed in less-skilled work (such as in motor car manufacture) effectively destroy knowledge-creating capacity. Glaeser illustrates this by comparing Detroit (historically dominated by a single manufacturing industry employing hundreds of thousands of less-skilled workers in three motor vehicle firms), with New York, which rose as a financial centre while Detroit continued its decline (see Fig. 3.1) (at least until recent signs of revitalisation). The face-to-face contact provided in central New York, particularly in areas such as Wall Street where land use allows firms to closely cluster, helps to create the type of 'intellectual explosions' where one smart idea helps to generate others (Glaeser, 2011, p. 56).

In contrast to the economic benefits of walking, some estimates suggest that freeways destroy more real estate value than the cost of building them (Mouzon, 2012). Yet politicians have a history of supporting the construction of these freeways. One of the reasons that city transport systems have been designed for speed is that politicians can use large scale freeway and bridge investment projects to promote the view that they are working towards solving

FIGURE 3.2 On August 4, 2017 the AU$246m Mitchell Freeway extension in the northern suburbs of Perth, Australia, was officially opened by the then Prime Minister Malcolm Turnbull and a number of other politicians and dignitaries. *(Credit: Pro Star Pics)*

city transport problems. While, as this book demonstrates, such investment is ineffective for solving transport problems, and building sidewalks and cycleways and developing new bus routes are much more effective solutions, the infrastructure for these 'slower' modes is small-scale, low cost, and less visible, and hence does not generate headlines in the press. It is easy to find photographs of opening ceremonies for new freeways and bridges over the last 100 years (Fig. 3.2), but much harder to find images of politicians opening a new sidewalk. The large-scale investments needed to support freeways are often misrepresented in terms of overestimating their benefits and underestimating their costs. High-speed freeways 'are constructed not because they offer an appropriate solution … but for their prestige value' (Cox, 2013, p. 19).

A similar argument can be found in Adam Smith's 1776 *The Wealth of Nations (Book V)*:

> *'The proud minister of an ostentatious court may frequently take pleasure in executing a work of splendour and magnificence, such as a great highway, which is frequently seen by the principal nobility … But to execute a great number of little works, in which nothing that can be done can excite the smallest degree of admiration in any traveller, and which … have nothing to recommend them but their extreme utility, is a business which appears in every respect too mean and paltry to merit the attention of so great a magistrate. Under such an administration, therefore, such works are almost always entirely neglected' (Smith, 2007 (digital edition), pp. 564–565).*

Thus a city transport system that encourages high-speed travel can lead to economic vulnerability. But there may be an even deeper problem associated with the 'progress' enabled by speed in the city, and here we turn to the second argument about economic growth—its impact on ecological sustainability. Although most city and national governments base their transport policies on the assumption that economic growth and globalisation represent 'progress' and are laudable, high priority goals, whether these goals are good for the well-being of people and the planet is a question that is being increasingly asked. 'Far from improving the quality of our working lives, there is growing evidence that this progress is making us more miserable and more stressed' (Porritt, 2005, p. 44). The continued push for speed in the city is supported by constant advertising that convinces people that speed is a privilege bestowed on successful members of a capitalist society (Cox, 2013). 'We created a cultural story in which anyone could amass material wealth if he or she was sufficiently industrious and persistent … So ingrained is the story that we rarely question its implications' (Andrews & Urbanska, 2009, p. 216).

Capitalist economies were developed around fossil fuels (and earlier around waterpower), individualism and consumer spending. When capitalism first began to dominate economic systems, the negative consequences of constantly increasing speeds in city transport systems did not seem significant to many policy makers. However, what was not understood at the time was the long-term impacts of speed that relied on the increasing use of fossil fuels in a world where the human population was increasing rapidly.

When industrial capitalism became the dominant social-economic system in the 1930s, the global population was only a little over two billion. The ecological damage from industrial capitalism with this number of people was relatively minor. However, with a current global population of nearly four times that size, which is increasingly affluent, and with greater access to 'faster' transport, the implications of an economic and social system that depends on burning fossil fuels to promote consumer spending can no longer be ignored, as Chapter 6 demonstrates. The faster the global economic system expands, 'the faster the world's fragile living systems decline' (Andrews & Urbanska, 2009, p. 216).

Fortunately, there is a viable alternative to this story. This alternative involves a slowing of our lives, our cities and our transport systems, instead of a continued push for greater speed and productivity to drive economic growth. This will require a change in the way we think about speed and the way we glorify it.

3.3 Speed in visions of the modern city

3.3.1 The celebration of speed in visions of the modern city

It is not only in the cost of supporting the motor car industry or the construction of transport infrastructure that the continued pursuit of speed has impacted on cities. It can also be seen in the way in which speed became a central part of visions of the modern city, dating from the early 20th century, when the speed enabled by the use of fossil fuels in motor cars was associated with a futuristic view of the world. Filippo Marinetti, the Italian poet and founder of the Futurist movement, famously described this view in his Manifesto of Futurism:

> *'We affirm that the world's magnificence has been enriched by a new beauty: the beauty of speed. A racing car whose hood is adorned with great pipes, like serpents of explosive breath – a roaring car that seems to ride on grapeshot is more beautiful than the Victory of Samothrace' (Marinetti, 1909).*

Marinetti's vision of the future was based on the adulation of technology and the aesthetics of modernity. This vision of the Futurists helped to shape the way other leaders in the 20th century imagined the development of society, particularly in cities (Daly, 2017).

The celebration of the benefits of speed in urban transport became clearly evident in the first half of the 20th century. Modernist architects (or visionaries as they were sometimes called) such as Le Corbusier and Frank Lloyd Wright aimed to create cities that embodied their particular understanding of what it meant to be modern. Le Corbusier's utopian city plans have been described 'as the quintessence of high-modernist urbanism' (Hubbard & Lilley, 2004, p. 274). He saw the speed of private cars as the means to enable fast movement into and out of tall buildings, distant from each other and from centres of employment. Similarly, Frank Lloyd Wright envisaged an idealistic 'Broadacre City' (Fig. 3.3) in which every 'citizen has his own car' and 'multiple-lane highways make travel safe and enjoyable' (Wright, 1935, p. 348) so that urban civilization

FIGURE 3.3 Frank Lloyd Wright's sketch for his 'Broadacre City'. *(Credit: Wikimedia Commons, Kjell Olsen—originally posted to Flickr as Wright Sketches for Broadacre City 2, CC BY-SA 2.0, https://commons.wikimedia.org/w/index.php?curid=12036508)*

could be 'disgorged into the countryside along high-speed transportation routes' (Judd & Beach, 2010, p. 6). The speed of motorised transport became a central pillar of the planners' vision of an efficient city.

The fascination with speed on roads as a central part of a modern nation started in the 1930s. Hitler began the construction of his Autobahnen in 1933, and they soon came to be admired throughout the world, particularly in the United States. A delegation from the American Bureau of Public Roads, after a tour of Autobahnen in 1937, returned to the United States full of praise for the German roads, as wonderful examples of the best modern road building. Politicians in the United States were aware of the nationalism behind Hitler's road building, but modern engineering was recognised as 'necessary everywhere, regardless of ideology' (Duffy, 2009, p. 230).

The 20th century 'visionaries' were supported by technocrats who translated their visions into reality. One of the most famous of these, Robert Moses, facilitated the speed of the motor car by designing massive road projects in New York City and other US cities. During the 1950s Moses was hailed by many as an urban progressive, and his new roads, while not supported by all, were seen as a way to liberate people from cramped and dirty urban squalor, allowing every family to live in a house with a yard, and to spend a day in the country, all facilitated by the speed of the car (Gordon, 2017). While Moses' redevelopment of New York's transport system was on a huge scale, similar (if less extensive) motorway construction also occurred in European cities, for example the Seine expressway in Paris. In all cases, the destruction of existing communities in the inner city was deemed to be a price worth paying for increasing the speed of travel in the city 'especially when the sacrificed areas were working-class districts depicted as in urgent "need" of modernisation' (Hubbard & Lilley, 2004, p. 276). This speed enabled more and more urban space to be organised around the car, supposedly providing advantages for all. These benefits of speed were also assumed to apply to whole nations, or alliances of nations with similar political-economic systems.

Increasing the speed of transport was integral to post-war reconstruction in Europe after 1945. Highway engineers were tasked with remodelling existing cities to create faster movement of goods, capital, and people, all of which they assumed would create better cities and a better society (Hubbard & Lilley, 2004). Western Bloc nations referred to modernism in their propaganda to claim superiority in technological progress and economic growth. High-speed highways 'became potent symbols in the psychological gamesmanship between capitalism and communism' (Platt, 2014, p. 184). Architects, planners and political decision makers in Eastern Bloc nations also enthusiastically adopted the modernist conceptions of urban planning, where planning for motorised traffic became the primary concern. In the German Democratic Republic (GDR), design competitions for cities including Karl-Marx-Stadt (now known as Chemnitz), Leipzig, Dresden and Halle were strongly influenced by the desire for 'planning solutions aimed at optimization of traffic flows and speed' (Beyer, 2011, p. 80). The speed of travel of moving cars was often a dominant theme in descriptions of developing socialist cities in the post-war period. Providing for the fast movement of cars fitted well with 'attributes of a desirable modernity' (Beyer, 2011, p. 80). However, as we explain in the following section, a future vision for a city based on speed was not enthusiastically adopted by all urban residents, even in US cities.

3.3.2 Alternative visions for the modern city: the role of 'slower' modes

The plans for freeways through city centres were masterminded by members of the auto industry and highway engineers, who were trained to focus on ensuring that cars moved as fast as possible through the city, not to consider how freeways might affect the urban fabric, or to estimate the cost to future generations of their plans. Many of Moses' expressways now require expensive maintenance and/or rebuilding, prompting city planners to re-consider the future of expressways. One example is the Brooklyn-Queens Expressway in New York City (Fig. 3.4), where 'a 1.5-mile span of the highway between Atlantic Avenue and Sands Street is crumbling, and city and state officials are mulling ways to repair the roadway' (Spivack, 2019).

Not everyone shared the passion for the visions promoted by people like Robert Moses, and in many cases alternative visions for better cities included recognition of 'slower' modes and the value of places for people, rather than for speeding vehicles. A valuable way to illustrate the changing visions of the city, and how the glorification of speed in city transport started to give way to the recognition of the importance of people and life in the streets, is to examine the battle over Manhattan streets between Robert Moses and Jane Jacobs. Jacobs, a vocal opponent to the speed-dominated vision of the city, was a journalist, author and activist who had no formal training in urban planning. Shortly after Jacobs settled in Greenwich Village in 1955, Moses proposed a road through Washington Square Park, clearance of 'slums' in Greenwich Village, and a major new highway—the Lower Manhattan Expressway—that would cut through much of Manhattan. Unfortunately for Moses, all three of these projects directly affected Jacobs where she lived (Lawson, 2017).

Jacobs took on the might of not only Robert Moses, but also James Felt, the head of the City Planning Commission, and several mayors. These powerful men were intent on putting into place a vision for central New York based on bold modern expressways, built to channel high-speed traffic through the city to the suburbs. This was seen as the ideal, modern vision of a city that would scrape away old and decaying neighbourhoods. Jane Jacobs saw these men as 20th century wreckers, and she developed her own philosophy on what the ideal city should look like. She argued that a vibrant city life required four urban conditions:

FIGURE 3.4 The Brooklyn-Queens Expressway, New York City, one of the expressways designed by Robert Moses, now in urgent need of expensive repair. *(Credit: Paul Tranter)*

1. mixed land use where each district would serve more than two primary functions, and this would attract people who are there for different purposes;
2. small blocks, with lots of corners to promote contact opportunities between people;
3. a mix of buildings in terms of age and form, meaning that high-rent and low-rent tenants could exist side by side; and
4. a sufficiently high density of people.

Jacobs' book *The Death and Life of Great American Cities* (1961) was released at the peak of the modernist urban renewal push towards high-speed city transport. This book is widely regarded as the most influential work in American planning history (Fulford, 1992). While Jacobs' book did not specifically focus on 'slow cities' or a critique of speed, it is based on the premise that urban planners should consider that cities are for people. They should discover how places with people work and then enhance those places, rather than destroy them with large projects that see homogeneity and fast movement in motorised vehicles as the ultimate goal. Jacobs' vision of the ideal modern city was in stark contrast to that of Robert Moses, whose belief was that 'cities are created by, and for [motor] traffic' (Chantry, 2018).

Jacobs did not believe in banning cars, but did encourage the 'slower' modes, particularly walking. She argued that 'automobiles are hardly inherent destroyers of cities … the internal combustion engine, as it came on the scene, was potentially an excellent instrument for abetting city intensity' (Jacobs, 1961, p. 343). Like many other commentators, she identified the surge in the numbers of cars as a problem, and the futility of attempts to increase speed in the city when there were large numbers of cars:

> *'We went awry by replacing, in effect, each horse on the crowded city streets with half a dozen or so mechanized vehicles, instead of using each mechanized vehicle to replace half a dozen or so horses. These mechanical vehicles, in their overabundance, work slothfully and idle much. As one consequence of such low efficiency, the powerful and speedy vehicles, choked by their own redundancy, don't move much faster than horses' (Jacobs, 1961, p. 343).*

When Jacobs started to win support in her opposition to this traffic-based vision, 'Moses' only argument was that Jacobs and her coalition were simply too stupid to understand his plans and visions for the city' (Chantry, 2018). The battle between Jacobs and Moses attracted wide media attention, and Moses' superhighway projects lost political support. Despite, or perhaps because of, her lack of planning education, Jane Jacobs achieved remarkable success. In 1962 Moses' Lower Manhattan Expressway was rejected by the City Commission, who accepted the argument that people were more important than expressways.

While Jane Jacobs was engaged in her opposition to the plans of Moses, another battle over visions of the future city was emerging in Europe. During the post-war decades, car ownership and use began to rise rapidly in European cities. As had occurred in the United States, transport planners and traffic engineers in Europe convinced politicians and policy makers that an appropriate vision for future cities was to cater for forecast growth in cars by building bigger and faster roads. These visions were based on the transport modelling of the time, which the planners (mistakenly) argued provided 'objective' and 'unbiased' predictions of increasing personal incomes, associated with growing car ownership and use, and declining mode shares for walking, cycling and public transport. Their modelling created self-fulfilling results. Predicting growing traffic led to building wider roads, which facilitated further growth in traffic.

In Britain, the influential Buchanan Report advocated the use of a hierarchy of urban roads, with through-traffic diverted away from 'environmental areas', onto primary arteries (Buchanan, 1963). An analogy was seen with large hospitals, where the quiet of areas like wards and theatres is preserved by diverting traffic along major corridors. However, 'In reality the distinction between "corridors" and "rooms" is not clear, for the city is more like an open-plan office, where spaces between the desks carry long- and short-distance traffic as well as much interaction between those sitting nearby' (Tolley & Turton, 1995, p. 210). In the crisis-ridden post-war British economy, there was never likely to be enough money available for tunnels and elevated freeways, so it became clear that catering for traffic growth would involve 'funnelling increasing volumes of traffic through this multi-purpose space' which would have created enormous problems of disruption to daily functions such as shopping and living. Unsurprisingly, strong public opposition to urban road construction emerged in the 1970s. The 'objective' modelling of the transport planners was met with concerted opposition from those who could imagine an alternative vision of a future modern city based on liveability rather than speed. Indeed, in both British and continental European cities, before plans for these faster roads could be fully implemented, enough citizens and politicians realised that such plans would destroy the rich character and architecture of their cities, and many plans for high-speed roads were rejected.

While Moses was busy constructing cities for high-speed traffic, German cities began building their U-Bahn and S-Bahn (public transport) systems, along with networks of human-scaled pedestrian plazas and streets with vibrant marketplaces (see Fig. 3.5). Alongside the injection of federal funds into public transport there was a cutting back of spending on roads. Kenworthy identifies the significance of this in terms of alternative visions of the modern city:

FIGURE 3.5 Part of the extensive pedestrianised area in Munich, Germany, serviced by U-Bahn and S-Bahn public transport systems. The 'U' and 'S' signs on both sides of the street mark the underground stations. *(Credit: Rodney Tolley)*

'The solution to the problem continental European cities were facing did not come out of relying on the guidance of technical transport planning methodologies. It came out of a political process involving a sense of vision which had to be fought as hard as anywhere in the world, and it had to go largely against the mechanistically determined view of the future as prescribed by conventional transport planning' (Kenworthy, 2012, p. 11).

In the previous section, we explained how a fundamental goal in post-war reconstruction in Europe was increasing speed. Yet, this only tells part of the story about how cities in the GDR (and other countries in the so-called Eastern Bloc) developed in the 1960s. Although Eastern Bloc urbanists did follow models developed in capitalist nations, promoting individual mobility by car, speed (via private motorised transport) was not the sole objective of city planners. In many Eastern Bloc cities, central urban spaces were given a distinctive socialist character through the provision of generous freedoms to walk and to sit and stay (see Fig. 3.6). In marked contrast to the way US cities were developing in the 1960s, these public spaces were also accessible to the majority of residents via public transport, even if not in the most comfortable vehicles (Beyer, 2011).

FIGURE 3.6 In the Eastern Bloc, many post-war city centres reflected socialist ideals through the provision of large urban spaces serviced by public transport, as seen in Red Square, Moscow. *(Credit: GuyDecker Studio, Flickr Public Domain https://www.flickr.com/photos/guydeckerstdio/30280927442)*

Although the process of widening streets and demolishing buildings to encourage higher traffic speeds is still taking place in some cities, Jane Jacobs' stand against the brutalist city visions of Moses and his colleagues may have marked a turning point towards a more human-focussed approach to city transport planning. Not only have freeway plans in many Western cities been abandoned, but now urban freeways throughout the world are being seen as candidates for removal (see Box 3.2). Yet the dominant narrative that higher speeds represent progress continues, with the belief by transport modellers that with speed comes time savings.

3.4 Speed and time savings in transport modelling and planning

3.4.1 Speed and time savings: the myth

The claimed benefits of speed in urban transport were given technocratic legitimacy in city-wide transport modelling exercises, starting with the 1959 Chicago Area Transport Study (CATS), the first major city transport plan. Partly because of the immense scale of data and the assumed statistical rigour employed in its modelling, CATS became an influential model for subsequent urban transport planning. The planners and highway engineers used their transport models 'to reduce travel frictions by the construction of new facilities so that people and vehicles ... can move about within the area as rapidly as possible' (Adams, 1981, p. 195). To achieve this goal, they identified six objectives. The first on their list was 'increasing speed' (Throgmorton & Eckstein, 2000, p. 4).

Cost–benefit analyses have been the dominant tool in the appraisal of transport projects throughout most of the world for several decades (Martens, 2011). These analyses aggregate the costs and benefits produced by any transport project into net benefits and losses. Typically, 80 per cent (or more) of the economic benefit of new transport projects as calculated in cost–benefit models comes from time savings (Metz, 2008). Other claimed benefits include lower fuel consumption, lower rates of crashes and reduced pollution, though all of these are regarded as minor benefits in comparison to time savings. Consequently, calculating the economic value of the time saved in transport through reducing congestion with new roads or widening existing roads has supposedly demonstrated the value of spending public money on infrastructure. The assumed wisdom of this has been powerfully transmitted to the public by bureaucrats tasked with designing transport systems or by politicians aiming to justify funding decisions.

Politicians continue to support road building policies to 'reduce congestion', citing the costs of congestion to individuals and to the economy. Announcing a multi-billion-dollar investment in Victoria to unclog daily traffic jams in Melbourne, Australia's Prime Minister Scott Morrison said his government was making record investments in 'congestion busting projects' which would 'help people get home sooner and safer and fix local traffic headaches' (Kelly, 2019).

FIGURE 3.7 Even on roads designed for high-speed travel in low-density cities, such as the Tuggeranong Parkway in Canberra, Australia, pictured here, induced traffic leads to congestion. *(Credit: Sue Tranter)*

Yet, evidence suggests that this investment is unlikely to help people 'get home sooner' (see Fig. 3.7).

3.4.2 Debunking the time saving myth: how speed induces destinations to move further apart

While transport planners and modellers see cost–benefit analyses as objective and value-free, these analyses are in fact extremely value-laden and have been widely criticised for their numerous weaknesses. These include:

- inconsistent results (two studies of the same project based on different methodologies can produce fundamentally different conclusions);
- underestimates of costs;
- inaccurate traffic forecasts (usually overestimated by 20–60 per cent);
- difficulties in estimating the value of life;
- little consensus on the valuation of time and too much emphasis on travel time savings rather than health benefits;
- lack of accounting for network effects;
- little account of agglomeration or land use interactions;
- ignoring equity issues (e.g. that high-income groups gain more net benefits from a transport project than low-income groups);
- lack of life cycle assessment of environmental impacts;
- disputable calculation methods for examining environmental and health variables; and
- lack of recognition of the range of disbenefits to health from driving, including a narrow focus on road trauma (injury and death) while ignoring the effects of sedentarism (Beukers, Bertolini, & Te Brömmelstroet, 2012;

Jones, Moura, & Domingos, 2014; Martens, 2011; Woodcock, Givoni, & Morgan, 2013).

The arguments in the section earlier—suggesting that high-speed transport saves time—are based on assumptions which have been demonstrated, for almost a century, to be flawed. Transport planners using the cost–benefit approaches described earlier argue that expanding road transport infrastructure increases speed and saves time for society. There are multiple problems with this argument. Perhaps the most important issue is that speed may not save time in a city if the distribution of land uses alters in response to 'improvements' in the road system. Unfortunately (for those who believe in the advantages of speed) the distribution of all types of land use does alter when transport conditions change, and these changes in land use usually cancel out any advantages that speed is assumed to provide. This was identified by Lewis Mumford in *The City in History*. Mumford explained that the speed provided by motor roads:

> *'devours space and consumes time with increasing friction and frustration while, under the plausible pretext of increasing the range of speed and communication, it actually obstructs it and denies the possibility of easy meetings and encounters by scattering the fragments of a city at random over a whole region' (Mumford, 1961 (1984 reprint), p. 577).*
>
> *'By pushing all forms of traffic onto high-speed motorways, we burden them with a load guaranteed to slow down peak traffic to a crawl; and if we try to correct this by multiplying motorways, we only add to the total urban wreckage by flinging the parts of the city ever further away in a formless mass of thinly spread urban tissue' (Mumford, 1961 (1984 reprint), p. 579).*

The time savings that are the basis for the supposed 'benefits' that come from building new road capacity rarely eventuate. (Also, as we explain in Chapter 6, other claimed benefits of new roads, such as lower fuel use and pollution, can be shown to be non-existent when a holistic assessment is made of transport. Indeed, faster roads may lead to increased fuel use and pollution.) The efficacy of increasing speed to save time has been questioned in many studies (Ackerman & Heinzerling, 2001; Lave, 1996). When a new road is built, the small time-savings for a large number of individual drivers derived from an expected increase in average speed (often measured in seconds), are assumed to create a large time saving for society when all these 'saved' seconds are added together. This assumes that motorists can make effective use of small segments of 'saved' time, which is highly unlikely. In many cases, time savings do not occur at all.

Numerous studies have shown that when new roads are built, any increase in speed is consumed by motorists not as a form of time saving, but as an opportunity to travel more or further (Buchanan, 2016; Metz, 2008). Thus building 'faster' roads leads to a spreading out of the city, and hence more pressure to build yet faster roads. Also, because of the phenomenon of 'induced traffic' (Zeibots & Elliott, 2011), many new roads quickly become as congested as the existing roads were before the investment in new capacity. Adding lanes almost always adds traffic on already congested roads (Litman, 2018), a phenomenon known as 'traffic generation'. Investing more money in roads increases the costs of urban traffic congestion. Yet groups who advocate for the (supposed) 'freedom and opportunity that comes from personal mobility' (AHUA, 2018) seem incapable of recognising the futility of expanding road capacity to save time for motorists (see Box 3.1 for an example of a major expansion of road capacity that failed).

A fundamental issue in the impact of speed on time saving is the difference between accessibility and mobility. For the last few decades, when transport planners evaluated the performance of a city transport system, the main criterion for success was 'faster vehicle operating speed'. This focus has meant that 'mobility' (the ease and speed of movement) has been seen as more important than 'accessibility' which can be defined as 'the potential of opportunities for interaction' (Hansen, 1959) or the 'ease of reaching places where people want to go' (Cervero, Guerra, & Al, 2017, p. 3). Herriges (2018) puts it simply: 'Mobility is *how far you can go* in a given amount of time. Accessibility is *how much you can get to* in that time'.

Transport policies that aim to enhance mobility and speed instead of accessibility can induce destinations to move further apart. The focus on increasing mobility is, as explained by Whitelegg (2012, p. 111) 'a result of subsidy and political prioritization … justified by a false conceptualization of the importance of time savings'. He further explains that the impact of a focus on mobility (instead of accessibility) is that more people have to travel further 'to access the same kind of things they used to access over shorter distances' (Whitelegg, 2012, p. 111). This can lead to a paradox where increased speed leads to 'more time and money spent in travel, rather than less' (Levine, Grengs, Shen, & Shen, 2012, p. 158). Planning cities for speed and mobility by motor car focusses on saving time (which is rarely achieved in practice) while 'planning for the accessible city focusses on time well spent' (Cervero et al., 2017, p. 3).

An important, but rarely considered, question about planning for speed is this: do higher speeds in low-density cities compensate for the greater distances between origins and destinations? According to Levine et al. (2012), who examined this question in relation to 38 of the largest cities in the United States, the answer is a clear 'no'. Their research demonstrated that low-density (high-speed) cities are also regions of low accessibility (even for car drivers). In contrast, in higher density regions (where speeds are lower) accessibility is greater. 'Having destinations nearby, as when densities are high, offers benefits even when the associated congestion slows traffic. Where land use policy frequently seeks to support low-development densities in part in an attempt to maintain travel speeds and forestall traffic congestion, our findings suggest that compact development can often improve transportation outcomes' (Levine et al., 2012, p. 157).

Levine (2013) argues that reform of transport and land use planning is needed: mobility-based evaluation (which prioritises speed) should be replaced with

BOX 3.1 How Katy failed to save time for motorists.

The Katy Freeway (Fig. 3.8) connects downtown Houston, Texas, to suburbia 30 miles to the west. Katy provides one of the most powerful examples of how induced traffic can foil the plans of traffic managers to save time for motorists by expanding road capacity. In 2004 the American Highway Users Alliance (AHUA) claimed that congestion on one of Katy's interchanges was wasting 25 million hours of commuters' time each year. For the traffic 'experts' of the time, the solution to this congestion problem was 'add more capacity, add more lanes to make the road wider'. This came at an immense cost to the state of Texas, which contributed over $2.8 billion into Katy's widening. By 2012 Katy was able to claim the title of the widest highway in the world, with 23 lanes. (In 2020 it had 26 lanes at its widest point: still the world's widest freeway.) The AHUA identified this widening as one of the nation's three most successful projects (AHUA, 2015), claiming that it had addressed congestion problems.

However, rather than saving time, congestion on Katy worsened since its expansion (Cortright, 2015). While trip time at rush hour declined immediately after the road widening, more recent data tell a very different story, turning the success story into one of dismal failure. Katy provided a powerful example of induced demand, whereby adding more road capacity generates more driving, longer trips and further sprawl. Data from the Houston Transtar consortium for two segments of the freeway show that commuting times increased significantly. 'Claiming that the Katy Freeway widening has resolved one of the nation's major traffic bottlenecks is more than just serious chutzpah, it shows that the nation's highway lobby either doesn't know, or simply doesn't care what "success" looks like when it comes to cities and transportation' (Cortright, 2015).

FIGURE 3.8 The Katy Freeway, Houston, Texas. *(Credit: iStock.com LUNAMARINA)*

accessibility-based evaluation. He suggests that roadways should be evaluated not just for their ability to speed traffic, but also for their potential to degrade accessibility through encouraging growth in distances between origins and destinations. Levine's arguments do not mean that mobility metrics should be entirely abandoned, as mobility is necessary, but that mobility should not be seen as the only goal: it would be considered as a 'means', not as an 'end', and within a framework where accessibility is the goal.

An emerging trend in urban traffic management turns traditional approaches on their heads. Instead of building more and 'faster' roads, many city governments are now removing or repurposing existing roads, particularly the grade-separated expressways that were seen by early transport departments as the solution to congestion. City governments are realising that there are better uses for city land, particularly for waterfront open space (see Box 3.2 and the Cheonggyecheon expressway removal example in Section 1.7). City freeways do not solve the traffic problems they were designed to fix, and often

BOX 3.2 What to do with the Buffalo Skyway?

Built in 1955, the Skyway in Buffalo (New York State), an elevated four-lane expressway routed along the Lake Erie shore and over the Buffalo River (see Fig. 3.9), was intended to facilitate goods movement to Buffalo's waterfront industry, now largely defunct. Since 2011 efforts have been made to begin regenerating the area,

FIGURE 3.9 The Skyway in Buffalo, USA, undergoing repair work in 1975. The Buffalo CBD is seen to the left and the land abutting the waterfront to Lake Erie, the harbour and the Niagara River to the right. *(Credit: Rodney Tolley)*

(Continued)

BOX 3.2 What to do with the Buffalo Skyway? *(Cont.)*

but the Skyway's massive infrastructure is often regarded as an obstacle to connecting the city to its waterfront for residents and visitors alike in order to better utilise new recreational opportunities.

The question about 'what to do with the Buffalo Skyway' (New York State, 2019) has been an ongoing topic of discussion, debating its removal or repurposing. In February 2019, Andrew M. Cuomo, the New York State Governor, announced a design competition for a future vision for the Buffalo Skyway Corridor in which urban designers, economists, planners and architects were invited to submit ideas for transforming the four mile (6.4 km) corridor (Congress for the New Urbanism, 2019). Traffic carrying functions may be sacrificed for local traffic movement in the city, but interestingly, the competition for ideas for its future embraced the possibility of retaining the Skyway and using it as a spectacular—if windy—walking and cycling trail like the High Line in New York City. As the environmental scientist Ray Vaughan points out, the Skyway offers several acres of extra waterfront open space that would not otherwise be there (Vaughan, 2014). Indeed, the winning design for the competition, announced in September 2019, involved the removal of part of the Skyway, along with access ramps, making 12 acres (nearly 5 hectares) available for redevelopment in the city downtown and Canalside. Part of the bridge would be re-purposed as a Skypark, providing iconic views.

Admittedly, the Skyway is only a tiny segment of the US highway system, but reimagining it by replacing motorised traffic with bicycles and shoes would be extraordinarily symbolic of new thinking about speed in the city. In a wider sense, Garfield (2018) points out that 'The growing movement to tear down freeway infrastructure symbolises the nation's changing attitudes about what future cities should look like'. Cities are realising that they can save money, boost their economies and improve the lives of their residents 'by not repeating the mistakes of the 20th Century' (Congress for the New Urbanism, 2019).

make them worse, while burdening residents with ongoing maintenance costs and damaging city liveability, sustainability, and economic vitality. Many cities now realise they can save huge sums of money by removing or repurposing freeways instead of repairing them. An extra bonus (for property owners if not for renters) is that when cities remove freeways, real-estate values increase in those neighbourhoods.

Another pleasant surprise for city transport departments and city residents is that freeway removal or repurposing does not, as predicted by supporters of high-speed transport, create traffic chaos. Instead, after freeway removals, much of the traffic disappears, or vehicle travel times actually improve: cars find other routes, people use different modes or they find alternatives to the trips they were making. This however should not be a surprise: it is entirely logical and predictable. Just as increasing road space leads to traffic 'generation', so decreasing road space leads to traffic 'degeneration'.

FIGURE 3.10 Despite the construction of elevated motorways in Bangkok, Thailand, traffic congestion continues to grow. *(Credit: Rodney Tolley)*

While there are good news stories about freeway removal projects in the United States and other nations, the news is not so positive in the Global South. For example, cities in Latin America, China and India followed the US lead and began building urban highways in the 1950s and 1960s. Many cities in South East Asia followed this trend later in the 20th century, building tollways and expressways (see Fig. 3.10). In Latin America, the debt crisis of the 1980s slowed freeway construction, but new freeways are now reappearing. In India and China, recent freeway construction is dramatic and rapid. In China all city land is owned by government, hence land acquisition is no obstacle to freeway building as it is in other nations (Bocarejo, LeCompte, & Zhou, 2012). How China deals with the issue of freeway construction will have an enormous influence on planetary health, as the country is expected to experience continued growth in vehicle ownership and mileage. Unfortunately, China does not appear to have learned from the US failures with freeway construction. For example, in Beijing, six new urban ring roads, built to accommodate a massive growth in motor car numbers, have failed to solve traffic congestion, and have created more pollution and further marginalised the 'slower' modes (Fig. 3.11) (Cervero et al., 2017).

It is not only with freeway removal that traffic levels can be reduced. Cairns, Atkins, and Goodwin (2002) report research from over 70 case studies of road space reallocation from eleven countries, where roads were abruptly

FIGURE 3.11 Intending bus passengers endure long waits amid heavy traffic and smog on Beijing's Second Ring Road. *(Credit: Peter Dowley, https://www.flickr.com/photos/pedronet/2661063011/)*

removed from the transport system. Examples in their research include: pedestrianisation schemes in European cities; bridge closures for maintenance and repairs (e.g. London's Westminster Bridge, Tower Bridge and Hammersmith Bridge); city-centre traffic re-routing; introduction of bus lanes in cities in Britain and Canada; street enhancement projects in towns in Norway; the Tasman Bridge collapse in Hobart, Australia; and the effects of earthquakes in Japan and the United States. They found that long-term disruption is rarely reported, and overall traffic levels can reduce by significant amounts (the mean traffic reduction in all their studies was 21.9 per cent). Despite research findings such as these, local newspapers typically warn of traffic chaos when road space is reallocated away from cars. A case in point is the redevelopment of London's Trafalgar Square in 2003. The work involved closing the eastbound road along the north side and diverting traffic around the other three sides of the square (Fig. 3.12) and inserting a wide set of steps to connect the square to a new pedestrianised terrace in front of the National Gallery (Fig. 3.13). Fears of traffic chaos have proved unfounded, reaffirming the typical comment that 'a lot of the traffic seems to have disappeared, and we don't know where it has gone' (Cairns et al., 2002, p. 14). A likely reason for this lack of understanding is that many city residents, as well as traffic planners and engineers, assume that nothing will get people out of their cars. A deeper belief behind this assumption is that cars represent the cultural freedom of people to move at speed through the city. Yet motorists seem able and willing to forego this

FIGURE 3.12 The closure of one side of Trafalgar Square in London to motorised traffic in 2003 created new space for people on foot and did not lead to predicted 'traffic chaos'. *(Credit: Rodney Tolley)*

FIGURE 3.13 Steps connecting Trafalgar Square to the new pedestrianised terrace (replacing the road) in front of the National Gallery. *(Credit: Rodney Tolley)*

supposed freedom, recognising that accessibility is more valuable than mobility and speed.

The answer to the question—where has the traffic gone—is in large part 'behaviour change by motorists'. These changes can involve: changing mode, visiting alternative destinations, changing trip frequency, combining trips, car sharing, or avoiding travel (e.g. by telecommuting). Long-term responses also include changing job and household location, or even changes in the choice of location for new construction by developers. 'Traffic reduction is partly explained by recognising that people react to a change in road conditions in much more complex ways than has traditionally been assumed in traffic models' (Cairns et al., 2002, p. 14).

Despite the dominance of assumptions about time savings from 'faster roads' during the 20th and early 21st centuries, planners, and traffic engineers have long questioned the logic of time savings from higher speeds. As early as the 1920s engineers were warning that new roads would not ease congestion, since the 'new capacity would invite new demand' and 'new roadways would be filled immediately by traffic which is now repressed because of congestion' (Norton, 2011, p. 156). The reaction from the automotive manufacturers was telling: they saw no threat in this pronouncement, and simply observed that this was 'an interesting thought from a sales standpoint' (Norton, 2011, p. 157). It appears that from very early in the history of car transport in cities, experts understood that the idea that new roads would save time was flawed.

Perhaps one explanation for why transport experts persist with approaches based on demonstrably faulty assumptions is that a belief system, or an ideology, has become so entrenched that the experts themselves are not aware that it exists. Northcott (2008) argues that the obsession that modern society has with speed in transport leads to an altered state of consciousness whereby any criticism or rational assessment of the value of speed is avoided. This desire for speed can be seen as pathological, 'because it curtails moral deliberation on the effects of speed' (Northcott, 2008, p. 222). Perhaps the experts value speed so highly that they are not aware of how this might influence their professional practice. This idea has been proposed by Charles Marohn, a highly qualified professional engineer and urban planner, who in 2017 was named one of the ten most influential urbanists of all time by Planetizen. (Number one in this list was Jane Jacobs.)

Marohn explains that when traffic engineers design a street, they begin with the design speed, then they consider the projected traffic volume, then safety and finally cost. 'This approach to design – speed then volume then safety then cost – reflects the ideology of the profession, an internal belief system so foundational that they don't recognize it as the application of a set of values' (Marohn, 2016). However, the priorities in the experts' set of values are changing, with increased recognition that increasing speed is not a useful goal in many circumstances. In Copenhagen, the renowned architect Jan Gehl sees an urban space as more successful when there is no movement:

when people are content to stay in a place rather than rushing through it, the place has become a place for people. Traffic engineers in America can identify their real, underlying priorities when prompted to reflect on this. When traffic engineers are asked about what they personally value, they identify safety first and speed last. 'Their actual values are nearly a perfect inversion of those they apply to their design ritual' (Marohn, 2016). This is a serious, systemic issue: long standing personal and societal addictions to speed (described in Chapter 2) have become so embedded in professional engineering praxis that they are akin to articles of faith, and thus much more deeply resistant to change than the individual views of engineers. (Section 10.4.4 provides further discussion of this issue.)

This belief system has evidently also influenced the way in which laws and regulations about urban development have evolved. The prioritisation of speed in laws and regulations regarding city planning can also force development to occur in ways that promote speed, despite the existence of preferences by urban residents for low-speed neighbourhoods. For example, many Americans would be willing to trade their larger home for a smaller home in a more walkable community (Andrews & Urbanska, 2009, p. 217). However, as we explain in Chapter 9 'many zoning and building codes effectively make the design of walkable, diverse neighbourhoods illegal, partly because they don't accommodate cars [or speed] well enough to fit the "normal" pattern. But a new normal is emerging, very quickly' (Andrews & Urbanska, 2009, p. 217), propelled by market forces. In Chapter 7 we discuss the pent-up demand for living in walkable places in US cities and the decline in appetite for suburban development.

There are also important equity issues surrounding assumptions about speed in transport planning and modelling. While some transport planners regard a high-speed, high-capacity road network as the ideal democratic transport system, it is inherently undemocratic. This is especially the case considering the large percentage of people (likely a minimum of 40 per cent of a city's population) that do not qualify as car drivers, due to their young age, infirmity through old age, defective vision, poverty, or being deprived of their right to drive because of traffic infringements (Adams, 1981).

An equitable transport system would measure improvements by the extent to which they aided access to basic needs, rather than simply mobility. Access can be improved either by increasing the speed of movement or by locating destinations closer to users. However, increasing the speed of cars requires increasing the space devoted to transport (as we explain in Chapter 6), which is neither efficient nor equitable (Cox, 2013). Some researchers have also identified ethical issues associated with seeking time savings from increased speed: 'We reject the ethically problematic paradigm in which loss of human life from increased speeds of travel is an accepted price worth paying for esoterically defined gains in time savings' (Richter, Berman, Friedman, & Ben-David, 2006, p. 126).

3.5 Conclusion

In the previous chapter we demonstrated how the supposed benefits of speed for individuals were largely illusory: 'speed was much overrated' (Reid, 2015, p. 94). In this chapter, we showed how the dominant narrative about speed being of value to modern economy and society is based on questionable assumptions and is increasingly being challenged, helping society to conquer its addiction to speed. A careful examination of the arguments about the supposed value of speed for economic growth, the role of speed in visions of the modern city, and the claims about the time saving benefits of speed, revealed that all of these arguments are based on faulty assumptions. Later chapters also challenge assumptions that speed brings benefits to health and sustainability.

The value of high-speed city transport for the economy was shown to be weakened by factors such as the huge road maintenance and repair bills, and the susceptibility of the sprawling outer suburbs (made possible by high-speed roads) to the mortgage crisis during the Global Financial Crisis. In addition, while capitalism (and the belief in economic growth and consumer culture) continues to dominate societies throughout most of the world, the unsustainability of economic growth is now widely acknowledged. As Thackara (2006, p. 29) argues 'the signs are that speed is a cultural paradigm whose time is up. Economic growth, and a constant acceleration in production, have run up against the limited carrying capacity of the planet'.

In the 20th century, high-speed transport for motor cars was claimed to represent the ideal vision for a modern city. Fortunately, visions of the modern city based on high-speed transport systems are increasingly being recognised as outmoded, and unable to meet the challenges of the 21st century. New urban visions based on cities for people, focussing on liveable and healthy environments, are emerging in cities throughout the world. This has led to a reappraisal of the value of road systems that were seen as symbols of a modern world when they were built. In many cases this reappraisal has resulted in reduction of roadway capacity and sometimes freeway removal.

In this chapter we also explored how technocrats (particularly transport modelling experts) played a role in supporting the dominant narrative about the value of speed. They used a technical strategy that was purported to be value-free and objective (e.g. cost-benefit analysis) that they claimed demonstrated the time-saving benefits of speed. In reality their tools were heavily value-laden and produced results that were fundamentally flawed: higher speeds rarely created the claimed time savings, partly because city land use changes when speeds increase. City planners and transport modellers increasingly appreciate that their goal should be to increase accessibility, not just mobility. In many cases, increasing speed leads to a paradox whereby more time and money is spent on transport.

In the following chapter we examine in more detail the paradox of speed, explaining that not only does speed in city transport systems fail to deliver on its promises, it can steal our time, our money and our health. By taking a holistic perspective on speed, we show that cities where walking, cycling and public transport become the dominant modes will also be cities where the least time and money is devoted to transport.

References

Ackerman, F., & Heinzerling, L. (2001). Pricing the priceless: Cost-benefit analysis of environmental protection. *The University of Pennsylvania Law Review*, *150*, 1553.

Adams, J. (1981). *Transport planning: Vision and practice*. London: Routledge and Kegan Paul.

AHUA. (2015). *Unclogging America's Arteries 2015: Prescriptions for healthier highways*. Available from: https://www.highways.org/wp-content/uploads/2015/11/unclogging-study2015-low-res.pdf.

AHUA. (2018). Who we are. *American Highways Users Alliance*. Available from: https://www.highways.org/about/whoweare/.

Amadeo, K. (2018). Auto industry bailout: Was the Big 3 bailout worth it? *The Balance*. Available from: https://www.thebalance.com/auto-industry-bailout-gm-ford-chrysler-3305670.

American Society of Civil Engineers. (2017). *2017 infrastructure report card: Roads*. Available from: https://www.infrastructurereportcard.org/wp-content/uploads/2017/01/Roads-Final.pdf.

Andrews, C., & Urbanska, W. (2009). *Less is more: Embracing simplicity for a healthy planet, a caring economy and lasting happiness*. Gabriola Island, BC: New Society Publishers.

Banister, D., & Berechman, J. (2003). *Transport investment and economic development*. London: UCL Press.

Beukers, E., Bertolini, L., & Te Brömmelstroet, M. (2012). Why cost benefit analysis is perceived as a problematic tool for assessment of transport plans: A process perspective. *Transportation Research Part A: Policy and Practice*, *46*(1), 68–78.

Beyer, E. (2011). Planning for mobility: Designing city centers and new towns in the USSR and the GDR in the 1960s. In L. H. Siegelbaum (Ed.), *The socialist car: Automobility in the eastern bloc* (pp. 71–91). Ithaca: Cornell University Press.

Bocarejo, J., LeCompte, M., Zhou, J. (2012). *The life and death of urban highways*. Available from: https://3gozaa3xxbpb499ejp30lxc8-wpengine.netdna-ssl.com/wp-content/uploads/2014/07/42.-LifeandDeathofUrbanHighways_031312.pdf.

Buchanan, C. (1963). *Traffic in towns: A study of the long term problems of traffic in urban areas: Reports of the Steering Group and Working Group Appointed by the Minister of Transport*. London: HM Stationery Office.

Buchanan, P. (2016). Transport, land use and economics. *Journal of Urban Regeneration Renewal*, *9*(2), 149–155.

Cairns, S., Atkins, S., & Goodwin, P. (2002). Disappearing traffic? The story so far. *Municipal Engineer*, *151*(1), 13–22.

Cervero, R., Guerra, E., & Al, S. (2017). *Beyond mobility: Planning cities for people and places*. Washington: Island Press.

Chantry, E. (2018). Urban designer series: Jane Jacobs. Available from: https://www.smartcitiesdive.com/ex/sustainablecitiescollective/urban-designer-series-jane-jacobs/92116/.

Congress for the New Urbanism. (2019). Freeways without futures. Available from: https://www.cnu.org/highways-boulevards/freeways-without-futures/2017.

Cortright, J. (2015). Reducing congestion: Katy didn't. *City Commentary*. Available from: http://cityobservatory.org/reducing-congestion-katy-didnt/.

Cox, P. (2013). *Moving people: Sustainable transport development.* London: Zed Books Ltd.
Daly, S. (2017). How the Italian Futurists shaped the aesthetics of modernity in the 20th century. *The Conversation.* Available from: https://theconversation.com/how-the-italian-futurists-shaped-the-aesthetics-of-modernity-in-the-20th-century-73033.
Duffy, E. (2009). *The speed handbook: Velocity, pleasure, modernism.* Durham: Duke University Press.
Eliot Hurst, M. E. (1981). Cars and capitalism: The political economy of urban transportation. *Geoforum, 12*(1), 71–84.
Fulford, R. (1992). When Jane Jacobs took on the world. *The New York Times.* Available from: https://archive.nytimes.com/www.nytimes.com/books/01/04/08/specials/jacobs.html.
Garfield, L. (2018). American highways are so expensive that cities are tearing them down -- here's what they're turning into. *Business Insider.* Available from: https://www.businessinsider.com.au/highway-closing-city-transformation-2018-5?r=US&IR=T.
Glaeser, E. (2011). *Triumph of the city.* New York: Pan Macmillan.
Gordon, C. (2017). Carbarism: Civilising the automobile. *World Transport Policy & Practice, 23*(1), 27–39.
Hansen, W. G. (1959). How accessibility shapes land use. *Journal of the American Institute of Planners, 25*(2), 73–76.
Harris, P., Lewis, J., & Adam, B. (2004). Time, sustainable transport and the politics of speed. *World Transport Policy and Practice, 10*(2), 5–11.
Hathaway, J. (2015). Taxpayers lose billions as auto industry bailout ends. *Human Events.* Available from: http://humanevents.com/2015/01/06/taxpayers-lose-billions-as-auto-industry-bailout-ends/.
Herriges, D. (2018). The difference between mobility and accessibility. *Strong Towns.* Available from: https://www.strongtowns.org/journal/2018/10/17/the-difference-between-mobility-and-accessibility.
Homer-Dixon, T. (2006). *The upside of down: Catastrophe, creativity, and the renewal of civilization.* Toronto: Knopf.
Hubbard, P., & Lilley, K. (2004). Pacemaking the modern city: The urban politics of speed and slowness. *Environment and Planning D: Society and Space, 22*(2), 273–294.
Jacobs, J. (1961). *The death and life of great American cities.* New York: Random House.
Jaffe, E. (2015). America's infrastructure crisis is really a maintenance crisis. *Citylab.* Available from: https://www.citylab.com/solutions/2015/02/americas-infrastructure-crisis-is-really-a-maintenance-crisis/385452/.
Jones, H., Moura, F., & Domingos, T. (2014). Transport infrastructure project evaluation using cost-benefit analysis. *Procedia-Social Behavioral Sciences, 111*, 400–409.
Judd, R. W., & Beach, C. S. (2010). *Natural states: The environmental imagination in Maine, Oregon, and the nation.* Washington: Resources for the Future.
Kelly, J. (2019). Coalition targets traffic jams with a $155m fix. *The Australian.* Available from: https://www.theaustralian.com.au/nation/politics/coalition-targets-traffic-jams-with-a-155m-fix/news-story/1f3864a8d81c5cc488e40287a634c151.
Kenworthy, J. (2012). Don't shoot me I'm only the transport planner (apologies to Sir Elton John). *World Transport Policy and Practice, 18*(4), 6–26.
Lave, L. B. (1996). Benefit-cost analysis: Do the benefits exceed the costs? In R. W. Hahn (Ed.), *Risks, costs and lives saved: Getting better results from regulation* (pp. 104–134). AEI Press: Washington, DC.
Lawson, W. (2017). *The woman who saved New York City from superhighway hell.* Available from: https://www.vanityfair.com/culture/2017/04/jane-jacobs-citizen-jane-documentary.

Levine, J. (2013). Urban transportation and social equity: Transportation planning paradigms that impede policy reform. In N. Carmon, & S. S. Fainstein (Eds.), *Policy, planning, and people: Promoting justice in urban development* (pp. 141–161). Philadelphia: University of Pennsylvania Press.

Levine, J., Grengs, J., Shen, Q., & Shen, Q. (2012). Does accessibility require density or speed? A comparison of fast versus close in getting where you want to go in US metropolitan regions. *Journal of the American Planning Association, 78*(2), 157–172.

Litman, T. (2018). *Generated traffic and induced travel: Implications for transport planning*. Available from: http://www.vtpi.org/gentraf.pdf.

Low, N., & Odgers, J. (2012). Rethinking the cost of traffic congestion, lessons from Melbourne's city link toll roads. *Urban Policy and Research, 30*(2), 189–205.

Marinetti, F. (1909). *The futurist manifesto*. Available from: https://www.societyforasianart.org/sites/default/files/manifesto_futurista.pdf.

Marohn, C. (2016). *The ideology of traffic*. Available from: https://www.strongtowns.org/journal/2016/12/4/the-ideology-of-traffic.

Martens, K. (2011). Substance precedes methodology: On cost–benefit analysis and equity. *Transportation, 38*(6), 959.

Metz, D. (2008). The myth of travel time saving. *Transport Reviews, 28*(3), 321–336.

Mouzon, S. (2012). Cheapways. *Original Green*. Available from: http://www.originalgreen.org/blog/2012/cheapways.html.

Mumford, L. (1961 (1984 reprint)). *The city in history: Its origins, its transformations, and its prospects*. Harmondsworth: Penguin.

New York State. (2019). Aim for the sky: The Buffalo Skyway Corridor competition. *Empire State Development*. Available from: https://esd.ny.gov/skyway.

Northcott, M. (2008). The desire for speed and the rhythm of the earth. In S. Bergmann, & T. Sager (Eds.), *The ethics of mobilities: Rethinking place, exclusion, freedom and environment* (pp. 215–232). Aldershot: Ashgate.

Norton, P. D. (2011). *Fighting traffic: The dawn of the motor age in the American city*. Cambridge, Massachusetts: MIT Press.

Platt, H. (2014). Planning modernism: Growing the organic city in the 20th century. In D. Brantz, S. Disko, & G. Wagner-Kyora (Eds.), *Thick space: Approaches to metropolitanism* (pp. 165–212). London: Transaction Publishers.

Porritt, J. (2005). Too many, too fast. In T. Aldrich, & M. Kaiser (Eds.), *About time: Speed, society, people and the environment* (pp. 39–52). Sheffield: Greenleaf Publishing.

Powell, W. W., & Snellman, K. (2004). The knowledge economy. *Annual Review of Sociology, 30*, 199–220.

Reid, C. (2015). *Roads were not built for cars: How cyclists were the first to push for good roads and became the pioneers of motoring*. Washington: Island Press.

Richter, E. D., Berman, T., Friedman, L., & Ben-David, G. (2006). Speed, road injury, and public health. *Annual Review of Public Health, 27*, 125–152.

Smith, A. (2007 (digital edition)). *An inquiry into the nature and causes of the Wealth of Nations, Books I, II, III, IV and V*. New York: MetaLibri. Available from: https://www.ibiblio.org/ml/libri/s/SmithA_WealthNations_p.pdf.

Spivack, C. (2019). Transform or tear down? The BQE reconstruction, explained. *Curbed, New York*. Available from: https://ny.curbed.com/2019/3/12/18248873/brooklyn-heights-bqe-repair-dot.

Sweezy, P. M. (2000). Cars and cities. *Monthly Review, 51*(11), 18.

Thackara, J. (2006). *In the bubble: Designing in a complex world*. Cambridge, Massachusetts: MIT press.

Throgmorton, J. A., & Eckstein, B. (2000). *Desire lines: The Chicago area transportation study and the paradox of self in post-war America. Literary and Visual Representations of Three American Cities, 1870s to 1930 A project web site of the 3 Cities Project of the Universities of Nottingham and Birmingham, United Kingdom.* Available from: https://ir.uiowa.edu/urban_pubs/8/.

Tolley, R., & Turton, B. J. (1995). *Transport systems, policy and planning: A geographical approach.* Longman, Harlow.

Tomlinson, J. (2007). *The culture of speed: The coming of immediacy.* Los Angeles: Sage.

Vaughan, R. (2014). CNU 22: Buffalo Skyway - Can CNU's Bad Boy Become a Beautiful Elevated Linear Park? *YouTube.* Available from: https://www.youtube.com/watch?v=2_PRoEQLbIk.

Whitelegg, J. (2012). How much transport can landscape tolerate: New ways of thinking about traffic, landscape and nature? In S. Koerner, H. Holzapfel, & F. Bellin-Harder (Eds.), *Landschaft und Verkeher.* University of Kassel, Germany. Available from: http://www.uni-kassel.de/upress/online/frei/978-3-86219-358-5.volltext.frei.pdf.

Woodcock, J., Givoni, M., & Morgan, A. S. (2013). Health impact modelling of active travel visions for England and Wales using an Integrated Transport and Health Impact Modelling Tool (ITHIM). *PLoS One*, *8*(1), e51462.

Wright, F. L. (1935). Broadacre City: A new community plan. *Architectural Record*, *77*(4), 243–254.

Wright, L. (2019). *Keynote: Financing the Walkable City.* Paper presented at the Walk21 Conference, Rotterdam, The Netherlands.

Zeibots, M. E., & Elliott, J. R. (2011). Urban road building and traffic congestion: What went wrong? *World Transport Policy & Practice*, *17*(3), 6–26.

Chapter 4

The 'slow paradox': how speed steals our time

'I have learned that the swiftest traveller is he that goes afoot'.

Henry David Thoreau, *Walden*, 1854

Abstract

Conventional transport planning in the past assumed that travel time should be kept to a minimum, and the way to achieve this was to increase the speed of travel, particularly by car. Increasing speed was assumed to make individuals and economies more productive. According to this logic, travelling by private motorised transport is more efficient than travelling via the slower modes. In this chapter, we question this logic. We explore the 'slow paradox' that 'slow cities' 'save time' in several ways. This is demonstrated using the concept of effective speed, which considers all the time costs of transport, not simply the time spent moving. Even when only trip speeds are examined, surprising findings emerge about the benefits of slowing city transport. In some circumstances, slowing traffic may reduce the overall journey time for all drivers. Also, cities with higher levels of walking, cycling and public transport spend less time travelling each day than cities dominated by private motor cars. This chapter ends with a caveat: we are not arguing that increasing speed or saving time is a useful policy goal. The promotion of health should be the primary goal, and any focus on increasing speed (even effective speed) may be counterproductive.

4.1 Introduction

'When you feel the need to speed up, slow down' is the title of a TedX talk by Kimi Werner (2014), a champion free diver. She described this as 'the best advice she was ever given about free diving'. The logic of this is clear when diving in deep water. When something goes wrong it can be a natural reaction to want to speed up and swim faster if you think that you are running out of time. Yet, this strategy will simply use up your energy and your air. In contrast, if you slow down, you use less energy, conserve your air and think more clearly, allowing you to make better decisions. Comparable logic applies to drivers in city traffic. Slower, smoother driving uses less energy (fuel) and gives drivers more time to make better decisions, hence reducing driving errors and crashes. Unfortunately, the culture of speed is so deeply entrenched in modern societies that when people experience time pressure, their most likely response is to hurry, to speed up.

Slow Cities. http://dx.doi.org/10.1016/B978-0-12-815316-1.00004-6

Could the advice given to Kimi Werner be adapted for transport policy and planning? Could we ask transport planners: 'whenever you feel you need to make traffic go faster, consider the possible benefits of slowing city transport'? The conventional transport paradigm that dominated city planning in the 20th century assumed that travel time should be kept to a minimum, and the way to do this was to increase the speed of travel, particularly by car. It was assumed that if we do things faster, we will get more things done and become more productive, and if we travel faster, we will save time. According to this logic, travelling by private motorised transport is more efficient than travelling via the 'slower' modes. In this chapter, we question this logic. Usually, encouraging faster driving simply makes us drive further, or more often, or both.

This chapter resolves an apparent paradox—that slowing city transport 'saves time' in several ways. We demonstrate that while speed can steal our time, money and health, slowing city transport can make us less time pressured, wealthier and healthier. While modern society may have largely accepted the view that 'faster is always better', an increasing number of people are questioning this view in many aspects of their lives. Here, we apply the idea that 'faster is not always better' to city transport.

In explaining the 'slow paradox', we begin by examining the actual speeds of motorists in cities today, showing that despite advances in technology and massive investment in road building, traffic speeds in many cities have changed little from pre-motor car times. We then outline the concept of effective speed, where the overall time costs of any mode of transport are considered, not simply the time spent travelling. This reveals the hidden time costs of speed. The way in which feelings of time pressure are increasing, despite our attempts to go faster, is also discussed. We then consider the possibility that slowing traffic down may reduce the overall journey time for all drivers, by enabling traffic to move freely. This requires the recognition of the collective impact of individual decisions by drivers to 'save time' by driving faster. We also describe research indicating that cities that have higher levels of walking, cycling and public transport have lower travel time budgets (TTBs) (Joly, 2004b): in cities where the 'slower' modes are more prevalent, residents spend less time travelling per day.

4.2 The quest for speed in the city

'Let's consider what the quest for speed has done to the city. In New York, London, Paris, Tokyo, road traffic speeds are more or less the same now as they were one hundred years ago. The modern motor-car goes no faster through the metropolis than did the horse and carriage. The whole paraphernalia of today's transport infrastructure—underpasses, flyovers, roundabouts, traffic-lights – has left city travel just as slow, just as far, as it ever was. This is despite the wholesale destruction of community assets (housing, parks, footpaths, pubs, shops) to make way for the car and lorry, and despite the vast financial cost' (Hamilton & Hoyle, 1999, p. 60).

Hamilton and Hoyle provide an indictment of the ability of transport planning to achieve high transport speeds in modern cities, and perhaps a reminder that we need to ask, 'how fast are we really going?' The answer, so it seems, as the cover of this book suggests, is 'Not so fast'. Has our attempt to increase (or even to maintain) the speed of cars been successful? Despite decades of transport modelling justifying higher speeds, and despite massive investment in road transport infrastructure, increases in speeds have not always been achieved, particularly in central areas of cities. In 2017, average taxi speeds in Manhattan were 7.1 mph (11.4 km/h), and in the Midtown Core, 5 mph (8 km/h) (NYC Department of Transportation, 2018). In many cases in Manhattan, walking is faster than a taxi, as walking allows shortcuts that are not available to taxis. Motorised traffic speeds in many cities in the Global South are even lower than in New York. In New Delhi, average driving speeds are now approaching walking speed (Thorpe, 2015). In San José, Costa Rica traffic speeds are so low that cars are sometimes barely faster than cart vendors walking in the city centre (see Fig. 4.1).

The average inner-city last mile speed (the speed at which a driver can expect to travel one mile into the central business district [CBD] during peak hours) for 220 cities from all over the world, as calculated by INRIX in 2018 was 12.9 mph (20.7 km/h). Of the 220 cities investigated, 61 had average inner-city

FIGURE 4.1 In some streets during peak hours in central San José, Costa Rica, travel speeds are the same for everybody, whether they are in cars or pushing carts. *(Credit: Nick Tranter)*

speeds of 10 mph (16 km/h) or less (INRIX, 2019). Some cities have low travel speeds even outside the CBD. London is an interesting case. Mogridge (1997) observed that traffic speeds in London had changed little in the previous several decades, and Simms and Boyle (2009) reported that traffic speeds in London had remained virtually unchanged between 1900 and 2008, at around 12 mph (19.3 km/h) in 1900 and 11.8 mph (19 km/h) in 2008. 'The extraordinary aspect of this loss of 0.2 mph in a century is that it comes, not just after billions spent on traffic management and urban motorways – on the North and South Circular roads and the M25 – but after the congestion charge introduced by Mayor Ken Livingstone in 2003' (Simms & Boyle, 2009, p. 65).

Mean trip speeds by car in many cities are now declining, and trip duration is increasing, as is trip distance. Between 1995 and 2008, the mean trip speed in the 100 largest metropolitan statistical areas (MSAs) in the United States fell from 26.8 mph (43.1 km/h) to 23.9 mph (38.5 km/h), while mean trip distance increased from 12.5 to 12.8 km. The mean trip duration increased even further (from 15.1 to 17.5 minutes) (Couture, Duranton, & Turner, 2012). More dramatic declines in trip speeds can be found in cities in the Global South. For example, average taxi speeds in Tianjin, the fourth largest city in China, fell from 17.9 mph (28.8 km/h) in 2007 to 10.7 mph (17.2 km/h) in 2017 (Zacharias & Sheng, 2019).

While there is little doubt that motor traffic speeds in cities throughout the world are falling as the number of cars increases, for the average driver in most cities, the time spent driving is only a minor component of the total time devoted to transport. In this chapter, we argue that more attention needs to be focussed on the multitude of other time costs associated with transport. For car drivers, these costs are far higher than for people walking, cycling or using public transport. Even when the car appears to provide a speed advantage over other modes of transport, this advantage is questionable when the total time devoted to the car is considered.

4.3 The 'slow paradox' and effective speed

Almost everyone will have heard of Aesop's fable about the Tortoise and the Hare, which represents a simple example of how slow travel can be more effective than faster travel. While 'slow and steady wins the race' is central to the 'slow paradox' we describe here, the reasons why 'slower' transport might save time are numerous. We start with an explanation of how machines that supposedly save us time (including motor cars) may not be as useful as we might believe. The possibility that machines may not deliver on the promise of saving time can be illustrated in the following story:

> *Imagine living in a future world that has been devastated by catastrophic climate breakdown and resource wars. You live in a small isolated community, where your assigned task is to walk to a nearby creek each day and bring back buckets of water. This takes you an hour each day. To save time, you build a machine to collect the water for you. Your machine has a system of springs, pulleys, cogs, cables and*

levers. All you have to do to get the water is to pull on a lever, and the bucket is taken to the creek, filled with water and brought back. However, while it appears to save time, there's a catch. To make the machine work you need to spend an hour each day winding up a spring.

This machine has not saved time. When the time taken to wind up the spring (as well as the time taken to build and maintain the machine) is taken into account, using the machine consumes more time than walking to the creek. The equivalent of 'winding up the spring' for people today is the time required in paid employment to cover the costs associated with their 'time-saving' machines, including their motor cars. When this time is considered, it is possible to estimate what we refer to as the 'effective speed' of any form of travel (Tranter, 2012).

The calculation of effective speed includes the time devoted to all aspects of transport: not simply the time spent moving, but also the time required to facilitate this movement. Effective speed uses the standard formula—speed equals distance divided by time. The time includes every activity that is required to enable travel to occur or to pay for the costs of this travel. These costs include both direct costs (e.g. the cost of fuel for cars) and indirect or external costs (e.g. health and environmental costs borne not by individuals, but by the whole community and future generations). Most motorists spend less time travelling than they spend at work earning the money to cover the various costs of motor car travel. When the concept of effective speed is taken into consideration, it is possible to identify many circumstances where cycling, and even walking, can be 'effectively' faster than driving.

Ideas about 'slower' modes of transport outperforming faster modes can be identified in literature dating back to the 1850s, and various writers and thinkers since this time have outlined the ideas behind 'effective speed'. Two of the most important of these were Henry David Thoreau and Ivan Illich (see Fig. 4.2). The American philosopher Henry David Thoreau, in his book *Walden*, first published in 1854, was likely the first to describe the ideas behind the concept of effective speed. In *Walden* Thoreau compares his own walking speed with the speed of a friend who might take the train to a nearby town:

'One says to me, 'I wonder that you do not lay up money; you love to travel; you might take the [railroad] cars and go to Fitchburg today and see the country.' But I am wiser than that. I have learned that the swiftest traveller is he that goes afoot. I say to my friend, suppose we try who will get there first. The distance is thirty miles; the fare ninety cents. That is almost a day's wages ... Well, I start now on foot, and get there before night ... You will in the meanwhile have earned your fare, and arrive there some time tomorrow, or possibly this evening, if you are lucky enough to get a job in season. Instead of going to Fitchburg, you will be working here the greater part of the day. And so, if the railroad reached round the world, I think that I should keep ahead of you; and as for seeing the country and getting experience of that kind, I should have to cut your acquaintance altogether' (Thoreau, 1854 (1960), p. 47).

FIGURE 4.2 A statue of Henry David Thoreau outside a replica of his cabin at Walden Pond, Massachusetts, and Ivan Illich, author of *Energy and Equity*. *(Credit (Thoreau): Anne Meadows, Henry David Thoreau Statue, https://www.flickr.com/photos/ameadows/5091313219. Credit (Illich): Adrift animal—own work, CC BY-SA 4.0, https://commons.wikimedia.org/w/index.php?curid=73602782)*

Thoreau was aware that there was no 'effective' speed advantage in train travel in the 19th century, at least for people who were not wealthy. For Thoreau, walking was faster than going by train: his reasoning was that in order to travel by train, travellers had to first earn the fare, and for many people, that would take longer than the time it took to walk the distance.

In 1974, Ivan Illich wrote his remarkably incisive book *Energy and Equity*, which brought Thoreau's arguments into the 20th century. Illich explained:

> *'The typical American male devotes more than 1,600 hours a year to his car. He sits in it while it goes and while it stands idling. He parks it and searches for it. He earns the money to put down on it and to meet the monthly installments. He works to pay for petrol, tolls, insurance, taxes and tickets. He spends four of his sixteen waking hours on the road or gathering his resources for it. And this time does not take into account the time consumed by other activities dictated by transport: time spent in hospitals, traffic courts and garages, time spent watching automobile commercials or attending consumer education meetings to improve the quality of the next buy. The model American puts in 1,600 hours to get 7,500 miles: less than five miles per hour' (Illich, 1974, pp. 30–31).*

Illich explained that in countries where walking is still a major mode of transport, people manage to achieve similar speeds, while allocating only three to eight per cent of their society's budget to traffic, instead of 28 per cent as in the United States. In rich countries, people are forced to spend 'more hours of compulsory consumption of high doses of energy, packaged and unequally distributed by the transportation industry' (Illich, 1974, p. 31).

In *Energy and Equity*, Illich develops arguments that are central to understanding the value of 'slow cities'. He demonstrates the power of the mobility systems in high-speed cities to shape and design not only landscapes, but also daily lives. High-speed transport systems shape how people see themselves (as consumers who constantly demand increased speed): 'the passenger who agrees to live in a world monopolized by transport becomes a harassed, overburdened consumer of distances whose shape and length he can no longer control' (Illich, 1974, p. 57).

Illich explains that as high-speed societies become more dependent on the use of energy (particularly oil), they suffer from degraded social relations. 'High speed is the critical factor which makes transportation socially destructive' (Illich, 1974, p. 24). He argues that when mobility accelerates to speeds greater than 15 mph (24 km/h)—the speed of a bicycle—there is both a decline in equity and an increased scarcity in time and space: 'Beyond a critical speed, no one can save time without forcing another to lose it' (Illich, 1974, p. 42). As speeds increase in a society, alternative mobility systems (e.g. walking and cycling) become less effective, because the higher speed mode dictates the configuration of space. 'Beyond a certain speed, motorized vehicles create remoteness which they alone can shrink. They create distances for all and shrink them for only a few' (Illich, 1974, pp. 42–43). Consequently, 'an elite packs unlimited distance into a lifetime of pampered travel, while the majority spend a bigger slice of their existence on unwanted trips' (Illich, 1974, p. 29).

The French social and political philosopher André Gorz offered similar arguments in his essay 'The social ideology of the motor car'. He argued 'The more widespread fast vehicles are within a society, the more time—beyond a certain point—people will spend and lose on travel ... In the final analysis, the car wastes more time than it saves and creates more distance than it overcomes' (Gorz, 1973). Gorz noted the impact of speed on distance: 'To make room for the cars, distances have increased. People live far from their work, far from school, far from the supermarket—which then requires a second car so the shopping can be done and the children driven to school' (Gorz, 1973).

4.4 Effective speeds of different modes

The ideas described by Thoreau, Illich and Gorz regarding the illusory time-saving benefits of faster modes of transport inspired several researchers to further investigate the effective speeds of different modes of transport. The basis of these investigations is the recognition that, while the adage 'time is money' might imply that moving faster will save money, increasing speed creates various costs. In modern cities, the costs of transport are often poorly understood and hidden.

In 1990, D. Seifried, a German sociologist, used the term 'social speed' to describe the average speed of a vehicle after hidden time costs are taken into account (Whitelegg, 1993a, 1993b). Seifried researched the time spent at work earning money to cover car operating costs, as well as the external costs of cars (e.g. crash costs). Seifried's calculations indicated that when all costs are considered, the 'social speed' of a bicycle can be faster than a car.

More recently, Kifer (2002) introduced the term 'effective speed'. He assessed the various costs of operating a motor car in the United States, including both direct costs used in the calculation of 'vehicle operating costs' by motoring organisations and indirect (or external and hidden) costs of cars. When only direct costs were examined, the 'net effective speed' of US motorists was estimated to be a mere 9.7 mph (assuming a trip speed of 25 mph as the probable US average for cars). (In Kifer's analysis, 'direct costs' did not include the costs of parking, fines, tolls or vehicle accessories.) When the highest estimates of external costs were included in the calculations, the 'net effective speed' fell to a mere 5.8 mph (9.3 km/h) (Kifer, 2002). He explains that 'in **all** of these cases, the speed of the automobile is no greater than that of a bicycle' (Kifer, 2002). Kifer's estimates of external costs were based on studies by the Conservation Law Foundation and the International Center for Technology Assessment. The second of these studies calculated that if US motorists had to pay the full costs of driving their cars, gasoline costs would increase from US$1 per gallon to between $5.60 and $15.40 per gallon. Updating this to 2019 prices shows that in the state with the median US gasoline price (Rhode Island) the cost would be around $14–$38.5 per gallon. The wide variation in these estimates is due to the difficulty of measuring or even defining external costs, particularly when some costs are likely to be paid by future generations.

Another researcher who examined the concept of effective speed is Todd Litman (Victoria Transport Policy Institute). In 2003, he estimated that an average Canadian motorist devoted nearly 20 per cent of their household budget to motor cars, requiring around 1.5 hours of work time per day. 'Combining this with the amount of time spent driving represents an overall speed of about 15 miles per hour (24 km/h) per working day' (Victoria Transport Policy Institute, 2003).

The idea of effective speed has also been researched by Tranter and co-authors (Tranter, 2010, 2012; Tranter & Ker, 2007; Tranter & May, 2005a, 2005b; Walks & Tranter, 2014). This research demonstrates that even in cities with high incomes and with relatively little traffic congestion, the effective speed of motor cars can be surprisingly low. Importantly, this research also demonstrates that any attempt to increase the effective speed of cars by increasing trip speeds is likely to be futile. Tranter and Ker (2007) introduced the term 'social effective speed' to indicate that both direct costs and indirect/external costs were being considered in the calculation of effective speed. Several recent papers have examined the way in which the concept of social effective speed can be used to improve sustainable urban mobility policies (Crozet, 2017; Meira, Andrade, & de Lima, 2017; Meira, de Mello, Castro, Oliveira, & Nascimento, 2020).

The concept of effective speed requires an assessment of all transport costs. If transport costs of any transport mode are high (for individuals or for whole cities or societies), then so too are the time costs involved in earning the money to pay all the costs associated with that transport. The transport modes that many city residents believe save the most time (e.g. cars) require significantly more time to pay for their costs, and they create other time commitments as well.

> *'The perceived gains derived by higher-speed, higher energy-consuming modes are illusory because the financial and time commitments demanded to support them ... create dependence and consume more time than lower-speed, lower-energy modes. The perceived benefits of higher speeds are actually offset by the amount of time people must labour to afford them, as well as the greater time commitment to travel created by greater trip distances' (Schiller, Bruun, & Kenworthy, 2010, p. 33).*

For the average car driver in any city, a time-consuming component associated with transport that is usually ignored is the work time required to earn the money to pay for the costs associated with the car. The 'fast' modes consume our time and our money—and because many motorists seem unaware that this is happening, it could be argued that their time and money have been quietly stolen. In contrast, the 'slower' modes—particularly walking and cycling—can be effectively used by individuals and societies to save time and money.

The calculation of effective speed (ignoring indirect/external costs for the moment) for any group or mode of transport is relatively straightforward. Individuals can calculate their own effective speeds as drivers, cyclists, walkers or users of public transport. The key data needed are:

1. the total distance covered;
2. the time spent travelling;
3. the costs of the mode of transport (e.g. fuel, depreciation, insurance, vehicle registration);
4. the annual income (or median income if a group, city or nation is being analysed) to estimate the time people need to spend at work to pay the transport costs; and
5. any other time devoted to transport (e.g. time spent washing the car).

Calculating 'social effective speed' is more difficult, because this relies on estimates of the external costs of factors such as pollution, congestion, road crashes and climate breakdown. External costs are rarely considered in choices made by individual motorists, hence, an understanding of external costs is not as influential in affecting travel behaviour as an understanding of direct costs. However, the awareness of issues such as the link between transport and the climate emergency is rapidly growing, so that in the future individuals may give more thought to the collective impact of their own travel decisions. Whether or not individuals consider the external costs of their actions, planners and policy-makers have a responsibility to consider these costs and the social effective speeds that result.

Estimates of effective speed in cities for different types of car and for different types of costs (direct and indirect) show that the 'fastest' new car (in terms of effective speed) is a small, inexpensive, fuel-efficient car (i.e. the car with the lowest operating costs, including insurance, fuel, tyres, servicing, registration, maintenance, repairs and depreciation). When a comprehensive assessment is made of the time devoted to transport, the social effective speed of a car driver (even in a new car with the lowest operating costs) is in most cases lower than a person on a bicycle, or a bus or train. In many cities in the Global South, the effective speed of drivers is likely to be lower than walking speeds.

One study of effective speeds, in fourteen cities throughout the world, calculated how fast a person on a bicycle needs to go to be effectively 'faster' than a car driver in the 'fastest' new car (Tranter, 2012). The cities were chosen to represent a range of densities, traffic speeds and economic development: car-dominated cities in the United States, Canada, Australia and New Zealand; European cities with medium densities; a high-density, developed Asian city (Tokyo); and three cities in the Global South, one in Africa and two in Asia. Trip speeds were estimated from Google Maps for areas within 15 km of the CBD in each city. Results from this study are presented in Fig. 4.3.

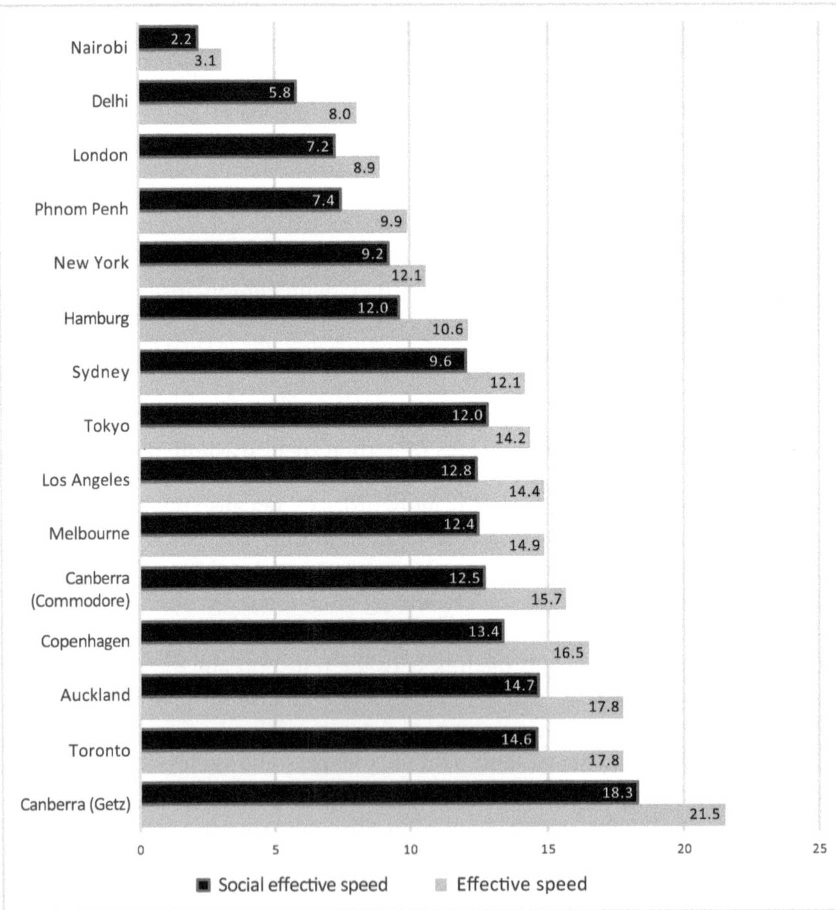

FIGURE 4.3 Cycling trip speeds (km/h) needed for the effective speed of cyclists to be faster than car drivers, showing both 'social effective speed' (including direct plus external costs) and 'effective speed' (direct costs only). *(Data from: Tranter (2012, p. 70))*

When both direct and external costs of transport were considered, a fit person on a bike could be faster than a car driver (driving the 'fastest new car' in each city) in all the cities examined. Even in Canberra, which INRIX has identified as one of the least congested cities in the world, someone riding a bike would have to travel at an average speed of just 11.4 mph (18.3 km/h) to be faster than the fastest new car (which at that time was a Hyundai Getz), but only 7.9 mph (12.7 km/h) to be faster than a Holden Commodore (Australia's top selling car at the time). Reasons for the variation in effective speed between cities include traffic congestion (high in London and New York, low in Canberra and Toronto), median incomes (high in Australian, New Zealand and North American cities and very low in Global South cities), and driving and parking costs (high in Tokyo and London, low in Australian cities). Box 4.1 provides a detailed analysis of effective speeds in Canberra in 2019.

An issue we discuss throughout this book is how autonomous vehicles might influence the 'slowing' of the city. There is potential for autonomous vehicles to produce significant increases in the effective speed of motor cars, at least if

BOX 4.1 Effective speeds in Canberra, a city designed for high-speed motor-car travel.

Canberra, Australia's national capital, has been planned as a series of relatively self-contained new towns, joined by high-speed roads such as the Tuggeranong Parkway (freeway). Recent estimates of effective speed in Canberra, examining the direct costs for individual drivers only (i.e. not taking into account external costs), suggest an effective speed of 12.1 mph (19.4 km/h) for car drivers in the 'fastest' new car. This figure is based on the Kia Rio, a small car with the lowest weekly operating costs in 2019, of AU$115.95 per week (not including parking or tolls) (Nicholson, 2019). Income estimates were based on average full-time adult weekly earnings (ABS, 2019). Average trip speeds, of 23 mph (37 km/h), were based on Google Maps data for peak-hour times for trips from the city centre to four shopping centres just under 15 km away. Parking cost estimates ($3,000 per year) were based on long-term parking costs averaged for the city centre and two new town centres. Compared to the effective speed in Canberra of the Kia Rio, the effective speed of Australia's most popular vehicle, the Toyota Hilux, would be only 9.4 (mph) 15.2 km/h, and for Tesla's Model X 100D SUV (one of the most expensive cars to run in Australia), the effective speed would be a mere 6.8 mph (11 km/h).

Canberra is likely to have higher effective speeds for car drivers than most other cities in the world. Australian incomes are high by international standards, and while fuel prices are higher in Australia than the United States, they are much lower than in European cities. Traffic congestion is low in Canberra, and there are no tolls on roads. Also, the operating cost figures used for the estimates in the previous paragraph were based on the assumption that the driver was 30 years of age or older. For younger drivers, incomes would be lower and insurance costs would be much greater, reducing effective speeds significantly. In the future, effective speeds for car drivers in most cities may fall, assuming continuing increases in fuel prices and traffic congestion.

they are operated in car share schemes with professionally managed fleets. This is because of the lower costs for individual households when they do not need to own and operate their own cars. However, individually owned autonomous vehicles would, because of the high cost of the technology, likely reduce effective speeds even if driving speed on the road is higher.

4.5 The futility of increasing trip speeds

Another important insight provided by examining effective speed is the way in which changes in trip speed influence the effective speeds of different modes. To appreciate the impact of changes in trip speed, it is important to understand that the time spent earning the money to pay for transport costs is a major component of the total time costs for drivers. This time requirement is a negligible component of the total time devoted to transport by people walking and cycling, and low for public transport users in most cities. In Chapter 7, we examine the cost, in Melbourne, of owning and operating a car in comparison to other modes. For example, a family with no cars that walks and cycles for local trips and uses public transport for trips to the city would save AU$240 per week (or more if parking costs were considered) compared to a household with two cars that never uses public transport (Rachele, Healy, Sallis, & Sugiyama, 2017).

For most car drivers in most cities in the world, because the time spent travelling is usually only a portion of the total time costs of their travel, any increase in trip speed will have little impact on effective speed, even assuming that an increase in car speed could be achieved at no extra cost. This assumption is unrealistic, because an increase in trip speeds for cars would involve considerable costs, including the significant cost of constructing 'faster' roads. This is a key observation as it indicates the futility of a transport planning approach that tries to save time by expanding road capacity in an effort to increase car speeds. It also indicates the futility of individual motorists attempting to 'save time' by driving faster. It may be possible to shave a few seconds off a trip in some instances, but the extra costs incurred by driving faster (e.g. more fuel used, more wear and tear on the car, possible speeding fines, increased crash risk) would reduce the effective speed of the car trip, because drivers would be obliged to devote more work time to paying for transport costs. In contrast, increases in trip speeds for public transport users, cyclists or walkers may produce significant increases in effective speed. This can be seen most clearly for walking, which has negligible time costs apart from time spent walking. Increasing walking speeds (even by only a small amount) would increase effective speeds by the same value. However, increasing trip speed by ten km/h for some car drivers would increase effective speeds by a mere one km/h, and even less if we factor in the massive costs of facilitating this increased speed (Tranter & Ker, 2007).

Any increase in cycling trip speed would also have a significant impact on the effective speed of people cycling. While there are some costs for cyclists (e.g. bike purchase and maintenance), these are minimal compared to the costs for car drivers. The external costs of cycling are negligible, and cycling generates benefits for society in terms of cleaner air and increased physical activity. As Tranter (2012, p. 71) explains using London as an example, 'if the average trip speed for cyclists increased by 10 km/h, the effective speed would increase by 8.7 km/h because the main time component for cyclists is the time spent cycling'. Increasing the trip speed of bicycles (even if only slightly) is easily accomplished compared to increasing the speeds of cars, for example by transferring road space to bicycles or by the use of the 'green wave'. The green wave system in Odense, Denmark, consists of bright green lights on bollards beside the cycle paths that pulsate in a wave-like motion, leading cyclists to the next green traffic signal at 20 km/h. When they maintain this pace, every traffic light they encounter during their trip will be green (Pucher & Buehler, 2008). The return on investment for increasing trip speeds for people cycling or walking is far greater than any return on increasing the speeds of people driving cars.

If increasing speed of transport is the goal of transport planning, which we are not suggesting should be the case, then it is much more helpful to increase the speed of the 'slower' modes. Not only will this provide a better return in terms of increasing effective speeds, it is likely to be much easier to achieve. While the focus of this book is on how 'slower cities' will improve health, an important part of the argument is that there should be a mode shift from motor cars to the (supposedly) slower modes of walking, cycling and public transport. Anything that promotes this mode shift should be considered, including increasing the speeds of these modes, particularly for walking and cycling. While this may seem contrary to the arguments of the book, a slight increase in the speed of these 'slower' modes would reduce one of the perceived advantages of motor cars.

Chapter 9 examines ways of promoting the 'slower' active travel modes, but the idea of increasing speeds for cycling and walking may be introduced at this point. Many cities have implemented and/or are planning to implement strategies to increase speeds of these modes. For example, the 'Radbahn Berlin' project (Mullova, 2019) (Fig. 4.4) is a pioneering plan for a covered cycle path, over 9 km long, clearly separated from cars and equipped with a green wave system, with overhead displays to inform people cycling of the 'optimal riding speed in order to keep hitting green lights at every intersection' (Wardell, 2018).

Walking speeds in many cities have also been increased by changing traffic control signals to give more time for people crossing on foot (Levinson, 2018; Selman, 2008). Providing countdown indicators on pedestrian phases at crossings increases walking speeds by giving people on foot confidence that they need not wait, because they can see that they have enough time to complete the crossing (Fig. 4.5). The construction of new bridges for people on foot and bicycle to reduce the barrier effect of waterways in city centres achieves the same ends (Fig. 4.6). Similarly, topography in some cities warrants provision of specialised facilities that allow direct walking without delay. An example is Hong Kong, where escalators and travelators assist people on foot to overcome steep gradients and avoid diversions (Fig. 4.7). Priority lanes for buses and intelligent

FIGURE 4.4 An artist's rendering of the proposed 'Radbahn Berlin' project, a cycle path under the elevated U1 U-Bahn line, transforming derelict space used for makeshift car parking into a public space not just for city mobility, but also for leisure. *(Credit: Matthias Heskamp)*

FIGURE 4.5 Countdown indicators on pedestrian phases at crossings such as this one in Washington, DC, speed up walking by removing doubt over whether there is enough time to complete the crossing. *(Credit: Paul Tranter)*

FIGURE 4.6 The Jubilee Bridge in Singapore, designed to cater for large crowds of people walking or cycling, provides a seamless and scenic link between two famed landmarks—the Esplanade Theatre and the Merlion statue. *(Credit: Adhitya Andanu, https://www.pexels.com/photo/group-of-people-on-jubilee-bridge-1561806/)*

FIGURE 4.7 The Central-Mid-Levels escalator walkway system in Hong Kong, opened in 1993, speeds people on foot on their upward journey of 443 feet (135 m) using 20 escalators and three inclined moving walkways (travelators). *(Credit: Ian and Wendy Sewell, https://commons.wikimedia.org/w/index.php?curid=3206124)*

traffic signals giving priority to trams are cost-effective ways to increase speeds for public transport.

Faster cars may steal our time, whereas faster buses, trains, cycling and walking may save us time. If we consider the combined impact of the low effective speeds of cars and other effects of mass car use, we can appreciate that cars consume more time and distance than they save, as Illich and Gorz observed in the 1970s: the extensive use of cars has contributed to the spreading of cities and the closure of local schools, shops and services. There are now longer distances and travelling times to access schools, goods, services and social contacts that were previously available within walking or cycling distance.

Planning for fast modes has spread the city and land uses, negating the assumed benefits of speed by making destinations further away. As we explained in Chapter 2 using Melbourne as an example, the number of land uses accessible to residents, particularly in new suburbs, has declined significantly in the last few decades. There are significant equity and health impacts of these changes, making it difficult for some groups of people to maintain their daily activity routines without a car, as Chapter 5 examines.

One of the important advantages of the concept of effective speed is that it allows individuals, policy-makers and planners to think differently about speed and the ways that transport systems are designed in cities. For individuals, an understanding of effective speed might help promote a shift to the 'slower' modes of transport. For policy-makers and planners, the incorporation of effective speed into their thinking allows new understandings of the value of transport investments. Yet, despite the likely advantages of effective speed as a concept in city and transport planning, there is a considerable level of cognitive dissonance surrounding the concept.

Many individuals cling to the idea that 'faster is always better', despite evidence that this is not the case. There is also evidence of bias in commuters' perceptions of travel times and costs of transport by different modes. In terms of perceived travel times and costs 'the car is assessed as being better than it really is, its alternatives worse' (Brog, 2000, p. 7). Drivers typically underestimate the costs and overestimate the speeds of their trips. Car drivers in a German study estimated their costs at 42 per cent of actual costs and estimated travel times by car at only 82 per cent of the actual time (Brog, 2000). A study by the Royal Automobile Club in the United Kingdom also found that drivers grossly undervalue the costs of motoring, estimating their expenditure at less than 40 per cent of the real average costs as calculated by the RAC, very similar to the German drivers (Tranter & Ker, 2007). The situation was reversed for users of public transport, who estimated their costs as 120 per cent of actual costs, and travel times at 143 per cent of actual times (Brog, 2000). Not only do car drivers underestimate the time they spend in their cars, they also rarely consider the total time devoted to these machines.

4.6 Countering arguments against effective speed

One of the authors of this book has given many conference presentations and seminars relating to effective speed. While delegates at cycling or walking conferences are delighted to discover that when all the time costs are considered, these modes are often more 'effective' than driving, some car drivers and transport planners seem unsettled by the idea of effective speed. They find it difficult to accept that their cars may not be as effective as they had been led to believe. Here, we refute arguments about why effective speed might not be a useful concept, or why it might not be relevant to particular drivers.

One argument is 'There's no choice but to drive'. Given decisions of policy makers, planners and residents about employment and residential location that have reduced active travel options, there may well be no reasonable choice for some people at present. They are caught in a 'social trap' from which they can see no easy escape, as section 10.2.4 explains. However, when they next make a locational decision—about where to live or work or send their children to school—the effective speed concept can highlight the time they have been spending at work to earn the money to cover the costs of their former reliance on cars—and thus encourage them to consider more accessible locations. The concept of effective speed may also prompt policy makers to implement changes to enable people to choose more 'effective' modes in the future. These include changes in land use, better provision of and support for public transport and a 'local' location policy for schools, medical facilities, shops and services.

Some people understand the effective speed concept, but still claim that they need to have their second car. One of the stated reasons is that they need this car to drive their child to school, because of the traffic dangers created by parents driving children to school. Apart from the irony in this argument, if these drivers could find a way to survive without the second car, and as a consequence could work fewer hours each week, they may have enough time to walk with their children to school and to other locations. This would provide multiple benefits, including increased levels of social connection in stronger neighbourhood-based communities, which, as we explain in the following chapter, can enhance levels of human health.

A related argument is 'I have to work nine to five, Monday to Friday, so even if I didn't have a car, I still could not work any less each week'. While this seems like a valid argument, it does not mean that they could not work less in the longer term. They could afford longer holidays, or they could retire earlier. For a person on an average income, depending on what type of car they choose 'not' to own, they could retire 10 to 20 years earlier if they invested the money saved. The 'must work nine to five' argument also highlights the potential for more flexible working hours to encourage a shift to the active transport modes.

Another argument is 'I like the convenience of the car'. There are a number of problems with this argument. Many city residents believe that the speed of the car has provided advantages in terms of convenience. However, while

FIGURE 4.8 As the use of cars increases, services such as shops, schools and hospitals become larger and more distant, and therefore more difficult to access, whilst local smaller facilities, accessible on foot and by bike, face closure: St Vincent's Hospital, New York. *(Credit: Dave Winer, St Vincent's closed, https://www.flickr.com/photos/scriptingnews/4669941472/)*

there may be convenience in terms of being able to depart immediately by car, instead of waiting for a bus or tram, as well as the ability to visit several locations that are not on the same public transport route, it can also be argued that this speed has given city residents enormous disadvantages. Widespread use of the car has contributed to the spreading out of cities, and the closure of local shops, schools, medical facilities and services (Fig. 4.8), as well as an erosion of public transport, walking and cycling. As a result, the speed provided by the car consumes more time and distance than it saves. More and more people now have to endure the inconvenience of being forced to drive to places that used to be within walking or cycling distance. A more serious perspective on the convenience argument requires a long-term view. Future generations suffering the effects of global heating will likely be underwhelmed by the realisation that their parents and grandparents believed the convenience of driving to the shops was more important than maintaining planetary health.

Some drivers, particularly young men, have used another argument about why effective speed does not apply to them. They claim: 'I'm a skillful driver and so I drive faster than everyone else'. If they understood the concept of effective speed, they would appreciate that increasing trip speed (how fast they drive) is likely to decrease their effective speed, as the extra costs created (even for extra fuel) would necessitate more time at work to earn the money to pay for the transport. This extra time would likely be much greater than the minimal time they might save by driving faster, particularly considering that younger drivers have lower incomes (Kiersz, 2018). Indeed, compared to drivers over 25 years old (who earn much more on average), the effective speeds of young drivers are likely significantly lower.

Some people have argued that car drivers do not just pay for higher speed, they pay for the wider choice in locations (jobs, schools and shops) that this higher speed provides. This argument demonstrates a lack of understanding of the way in which transport systems affect accessibility, and the difference between increasing speed (mobility) and improving accessibility. We have already addressed the issue of how high speeds are (wrongly) assumed to provide an advantage in choice of destinations in Chapters 2 and 3, but this is worth revisiting.

In Section 3.4.2, we asked: do higher speeds in low-density cities compensate for the greater distances between origins and destinations? According to Levine, Grengs, Shen and Shen (2012), the answer to this question is 'no'. Some people are likely to see this answer as counterintuitive. Yet, evidence shows that low-density (high-speed) cities are also regions of low accessibility (even for car drivers). In contrast, in regions where speeds are lower, accessibility can be increased. The argument about the wider choice of destinations that higher speed provides ignores the impact of creating cities where speed contributes to the spreading out of the city and the closure of local shops, schools and services, hence reducing accessibility. These destinations become further apart when speeds are increased. 'Paradoxically, a reduction in speed and its concomitant reduction in journey length gives people more time, reversing the historic tradeoff between speed and distance' (Whitelegg, 1997, p. 112).

As Walks and Tranter (2014, p. 129) explain, 'automobiles, car drivers and destinations do not exist in isolation or on some abstract limitless plain ... As the city grows in a dispersed fashion and its form becomes ever more monomodal, the benefits of automobile-based mobility are eroded and transformed ... In the modern dispersed city, many are "driven to drive" by long trip distances, the lack of alternatives, and the political and cultural "lock in" created by the weight of so many interests vested in the maintenance of automobility'.

A final argument used against the effective speed concept is that it is not needed because transport economists already have the tool of cost–benefit analysis (CBA). We have addressed some of the shortcomings of CBAs in the previous chapter. But we can add more to the list of deficiencies now that we have introduced the concept of effective speed.

While CBAs struggle with the calculation of the monetary 'value of travel time saved' because of different values used for different modes and different types of travel, using the effective speed concept avoids the issue of valuing travel time, as all costs are expressed as units of time. This provides an advantage compared to basing the value on access to money: 'While money is unequally distributed, the amount of time available is distributed equally. Also, unlike money, time is a concept that is instantly recognizable and understood, and is directly rooted in universal human experience' (Walks & Tranter, 2014, p. 129).

Another fundamental weakness of CBAs is that, unlike the effective speed concept, they ignore a major time component for motorists—the time spent earning the money to pay for the costs of cars. CBAs are based on a premise that households already own their cars and will continue to do so. In a hypothetical comparison of a new rail service with a new freeway, where both projects lead to the same increase in speeds, a CBA would rate both projects equally in terms of time savings. However, if instead of conducting a CBA to compare the rail service with the freeway, the total time costs for motorists were considered using effective speed; this would likely show a greater 'benefit' in terms of total time savings for the rail service, as at least some households would not need their second cars if the new rail service obviated the need for a car.

Perhaps the most significant problem with CBA is that it does not have a defensible legacy: its use has justified enormous expenditures on transport infrastructure, often destroying the physical and social fabric of neighbourhoods. Instead of saving time, the increased speed provided by new infrastructure is used by motorists to drive further or more often. As Whitelegg (2012, p. 108) explains, 'in empirical terms this means that time savings have the effect of increasing distance travelled, space required for that travel, costs and the consumption of landscape by new transport infrastructure. The whole time saving logic is based on the fiction that time savings provide individual and societal gains when they do not'.

Thus, the use of CBAs has justified the continued striving for more speed, and facilitated the increased use of private motor cars. While this may have seemed an appealing outcome decades ago when car ownership levels were low, there is now greater concern over the multiple costs associated with this strategy. As Banister (2011) argues, concerns around climate breakdown as well as energy security suggest that transport priorities should change. As long as CBAs based on questionable time savings and low values assigned to greenhouse gas emissions (see Box 6.2) remain the dominant decision-making tool for city transport systems, this change seems unlikely.

4.7 Increasing speeds, yet increased time pressure

The continued use of CBA analysis that focusses on the desire to speed up traffic may also contribute to the growing sense of time pressure in modern society. Despite the application of CBA and advances in technology that supposedly increase the speed of travel within cities, many city dwellers now have less free time and feel more time pressured than ever before. As the industrial revolution progressed, efficient time use became an imperative in production. This may have helped raise living standards, but it also contributed to feelings of time scarcity. 'Time became viewed as precious and valuable: it was to be used 'economically'—saved or spent but not wasted' (Strazdins et al., 2011, p. 547). Pemberton and Cox (2011, p. 83) explain how since the late 18th century the pace of life has sped up. 'People feel more rushed ... in all areas of life, including work, home maintenance and leisure ... [we] lose connections to the natural rhythms of night and day. We are experiencing increasing time pressure as every moment of the day fills with constant activity'. Zuzanek (1998, p. 26) agrees: 'Employed people in industrial societies feel more pressed for time and psychologically more stressed than ever before'.

As we discussed in Chapter 2, Honoré (2013) coined the expression 'the virus of hurry', describing how the culture of speed now dominates modern city living and requires individuals to use time more 'productively'. For people afflicted by the hurry virus the default mode is to attempt to do everything as quickly as possible. They attempt to do more things in less time, meaning that they can do very few things as well as they would like. This hurry virus has become so entrenched that even activities that aim to slow people down have been affected: there are now 'speed yoga' sessions for time-pressured people (Honoré, 2013).

Margaret Atwood, the Canadian poet, novelist and environmental activist, satirically describes the tyrannies of speed and our desire to go 'Faster' in *The Tent*, a collection of insightful essays:

> *'FASTER*
>
> *'Walking was not fast enough, so we ran. Running was not fast enough, so we galloped. Galloping was not fast enough, so we sailed. Sailing was not fast enough, so we rolled merrily along on the long metal tracks. Long metal tracks were not fast enough, so we drove. Driving was not fast enough, so we flew.*
>
> *'Flying isn't fast enough, not fast enough for us. We want to get there faster. Get where? Wherever we are not. But a human soul can only go as fast as a man can walk, they used to say. In that case, where are all the souls? Left behind. They wander here and there, slowly, dim lights flickering in the marshes at night, looking for us. But they're not nearly fast enough, not for us, we're way ahead of them, they'll never catch up. That's why we can go so fast: our souls don't weigh us down'.*
>
> *(Atwood, 2006)*

Children, at least in modern Western societies, are increasingly affected by the culture of speed, or, perhaps more specifically, by their parents' addiction to speed. Parents rush their children from one stimulating extra-curricular activity to another, to give their own child a competitive edge in a consumerist world. However, as Honoré (2004) explains, children have paid a price for this speed, with more upset stomachs, depression and eating disorders relating to the pressure of being rushed. Adult health is also affected by time pressure, which is linked with stress, depression, obesity, poor diets and low levels of physical activity. 'People who experience time pressure often eat fast food, thinking that this will save them time, yet they still do not get enough time for regular exercise. This combination of unhealthy eating and lack of exercise leads to increased levels of obesity' (Tranter, 2014, p. 67).

Time pressure has emerged as a modern malaise, and evidence suggests that this pressure is increasing, despite, or perhaps because of, advances in the speed of transport (May, Tranter, & Warn, 2008). During the 20th century, as the speed of urban transport, particularly by private motor cars, increased, so too did land uses become more dispersed. This often led to a reduction in accessibility, and increased pressure on individual motorists to drive more quickly to their destinations to 'save time'. As more households attempted to save time by using their cars for more trips, attempting to drive faster when they did, this led to more and more pressure to drive, including driving children to school and other locations. Not only were these motorists trapping themselves into continual striving for greater speed, any gains in speed were unlikely to save them time when all time costs of speed are considered. They might also save more time on each trip by slowing down, as the following section explores.

4.8 Slowing down to speed up in city traffic

Some motorists mistakenly believe that reducing speeds in city streets (e.g. to 20 mph from 30 mph, or to 30 km/h from 50 km/h) will impede traffic flow. In fact, the opposite occurs, particularly where there are many intersections. Evidence from cities that have streets with design speeds of 30 km/h per hour (18.6 mph), as in many European cities, demonstrates 'that slower speeds improve traffic flow and reduce congestion' (Baker, 2004).

Understanding why this might be the case requires the consideration of the limitations of human perception. An individual's ability to interact with other road users reduces significantly at speeds greater than 20 mph or around 30 km/h. One reason that slower speeds improve traffic flow is that the average speed in urban areas depends largely on the way that intersections perform. At higher speeds (e.g. 30 mph) traffic control signals are often installed, resulting in no traffic flow for significant periods. At lower speeds, ideally 15 mph (24 km/h), vehicles move more closely together, and motorists use eye contact to engage with other drivers and make decisions about moving through an intersection. Traffic control signals are not needed, and as a result there is a much higher throughput of cars (Hamilton-Baillie & Jones, 2005). Slower speeds can also reduce average journey times on freeways, as explained in Box 4.2.

4.9 Travel time budgets: 'slower cities' spend less time travelling

It is frequently asserted that the time spent travelling per day—a person's travel time budget (TTB)—is constant across cities and has remained largely unchanged for several decades, if not centuries at around one hour (Cervero, 2011). This has been referred to as Marchetti's constant (Marchetti, 1994). Indeed, the 'one-hour' wide city has been shown to have been ubiquitous in the United

BOX 4.2 Do lower speeds help us get there sooner?

Even on freeways and major arterial roads there is a strong case for reducing speeds to improve traffic flow, as in smart motorways in the United Kingdom (see Section 2.7). In an article with the intriguing title 'Does slower driving make us go faster?' Bliemer and Raadsen (2018) explain 'we can all be faster by slowing down during peak periods'. Many drivers seem to have an innate desire to 'save time' by driving as fast as possible and (perhaps) legal, even if this gains them only a few seconds. This focus on individual time gains can have negative impacts when the collective impact of multiple individual decisions leads to a loss of time for all motorists (and indeed, for all city residents). Many traffic experts argue that 'lower speeds can improve fluidity and lower travel times by limiting the so-called accordion effect' where cars braking and accelerating can create traffic jams (O'Sullivan, 2019). 'One person brakes, then all these shockwaves go through the system. If there's fewer shockwaves, there's actually smoother travel ... and we would find less rear-end crashes' (Larkins, 2018).

These explanations are supported by the University of Tokyo's Professor Katsuhiro Nishinari, who studies the mathematics of traffic jams. Nishinari showed that slowing down on motorways gets motorists to their destination quicker. He demonstrated this paradox using an experiment on the Shuto Expressway in Tokyo, Japan's busiest motorway (Fig. 4.9), where there was a regular 10 km traffic jam at 4 p.m. He asked eight cars to drive more slowly than the other cars, keeping a large headway. 'With just eight cars the jam didn't appear for 40 minutes. If you continuously had all cars (keeping headway) maybe you can shift the onset again and have no traffic jam' (Brook, 2018).

FIGURE 4.9 Kasai Junction, Shuto Expressway in Tokyo, Japan's busiest motorway. *(Credit: Comyu—Japanese Wikipedia, CC BY-SA 3.0, https://commons.wikimedia.org/w/index.php?curid=4318722)*

Kingdom for six hundred years (SACTRA, 1994). As transport speeds increase, the city expands. Walking cities were around five to eight km (three to five miles) in diameter and car-based cities grew to 40 to 50 km (25 to 31 miles) in every direction. As Newman (2003, p. 52) observes, 'this journey time appears to be built into human psychology/biology and urban economy as a fundamental organising force'. However, there is evidence of differences in the time spent travelling each day between cities with different mode splits. Advocates for high-speed cities might expect lower travel time budgets to exist in cities with higher motorised traffic speeds. Evidence suggests that the opposite is the case (Joly, 2004a, 2004b).

Joly (2004b) compared cities with different urban structures: extensive urban model cities (North American cities) characterised by high speeds, low densities and a predominantly car-based transport system; and intensive urban model cities (Western European cities) with high urban densities, lower motorised traffic speeds and a greater role for public transport. In North American cities in Joly's research, less than six per cent of trips were by public transport, compared to 25 per cent in Western European cities. In the Western European cities (with high use of 'slower' modes) people spend less time travelling per day than people in North American cities (the United States and Canada), where the car is dominant. The daily motorised TTBs were higher in the cities with higher speeds and higher car ownership, and lower in cities with higher levels of public transport (see Fig. 4.10).

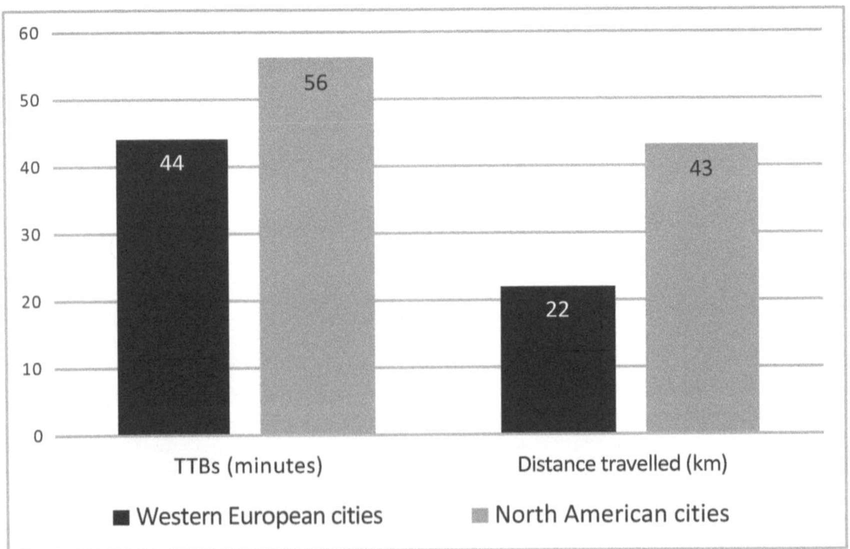

FIGURE 4.10 Average daily motorised travel time budgets (TTBs) and distance travelled in Western European cities and North American cities. *(Data from: Joly (2004b))*

Western European cities had daily motorised TTBs of 44 minutes, travelling approximately 22 km. In contrast, North American cities had TTBs of about 56 minutes, with 43 km distances. The increased speed provided by motor cars in North American cities was not used to save time but to cover more distance. As cities expand (or as jobs, services, schools and shops are more dispersed), ever more speed is required to overcome longer distances. However, the increases in speed may not fully compensate for the increased distances, and hence high-speed 'cities pay for their spatial extension and dispersion by an increase in travel times' (Joly, 2004a). Speed fails to reduce TTBs, and instead increases them. Importantly, Joly did not consider the total time devoted to transport. If the time required to earn the money to pay for the transport was considered (applying the effective speed concept), then the contrast between the North American cities and the Western European cities would have been even more pronounced. Clearly, high speeds are not saving time for city dwellers. 'Slower cities' can save time, and not just in the time spent travelling, as we explain in the following section.

4.10 Other ways the 'slower' modes save time

Active modes, particularly walking and cycling, save time for people in terms of the time needed at the gym for regimented physical activity. As we explain in the following chapter, people who regularly use the 'slower' modes will also likely spend less time visiting doctors or psychologists, due to the health benefits of an active lifestyle that provides opportunities for social connection each day. Active travel contributes to longer life expectancy, and longer healthy life expectancy. Public transport users can also use time for other activities that drivers will find difficult or illegal, including texting friends or reading.

Another way in which slowing city transport can save time involves the impact of slower (and safer) streets on the likelihood that parents will allow their children to walk and cycle to school. Common reasons that parents drive their children to school include concerns about traffic and 'stranger danger', and when streets have lower speeds, both of these concerns are reduced. If this results in more children walking and cycling to school, traffic will flow more freely, as there will be fewer cars making 'serve passenger' trips.

Perhaps the most critical way in which 'slower' modes of transport save time relates to the impact of transport choices on the earth's ever-worsening climate crisis. If there is a successful slowing of city transport in the next decade, then future generations are likely to have to devote less time and energy to repairing the damage created by climate breakdown. If cities continue their commitment to high-speed transport, then the future of the human race may be compromised; the ultimate loss of time.

4.11 Conclusion

'When evaluating the performance of a transportation system, the fundamental criterion for success has long been faster vehicle operating speed' (Levine et al., 2012, p. 158). However, gains in speed have failed to 'save time'. Clearly, a different criterion for success is needed. We have argued in this chapter that slowing city transport will, paradoxically, save time for city residents. In many cases, slowing motor car traffic or switching from the car to other modes might 'speed up' city transport. However, we should be clear that we are not arguing that increasing speed or even saving time is a goal we should be striving for. Any policy that promotes increases in speed—even effective speed—as a goal of city transport planning can conflict with the goals of promoting human, economic and environmental health. We argue that the promotion of health and sustainability should be the primary goal of city planning, and that a focus on increasing speed is likely to be counterproductive.

What we do argue is that the way we value speed and time is an important factor in the health of cities. To address the issue of the amount of time (and money) devoted to transport requires a reappraisal of the priorities of city transport systems, particularly in car-dominated cities. Switching to 'slower' transport modes will not only save time, but it will also lessen the health-damaging impacts of transport. Also, because the total time devoted to transport is lower in cities where walking, cycling and public transport are prioritised, time pressures are less likely to impose barriers to healthy lifestyles. The following chapters examine the various ways in which a focus on slowing city transport can enhance human, environmental and economic health.

References

ABS. (2019). 6302.0—average weekly earnings, Australia. *Australian Bureau of Statistics*. Available from: https://www.abs.gov.au/ausstats/abs@.nsf/Lookup/6302.0main+features1May%202019.

Atwood, M. (2006). *The Tent*. New York: Doubleday.

Baker, L. (2004). Why don't we do it in the road? SALON. Available from: https://www.salon.com/2004/05/20/traffic_design/.

Banister, D. (2011). The trilogy of distance, speed and time. *Journal of Transport Geography*, *19*(4), 950–959.

Bliemer, M., & Raadsen, M. (2018). Does slower driving make us go faster? Thinking outside the box. University of Sydney Business School. Available from: https://sydney.edu.au/business/news-and-events/news/2018/12/21/does-slower-driving-make-us-go-faster-.html.

Brog, W. (2000). *Switching to public transport.* Paper presented at the UITP: 2nd Asia Pacific Congress. Melbourne, October 10–13.

Brook, B. (2018). Simple road rule that could end traffic jams forever. Available from: https://www.news.com.au/technology/innovation/motoring/on-the-road/simple-road-rule-that-could-end-traffic-jams-forever/news-story/3f11ec52d082a6b436929b7819c72119#.qvlml.

Cervero, R. (2011). *Beyond travel time savings*. Washington, DC: World Bank.

Couture, V., Duranton, G., & Turner, M. A. (2012). *Speed.* Available from: http://individual.utoronto.ca/gilles/Papers/Speed.pdf.

Crozet, Y. (2017). Appraisal methodologies and the limits to speed gains. *Transportation Research Procedia,* 25, 2898-2912.

Gorz, A. (1973). The social ideology of the motor car. Le Sauvage. Available from: http://www.copenhagenize.com/2009/11/social-ideology-of-motorcar.html.

Hamilton, K., & Hoyle, S. (1999). Moving cities: Transport connections. In J. Allen, D. Massey, & M. Pryke (Eds.), *Unsettling cities movement/settlement* (pp. 54–100). London: Routledge.

Hamilton-Baillie, B., & Jones, P. (2005). Improving traffic behaviour and safety through urban design. *Proceedings of the Institution of Civil Engineers—Civil Engineering, 158*(14014), 39–47.

Honoré, C. (2004). *In Praise of Slow: How a worldwide movement is challenging the cult of speed.* London: Orion.

Honoré, C. (2013). *The slow fix: Solve problems, work smarter and live better in a fast world.* New York: HarperCollins.

Illich, I. (1974). *Energy and equity.* London: Calder and Boyers.

INRIX. (2019). INRIX 2018 global traffic scorecard. Available from: http://inrix.com/scorecard/.

Joly, I. (2004a). *The link between travel time budget and speed: A key relationship for urban space-time dynamics.* Paper presented at the European Transport Conference. Strasbourg, France.

Joly, I. (2004b). *Travel time budget - decomposition of the worldwide mean.* Paper presented at the International Association of Time-Use Research Annual Conference. Rome, Italy, October 27–29.

Kiersz, A. (2018). Here's what the typical American worker earns at every age. *Business Insider.* Available from: https://www.businessinsider.com.au/typical-salary-americans-at-every-age-2018-6?r=US&IR=T.

Kifer, K. (2002). Auto costs versus bike costs. Available from: http://www.phred.org/~alex/kenkifer/www.kenkifer.com/bikepages/advocacy/autocost.htm.

Larkins, D. (2018). M1 speed limit drop will improve congestion and travel times, experts say. *ABC News.* Available from: https://www.abc.net.au/news/2018-03-01/m1-speed-limit-drop-to-improve-commonwealth-games-commute-time/9497532.

Levine, J., Grengs, J., Shen, Q., & Shen, Q. (2012). Does accessibility require density or speed? A comparison of fast versus close in getting where you want to go in US metropolitan regions. *Journal of the American Planning Association, 78*(2), 157–172.

Levinson, D. (2018). How traffic signals favour cars and discourage walking. *The Conversation.* Available from: https://theconversation.com/how-traffic-signals-favour-cars-and-discourage-walking-92675.

Marchetti, C. (1994). Anthropological invariants in travel behavior. *Technological Forecasting and Social Change, 47*(1), 75–88.

May, M., Tranter, P., & Warn, J. (2008). Towards a holistic framework for road safety in Australia. *Journal of Transport Geography, 16*(6), 395–405.

Meira, L. H., Andrade, M. O., & de Lima, J. H. (2017). Conceito de velocidade efetiva social como argumento de reforço à implantação de políticas de mobilidade urbana sustentável no Brasil. *Transportes,* 25(2), 64-77.

Meira, L. H., de Mello, C. A., Castro, Y. M., Oliveira, L. K., & Nascimento, C. (2020). Measuring social effective speed to improve sustainable mobility policies in developing countries. *Transportation Research Part D: Transport and Environment,* 78, 102200.

Mogridge, M. J. (1997). The self-defeating nature of urban road capacity policy: A review of theories, disputes and available evidence. *Transport Policy, 4*(1), 5–23.

Mullova, J. (2019). Berlin's pioneering bike path project gets the green light. *RESET.* Available from: https://en.reset.org/blog/berlins-pioneering-bike-path-project-gets-green-light-05072019.

Newman, P. (2003). Walking in a historical, international and contemporary context. In R. Tolley (Ed.), *Sustainable transport: Planning for walking and cycling in urban environments* (pp. 48–58). Cambridge: Woodhead Publishing Limited.

Nicholson, T. (2019). The real cost of a running a car. *Royal Automobile Club of Victoria.* Available from: https://www.racv.com.au/royalauto/moving/news-information/car-running-costs.html.

NYC Department of Transportation. (2018). *New York City mobility report.* Available from: http://www.nyc.gov/html/dot/downloads/pdf/mobility-report-2018-print.pdf.

O'Sullivan, F. (2019). Traffic is unbearable on Paris's beltway. The Fix? Remove Lanes. Available from: https://www.citylab.com/transportation/2019/05/paris-beltway-speed-limit-traffic-congestion-lane-removal/590362/.

Pemberton, S., & Cox, D. (2011). What happened to the time? The relationship of occupational therapy to time. *The British Journal of Occupational Therapy*, *74*(2), 78–85.

Pucher, J., & Buehler, R. (2008). Making cycling irresistible: Lessons from the Netherlands, Denmark and Germany. *Transport Reviews,* 28(4), 495-528.

Rachele, J., Healy, A., Sallis, J. F., & Sugiyama, T. (2017). Designing suburbs to cut car use closes gaps in health and wealth. *The Conversation.* Available from: https://theconversation.com/designing-suburbs-to-cut-car-use-closes-gaps-in-health-and-wealth-83961.

SACTRA (1994). *Trunk roads and the generation of traffic.* London: HMSO.

Schiller, P. L., Bruun, E. C., & Kenworthy, J. R. (2010). *An introduction to sustainable transportation: Policy, planning and implementation.* London: Earthscan.

Selman, M. (2008). The 50 metre dash – trials and tribulations of the walking journey to school. *World Transport Policy and Practice*, *14*(1), 48–55.

Simms, A., & Boyle, D. (2009). *The new economics: A bigger picture.* London: Earthscan.

Strazdins, L., Griffin, A. L., Broom, D. H., Banwell, C., Korda, R., Dixon, J., et al. (2011). Time scarcity: Another health inequality? *Environment and Planning A*, *43*(3), 545–559.

Thoreau, H. D. (1854 (1960)). *Walden.* New York: New American Library.

Thorpe, D. (2015). In which cities is it quicker to walk, cycle than drive a car? *World Economic Forum.* Available from: https://www.weforum.org/agenda/2015/05/in-which-cities-is-it-quicker-to-walk-and-cycle-than-drive-a-car/.

Tranter, P. (2010). Speed kills: The complex links between transport, lack of time and urban health. *Journal of Urban Health*, *87*(2), 155–166.

Tranter, P. (2012). Effective speed: Cycling because it's faster. In J. Pucher, & R. Buehler (Eds.), *City cycling* (pp. 57–74). Cambridge, MA: MIT Press.

Tranter, P. (2014). Active travel: A cure for the hurry virus. *Journal of Occupational Science*, *21*(1), 65–76.

Tranter, P., & Ker, I. (2007). *A wish called $quander: (In)effective speed and effective wellbeing in Australian cities. Proceedings of the State of Australian Cities 2007 National Conference*, November 28–30, University of South Australia and Flinders University, Adelaide, Australia.

Tranter, P., & May, M. (2005a). Questioning the need for speed: Can "effective speed" guide change in travel behaviour and transport policy? *Proceedings of the 28th Australasian Transport Research Forum,* September 28–30, Sydney.

Tranter, P., & May, M. (2005b). Using the concept of effective speed as a stimulus for travel behaviour change and policy development. *A Report for the Australian Greenhouse Office.* Department of Environment and Heritage, Australia.

Victoria Transport Policy Institute. (2003). The cost of driving and the savings from reduced vehicle use. Available from: http://www.vtpi.org/tdm/tdm82.htm.

Walks, A., & Tranter, P. (2014). Driving mobility, slowing down the poor. In A. Walks (Ed.), *The urban political economy and ecology of automobility: Driving cities, driving inequality, driving politics* (pp. 129–151). New York: Routledge.

Wardell, S. (2018). Project Radbahn: Transforming Berlin's U1 into a covered bike path. *Bike in Berlin.* Available from: https://bikeinberlin.com/index.php/2018/05/15/project-radbahn-transforming-berlins-u1-covered-bike-path/.

Werner, K. (2014). Kimi Werner – when you feel the need to speed up, slow down. *TedX Talks.* Available from: https://tedxmaui.com/kimi-werner-when-you-feel-the-need-to-speed-up-slow-down/.

Whitelegg, J. (1993a). Time pollution. *The Ecologist*, *23*(4), 131–134.

Whitelegg, J. (1993b). *Transport for a sustainable future: The case for Europe*. London: Belhaven Press.

Whitelegg, J. (1997). *Critical mass: Transport environment and society in the twenty-first century.* London: Pluto Press.

Whitelegg, J. (2012). How much transport can landscape tolerate: New ways of thinking about traffic, landscape and nature? In S. Koerner, H. Holzapfel, & F. Bellin-Harder (Eds.), *Landschaft und Verkeher.* University of Kassel, Germany. Available from: http://www.uni-kassel.de/upress/online/frei/978-3-86219-358-5.volltext.frei.pdf.

Zacharias, J., & Sheng, Q. (2019). Why cycling in 2007 was faster than being driven in 2017 in Tianjin. *Journal of Traffic and Transportation Engineering*, *7*, 1–12.

Zuzanek, J. (1998). Time use, time pressure, personal stress, mental health, and life satisfaction from a life cycle perspective. *Journal of Occupational Science*, *5*(1), 26–39.

Part II

Health

Chapter 5

Keeping the doctor away: promoting human health through slower travel

'For fast acting relief, try slowing down'.

Lily Tomlin

Abstract

This chapter is the first of three in Part Two of the book that discuss the implications of 'slower cities' for health. We begin with an introduction to the deleterious consequences for physical, mental and community health when faster, motorised modes dominate city movement. Subsequent chapters contrast the environmental and economic health of the slow and fast city. For human health, 'slower' active travel brings a health dividend not only from the physical activity itself, but also from incidental outcomes of walking, cycling and public transport, such as better air quality, reduced greenhouse gas emissions, enhanced social connectedness and fewer and less serious road crashes. In many existing cities where fast travel divides communities and spreads development, access to health-nurturing opportunities—green space, work opportunities and friends—is diminished for all and especially for those who rely on their own steam to get around. Such transport deprivation reduces health equity and produces unequal—and unfair—opportunity surfaces for residents, leading to declining political, social, cultural and community 'health' across the city.

5.1 Introduction

The definition of human health adopted in this book is based on the World Health Organization Constitution, where 'health is a state of complete physical, mental and social well-being and not merely the absence of disease or infirmity' (World Health Organization, 2019). This chapter discusses the health-nurturing and health-damaging consequences of our collective transport decisions. It examines the reduced health associated with faster, motorised modes and the physical and mental health benefits of 'slower' modes, and reviews other likely health changing issues of 'slow cities', such as better air quality and fewer road crashes. There is a focus too on the wider issues of access to health-nurturing

Slow Cities. http://dx.doi.org/10.1016/B978-0-12-815316-1.00005-8

opportunities, such as work, health care and green spaces and how such access has been compromised as facilities have scattered under the influence of increasing speed and motorisation. For many people the response to access reductions has been to get a car and try to reach destinations faster, with each such personal solution making everyone else's problem that little bit worse. This tyranny of small decisions—perceived individually as rational, sensible choices—has led to unforeseen consequences when taken by everyone. In no other sphere is this more profoundly important than in that of human health.

5.2 Promoting personal physical health through the 'slower' modes

5.2.1 Introduction

We have come a long way in our understanding of the relationship between health and transport since the Health Commissioner of New York City in 1922 observed that:

> *'It is from the waist upward that flabbiness usually sets in. The slight, but purposeful effort demanded in swinging the steering wheel, reacts exactly where we need it most. Frankly I believe that steering a motor car is actually better exercise than walking' (quoted in Long, 1924, p. 19).*

We cannot agree with that view. Indeed, it is clear that most populations have insufficient levels of physical activity in general and that active travel has significant advantages over other forms of exercise and physical activity, and so has great potential to enhance public health. In short, the 'slower' city will be a healthier city, providing a faster route to health. Slower travel can indeed make us fitter and stronger, faster.

5.2.2 Physical activity and health

Physical inactivity is a serious public health problem, being one of the two largest contributors to non-communicable disease (along with unhealthy diets) (Giles-Corti et al., 2016). Ding et al. (2016) refer to 'a pandemic of physical inactivity'. It is now more than 60 years since the publication of the groundbreaking research into the heart health of bus crews at London Transport, which showed that conductors, who spent their work shift walking up and down the aisles and stairs of the buses collecting fares, were considerably less likely to die from heart disease than their driver colleagues, who were sedentary all day (Morris, Heady, Raffle, Roberts, & Parks, 1953). Since then, multiple large-scale studies have substantiated and extended the finding that being physically active lowers risk of illness and death. One of the most recent, for example, is a Cambridge University research study which followed over 300,000 Europeans for 12 years and showed that the annual number of deaths attributable to inactivity was double that from obesity (Ekelund et al., 2015).

Obesity, itself a major health issue throughout the world, and especially in the United States, is also associated with both physical inactivity and time spent sitting in cars. A study involving over 10,000 participants in Atlanta, Georgia, found that 'Each additional hour spent in a car per day was associated with a 6% increase in the likelihood of obesity. Conversely, each additional kilometer walked per day was associated with a 4.8% reduction in the likelihood of obesity' (Frank, Andresen, & Schmid, 2004, p. 87)

Physical activity helps us to live longer lives, and it also helps us to have healthier lives, as the Centers for Disease Control (CDC) in the United States have summarised. Physical activity:

- helps to control weight;
- reduces risks of cardiovascular disease, type 2 diabetes, metabolic syndrome and some cancers;
- strengthens bones and muscles;
- improves mental health and mood;
- improves ability to do daily activities and prevent falls (CDC, 2018).

A further benefit of physical activity is that it reduces time spent sitting. Recent evidence shows that longer time spent in sedentary posture is significantly associated with higher coronary heart disease risk and larger waist circumference (Tigbe, Granat, Sattar, & Lean, 2017). This affirms a strong growth of evidence in recent years that large amounts of sedentary behaviour are associated with increased risks of several chronic conditions and mortality—and indeed that physical activity may not even be able to attenuate or eliminate the detrimental effects of prolonged sitting. Ekelund et al. (2016) examined these associations in a meta-study involving over a million individuals and found that high levels of moderate intensity physical activity (i.e. about 60–75 minutes per day) were required to completely counteract the increased risk of death associated with high-sitting time. Such amounts of physical activity do not have to be achieved all at once, but can be accumulated in two or more sessions. Abandoning pursuing more speed in the car and instead commuting or accessing services by active, 'slower' modes fits this pattern perfectly—and it is to this type of physical activity that we now turn.

5.2.3 Active travel as a beneficial form of physical activity

Active travel

Active travel is that which requires only the use of the human body for propulsion. It includes the use of skateboards, scooters, in-line skates and various other devices, but these are all relatively unimportant compared with walking and cycling. Active travel also includes public transport, because of its potential combination with walking and cycling. For example, many trips involve a walk (or a bike ride) to the bus or train followed by a walk to the final destination (Fig. 5.1). In other cases, the bike might be carried on the public transport

FIGURE 5.1 Integration of active travel modes, as walkers become tram riders and vice versa in Brno, Czech Republic. *(Credit: Rodney Tolley)*

vehicle itself and used for onward travel. Depending on the proportions of the stage lengths, public transport passengers may gain significant physical activity benefit. Indeed, evidence on the amount of walking and cycling accomplished by public transport users shows that using public transport could make a significant contribution to attaining recommended levels of daily physical activity. Research in Bogotá, Colombia found that living within one kilometre of one or more TransMilenio busway stations increased the odds of walking 30 minutes or more each day for utilitarian purposes by 72 per cent compared to those living in areas without a busway station. Thus the TransMilenio busway not only 'confers numerous environmental and mobility benefits, it also appears to provide a public health benefit—specifically, inducing more walking per day, controlling for socioeconomic factors like age and car ownership' (Cervero, Sarmiento, Jacoby, Gomez, & Neiman, 2009, p. 217).

Walking

Walking and cycling have significant potential to enhance public health, with great advantages over other forms of exercise and physical activity (Pucher & Dijkstra, 2003). Not only do they provide valuable physical activity on a daily basis, but they also create virtually no noise or air pollution, and consume far fewer non-renewable energy resources than motorised transport

(Pucher & Buehler, 2010). To take walking first, Sussman and Goode, in *The Magic of Walking*, comment that:

> *'Walking is the exercise that needs no gym. It is the prescription without medicine, the weight control without diet, the cosmetic that is sold in no drugstore. It is the tranquilizer without a pill, the therapy without a psychoanalyst, the fountain of youth that is no legend' (Sussman & Goode, 1967, p.19).*

As the most natural form of physical activity, walking has distinct advantages over other forms of exercise. It is low cost for the individual, requiring no equipment and is accessible for all ages, fitness levels and abilities, whether alone or in groups. It is the most common adult activity and is easy to fit into daily lives and split into easily manageable sessions, so that it is more likely to be taken up by people and maintained. It has been shown to have multiple benefits to physical health, such as:

- decreasing premature death from all causes and cardiovascular-related death;
- reducing development of and improving management of diabetes;
- lowering risk of cancer (breast and colon);
- assisting the treatment of hypertension;
- lowering the risk of osteoporosis and fractures; and
- mitigating the risks of obesity.

Other specific impacts of walking on health are pictured in Fig. 5.2, and these—and many other benefits—have been confirmed by multiple studies over many years (e.g. Cavill, 2003; Morris & Hardman, 1997; U.S. Department of Health and Human Services, 2015).

Unsurprisingly given these benefits, a review of physical activity promotion strategies concluded that 'Brisk walking has the greatest potential for increasing the overall activity levels of a sedentary population and meeting current public health recommendations. It is also the kind of exercise most likely to be adopted by a range of ages, socioeconomic, and ethnic groups as well as both sexes' (Hillsdon & Thorogood, 1996, p. 88). Perhaps more eloquently, Robert Sallis, a practising physician from California, has described walking as 'the long sought vaccine to prevent chronic disease and extend life' and continued 'If we had a pill that conferred the proven health benefits of walking, physicians would prescribe it to every patient and healthcare systems would find a way to make sure every patient had access to this wonder drug' (Sallis, 2013).

These undoubted health benefits of walking beg the question of what type of walking we are discussing. To a degree the faster the walk the better, as this improves aerobic fitness, but that is to downplay that *all* walking, of whatever speed or purpose, is beneficial to physical health. In a book about 'slow cities' it would be ironic if we were promoting high-speed walking as the desirable goal. In any case, advocating fast walking for health ignores the reality of normal walking (e.g. carrying shopping, accompanying children), which dictates

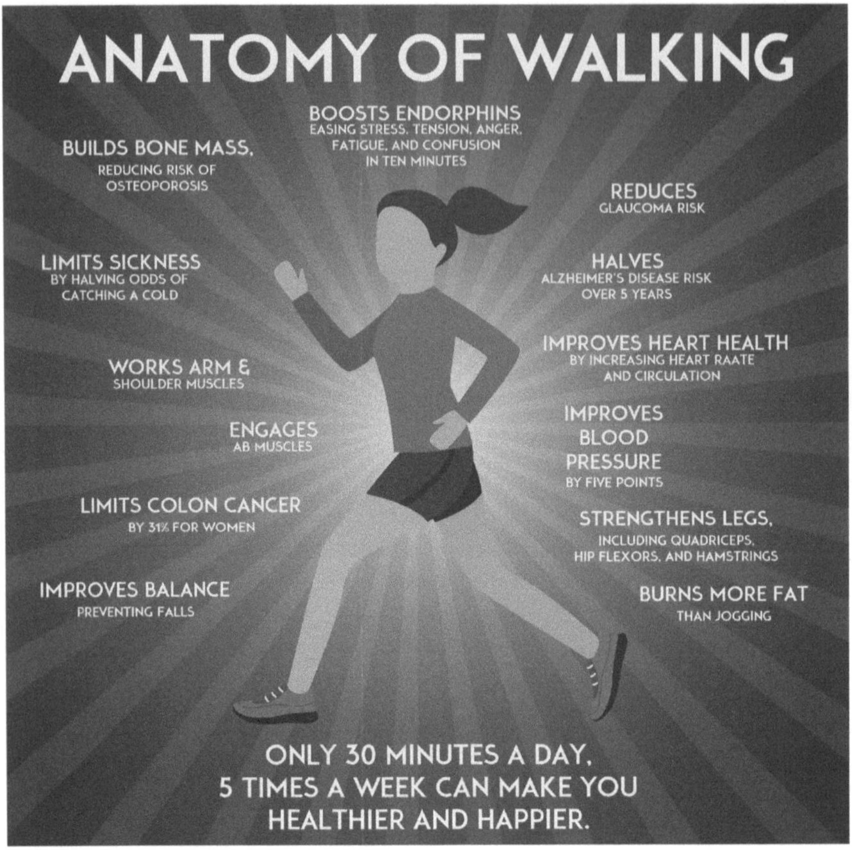

FIGURE 5.2 Walking confers multiple health benefits, and these have been proven in numerous studies over a long period. *(Credit: Shutterstock.com/SkyPics Studio)*

a slower pace. But that slower pace is available to everyone, to gain physical health benefits by incidental walking—to the shops or work—as part of normal, everyday activity. Not surprisingly then, the overall population health benefits from walking are greater than from any other physical activity.

Cycling

Many of the advantages of walking also apply to cycling, including the fact that they are both affordable for most people and hence are the 'most equitable of all transport modes' (Pucher & Buehler, 2010, p. 391). The health benefits of cycling are also well-documented, but there are two significant differences from the walking case. First, on the positive side, there is an argument that the personal health benefits of cycling are even greater than walking, because it is an aerobic activity which uses major muscle groups; has the potential to raise the heart rate to an extent that benefits cardiovascular health; and expends significant amounts of energy (Cavill, 2003, p. 153). The results have been well-documented: regular cyclists are fitter and live longer than non-cyclists (Hillman & Morgan, 1992). To take just one example, the Copenhagen Heart Study found that those who did not cycle to work experienced a 39 per cent higher mortality rate than those who did (Andersen, Schnohr, Schroll, & Hein, 2000).

Second, and on the other hand, there are reasons why the cycling contribution to health may be much less significant than that of walking when considered at a population level. Whereas most people can walk, not everyone can ride and not everyone can access a bicycle. Many trips are very short and are quicker and more convenient to walk than cycle, when one considers access and parking. The combination of walking and public transport is frequently smoother than accessing public transport by bike. Even in the most bicycle-orientated cities, the share of trip stages by bike rarely climbs above 50 per cent. Of course, encouraging more cycling is necessary and desirable, especially for the longer trips. However, we need to keep in mind that it is walking that is closer to a universal activity and should therefore be the primary focus when encouraging active travel.

There is a further difference between walking and cycling, and that is in terms of perception of traffic danger. As far as walking is concerned, this perception is frequently cited as a reason to walk less or for particular journeys, but for cycling, it is much more commonly voiced as a reason not to ride at all. The view that cycling is 'dangerous' can be supported by higher killed and seriously injured rates per km travelled compared to car use. However, the fatality rate in road crashes should relate the loss of 'life years' (the life expectancy at age of death of all cyclists) in cycle fatalities to the gain of 'life years' through improved fitness among regular cyclists. Regular cyclists increase their longevity, particularly as a result of a lowered rate of heart disease. Mayer Hillman has argued that even in the generally hostile traffic environment for cycling in Britain, the benefits gained from regular cycling in terms of life years gained outweigh the loss of life years in cycling fatalities, perhaps by 20 to 1 (Hillman, 1993).

In summary, the potential for walking and cycling to improve public health is considerable. Even under existing conditions, these modes are more appealing to larger numbers of people than traditional sports or exercise. Moreover, slowing motor car traffic and providing safer and more convenient walking and cycling networks would not only make these modes safer for existing users, as is the case in the Netherlands, Denmark and Germany for example (Pucher & Buehler, 2008), but it would likely release considerable latent demand amongst those who are currently too fearful of the dangers from motorised traffic. The potential for increased participation and consequent improved individual and population health is therefore very great indeed.

5.3 'Slower' modes and personal mental health

5.3.1 How can walking and cycling improve mental health?

There are strong connections between physical activity in general and mental well-being. Being active: promotes mental health; improves self-perception and self-esteem, mood and sleep quality; and reduces anxiety, fatigue and stress (Fig. 5.3). Active adults are 30 per cent less likely to feel distressed and 20–30 per cent less likely to develop depression and dementia (de Moor, 2013).

In terms of cycling or walking specifically, there are also studies that have documented beneficial mental health outcomes (Pucher & Dijkstra, 2003). To take cycling first, Cycling UK (2017) argues that cycling reduces stress and anxiety, promotes calmer thinking and combats depression (Cyclescheme, 2017). It seems that there are both physiological mechanisms such as the release of endorphins, which trigger a positive feeling in the body, and psychological mechanisms, such as improvements in self-esteem.

In relation to walking, research findings currently indicate that walking can:

- reduce physical symptoms of anxiety associated with minor stress;
- improve sleep quality;
- elevate affective response (e.g. pleasure), resulting in increased psychological well-being for individuals with type 2 diabetes;

FIGURE 5.3 Stress-free walking in a suburban street, Vancouver, Canada. *(Credit: Paul Tranter)*

- increase the size of the hippocampus and prefrontal cortex, potentially beneficial for memory;
- improve cognitive performance in mental processes such as thinking, understanding and remembering (C3 Collaborating for Health, 2012).

Of course, the idea that walking helps creative thought is hardly revolutionary, given Friedrich Nietzsche's observation that 'All truly great thoughts are conceived by walking'. Indeed, researchers at Stanford University who compared creativity amongst participants when sitting and walking, found that across the board, creativity levels were consistently and significantly higher (60 per cent on average) for those walking compared to those sitting (Oppezzo & Schwartz, 2014). Every participant who walked outside generated at least one novel, high-quality idea, compared with only 50 per cent of those seated inside. However, it was the act of walking itself, and not the environment, that was the main factor: creativity also improved for those walking indoors on a treadmill, facing a blank wall. Similar outcomes have been reported for cycling, where participants scored higher on memory, reasoning and planning after cycling, and they were able to finish tests more rapidly than before (Andrews, 2015).

Research also demonstrates mental health benefits for at-risk populations, indicating that walking can relieve symptoms of depression and anxiety, and that riding a stationary bike for just a few minutes can reduce levels of the stress hormone cortisol. Another review of international trials found that walking and other aerobic exercise significantly improves motor action, balance and walking ability in people with Parkinson's Disease (Shu et al., 2014).

One of the most important health benefits of walking and cycling is their positive impact on social connection and hence their beneficial effect on the reduction of loneliness. Loneliness is increasingly recognised as a major and growing public health issue, with its impact on mortality comparable with well-established risk factors such as obesity (Holt-Lunstad, Smith, Baker, Harris, & Stephenson, 2015). Loneliness and social disconnection are increased by rising speeds of city transport, as Box 2.1 demonstrates.

5.3.2 Mental health effects of transport choice by journey purpose

The journey to work

Driving more than 10 miles (16 km) each way, to and from work, is associated with a set of negative physical impacts, including higher blood sugar and cholesterol levels. Research also shows temporary spikes in blood pressure when driving in rush hour and long-term higher blood pressure associated with the length of the car commute, as well as lower cardiovascular fitness, back and posture problems, lower sleep quality and more exhaustion (Kylstra, 2015). Moreover, we now understand better the health dangers of sitting, including in a car, as discussed earlier in Section 5.2.2.

Commuting by car is associated not only with physical health risks. The UK's Office of National Statistics finds that people who commute more than half an hour to work each way report higher levels of stress and anxiety and lower life satisfaction and happiness than people with shorter commutes or no commutes at all (Office for National Statistics, 2014). Stutzer and Frey (2008) found that a person with a one-hour car commute has to earn 40 per cent more money to be as satisfied with life as one who walks to the office. For a single person, exchanging a long car commute for a short walk to work has the same effect on happiness as finding a new love (Viry, Kaufmann, & Widmer, 2009). In England, Hewlett-Packard research found that whether they were driving or taking the train, peak-hour travellers 'suffered worse stress than fighter pilots or riot police facing mobs of angry protesters' (Montgomery, 2013, p. 185). Only one group of commuters reported enjoying themselves—people who rode bicycles, or ran or walked.

Higher-speed transport encourages urban sprawl. According to Professor Billie Giles-Corti, this 'means that when people are having to drive long distances and are spending a lot of time outside their community ... they're not engaging with people locally. That's weakening social networks' (Norrie, 2012). In many cities in the Western world, driving to work is typically done alone, and interactions with other drivers, who are often seen as rude or aggressive, can be stressful and frustrating rather than friendly. While walking and cycling promote social connection, there is strong evidence that streets with high levels of fast moving traffic 'reduce neighbourly interaction and friendships' (Kelly et al., 2012, p. 55). This in itself is a strong argument for the introduction of measures to reduce speeds.

Commuting on foot produces positive outcomes for mental health. UK research using 18 years of data on 18,000 18–65-year-old commuters examined psychological health including feelings of worthlessness, unhappiness, sleepless nights, and being unable to face problems. The researchers identified 'a positive relationship between time spent walking and wellbeing which ... indicates a dose–response relationship' (Martin, Goryakin, & Suhrcke, 2014, p. 300). Significantly, while improved mental health is generally associated with reduced commuting times, the benefits of walking outweighed the benefits of a short commute: 'the potential benefits available to car drivers if they switched to active travel ... and walking in particular ... exceed any potential benefits associated with reducing commuting time' (Martin et al., 2014, p. 301). This is yet another example of the damaging relationship between well-being and our addiction to speed in the city.

The journey to school

Using active travel to school improves the mental well-being of children. One study involving some 20,000 Danish school children found that children who walk or cycle to school rather than being driven by their parents have increased powers of concentration, and this effect lasts for up to four hours after they get to school (Goodyear, 2013).

FIGURE 5.4 West Boulevard Elementary walking school bus, Boardman, Ohio. *(Credit: MoBikeFed, Flickr https://www.flickr.com/photos/mobikefed/3452932586)*

There is also evidence of effects of active school travel on wider mental awareness of children, though this has been less commonly researched. A study of 8-to-11-year-old children in Rome found that children who walked to school on their own or with other children or accompanied by an adult had greater environmental knowledge of their neighbourhoods than those driven by car. Children who walked had the best performance in sketch maps of their home-school area and in drawing their movements on a blank map of their neighbourhood (Rissotto & Tonucci, 2002).

Another (small-scale) study undertaken at Pirehill School in Staffordshire in the United Kingdom reviewed children's drawings of their journey to school. Some children were driven, some walked and others were part of a 'walking school bus', where children walk to school accompanied by one or more adults, using a set route, as illustrated in Fig. 5.4. The drawings produced by children who were car passengers (such as the top two images in Fig. 5.5) indicated an isolated experience, whereas the walkers (such as the example at bottom left) displayed more social and spatial awareness. Still others who used the walking school bus (bottom right) drew images that showed elements of nature and joyful interaction with others (Bickerstaff & Shaw, 2000). An Australian study of walking school buses identified similar trends: children's drawings of their journey to school showed that walking not only improved the children's understanding of their social networks in their community, it also enhanced 'their awareness of the physical and social space in which they move' (Rooney, 2008, p. 44).

FIGURE 5.5 Children's drawings of their journey to school at Pirehill School in Staffordshire, UK, according to mode of travel: car passengers (*top* two); independent walking (*bottom left*); participants in the walking school bus (*bottom right*). *(Credit: Rodney Tolley)*

Walking for social connection

'Walking *is* Transport' was the title of one of the first books to focus on the importance of walking in the city (Hillman & Whalley, 1979). The point was well made to counteract the way that walking had been forgotten in transport planning and needed to be re-discovered. However, this is not to say that all everyday walking is *only* transport. The commuter walker may indeed require a clear and fast route, whilst the walk to the shops is often merely functional, although perhaps with a more aesthetic aspect. However, children walking may want a mazy environment that encourages exploration, whilst the needs of those walking to think or de-stress may only be met when there is some beauty, a view, or a place to sit and cry.

The point is that much slow travel has a strong social purpose. Transport is usually conceptualised as getting from A to B, but for walkers, what is between A and B is just as critical: places to stand and sit; opportunities for conversations and play; things to see such as interesting shops and street vendors; greenery and trees; combinations of sun, shade, and protection from wind; art installations that make you curious and want to linger and observe (Fig. 5.6); and other displays that make you smile and possibly join in, such as street entertainers, live music and dancing. Above all, of course, there have to be people: as William Whyte observed, 'What attracts people most, it would appear, is other

FIGURE 5.6 Lingering to observe and contemplate the *Forgotten Songs* sound sculpture in Angel Place, Sydney, Australia. Combined with suspended bird cages, sound rises from below in waves of calls from 50 birds that were once heard in the city, now either forced to the city edge or drowned out by transport and development noise. *(Credit: Rodney Tolley)*

people' (Whyte, 1980, p. 19) (see Fig. 5.7). When all or most of these conditions are met, people will go there and stroll, linger and sit: in the European phrase, they will sojourn. The presence of such places encourages people to walk to them and through them, and has a major indirect impact on the amount of walking that residents do.

The fact that people in these scenarios are not trying to get somewhere in a hurry does not in any way diminish the role of walking in the range of transport modes. Walking for social purposes is an absolutely legitimate justification for walking. Sitting down for a coffee or to chat needs to be understood in much the same way as a car driver may park for a while in a multi-stage journey.

FIGURE 5.7 As Jan Gehl observes 'There is so much more to walking than walking': people sitting and watching other people walking in Strøget, Copenhagen, Denmark. *(Credit: Rodney Tolley)*

The sidewalk coffee drinker is a 'parked pedestrian' in a multi-faceted activity whose purpose is not about saving time—our traditional perspective on transport—but about spending time. As we have alluded to in Chapter 1, as Jan Gehl has famously said, 'in cities there is so much more to walking than walking' (Gehl, 2010, p. 19).

It is undeniable that walking and spending time in social spaces and situations gives many people pleasure. However, there is a need for more research into the relationship between the social context of walking and its effect on specific mental health outcomes—for example, how walking can help to overcome social exclusion, which itself has health consequences. This is demonstrated by Australia's Heart Foundation walking programmes of organised walking groups, which are some of the most successful in the world, with over 27,000 active participants in over 1,250 regular groups (Heart Foundation, 2016). They engage population groups that are least likely to be active—80 per cent female, 75 per cent over 60, 26 per cent living alone—yet achieve exceptional retention rates of 77 per cent after six months and 73 per cent after a year. There are many reasons for success, but feedback indicates that the social connection element—sharing stories, having a laugh and making friends—is just as important for the participants as feeling healthy and getting in shape. More than 80 per cent of walkers join for the health benefits, but the major motivations for staying are the social benefits such as friendship. Chau (2007) has shown that

FIGURE 5.8 Walking in natural surroundings amplifies the mental health benefits of walking: Stanley Park, Vancouver, Canada. *(Credit: Paul Tranter)*

these are mutually reinforcing relationships. On the one hand, walking groups are effective for increasing socialisation and fostering a greater sense of community spirit and participation, and on the other, having strong social networks is associated with being physically active.

Though indoor walking and cycling both produce positive health outcomes, doing them outdoors in natural surroundings (Fig. 5.8) magnifies these benefits. The UK mental health charity MIND questioned people in groups active in gardening, conservation and cycling as well as walking: 90 per cent said that they feel that 'green exercise' benefits their physical health but an even higher proportion, 94 per cent, felt that it improves their mental health (MIND, 2007, p. 1). Green exercise can reduce stress and decrease symptoms of depression and anxiety, as well as increasing enjoyment and motivation.

Jody Rosenblatt-Naderi's (2014) review of research on walking for contemplation and renewal extends this connection. She points out that people who walk for deep thinking or trying to connect with nature are the most demanding of the environment. They will go out of their way to take a route that has certain aesthetic attributes and no interruptions. 'To take an uninterrupted one kilometre walk in the city, in my mind is the pinnacle walking experience, in the sense that if you can do that, then you have pretty much a city that can do all the rest of it too' (Rosenblatt-Naderi 2014, p. 5). Given that the 'slower city' of the future may be able to re-purpose much road and car parking space into green space close to where people live, the potential for benefiting health by incorporating nature into our daily lives may be very large indeed.

5.4 Incidental public health benefits of active travel

5.4.1 Reduction in the frequency and severity of crashes

It is to the devastating consequences of speed and crashes that we turn in this section. Global statistics on road deaths show that the total number continues to rise, reaching 1.35 million in 2016, or nearly 3,700 deaths each day (World Health Organization, 2018b). More people die due to road crashes than from HIV/AIDS, tuberculosis or diarrhoeal diseases, yet there is less political commitment and financial investment in road safety compared to that invested in combatting these diseases. Over half of global road crash deaths involve vulnerable road users—people on foot and on bicycles, and motorcyclists. This is a particular problem in the Global South, where lack of provision for people walking and cycling exacerbate this vulnerability. A concerning example is Ethiopia, a nation with a road traffic fatality rate of over 25 per 100,000 population, amongst the highest in the world (Abegaz & Gebremedhin, 2019), and almost nine times higher than in Sweden. Ethiopia's rate has been increasing in recent years, as motor vehicle numbers continue to rise and as conditions for vulnerable road users remain appalling (see Fig. 5.9). More than 270,000 people are killed on the world's roads annually while walking, or over 700 per day.

Road crashes are the leading cause of death for young people (aged 5–29 years). The WHO Global Status Report on Road Safety 2018 sees this as a heart-breaking statistic and argues: 'No child should die or be seriously injured while they walk, cycle or play. We must return our streets to our children. They

FIGURE 5.9 Room for improvement in conditions for walking in Addis Ababa, Ethiopia. *(Credit: Carlos Felipe Pardo, Addis Ababa, Ethiopia November 2014, https://www.flickr.com/photos/carlosfpardo/15569928347)*

have a right to feel safe on them' (World Health Organization, 2018b, p. vii). Even though many world leaders have made a commitment to halve the number of road crash deaths by 2020, little progress has been made towards this goal in most nations. From 2013 to 2016 there was no reduction in the number of road crash deaths in any nation of the Global South, while minor reductions were evident in 48 middle- and high-income nations. During the same period, numbers of deaths increased in over 100 nations (World Health Organization, 2018b).

It is clear that the speed of motorised vehicles is a critical factor in this scourge. City planners, traffic engineers and residents in cities throughout the world have an innate understanding that reducing the speed of motorised traffic will reduce the frequency and severity of crashes. To understand why lower speeds are important for road safety, it is necessary to consider five factors:

1. the limits of human perception;
2. the laws of physics;
3. the biomechanics of human bodies;
4. the psychology of living in a low-speed environment; and
5. the feedback impacts of slowing city transport on other human behaviours and on land use.

Road safety researchers and practitioners recognise that speeds of motorised traffic above 20 mph (or 30 km/h) are not compatible with environments where there are vulnerable road users. As speeds increase, there is a narrowing of our field of vision, as Fig. 5.10 illustrates. At 25 km/h (15 mph), all of the

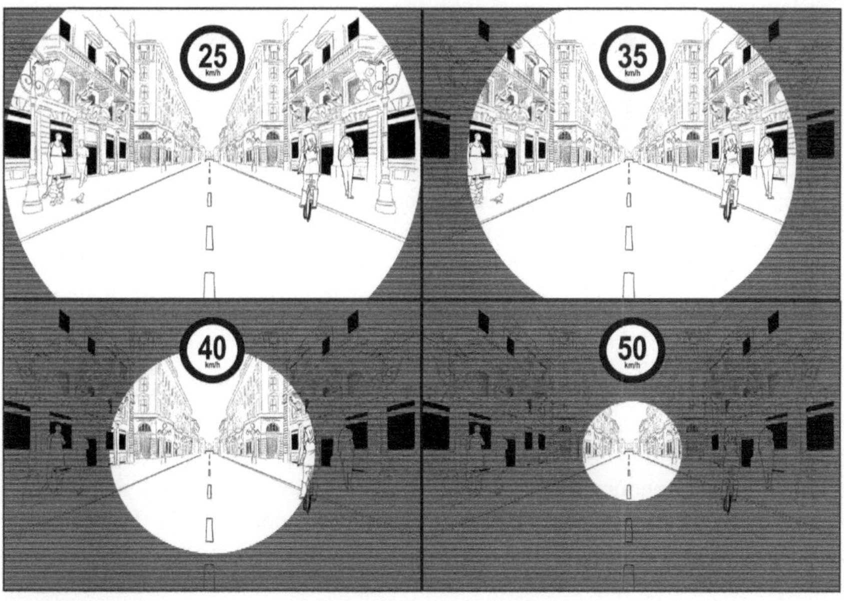

FIGURE 5.10 Driver's cone of vision shrinks with increasing speed. *(Credit: Claudio Olivares Medina)*

people on foot or bicycles are clearly visible (top-left image) and the driver can observe vulnerable road users (e.g. a child playing) and compute likely scenarios. At just 50 km/h (31 mph) (bottom-right image—and itself below the speed limit in many cities)—the driver would be oblivious even to the presence of people on foot or bicycles, let alone to the likelihood of unanticipated movements.

To appreciate the significance of the limits of human perception, we also need to consider the influence of speed on stopping distances, and this requires the consideration of some basic physics. 'To the extent that the world's roads and cities remain shaped around the worship of smooth car traffic flow, the laws of physics will continue to make them dangerous places for everyone, especially those not protected by a steel frame and airbags' (Baker, 2019). Physics helps to explain the connection between increasing speed and rising vulnerability. The kinetic energy (KE) of a moving object is directly proportional to the mass of that object and to the square of its velocity. The formula to explain this is KE = $1/2 \text{ m} \times v^2$. This means that if the speed of an object doubles, its kinetic energy increases to four times the initial kinetic energy. If the speed triples, kinetic energy increases by nine times.

To put these figures into perspective, if a car weighing 1,500 kg travels at 20 km/h, it has a KE of 23,148 joules. The same car at 60 km/h has a KE of 208,333 joules. A slight increase in velocity produces a much greater increase in KE and risk of injury in a collision. If a person walking is hit by a car at 50 km/h, the fatality risk is more than twice as high as the risk at 40 km/h and more than five times higher than the risk at 30 km/h (Rosén & Sander, 2009). The laws of physics also explain why the chances of avoiding a collision are higher at lower speeds: stopping distances are much lower at lower speeds. Stopping distance is directly proportional to the square of the speed of the car at the instant the brakes are applied.

When total stopping distances are calculated for different speeds, assuming a reaction time of one second, the differences between 30 and 50 km/h may be a surprise to most people: 'a driver who could stop from 30 km/h in front of an obstacle would hit that obstacle at a speed of 50 km/h if she drove at 50 km/h under the same conditions' (Svenson, Eriksson, & Gonzalez, 2012, p. 488) (see Fig. 5.11). Whilst distance travelled during reaction time increases in a consistent arithmetic function with the increase in speed, braking distances increase exponentially.

In addition to the laws of physics, the adoption of 30 km/h speed limits is based on a sound understanding of biomechanical tolerance that recognises the human body's ability to survive sudden impacts. Human evolution has given us the ability to endure the impact of colliding with a stationary solid object at maximum running speed (Hamilton-Baillie & Jones, 2005). Few humans can run faster than 30 km/h. At impact speeds above 30 km/h, injury severity increases markedly: the chances of surviving being hit by a car decrease rapidly (Brown, Moodie, & Carter, 2017). To help appreciate the significance of

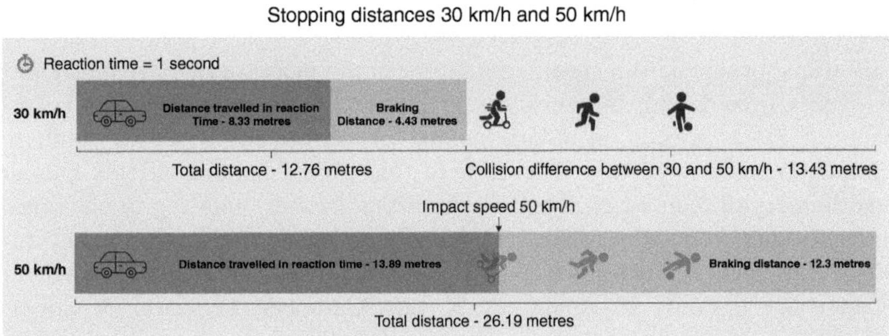

FIGURE 5.11 Reaction time and braking distance for cars travelling at 30 and 50 km/h. *(Credit: Jeff Steinacker)*

increasing speed from 30 to 60 km/h, think of falling from a multistorey building. A person falling from the first floor (called the second floor in the United States) will hit the ground at just below 30 km/h, and very likely survive with only minor injuries. To produce an impact speed of 60 km/h would entail falling from the 4th floor (5th in the United States), a terrifying prospect that would lead to a risk of death of around 75 per cent.

Another benefit for road safety of lower vehicle speeds is the psychology associated with low-speed environments. When people walk, cycle or scooter around a street where vehicles move at 30 km/h or less, the streets 'feel' safer. The reasons for this relate partly to the psychology of human perception. The ability of humans to retain eye contact with others reduces when we are travelling faster than a fast running speed (above 30 km/h). This reduces our ability to communicate non-verbally, and verbal communication effectiveness is also reduced. This means that when vehicles are travelling more slowly, the pace is more comfortable for human interaction.

The final factor in understanding the importance of lower speeds for road safety concerns feedback impacts on behaviours and land use. One result of a psychology of increased safety in low-speed streets is that more people of all ages are likely to walk and cycle in their neighbourhoods, thus creating a 'safety in numbers' feedback effect (Jacobsen, 2003). Parents become more confident in letting their children walk or cycle to school, or play in (or near) the street, because of both lower traffic danger and lower fears of stranger danger that result from higher levels of passive surveillance in communities with more social interaction (Tranter, 2016). Evidence that lower speeds encourage more active transport can be found in a study in Bristol, where low-speed areas (with 20 mph signs only), led to increased walking and cycling and also increased levels of children's independent mobility (Brown et al., 2017). This in turn creates a virtuous circle: more people walking and cycling mean that more people use local shops and services. This increased support for local shops strengthens local communities, which in turn reduces concerns about strangers.

5.4.2 Reduction in pollution and greenhouse gas emissions

City transport speed is a significant factor in the increase in extreme weather events linked with human-induced climate breakdown. Whilst the impacts of lower speeds on environmental health are discussed in detail in Chapter 6, it is important to note here that global heating affects human health in significant ways, the most important of these relating to increased intensity and frequency of heat waves, fires, floods and droughts, and increased impacts of vector-borne diseases, food insecurity and displacement (Capon & Corvalan, 2018; Haines, Kovats, Campbell-Lendrum, & Corvalan, 2006). Whilst low-income nations in the Global South are likely to be the worst affected, recent heat wave events in the United States and Europe indicate that high-income nations are also likely to suffer these negative impacts. In 2003 more than 70,000 people died in heat waves in Europe (Robine et al., 2008), and in 2018, there were heat waves in Quebec, across Europe and in Japan, where 65 people died and 22,647 went to hospital (Agence France-Presse, 2018).

Whilst greenhouse gas emissions are a global-health risk, pollution from road traffic is a significant hazard at the city and street level, implicated in aggravating cardiovascular and respiratory illness, reducing lung capacity and contributing to the development of diseases including bronchitis, emphysema and cancer. The statistics on pollution are damning: in the United States in 2005, for example, some 53,000 premature deaths per annum were attributable to particulate matter from road transport, larger even than the 43,000 crash fatalities—and this in a country with a poor road safety record (Caiazzo, Ashok, Waitz, Yim, & Barrett, 2013). These effects are not evenly distributed among the population. For example, chronic exposure to air pollution is linked to impaired cognitive performance, with the negative impact increasing with age, and particularly affecting men with the poorest education (BBC, 2018). In general, the groups most impacted are pregnant women, the elderly, people with existing chest, heart or lung problems, and children. The impacts of pollution on children deserve more detailed inspection (see Box 5.1).

In order to appreciate the link between high-speed transport and pollution, it is important to consider the whole transport system, rather than individual vehicles. Whilst tail-pipe emissions from individual internal combustion engine vehicles may be higher at lower speeds in some circumstances (e.g. 30 km/h compared to 50 km/h assuming that cars are travelling at a constant speed rather than frequently braking and accelerating), this does not mean that the solution to health-damaging pollution is to increase the average speed of cars in city streets. Increasing car speeds will simply encourage more car use and discourage active transport. Instead, reducing overall speed in the transport system by encouraging a modal switch to less polluting modes will reduce pollution in a much more extensive way.

BOX 5.1 Pollution impacts on children.

Children are especially susceptible to pollution caused by transport systems based on speed. Their developing tissues and organs are more sensitive to toxins, partly because they eat, drink and breathe more per unit of body weight. They are more vulnerable to air pollution because of their small stature: children walking near roads are exposed to a third more air pollution than adults due to breathing air closer to passing motor car exhausts (Edwards & Whitehouse, 2018).

Recent research on the impact of air pollution on child health shows that high-speed cities present significant and hitherto largely unappreciated risks for children. A UNICEF report found that children in the United Kingdom were at daily risk from particulate air pollution that could be 'stunting their lung growth, increasing their risk of asthma and potentially damaging their brain growth' (Edwards & Whitehouse, 2018, p. 2). The report found that the majority of this pollution comes from vehicle emissions and that children are disproportionately exposed to higher doses of pollution during their journey to school. Now in the United Kingdom, many local governments are intending to target air pollution from engine-idling near schools, given the estimate that an idling car produces enough exhaust emissions to fill 150 balloons a minute (Busby, 2019).

An important finding regarding children's exposure is that air pollution is more harmful to children (and adults) *inside* cars than when they are walking or cycling. Outside vehicles, emissions are dissipated into the air, reducing exposure. In cars, emissions are circulated and build up inside the vehicle. Research in a Canadian city found children who are driven to school (either in cars or in buses) are exposed to higher $PM_{2.5}$ (fine particle) concentrations than those who walk to and from school (Gilliland et al., 2019). Research in the United States showed that benzene concentrations inside cars can exceed concentrations in roadside air by up to four times and carbon monoxide concentrations can be 10 times higher inside cars than beside the road (International Center for Technology Assessment, 2000).

Whilst the dangers of in-car pollution have been known to researchers for many years, these dangers have recently attracted media attention focussing on the particular and significant dangers to children (Carrington, 2017). As one article pointed out, even drivers of cars with cleaner engines than others are still collecting toxic gases from all the vehicles around them: 'being in your car does not make you or your children immune to the deadly effects of air pollution ... smoking in cars is banned. But children still inhale toxic fumes in backseats' (King, 2017).

5.4.3 Enhancing social capital

Lower speeds lead to an increase in levels of social connection and social capital, whereas growth in the volume and speed of traffic leads to increasing community severance, as people are cut off from their neighbours, friends, family and community, as well as from essential services. However, the problem is not just the barriers produced by traffic speed and volumes and road infrastructure in the city: the street itself has increasingly been sacrificed for one purpose—high-speed travel by car. Amongst the activities driven out are nature, recreation, street trades, meetings, celebrations and parades, and of course children and children's games.

John Adams referred to the dystopian future that faced us if trends in mobility at the time continued continued:

> *'Street life will disappear. The spread-out scale will defeat pedestrians and traffic will make cycling too dangerous. There will be no local shops to walk to. Children will become captives of the family chauffeur in a world too full of traffic and alienated strangers for them to be permitted their traditional independence ... Present priorities ... by actively promoting developments that are relaxing constraints on access and mobility, are fast creating a bleak, dangerous, alienated, selfish, polarized, dehumanized world' (Adams, 1997, p. 97).*

There is plentiful evidence that the street as a meeting place is under threat. Fifty years ago, ground-breaking research in San Francisco showed how heavily trafficked streets damaged the social use of the street (Appleyard & Lintell, 1972). More recent studies have validated these findings. In Bristol, England, people living on lightly trafficked streets had five times as many friends and twice as many acquaintances as those on streets with heavy traffic. Lightly trafficked streets had three times the number of 'gathering spots' and residents were more likely to live at the front of the house and to let their children play in the street (Hart, 2008).

A study of similar arrangements in Switzerland showed that streets with slow moving traffic, limited space for parking and good environmental qualities, 'offer a large potential for personal development, contentment and social integration' (Sauter & Huettenmoser, 2008, p. 67). Ben Rossiter from Victoria Walks has extended this argument to sidewalks, which he says 'are not transport routes: they are for walking, talking, playing, living, loving and learning' (Rossiter, 2016).

Because public space fosters civic, social, commercial and political life, its loss or deterioration has grievous impacts on well-being, whether those are due to reduced active travel in the street or the loss of community benefits that come from use of the street for meeting, trading and creativity. People in public space attract people. In other words, living in walkable and cyclable neighbourhoods is related not only to more physical activity, but also to feeling more connected with people in the community (Fig. 5.12).

There is evidence that social relationships (or a lack of them) are as important for mortality risk as tobacco, and more important than obesity (Holt-Lunstad, Smith, & Layton, 2010). As Putnam explains, 'the evidence for the health consequences of social connectedness is as strong today as the evidence for health consequences of smoking at the time of the first surgeon general's report on smoking' (Putnam, 2001, p. 327). Research in sociology indicates that walking in one's own neighbourhood is important for building social capital. The bottom line is that social connection is a critically important factor in well-being because maintaining social contacts contributes to mental health and quality of life, and is particularly important for children, older people and

FIGURE 5.12 Slow travel makes space and time for social interaction. Brescia, Italy. *(Credit: Rodney Tolley)*

vulnerable populations. For children in Japan, where there is a societal expectation that children will walk to school, walking is associated with more frequent opportunities for children to have contact with people, particularly people that they know (Waygood, Sun, & Letarte, 2015). The value of these connections for children in Japan is enhanced compared to children in nations such as Australia, the United States and the United Kingdom because 'greeting people (*aisatsu*) is a culturally valued behaviour and children and adults alike are encouraged to greet each other' (Waygood & Friman, 2015).

5.4.4 Increasing accessibility for the transport deprived

Enrique Peñalosa, as Mayor of Bogotá, Colombia (renowned for its people-centred transport interventions) said: 'What are our needs for happiness? We need to walk, just as birds need to fly. We need to be around other people. We need beauty. We need contact with nature. And most of all, we need not to be excluded' (Montgomery, 2013, p.4).

A more formal way of debating these issues is to use the concept of 'health equity', defined as the fair and just opportunity for everyone to be healthier (Robert Wood Johnson Foundation, 2017). Achieving this requires removing obstacles to health such as poverty and discrimination, and their consequences, which include aspects of transport disadvantage such as lack of access to good jobs, health care and safe environments. Such disadvantage follows familiar lines of structural social inequality and impacts the economically disadvantaged, those with disabilities, the elderly, the young and women. This section will examine each of these groups, whilst recognising that there is considerable overlap between them.

The economically disadvantaged

Poverty itself has serious health implications, but the pursuit of higher-speed travel in the city has exacerbated them for those on low or no incomes. In the typical US city, high-speed travel has undermined the viability of public transport which, for the 25 per cent of Americans living in poverty who do not own a motor vehicle, means less ability to access healthy foods, health care, parks and well-paying jobs and educational opportunities. Their communities have been divided by freeways connecting downtowns with suburbs, resulting in elevated air pollution and noise levels and making active travel more dangerous as a result of high volumes of fast-moving through traffic: in the United States pedestrian fatality rates in the poorest counties are over 80 per cent higher than the national average (Smart Growth America, 2017). In the United Kingdom, it has been estimated that there would be 600 fewer fatalities if all adults were as likely to be involved in a road traffic crash as those in the highest social class (Christie et al., 2010). As Allen and Allen (2015, p. 100) explain, 'reducing vehicular speed is likely to have a greater impact lower down the social gradient, thereby "levelling up" outcomes'.

Residents' health in disadvantaged areas is impacted disproportionately. There is both a lack of access to health-giving facets of the city and excessive exposure to health-damaging aspects. Having the poorest access to opportunities in the city and simultaneously suffering the worst effects of other people's movement doubly disadvantages them.

Nor is this just an inner-city problem. In Australia's large cities, for example, rising housing prices have forced many low-income families to live in sprawling, outer suburbs, where public transport is usually rudimentary, if it exists at all. Here owning one or more cars per family is often regarded as necessary for survival, to simply get to work and take children to school. Not only does this mean long and unhealthy commutes, but also access to health care and healthy food is undermined. Household finances are stretched and are vulnerable to uncontrollable changes in prices, such as for fuel and mortgage repayments, as shown in the VAMPIRE (Vulnerability Assessment for Mortgage, Petroleum, and Inflation Risks and Expenditure) studies of Australian cities (Dodson & Sipe, 2008) (see Fig. 5.13). The mortgage foreclosure crisis in US cities during the GFC in 2008 was led by the distant outer suburbs of sprawled southern metro areas, as people abandoned homes and lifestyles that had become impossible to access and maintain in any affordable way in new times of higher prices. For those that leave, it is difficult to imagine a more damaging impact on health than homelessness. For those remaining,

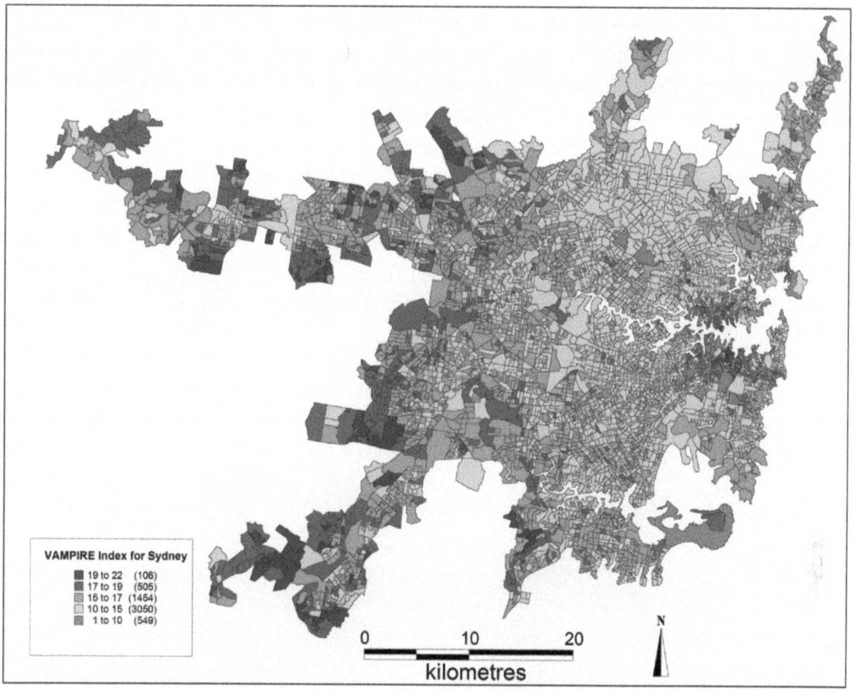

FIGURE 5.13 Mortgage and oil vulnerability in Sydney according to the VAMPIRE index (Vulnerability Assessment for Mortgage, Petroleum and Inflation Risks and Expenditure). The highest scores are in the outer western and south-western suburbs, indicating higher vulnerability to rising fuel costs on the basis of car dependence, incomes and mortgages. *(Dodson and Sipe, 2006)*

the continuing stress of high transport costs is an additional health burden (Rachele, Healy, Sallis, & Sugiyama, 2017).

People with a disability

According to the World Health Organization (2001), disability has three dimensions: impairment, activity limitation and participation restrictions, so this is a very diverse group that does not lend itself to generalisations when it comes to transport limitations. It is a large group, too: in the United States, for example, there were 36 million people in 2011 who had at least one disability, about 12 per cent of the total US population, rising to 37 per cent of adults 65 and older (US Census Bureau, 2011).

In general, people with disabilities are less likely to drive and are more likely to rely on public transport, community transport or assistance from friends, family or colleagues. Accessibility on foot to public transport services or stations is obviously key, with many countries using disability access laws to ensure that appropriate physical infrastructure—such as ramps and tactile indicators—is in place. However, though this might make a trip feasible, for many people it will still remain extraordinarily daunting. For example, Burtt (2014, p. 3) has pointed out that people on foot with vision impairment not only face the same dangers and distractions as others but they 'have fewer cues about the physical environment, fewer cues about approaching dangers, often restricted mobility to get out of danger quickly and are often pre-occupied with the need to avoid a fall or obstacle'.

A solution for many is to use mobility devices such as wheelchairs or motorised scooters, but these too have limitations in complex walking environments, and they are less likely to be used in streets with high-speed traffic (see Fig. 5.14). For example, the Dutch City of Breda, a leader in the accessibility

FIGURE 5.14 The setting of low speed limits is crucial for those using wheelchairs. Where speed limits are high, gaps to cross roads are hard to find, as in (A) Dandenong, Melbourne, Australia. However, where area-wide speeds are low, co-existence with other modes becomes normal. This is the case in (B) from the Maldives, where a speed limit of 30 km/h (25 km/h for two-wheelers) increases the safety of people using wheelchairs and provides a tranquil environment. Road traffic fatality rates here are among the lowest in the world. *(Credit: Photo (A), Paul Tranter; Photo (B), Asad Photo Maldives, https://www.pexels.com/photo/asian-people-2245218/)*

field, has flattened all of the cobblestones that pave its historic centre in order to improve comfort for wheelchair users, an example of its perspective that it is the environment in which people live that is disabled, rather than people themselves (Yates, 2019).

Disabled and elderly people have the most to gain from walking and cycling becoming safer active travel options, as they exercise the least and are most at risk of additional health complications. Speeding traffic is clearly incompatible with this goal. The real and perceived barriers that speed produces restrict daily time-space prisms for all people but especially so for this group, reducing access to employment, education, and other health-enhancing activities and increasing health-damaging social exclusion and inequality.

Older people

In richer countries, the current generation of older people is the first to have grown up with mass car ownership, and as a result many older people have lifestyles and travel patterns based around the car. They have been at the forefront of the decentralisation of the city and unfortunately many will suffer the consequences of this in their old age. The ageing process frequently brings reductions in car use through decline in physical ability to drive (and decreased confidence to do so), loss of a driving partner, and reductions in disposable income. This may have serious impacts on mental and physical health, as for older people there is a correlation between lack of car access and multiple social exclusions, especially where public transport is unsatisfactory.

On the other hand, more active travel 'can contribute substantially to the accumulation of health-enhancing levels of physical activity in older adults' (Cerin, Nathan, Van Cauwenberg, Barnett, & Barnett, 2017). Evidence for this is found in the longer life expectancy and longer 'healthy life' expectancy in Germany and the Netherlands—two years longer than in the United States. This is likely at least partly due to the higher levels of walking and cycling among the elderly in Germany and the Netherlands. For example, 'the Dutch and Germans who are 75 and older make roughly half their trips by foot or bike, compared with only 6% of Americans aged 65 and older' (Pucher & Dijkstra, 2003, p. 1510).

Walking and cycling also likely contribute to a lowered incidence of cognitive impairment and depression. There is a growing body of work on the protective effects of walking on rates of dementia and its onset. For example, increased walking was associated with greater grey matter volume nine years later in several brain areas including the hippocampus, which may be associated with a reduced risk of Alzheimer's disease (Erickson, Weinstein, & Lopez, 2012). The Australian Heart Foundation evaluated fifteen walking groups across Australia, inclusive of people with dementia, and found improvements in behavioural and psychological symptoms of dementia, with statistically significant enhancements seen in family relationships, sleep and overall quality of life (Morley, 2011).

FIGURE 5.15 Attractive and accessible seating (with armrests), located in socially safe spaces is vital for the elderly to rest, meet friends and to feel socially included. Oaxaca, Mexico. *(Credit: Rodney Tolley)*

However, for more seniors to engage in or increase their level of active travel, there would need to be perceived and real improvements in the neighbourhood physical environment. Well-maintained, plentiful and accessible toilets are essential to provide confidence to get out and about. High quality seating, appropriately located, provides essential resting places and opportunities for social contact (Fig. 5.15). However, a survey of seniors in Victoria, Australia found extensive perceived barriers to walking, including the barrier effect of heavy traffic and short walk cycles at lights (Garrard, 2013). In the United Kingdom, traffic light crossings are set to accommodate a walking speed of 1.2 m per second, but of those over 65 years old, 76 per cent of men and 85 per cent of women, are unable to walk at this speed (Asher, Aresu, Falaschetti, & Mindell, 2012) (see Box 8.1). Due to their frailty, if hit by a car at 30 mph, those over the age of 60 are seven times more likely than average to be killed (Sustainable Development Commission, 2011).

The quality of footpaths is also key for the elderly, because falling is a major cause of personal injury due to trips, slips and stumbles. Garrard (2013, p. 3) noted that 'narrow, uneven, sloping, or slippery footpaths, obstacles such as tables, chairs and advertising signs on footpaths present a greater hazard to older pedestrians. In general, older adults require higher standards of both design and maintenance of pedestrian infrastructure'.

Worldwide, there are an estimated 646,000 fatal falls each year, the second largest group of accidental deaths behind road crashes (although fall injuries probably outnumber traffic injuries) (World Health Organization, 2018a). The risk of falling is greater for women than men and increases with age due to disturbances to gait and balance, and changed reflexes due to visual, sensory, motor and cognitive impairment, and medications. Falls are the leading cause of death from injury among people 65 and older—and moreover, fracturing a hip from a fall can have catastrophic health consequences, with, for example, a quarter of such events in the United States leading to death within six months (Shellpoint, 2012). Many people who fall, even if they are not injured, become afraid of falling. This may cause them to cut down on their everyday activities, thus weakening the body and increasing the chances of falling again: indeed, falling once doubles the chances of falling again (CDC, 2016). However, the most profound impact of the fear of falling is withdrawal from public life and space, and the loss of functioning associated with independent living, with all of the family and societal costs this brings.

The problem for the elderly is that as society is speeding up, they are slowing down. Traffic infrastructure and volumes, together with dispersal of needed facilities and the unreliability of public transport, are all significant barriers to older people maintaining their independence and health—and all of these are exacerbated by the pursuit of more speed in motorised city transport.

Younger people

This is not the only place in this book that the point is made that higher speeds tend to result in longer distances, which in turn lead to sprawl and reduced accessibility to services for those without cars. Youth (12–18 years old) are profoundly disadvantaged by these trends, as they transition from relatively active children to less active adolescents.

O'Brien, Ramanathan, Gilbert, and Orsini (2009) note in their review of the literature on youth and sustainable transport that motorised transport may adversely affect the physical health of youth by:

- decreasing opportunities for physical activity;
- increasing exposure to poor air quality;
- creating stress via noise disturbances;
- posing safety hazards in high traffic and high-speed areas.

Conversely, using active forms of transport may have a positive impact on several aspects of emotional well-being among youth, including self-esteem, independence and psychological and social development. A fascinating picture of young people's travel patterns and attitudes emerged from an online survey of over a thousand 15–20 year olds in Victoria, Australia (Garrard, 2017). It showed that, as far as health is concerned, walking for transport plays a significant role in young people's physical activity and is more likely to increase physical activity by young people than recreational walking programmes. The most popular motivation for recreational walking was to relax and calm down when stressed, angry or anxious.

Overall, 85 per cent of the 15 to 20-year-olds surveyed by Garrard wanted to live in a walk-friendly environment, considerably more than the 57 per cent that wanted to be able to drive everywhere. Not surprisingly, concerns around traffic safety and walking infrastructure were cited as major barriers to walking. Only about half of the young people surveyed agreed that they can depend on drivers to obey the road rules and give way to people on foot when required—and this seems to apply most especially in suburban areas where travel by car is facilitated by slip lanes and other infrastructure that encourages higher speeds by cars, and consequent greater intimidation of those on foot.

In sum, walking, often in tandem with public transport, provides a critical opportunity for young people to lead independent lives. In a faster, more motorised world, suburban environments (where walking, cycling and using public transport are difficult) leave many young people reliant on parents or others to drive them, with all of the deleterious effects for both parties and the environment.

Women

Without doubt, gender inequalities in transport have been poorly recognised historically. It was only in 2009 that the UN first reviewed the issue, noting the transport implications of differences from men in the fields of domestic responsibilities, access to transport, and employment patterns and participation rates (United Nations Economic and Social Council, 2009). We now see the bigger picture more clearly—that the principal transport disadvantage suffered by women in the speeding city relates to the way in which the car has been stealing their space and time. The normal day of many women, especially mothers, involves accessing multiple activities—such as child care, household chores, paid work and elderly care—in complex journey chains, so it is important that destinations are within easy reach. Speed-induced sprawl undermines the viability of public transport and increases the separation of home and workplace, thus undermining essential tasks and compromising choices of job opportunities for women.

Vienna has done more than most cities to recognise these issues and try to rectify them (see also Box 2.1). In 1985 it pioneered gender mainstreaming, a set of rules and laws to ensure that everyone is provided with equal access to the city's infrastructure and resources, irrespective of gender. The city's approach was to counteract male-dominated thinking which had 'designed cities like there would be no other people than men going to work in the morning and coming back in the evening – everything else in between, they kind of had no idea' (Riss, quoted in Hunt (2019)). Eva Kail, the former head of Vienna's first Frauenbüro (women's office) notes that when a survey revealed that roughly two-thirds of car journeys were made by men, whilst two-thirds of those on foot were by women, 'That was really an "a-ha" moment' (Kail, quoted in Hunt (2019)). It demonstrated that men's and women's experiences of city living were different—and women's were being entirely overlooked. Hunt points out that 'When the city is viewed only as through a windscreen, women feel the absence of measures to benefit pedestrians in a way that men typically do not'. The city has since conducted about 60 gender-sensitive pilot projects, which typically involve street lighting improvements, prioritising people on foot at traffic lights, adding more seating, widening footpaths and removing barriers so as to better accommodate prams. Kail summarises the Vienna approach succinctly: 'if you want to do something for women, do something for pedestrians'.

Vienna's approach to gender mainstreaming is in stark contrast to most other cities, where there has been little or no progress. In most, the spatial separation of basic urban functions produces areas of uniform land use, which only have significant numbers of people present for part of the time, intensifying women's feelings of insecurity. In the Garrard (2017) survey of youth attitudes (discussed earlier), concerns around personal safety emerged as the primary barrier to walking for young women in particular and especially at night, when only 15 per cent said they felt safe. The response to this may be to modify routes, destination or travelling companions, or perhaps to use taxis instead of walking. But women can only choose not to walk if they can afford alternatives, which means that for teenage girls in particular, cost can be a barrier to safety. Abandonment of evening walking trips may be an outcome for some, thus restricting independent mobility and participation in public life.

Feeling unsafe in public space is doubtless one reason why, in almost every country in the world, women walk disproportionately fewer steps each day than men. An analysis of the smartphone data of over 700,000 people worldwide over 68 million days of activity showed that the 'gender step gap' between men and women was typically widest in high-obesity countries and much smaller in cities with higher walkability scores (Althoff, Hicks, King, Delp, & Leskovec, 2017). The implication is that activity inequality contributes to the burden of disease related to overweight and obesity, and that women in particular are disproportionately vulnerable.

The country whose people walk the least is Indonesia, where women took 611 fewer steps than men each day. Some journalists described this as 'laziness' (Matthews, 2017), but the reality is very different. Quite apart from the heat, poor access to public transport, and inadequate infrastructure, it is the threat of harassment than can stop women in their tracks. One student in Jakarta, Vivi Restuviani (quoted in Shadwell (2017)) says that she dreads the daily five-minute walk to her class. 'It's just so annoying,' she says of the incessant cat-callers who motivate her to keep that daily walk as short as possible. 'The construction workers, the motorbikes, people in the cars—they all honk. It's always gonna be there, and it's less than 100 metres—but I still have to find the motivation to walk ... it's exhausting'.

In sum, women's activity patterns demand short distances that are easily accessible by walking, but frequently women are choosing not to walk, due to harassment, more severe concerns about personal safety, street design, a lack of sidewalks or distance to destinations. The consequences for personal and public health are severe. 'Slower cities' reduce these negative consequences. As Thornton summarises, 'A walkable city increases physical activity for everyone but in particular, women's activity levels increase in more walkable communities, thus reducing the gender gap in activity and inequality' (Thornton, 2018, p. 1).

Transport deprivation: an overview

This Section 5.4.4 has argued that speed and car dependency increases health inequity, by undermining public transport, exacerbating the danger to active travel users and spreading the city beyond active travel range. The result is that while some people can access a wide range of opportunities and services in the city, others are prevented from doing so and thus are denied the opportunity to maximise their own well-being. As the UK's Sustainable Development Commission puts it: 'The inequality is two-fold. In general the people experiencing the worst access opportunities also suffer the worst effects of other people's travel. They are both "less travelled" and more "travelled-upon"' (Sustainable Development Commission, 2011, p. 8).

5.5 Conclusion

This chapter has outlined the damage to health that results from the use of faster, motorised modes of travel and has detailed the health benefits of the 'slower' modes, including better physical and mental health as well as reduced air pollution and crashes. It has also discussed the broader context within which travel decisions are made, demonstrating the decreased access to health-enhancing opportunities that has resulted for many people as a result of greater speed consumption by others.

Of course, this is not a static situation. Fleets of shared, electric, autonomous vehicles (discussed in more detail in Chapters 8 and 9) are predicted by some to eliminate pollution and crashes, but benefits of these innovations on human health may be much less than anticipated, and there may also be negative impacts. Apart from the risk of death and injury from crashes, as J. Sallis (2018) has highlighted, 'Virtually all of the health impacts of cars are due to increasing risks for very common chronic diseases. Therefore it will not matter if people are sitting in driverless or people-driven cars'. Every motor vehicle, including electric and autonomous ones, has health-damaging impacts: Alves (2017) puts it simply, 'we are all better off with carless drivers instead of driverless cars'.

In 'slow cities' vehicle speeds are lowered, whether by legislation or street design, or both. Former car-dominated space is reclaimed for people-centred uses, either permanently or temporarily and frequently. Cars are less desirable, parking places are scarcer and car sharing becomes normal. Active travel modes become more attractive and safer and are used by the majority of the population for everyday trips, as well as for freight delivery or transporting children. In time, land uses will adapt to the new travel realities, with higher densities and a greater variety and mixing of uses. The number of trips per person may not change fundamentally, but trips will be on average much shorter than at present.

Those currently using active travel modes will do so in future 'slow cities' in an improved physical environment, experiencing fewer crashes, with less noise and air pollution and reduced urban heat island effects, so their existing physical health benefits will be enhanced. So too will their mental health, through reduced stress from less traffic congestion and lower crash risk, and from increased personal safety, as there will be more 'eyes on the street'. As the city slows and travel conditions become more supportive for walkers and people on bikes, they will gain even more health benefits from more frequent and regular use of walking and cycling. Shorter distances will produce easier access to health-enhancing opportunities, such as jobs, healthy food, green space and health care facilities.

There will of course be some whose choice remains to drive, but even they will reap substantial health gains (though less than active travel users). They will make slower and shorter car trips and may make fewer of them too. They will gain physical health benefits from spending less time sitting, in less polluted conditions, and will improve their mental well-being as a result of experiencing less stress from driving in traffic. They will probably make more active travel trips (with the physical and mental health gains this entails) and will gain community benefits of more active use of public space.

In summary, it is apparent from this chapter that the 'slower city' (meaning slower motorised transport and increased use of the 'slower' modes) will bring benefits in physical, mental and community health to existing (and continuing) car-users as well as those currently (and in future) using active travel modes. Moreover, the benefits will be experienced by the old and young, women and men, the able and the less able, the economically advantaged and those less fortunate—in short, everyone.

Though the 'slower city' will bring health gains from changed individual behaviour, health is of course impacted by broader environmental conditions too, such as pollution of air or water, noise, visual blight and the unseen but crucially important rise in greenhouse gas emissions and their contribution to the climate emergency. What the arrival of 'slow cities' will mean for such environmental—rather than physical and mental—health is a topic for the next chapter.

References

Abegaz, T., & Gebremedhin, S. (2019). Magnitude of road traffic accident related injuries and fatalities in Ethiopia. *PLoS One*, *14*(1), e0202240.

Adams, J. (1997). Can technology save us? In R. Tolley (Ed.), *The greening of urban transport, planning for walking and cycling in western cities* (pp. 81–97). Chichester: Wiley.

Agence France-Presse. (2018). Unprecedented Japan heatwave kills 65 people in a week. *The Guardian,* Available from: https://www.theguardian.com/world/2018/jul/24/unprecedented-japan-heatwave-kills-65-people-week.

Allen, M., & Allen, J. (2015). Health inequalities and the role of the physical and social environment. In H. Barton, S. Thompson, S. Burgess, & M. Grant (Eds.), *The Routledge handbook of planning for health and well-being* (pp. 89–107). London: Routledge.

Althoff, T., Hicks, J. L., King, A. C., Delp, S. L., & Leskovec, J. (2017). Large-scale physical activity data reveal worldwide activity inequality. *Nature*, *547*(7663), 336–339.

Alves, M. (2017). Driven by distraction: Sustainable road safety and the impact of autonomous driving on vulnerable users (breakout presentation). *Journal of Transport & Health*, *7*, S65.

Andersen, L. B., Schnohr, P., Schroll, M., & Hein, H. O. (2000). All-cause mortality associated with physical activity during leisure time, work, sports, and cycling to work. *Archives of Internal Medicine*, *160*(11), 1621–1628.

Andrews, L.W. (2015). Bicycling can sharpen your thinking and improve your mood. *Psychology Today.* Available from: https://www.psychologytoday.com/us/blog/minding-the-body/201505/bicycling-can-sharpen-your-thinking-and-improve-your-mood.

Appleyard, D., & Lintell, M. (1972). The environmental quality of city streets: The residents' viewpoint. *Journal of the American Institute of Planners*, *38*(2), 84–101.

Asher, L., Aresu, M., Falaschetti, E., & Mindell, J. (2012). Most older pedestrians are unable to cross the road in time: A cross-sectional study. *Age and Ageing*, *41*(5), 690–694.

Baker, P., C. (2019). Collision course: Why are cars killing more and more pedestrians? *The Guardian.* Available from: https://www.theguardian.com/technology/2019/oct/03/collision-course-pedestrian-deaths-rising-driverless-cars.

BBC. (2018). Air pollution may harm cognitive intelligence, study says. Available from: https://www.bbc.com/news/health-45326598.

Bickerstaff, K., & Shaw, S. (2000). An evaluation of the walking bus at Pirehill First School: A report commissioned by The Staffordshire Walking Bus Partnership. The Centre for Alternative and Sustainable Transport, Staffordshire University.

Brown, V., Moodie, M., & Carter, R. (2017). Evidence for associations between traffic calming and safety and active transport or obesity: A scoping review. *Journal of Transport & Health*, *7*(A), 23–27.

Burtt, D. (2014). *Road safety audit tool for pedestrians who are vision impaired.* Melbourne: Victoria Walks. Available from: http://www.victoriawalks.org.au/Assets/Files/Vision_Impaired_Road_Safety_Audit_Tool.pdf.

Busby, M. (2019). Patience exhausted: UK drivers who sit with engines idling could face instant fines. *The Guardian.* Available from: https://www.theguardian.com/environment/2019/may/14/patience-exhausted-drivers-who-sit-with-engines-idling-could-face-instant-fines.

C3 Collaborating for Health. (2012). *The benefits of regular walking for health, well-being and the environment.* Available from: https://www.c3health.org/wp-content/uploads/2017/07/C3-report-on-walking-v-1-20120911.pdf.

Caiazzo, F., Ashok, A., Waitz, I. A., Yim, S. H., & Barrett, S. R. (2013). Air pollution and early deaths in the United States. Part I: Quantifying the impact of major sectors in 2005. *Atmospheric Environment*, *79*, 198–208.

Capon, A., & Corvalan, C. (2018). Climate change and health: Global issue, local responses. *Public Health Research and Practice*, *28*(4), e2841823.

Carrington, D. (2017). Air pollution more harmful to children in cars than outside, warns top scientist. *The Guardian.* Available from https://www.theguardian.com/environment/2017/jun/12/children-risk-air-pollution-cars-former-uk-chief-scientist-warns.

Cavill, N. (2003). The potential for non-motorised transport for promoting health. In R. Tolley (Ed.), *Sustainable transport: Planning for walking and cycling in urban environments* (pp. 144–158). Cambridge: Woodhead Publishing.

CDC. (2016). Important facts about falls. Available from: https://www.cdc.gov/homeandrecreationalsafety/falls/adultfalls.html.

CDC. (2018). The benefits of physical activity. *Physical Activity and Health.* Available from: https://www.cdc.gov/physicalactivity/basics/pa-health/index.htm.

Cerin, E., Nathan, A., Van Cauwenberg, J., Barnett, D. W., & Barnett, A. (2017). The neighbourhood physical environment and active travel in older adults: A systematic review and meta-analysis. *International Journal of Behavioral Nutrition and Physical Activity, 14*(1), 15.

Cervero, R., Sarmiento, O. L., Jacoby, E., Gomez, L. F., & Neiman, A. (2009). Influences of built environments on walking and cycling: Lessons from Bogotá. *International Journal of Sustainable Transportation, 3*(4), 203–226.

Chau, J. (2007). *Physical activity and building stronger communities.* Available from: https://www.activelivingnsw.com.au/assets/Uploads/PA-and-Building-Stronger-Communities-Report.pdf.

Christie, N., Ward, H., Kimberlee, R., Lyons, R., Towner, E., et al. (2010). *Road traffic injury risk in disadvantaged communities: Evaluation of the neighbourhood road safety initiative.* London: Department for Transport.

Cyclescheme. (2017). Cycling and the mental health benefits. Available from: https://www.cyclescheme.co.uk/community/featured/cycling-and-the-mental-health-benefits.

de Moor, D. (2013). *Walking works: Making the case to encourage greater uptake of walking as a physical activity and recognise the value and benefits of Walking for Health.* Available from: https://www.walkingforhealth.org.uk/sites/default/files/Walking%20works_LONG_AW_Web.pdf.

Ding, D., Lawson, K. D., Kolbe-Alexander, T. L., Finkelstein, E. A., Katzmarzyk, P. T., Van Mechelen, W., & Pratt, M. (2016). The economic burden of physical inactivity: A global analysis of major noncommunicable diseases. *The Lancet,* 388(10051), 1311-1324.

Dodson, J., & Sipe, N. (2006). *Suburban shocks: Assessing locational vulnerability to rising household fuel and mortgage interest costs.* Paper presented at the 29th Australasian Transport Research Forum.

Dodson, J., & Sipe, N. (2008). *Unsettling suburbia: The new landscape of oil and mortgage vulnerability in Australian cities. Urban Research Program Research Paper No. 17.* Brisbane: Urban Research Program, Griffith University.

Edwards, H., & Whitehouse, A. (2018). *The Toxic School Run, Unicef UK research briefing.* Available from: https://downloads.unicef.org.uk/wp-content/uploads/2018/09/UUK-research-briefing-The-toxic-school-run-September-2018.pdf?_ga=2.234006365.298981577.1537257494-289689197.1536231694.

Ekelund, U., Steene-Johannessen, J., Brown, W. J., Fagerland, M. W., Owen, N., Powell, K. E., et al. (2016). Does physical activity attenuate, or even eliminate, the detrimental association of sitting time with mortality? A harmonised meta-analysis of data from more than 1 million men and women. *The Lancet, 388*(10051), 1302–1310.

Ekelund, U., Ward, H. A., Norat, T., Luan, J. A., May, A. M., Weiderpass, E., et al. (2015). Physical activity and all-cause mortality across levels of overall and abdominal adiposity in European men and women: The European Prospective Investigation into Cancer and Nutrition Study (EPIC). *The American Journal of Clinical Nutrition, 101*(3), 613–621.

Erickson, K. I., Weinstein, A. M., & Lopez, O. L. (2012). Physical activity, brain plasticity, and Alzheimer's disease. *Archives of Medical Research, 43*(8), 615–621.

Frank, L., Andresen, M. A., & Schmid, T. L. (2004). Obesity relationships with community design, physical activity, and time spent in cars. *American Journal of Preventative Medicine, 27*(2), 87–96.

Garrard, J. (2013). *Senior Victorians and walking: Obstacles and opportunities: Summary Report.* Available from: http://www.victoriawalks.org.au/Assets/Files/FINALSeniorsSummary.pdf.

Garrard, J. (2017). *Young people and walking in Victoria: Full report.* Available from: http://www.victoriawalks.org.au/Assets/Files/Young-people-and-walking-Full-report.pdf.

Gehl, J. (2010). *Cities for People.* Washington: Island Press.

Giles-Corti, B., Vernez-Moudon, A., Reis, R., Turrell, G., Dannenberg, A. L., Badland, H., et al. (2016). City planning and population health: A global challenge. *The Lancet, 388*(10062), 2912–2924.

Gilliland, J., Maltby, M., Xu, X., Luginaah, I., Loebach, J., & Shah, T. (2019). Is active travel a breath of fresh air? Examining children's exposure to air pollution during the school commute. *Spatial and Spatio-temporal Epidemiology, 29*, 51–57.

Goodyear, S. (2013). The link between kids who walk or bike to school and concentration. *City Lab.* Available from: https://www.citylab.com/transportation/2013/02/kids-who-walk-or-bike-school-concentrate-better-study-shows/4585/.

Haines, A., Kovats, R. S., Campbell-Lendrum, D., & Corvalan, C. (2006). Climate change and human health: impacts, vulnerability and public health. *Public health, 120*(7), 585–596.

Hamilton-Baillie, B., & Jones, P. (2005). Improving traffic behaviour and safety through urban design. *Proceedings of the Institution of Civil Engineers - Civil Engineering, 158*(14014), 39–47.

Hart, J. (2008). *Driven to excess: impacts of motor vehicle traffic on residential quality of life in Bristol, UK.* MSc in Transport Planing. University of West England, Bristol.

Heart Foundation. (2016). *Walking: Summary evaluation.* Available from: http://walking.heartfoundation.org.au/uploads/pdf-files/HFW-2016-Evaluation-Report.pdf.

Hillman, M. (1993). Cycling and the promotion of health. *Policy Studies, 14*(2), 49–58.

Hillman, M., & Morgan, D. R. (1992). *Cycling: Towards health and safety.* Oxford: Oxford University Press.

Hillman, M., & Whalley, A. (1979). *Walking is transport.* London: Policy Studies Institute.

Hillsdon, M., & Thorogood, M. (1996). A systematic review of physical activity promotion strategies. *British Journal of Sports Medicine, 30*(2), 84–89.

Holt-Lunstad, J., Smith, T., & Layton, J. B. (2010). Social relationships and mortality risk: A meta-analytic review. *PLoS medicine, 7*(7), e1000316.

Holt-Lunstad, J., Smith, T. B., Baker, M., Harris, T., & Stephenson, D. (2015). Loneliness and social isolation as risk factors for mortality: A meta-analytic review. *Perspectives on Psychological Science, 10*(2), 227–237.

Hunt, E. (2019). City with a female face: How modern Vienna was shaped by women. *The Guardian.* Available from: https://www.theguardian.com/cities/2019/may/14/city-with-a-female-face-how-modern-vienna-was-shaped-by-women.

International Center for Technology Assessment. (2000). In-car air pollution. Available from: http://pureti.com/content/documents/ICTA-In-Car-Air-Pollution-Report.pdf.

Jacobsen, P. (2003). Safety in numbers: More walkers and bicyclists, safer walking and bicycling. *British Medical Journal, 9*(3), 205.

Kelly, J. F., Breadon, P., Davis, C., Hunter, A., Mares, P., Mullerworth, D., et al. (2012). *Social cities.* Melbourne: Grattan Institute.

King, D. (2017). Smoking in cars is banned. But children still inhale toxic fumes in backseats. *The Guardian.* Available from: https://www.theguardian.com/science/2017/jun/12/smoking-in-cars-banned-but-children-still-inhale-toxic-fumes-in-backseats.

Kylstra, C. (2015). 10 things your commute does to your body. *Time Health.* Available from: http://time.com/9912/10-things-your-commute-does-to-your-body/.

Long, J. C. (1924). The Motor's part in public health. *The Annals of the American Academy of Political and Social Science, 116*(1), 18–21.

Martin, A., Goryakin, Y., & Suhrcke, M. (2014). Does active commuting improve psychological wellbeing? Longitudinal evidence from eighteen waves of the British Household Panel Survey. *Preventive Medicine*, *69*, 296–303.

Matthews, S. (2017). Do YOU live in the world's laziest country? *Daily Mail*, Australia. Available from: https://www.dailymail.co.uk/health/article-4688148/Do-live-world-s-laziest-country.html.

MIND. (2007). *Ecotherapy: The green agenda for mental health*. Available from: https://www.mind.org.uk/media/211255/Ecotherapy_The_green_agenda_for_mental_health.pdf.

Montgomery, C. (2013). *Happy city: transforming our lives through urban design*. New York: Penguin Random House.

Morley, H. (2011). *Active body active brain: improving access to Heart Foundation walking for people with dementia*. Available from: National Heart Foundation of Australia, Adelaide: https://www.dementia.org.au/sites/default/files/1630-Morley.pdf.

Morris, J. N., & Hardman, A. E. (1997). Walking to health. *Sports Medicine*, *23*(5), 306–332.

Morris, J. N., Heady, J., Raffle, P., Roberts, C., & Parks, J. (1953). Coronary heart-disease and physical activity of work. *The Lancet*, *262*(6796), 1111–1120.

Norrie, J. (2012). Loneliness on the rise as our cities atomise. *The Conversation*. Available from: https://theconversation.com/loneliness-on-the-rise-as-our-cities-atomise-6068.

O'Brien, C., Ramanathan, S., Gilbert, R., & Orsini, A. (2009). *Youth and sustainable transportation: A review of the literature*. Winnipeg: The Centre for Sustainable Transportation at the University of Winnipeg.

Office for National Statistics. (2014). *Commuting and personal well-being*. Available from: http://webarchive.nationalarchives.gov.uk/20160107224314/http://www.ons.gov.uk/ons/dcp171766_351954.pdf.

Oppezzo, M., & Schwartz, D. L. (2014). Give your ideas some legs: The positive effect of walking on creative thinking. *Journal of Experimental Psychology: Learning, Memory and Cognition*, *40*(4), 1142–1152.

Pucher, J., & Buehler, R. (2008). Making cycling irresistible: Lessons from the Netherlands, Denmark and Germany. *Transport Reviews*, *28*(4), 495–528.

Pucher, J., & Buehler, R. (2010). Walking and cycling for healthy cities. *Built Environment*, *36*(4), 391–414.

Pucher, J., & Dijkstra, L. (2003). Promoting safe walking and cycling to improve public health: Lessons from the Netherlands and Germany. *American Journal of Public Health*, *93*(9), 1509–1516.

Putnam, R. D. (2001). *Bowling alone: The collapse and revival of American community*. New York: Simon and Schuster.

Rachele, J., Healy, A., Sallis, J.F., & Sugiyama, T. (2017). Designing suburbs to cut car use closes gaps in health and wealth. *The Conversation*. Available from: https://theconversation.com/designing-suburbs-to-cut-car-use-closes-gaps-in-health-and-wealth-83961.

Rissotto, A., & Tonucci, F. (2002). Freedom of movement and environmental knowledge in elementary school children. *Journal of Environmental Psychology*, *22*(1–2), 65–77.

Robert Wood Johnson Foundation. (2017). What is health equity? And what difference does a definition make? Available from: https://buildhealthyplaces.org/content/uploads/2017/05/health_equity_brief_041217.pdf.

Robine, J. M., Cheung, S. L. K., Le Roy, S., Van Oyen, H., Griffiths, C., Michel, J. P., et al. (2008). Death toll exceeded 70,000 in Europe during the summer of 2003. *Comptes Rendus Biologies*, *331*(2), 171–178.

Rooney, M. (2008). 'Oh, you're just up the street!': The role of walking school bus in generating local community for children and adults. *World Transport Policy and Practice*, *14*(1), 39–47.

Rosén, E., & Sander, U. (2009). Pedestrian fatality risk as a function of car impact speed. *Accident Analysis & Prevention, 41*(3), 536–542.

Rosenblatt-Naderi, J. (2014). Transcript of an interview with Jody Rosenblatt-Naderi. *Recorded over the Internet for Talking Walking, by Andrew Stuck.* Available from: http://www.talkingwalking.net/wp-content/uploads/2014/03/Transcript_JRN-interview.pdf.

Rossiter, B. (2016). *Designing streets for the walking dependent.* Paper presented at the Walk 21 Conference on walking and liveable cities, Hong Kong, October, 3–7.

Sallis, J. (2018). Driverless cars could be better or worse for our health – it's up to us. *The Conversation.* Available from: https://theconversation.com/driverless-cars-could-be-better-or-worse-for-our-health-its-up-to-us-87242.

Sallis, R. (2013). *Exercise is medicine.* Paper presented at the Everybody Walk! National Walking Summit, Washington DC, October, 2.

Sauter, D., & Huettenmoser, M. (2008). Liveable streets and social inclusion. *Urban Design International, 13*(2), 67–79.

Shadwell, T. (2017). 'Paying to stay safe': Why women don't walk as much as men. *The Guardian.* Available from: https://www.theguardian.com/inequality/2017/oct/11/paying-to-stay-safe-why-women-dont-walk-as-much-as-men.

Shellpoint. (2012). Ten shocking statistics about elderly falls. *Senior Health & Wellness Blog.* Available from: https://www.shellpoint.org/blog/2012/08/13/10-shocking-statistics-about-elderly-falls/.

Shu, H. F., Yang, T., Yu, S. X., Huang, H. D., Jiang, L. L., Gu, J. W., et al. (2014). Aerobic exercise for Parkinson's disease: A systematic review and meta-analysis of randomized controlled trials. *PLoS One, 9*(7), e100503.

Smart Growth America. (2017). Dangerous by design. Available from: https://smartgrowthamerica.org/dangerous-by-design/.

Stutzer, A., & Frey, B. S. (2008). Stress that doesn't pay: The commuting paradox. *Scandinavian Journal of Economics, 110*(2), 339–366.

Sussman, A., & Goode, R. (1967). *The magic of walking.* New York: Simon & Schuster.

Sustainable Development Commission. (2011). *Fairness in a car-dependent society.* Available from: https://research-repository.st-andrews.ac.uk/bitstream/handle/10023/2290/sdc-2011-car-fairness.pdf?sequence=1&isAllowed=y.

Svenson, O., Eriksson, G., & Gonzalez, N. (2012). Braking from different speeds: Judgments of collision speed if a car does not stop in time. *Accident Analysis & Prevention, 45*, 487–492.

Thornton, B. (2018). Women and walking. *Walk 21 Conference.* Available from: https://www.walk21.com/single-post/2018/05/22/Women-and-Walking.

Tigbe, W. W., Granat, M. H., Sattar, N., & Lean, M. E. (2017). Time spent in sedentary posture is associated with waist circumference and cardiovascular risk. *International Journal of Obesity, 41*(5), 689–696.

Tranter, P. (2016). Children's play in their local neighborhoods: Rediscovering the value of residential streets, living reference work entry. In B. Evans, J. Horton, & T. Skelton (Eds.), *Play, recreation, health and well being, geographies of children and young people* (pp. 211–236). (Vol. 9). Singapore: Springer.

U.S. Department of Health and Human Services. (2015). *Step It Up! The surgeon general's call to action to promote walking and walkable communities.* Washington: Office of the Surgeon General.

United Nations Economic and Social Council. (2009). Review of gender issues in transport. Available from: https://www.unece.org/fileadmin/DAM/trans/doc/2009/itc/ECE-TRANS-2009-08e.pdf.

US Census Bureau. (2011). Latest U.S. disability statistics and facts. Available from: https://www.disabled-world.com/disability/statistics/census-figures.php.

Viry, G., Kaufmann, V., & Widmer, E. D. (2009). Social integration faced with commuting: more widespread and less dense support networks. In T. Ohnmacht, H. Maksim, & M. M. Bergman (Eds.), *Mobilities and inequality* (pp. 121–144). Farnham: Ashgate.

Waygood, E., & Friman, M. (2015). Children's travel and incidental community connections. *Travel Behaviour and Society, 2*, 174–181.

Waygood, E., Sun, Y., & Letarte, L. (2015). Active travel by built environment and lifecycle stage: Case study of Osaka metropolitan area. *International Journal of Environmental Research and Public Health, 12*(12), 15900–15924.

Whyte, W. H. (1980). *The social life of small urban spaces*. Washington D.C.: The Conservation Foundation.

World Health Organization (2001). *International classification of functioning, disability and health: ICF*. Geneva: World Health Organization.

World Health Organization. (2018a). Falls: key facts. Available from: http://www.who.int/en/news-room/fact-sheets/detail/falls.

World Health Organization. (2018b). *Global status report on road safety 2018*. Available from: https://apps.who.int/iris/bitstream/handle/10665/276462/9789241565684-eng.pdf?ua=1.

World Health Organization. (2019). World health organization constitution. Available from: https://www.who.int/about/who-we-are/constitution.

Yates, E. (2019). 'People aren't disabled, their city is': Inside Europe's most accessible city. *The Guardian*. Available from: https://www.theguardian.com/cities/2019/may/28/people-arent-disabled-their-city-is-inside-europes-most-accessible-city.

Chapter 6

Advancing environmental health in future 'slow cities'

'... speed may in itself be as much the enemy of a sustainable future as the reckless consumption that powers our global economy'.

Porritt, 2005, p. 44

Abstract

This chapter outlines the complex environmental impacts of speed. These impacts occur at scales from local (e.g. air and noise pollution in residential streets) to global (where increased levels of greenhouse gases represent a threat to planetary health). We explain the complex ways in which increased speed can exacerbate many negative environmental impacts. For example, high-speed car transport fuels suburban sprawl, which in turn increases total urban travel and food miles, total energy used in transport (mainly fossil fuel), area of hard surfaces, heat island effects and urban air pollution, consumption of household goods, and loss of farmland, forest area and ecological diversity. Claims that increased efficiency of vehicles or traffic flow will reduce negative environmental impacts are critiqued. We argue that given the urgency created by global climate breakdown, slowing city transport is not only something that we should do, but something we must do. Whilst on its own, slowing city transport will not solve the climate crisis, it may be no exaggeration to say that if the city itself is to survive, all future cities must be 'slow cities'.

6.1 Introduction

To understand the environmental health impacts of 'slow cities', we must first examine the complex impacts of speed on environmental health. The German environmental researcher Wolfgang Sachs argues that 'speed is an under-recognized factor fuelling environmental problems' (Andrews & Urbanska, 2009, p. 185). If speed fuels environmental problems, is it possible that slowing city transport is an effective strategy in addressing environmental problems? The potential of this strategy, involving both reducing the speed of motorised transport and encouraging more use of the 'slower' modes, is outlined in this chapter.

The speed of city transport (as well as transport in other contexts) is a critical factor in the destruction of the environment. Higher speeds increase energy use, resource use and pollution (of all kinds). As Sachs (1996) observes: 'the speed regime of modern society drives up the rate by which nature is being used

Slow Cities. http://dx.doi.org/10.1016/B978-0-12-815316-1.00006-X

as a mine and as a dumping ground'. High-speed city transport necessitates the production and use of vehicles, roads, parking areas, electricity and electronic equipment, a robust legal system, police and emergency services, and even satellites and relay stations. All of this production requires a reliable and vast supply of energy and raw materials, including not only fossil fuels, but also steel, copper, zinc, magnesium, silicon, bauxite, cobalt, manganese, nickel, rubber, and many others.

As the speed of transport increases, so too does the speed at which nature is used as a waste sink. Air pollution, water pollution, noise pollution and waste all increase when efforts are made to increase transport speeds. The impact of speed on environmental health can be felt at different spatial scales. The impact can be local, for example in increased air pollution in residential streets with high traffic levels. It can be city wide, as can be seen in urban heat island impacts, and it can be global. The most serious form of pollution in terms of planetary health is greenhouse gas emissions, and transport is a major contributor. Globally, transport is one of the fastest growing sources of these emissions. In 2016 transport as a whole was responsible for one quarter of total CO_2 emissions, around 8 GtCO2, 71 per cent larger than in 1990 (International Energy Agency, 2018). Any efforts to reduce CO_2 emissions must involve the decarbonisation of the transport sector. Slowing city transport, particularly through the promotion of the 'slow' modes of walking, cycling and public transport, can contribute significantly to this goal (Buehler & Pucher, 2011).

In this chapter we begin by explaining the importance of examining the environmental impacts of speed—at a variety of scales of analysis—from a holistic perspective. We then move on to the implications of speed for the growing use of fossil fuels and the output of pollution. We show that speed has impacts on many kinds of pollution, including air, water, and noise, and on waste disposal, greenhouse gas emissions and even 'space pollution' (the increased need for space as speeds increase). The claim that higher-speed car travel (free flowing traffic) reduces fuel consumption is also critiqued.

6.2 Holistic assessments of speed's impact on environmental health

The ways in which speed affects environmental health are summarised in Fig. 6.1. The environmental impacts of speed are the result of a series of knock-on effects, as well as feedback impacts. Whilst this diagram does not illustrate the full range of effects and feedbacks, it provides an indication of the type of thinking and analysis required to understand how high-speed transport affects environmental health. For example, the negative impacts of speed are exacerbated when high-speed transport environments make streets too dangerous and distances too far for children to travel independently to school, friends or sport, and public transport less competitive. These factors lead to longer distances travelled by car, which lead to further pressure to increase or maintain higher

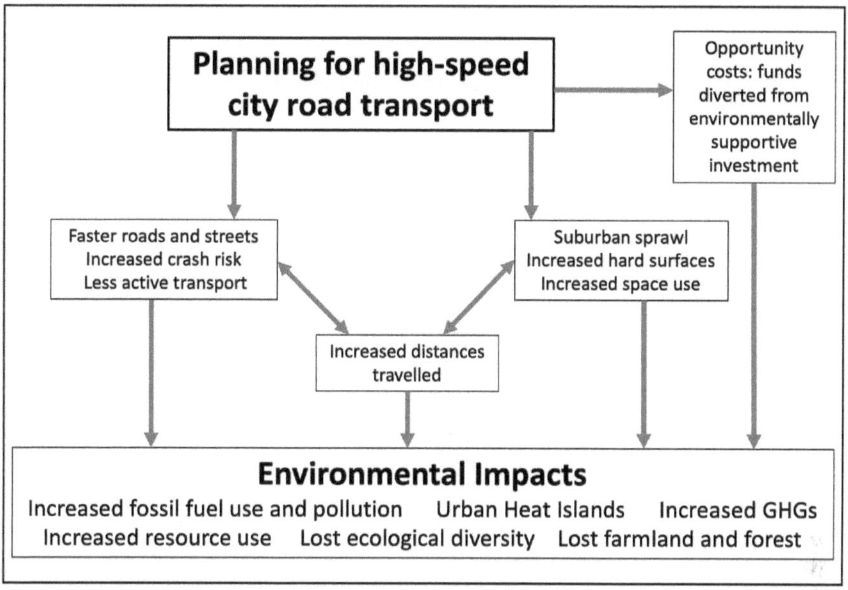

FIGURE 6.1 Impacts of high-speed city road transport on environmental health.

speeds of urban travel. This increases pressure to build more high-speed roads, and roadways and paved parking contribute to drainage impacts and the dissecting of local ecosystems.

High-speed roads promote urban sprawl, which increases travel by cars, leading to greater use of fuel and increased greenhouse gas concentrations, in addition to the loss of green space and prime agricultural land, and loss of natural habitats and wildlife. In addition, urban sprawl is associated with increased consumption generally (e.g. household goods and garden maintenance), which also increases energy use and greenhouse gas production. There are also opportunity costs associated with speed. Investment in speed means that there is less funding available for adaptation to global heating, local food production, tree planting, energy efficient housing, green energy investment and any other environmentally supportive programme. Whilst the impacts of speed on human health have been examined in Chapter 5 and the impacts on economic health are the focus of Chapter 7, this chapter focusses on environmental sustainability and revolves around the relationships depicted in Fig. 6.1.

6.3 Energy consumption

Transport requires the input of energy, and today most of this energy is provided by petroleum. In the United States in 2018, petroleum products accounted for about 92 per cent of the total US transportation sector energy use (US Energy Information Administration, 2019). Active travel modes are extraordinarily efficient users of energy. Though a human being on foot is 'thermodynamically more efficient than any motorised vehicle' (Illich, 1974, p. 59), riding a bicycle raises efficiency to unprecedented levels. The human powered bicycle uses five times less energy to go three to four times faster. As (Tolley, 1990, p. 13) has argued, 'Equipped with a bicycle, man is more efficient than all machines and all animals too'. However, going faster than a bicycle requires motorised movement that needs external, non-human energy inputs—and from that point on, every increment in speed requires more energy. For example, an individual seeking faster travel in the city might abandon the slower, collective transport bus and undertake more single-occupancy vehicle trips, since these appear to minimise delay. In doing so, a less fuel efficient vehicle replaces a more efficient one: passenger-miles per gallon are reported to average 20 for a car, compared to 115 for a city bus, 244 for a commuter train, and 653 for a bicycle (Litman, 2016, Section 5.12, 9). As we ascend the speed ladder, we consume more energy, primarily petroleum, with every step.

This becomes an environmental issue if the energy source is not renewable, so that we are depriving future generations of resources, and if its use causes other environmental damage. Both are clearly the case with the use of petroleum, including (as Litman, 2016 has argued) habitat disruption and landscape impacts from exploration and drilling activity, as well as air, noise and water pollution and spills. Depletion of relatively accessible oil fields will encourage development of higher-risk deep ocean wells and alternative sources such as tar sands and oil shales, the mining of which damages landscapes, expends large amounts of fresh water, threatens species viability and produces more greenhouse gases per unit of fuel (Litman, 2016, Section 5.12, 5).

The direct energy consumption in vehicle operation is augmented by 'embodied' or 'indirect' energy consumption in vehicle production (making steel, rubber and glass and other components), in vehicle disposal and in providing infrastructure, such as building roads and sourcing bitumen, stone and concrete. 'So important are these "indirect" forms of energy consumption that they make up a further 50% of road transport energy use over and above that for direct vehicle operation' (Vokolkova, 2008, p. 260).

Both asphalt and concrete, indispensable materials for roads, parking lots and bridges, have immense environmental impacts (Ma, Sha, Lin, Huang, & Wang, 2016). Concrete is an extremely destructive material. Its manufacture is highly emissions- and energy-intensive, largely due to the energy demands from the extreme heat required to produce cement (as high as 1,450°C). Producing one ton of cement generates nearly one ton of CO_2. 'If the cement industry were a country, it would be the third largest carbon dioxide emitter in the world with up to 2.8bn tonnes, surpassed only by China and the US' (Watts, 2019b). Recycling of these materials is limited. Concrete also adds to heat-island effects. Given that some cities have paved surfaces covering more than 30 per cent of their land cover (Ferguson et al., 2008), switching to lower speed transport systems could significantly reduce environmental impacts by reducing the need for these paved surfaces (Fig. 6.2). Reducing motorised transport could provide

FIGURE 6.2 Unnecessarily wide suburban streets have many deleterious environmental impacts, not least on global heating and the consumption of excessive amounts of asphalt and concrete (Red Deer, Alberta, Canada). *(Credit: Rodney Tolley)*

opportunities to convert much of this paved surface to urban agriculture or parkland with trees. Switching to electric cars will not reduce these impacts from embodied energy, and may exacerbate other environmental problems, including the destructive effects of mining lithium in large volumes.

It could be argued that these effects may be mitigated by the continuing improvement in the fuel efficiency of individual cars (e.g. an almost doubling of real world fuel economy from 1975 to 2017 for new light duty vehicles in the United States (USEPA, 2019)). However, this has been counteracted by the much greater growth in the global vehicle population. The total number of cars and trucks has risen sharply from 342 million in 1976 to 1.32 billion in 2016 (Petit, 2017), which raises the number of km driven and also means that the average occupancy per car falls, leading to a rise in fuel used per passenger-km. Of importance too is the trend towards buying larger, heavier SUV-type cars, which have greater fuel consumption and counteract the overall growth in fleet efficiency. Increases in vehicle numbers and vehicle use not only escalate fuel demands, but they also require more extensive infrastructure and thus further energy inputs to the system.

Higher average speeds of urban traffic (up to about 60 km/h) have been claimed to provide benefits for automotive fuel efficiency and lower emissions. For example, it is widely accepted by motoring organisations that higher average traffic speeds enabled on uncongested roads can make cars more efficient (Kenworthy, Newman, & Lyons, 1989). Researchers from the General Motors Research Laboratories in Michigan argued: 'we expect that improvements in traffic can reduce travel time which, in turn, can directly produce a reduction in fuel consumption' (Chang & Herman, 1978, p. 75).

The traffic engineering logic used by national governments and planning authorities led to the goal of 'free-flowing traffic systems for reasons of energy conservation and emissions abatement': free flowing traffic leads to higher average speeds, which in turn leads to lower fuel consumption and emissions in individual vehicles, which ultimately produces lower overall fuel consumption and emissions for an urban area (Kenworthy et al., 1989, p. 68). This logic is used as a justification for urban policy on roads and congestion. At first glance the logic seems sound. Indeed, in an analysis of fuel efficiency and emissions from automobiles in Perth (Western Australia), Kenworthy et al. (1989) report that the average speed of driving by motorists living at greater distances from the CBD increases markedly with increasing distance. Associated with this increase in speed, fuel efficiency per kilometre for individual vehicles improves, and emissions per kilometre (e.g. carbon monoxide (CO) and hydrocarbons (HC)) are lower, for individual vehicles. It would appear that higher speeds lead to lower pollution levels and lower fuel consumption for individual vehicles—and indeed such benefits of speed are identified in urban transport modelling.

Whilst the arguments presented above may seem convincing, they are based on what Kenworthy et al. refer to as 'linear assumptions' in transport. When the feedback impacts of increased speeds are considered, the impact of speed on total fuel use and pollution levels is the reverse of what the traffic engineering logic suggests. Kenworthy et al. demonstrate, using Perth data, that whilst fuel economy and pollution levels for individual cars per kilometre may be lower in areas with higher average vehicle speeds, the distances travelled in these areas are much higher, and the proportion of trips made by the 'slower' modes (walking, cycling and public transport) is much lower. These factors more than cancel out any advantages in fuel economy and pollution (Fig. 6.3). Residents of inner Perth areas, with low speeds, generate around 20 per cent less CO and HC, due to their lower use of cars and higher use of other modes. Residents in the outer areas, with higher-speed travel, generate over 20 per cent more emissions due to longer car travel distances and less use of walking, cycling and public transport. As Kenworthy et al. (1989, p. 72) conclude, 'higher average traffic speed appears to spread the city, creating lower density land use, a greater need for cars, longer travel distances and reduced use of other less polluting or pollution-free modes. The benefits gained in terms of less polluting traffic streams appear to be overwhelmed by the sheer amount of extra travel and the resulting bulk of emissions'.

Thus it appears that incorporating fuel and pollution savings into transport models that justify higher speeds has been based on faulty assumptions. However, this begs the question of what optimum speeds should be advocated in a book

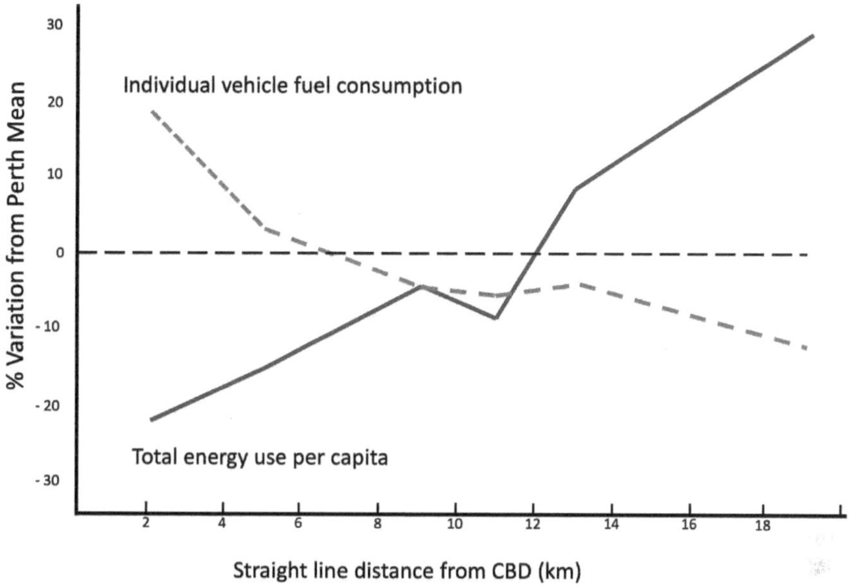

FIGURE 6.3 The trade-off between individual vehicle fuel efficiency and urban system fuel efficiency in Perth, Western Australia. *(Redrawn with permission from the author (Kenworthy, 1986, p. 431))*

about reducing speeds of movement. The laws of physics dictate that increases in speed can lead to much greater increases in the energy required to overcome friction and air resistance, so that a car travelling at 160 km/h consumes about four times (not double) the fuel of a car travelling at 80 km/h.

On the other hand, there are optimum speeds for an engine's best fuel consumption (at least for current internal combustion engine vehicles). Are these higher than the average speeds likely to be achieved in a walkable city, with its higher densities, small blocks and short distances? Once again feedback loops need to be considered. Any attempt to speed up vehicles in order to achieve optimal fuel consumption will result in walking, cycling and public transport trips being replaced by car movements, and thus an increase in consumption by the system as a whole. To promote an environmentally sustainable city transport system, motorised traffic speeds need to be lowered to encourage a mode shift to the 'slow' modes, as has been achieved for example in Germany's model sustainable city, Freiburg. In Freiburg, 90 per cent of residents live in traffic calmed areas with 30 km/h speeds (or lower), and emissions from transport have fallen since the early 1990s, even with strong economic and population growth (Buehler & Pucher, 2011).

Moreover, although this is an interesting discussion, it is actually completely irrelevant to the city's needs now and in the future. To discuss 'optimal' fossil fuel consumption in the people-centred streets of future 'slow cities' is oxymoronic. As the following sections demonstrate, the global crises of urban air pollution and climate breakdown demand that there can be no other goal than reducing use of fossil fuels in city transport to zero. It is no longer an issue of optimum efficiency for internal combustion engines: it is instead a case of optimal quality of life for people.

6.4 Pollution

6.4.1 Introduction

As we have just seen, higher-speed transport has a direct impact on the total amount of fuel consumed (which will increase pollution outputs), and higher speeds also lead to increased distance travelled and increased urban sprawl, which also contribute to increased pollution. 'The best way to reduce health and climate problems caused by transport pollution emissions is by reducing (particularly private vehicle-) kilometres of travel altogether, not necessarily by making traffic flow faster' (Agarwal, Zimmerman, & Kumar, 2018, p. 70). This section examines the air, noise, water and waste pollution that results from a focus on increasing speed, and also examines the implications for environmental damage and human health.

6.4.2 Air pollution

Data from the World Health Organization (2016) indicate that outdoor air pollution is the largest single killer in the world, with over four million deaths annually (more than three times the 1.25 million killed in road crashes). Globally, nine out of ten people breathe polluted air (World Health Organization, 2015). The impacts are becoming more severe: outdoor air pollution has grown eight per cent globally in the five years to 2016 according to data from more than 3,000 cities compiled by the World Health Organization (Vidal, 2016). About half of this total is attributable to road traffic and is being fuelled by rapid deterioration of air quality in cities throughout the Global South, 'where the growth in traffic has outpaced the adoption of tighter emission limits' (OECD, 2014) (Fig. 6.4). Indeed, in November 2019 Delhi was likened to 'a gas chamber' (BBC News, 2019) when background air pollution from traffic and construction was exacerbated by a spike in pollutants from stubble burning in surrounding rural areas and fireworks set off during the Diwali celebrations. The political response to the crisis was to issue five million masks to school students and attempt to halve the number of private vehicles on the city's roads by instituting a ban on odd and even number plates on alternate days.

The air pollutants with the largest impacts on environmental and human health include nitrogen oxides (NO_x), volatile organic compounds (VOCs), and fine particulates. NO_x is the major contributor to acid rain and when combined with VOCs produces low-level tropospheric ozone, an urban air pollutant contributing to respiratory ailments, eye irritation, and climate breakdown. Fine particulates are inhalable particles from tailpipes, brake linings and road

FIGURE 6.4 Pollution from car exhausts in a traffic jam at the entrance to markets in Lafia, Nasarawa State, Nigeria. *(Credit: Andrea Cook)*

surface abrasion that cause respiratory and cardiovascular morbidity (such as aggravation of asthma and respiratory symptoms) and mortality from cardiovascular and respiratory diseases and from lung cancer (World Health Organization, 2013). It is important to note that particles from non-exhaust sources (tyre, road surface and brake wear) are critically important in air pollution, in addition to pollution from exhaust sources (Grigoratos & Martini, 2014). In the United Kingdom 'particles from brake wear, tyre wear and road surface wear currently constitute 60 per cent and 73 per cent (by mass), respectively, of primary PM2.5 and PM10 emissions from road transport, and will become more dominant in the future' (Monks, 2019). This has important implications for the idea that electric cars will solve pollution problems, suggesting that for PM2.5 and PM10 emissions, they will only influence part of the problem.

The severity of pollution impacts continues to be revised upward. As the OECD (2014, p. 11) explains, recent figures on premature deaths caused by outdoor air pollution 'based on new technologies for measuring pollution and improved analysis of health data, are far higher than those from previous studies of premature death and illness from air pollution'. Barrett, quoted in (Chu, 2013) notes that 'In the past five to 10 years, the evidence linking air-pollution exposure to risk of early death has really solidified and gained scientific and political traction ... There's a realization that air pollution is a major problem in any city'. Litman cites research that indicates that people who live or work near busy

FIGURE 6.5 Traffic in Athens. In 2016 the city pledged to ban diesel vehicles from the city core in light of pollution concerns. *(Credit: Rakoon —Own work, CC0, https://commons.wikimedia.org/w/index.php?curid=73707272)*

highways experience significant increases in lung disease (Litman, 2016, Section 5.10, p. 4), a major concern given that the USEPA reports that 45 million Americans live or work within 300 feet (91 m) of major transport infrastructure (USEPA, 2017).

In Europe the problem is particularly acute, with diesel cars accounting for 50 per cent of new car sales in 2016, encouraged by incentives from governments attempting to reduce greenhouse gas emissions, as well as the high price of petrol and the promise from the manufacturers of a clean fuel. This promise proved to be false in the 2015 'dieselgate' emissions scandal, in which Volkswagen cars were detected to have been fitted with software to falsify emissions data, which was then followed by similar revelations about other large manufacturers (Forrest, 2017). Studies showing the huge health costs of diesel engines multiplied, with NO_x and particulate pollution so dangerous that the World Health Organization declared diesel exhaust a carcinogen, 'a cause of lung cancer in the same category as asbestos and mustard gas' (Kelland, 2012).

Now many European cities such as Paris, Athens, Amsterdam, Frankfurt, Brussels and Milan (Bendix, 2019) are instituting clean air zones and banning diesel cars, after years of promoting them as a clean solution to urban driving (Fig. 6.5). Drivers rail against what they see as hypocrisy, but for the scientific community and political establishment it is a sharp reminder of the complexity of inter-relations between the promotion of increasing amounts of mobility and the inevitable, if sometimes hidden, environmental and health consequences.

6.4.3 Noise pollution

Though noisy neighbours and dogs are common complaints in residential areas, road traffic noise is often the dominant factor. Noise is the second most harmful environmental stressor in Europe, behind air pollution, with effects arising mainly from the stress reaction it causes in the human body, which can potentially lead to premature death, cardiovascular disease, cognitive impairment, sleep disturbance and hypertension (European Environment Agency, 2017). It discourages outdoor recreation, disrupts conversation, and at the least, causes anxiety and annoyance—and so may dissuade some from walking or cycling, both of which are virtually silent forms of transport.

Noise from road vehicles includes that from engines, braking, slamming doors, loose loads, horns and alarm systems. Noise volumes are affected by vehicle and engine type, topography, road surface, driver behaviour and vehicle speed. Though slow stop-start traffic can generate considerable noise from engine acceleration and braking, as speeds increase, aerodynamic and tyre/road interaction noise becomes dominant, producing higher levels of background noise. Sandberg (2001) comments that 'No other single factor has such a prominent influence on tyre/road noise as speed', which is important because although electric vehicles—often touted as a solution to many pollution problems—may have extremely quiet propulsion systems, they are just as capable of generating intrusive road noise. Indeed, Sandberg suggests that exterior tyre/road noise of car tyres may have increased, partly due to a trend towards wider tyres more focussed on extreme high-speed performance.

US evidence shows that a rise in car speed from 30 to 40 mph (48 to 64 km/h) increases noise at 50 feet from 62 to 67 decibels and results in a 'substantial increase in noise for those living and working near highways', and that 'reducing vehicle speeds from 40 to 30 mph is as effective as removing one half the vehicles from the roadway' (Nonoise, n.d.). There is plentiful evidence that traffic noise depresses residential property values (Bagby, 1980) and that traffic volumes are a major reason why residents on busy streets retreat to rooms at the back of their houses (Appleyard & Lintell, 1972). No wonder then that one study of car alarm noise in New York City found that 91 per cent of respondents said that the annoyance of car alarms reduced their quality of life—so much so that whilst only five per cent have called the police to report a possible theft, 60 per cent have called them to complain about the noise of the alarms (Friedman, Naparstek, & Taussig-Rubbo, 2003).

6.4.4 Water consumption, pollution and waste disposal

Motor car manufacture and use puts considerable demands on water supplies. Water consumption for the life cycles of three Volkswagen cars was estimated to range from 52,000 litres to 83,000 litres (Berger, Warsen, Krinke, Bach, & Finkbeiner, 2012). Estimates of freshwater use in petroleum and ethanol gasoline production range from 1.4 to 8.6 litres per litre of gasoline (US Conventional Crude) to 8.7 to 160 litres per litre of corn ethanol (Wu & Xu, 2018). Whilst the water used in fuel production is unaffected by the speed of city transport, speed does have other impacts on water use. More speed results in higher fuel consumption, more consumption of distance and more sprawl, which all result in higher levels of water consumption in city transport. More sprawl also requires extended road infrastructure in circumstances where cement uses almost a tenth of the world's industrial water use (Watts, 2019b) and more sprawl also leads to larger houses with more bathrooms, hot tubs, swimming pools and water-thirsty lawns.

In addition to their impact on water consumption, motor vehicles, roads and parking facilities are a major source of water pollution, such as from: petroleum leaks and spills during extraction, processing, and distribution; road de-icing salts leaking into watercourses; and herbicide dispersal from roadside vegetation control. Also important is surface settlement of air pollution, such as particles of lead, which for over 50 years was used as an additive to vehicle fuels and is associated with high blood pressure, kidney and liver damage and retarded cognitive development in children. Collectively, these impacts result in polluted surface and ground water, contaminated drinking water and wildlife habitat damage, as Litman (2016, Section 5.15, p. 1) has detailed.

About 80 per cent of the material in life-expired cars—mostly the metals—can be recycled, but the rest increases the burden on landfill sites. Moreover, many tyres are illegally dumped, and the inappropriate disposal of oils and other substances is a further source of ground and water pollution and is often extremely toxic to humans and nature. These impacts relate to the amount of vehicle usage, not the speed of those vehicles. However, insofar as the quest for speed demands more road space and more vehicle usage, these water pollution impacts must be counted as a major cost of travelling faster and further. It might be noted that the water pollution and waste disposal impact of shoes and bicycles is barely discernible.

6.5 Greenhouse gas levels

'Slower cities' can play a critical role in reducing global greenhouse gas levels, as they reduce the fossil-fuel energy consumed. Greenhouse gases are those that increase atmospheric solar heat gain and include carbon dioxide and monoxide, CFCs, hydrocarbons and methane (Litman, 2016). The Intergovernmental Panel on Climate Change is the most authoritative source on the issue and its principal conclusions are that:

- 'Human influence on the climate system is clear, and recent anthropogenic emissions of greenhouse gases are the highest in history' (IPCC, 2014, p. 2);
- 'Recent climate changes have had widespread impacts on human and natural systems' (IPCC, 2014, p. 2); and
- 'Continued emission of greenhouse gases will cause further warming and long-lasting changes in all components of the climate system, increasing the likelihood of severe, pervasive and irreversible impacts for people and ecosystems' (IPCC, 2014, p. 8).

If a few politicians still refuse to accept the evidence from climate scientists about global heating, they may be convinced by the insurance industry, which is

FIGURE 6.6 A warmer atmosphere can hold more moisture, resulting in more extreme rainfall events, such as seen here in Brisbane, Queensland, Australia in April 2017. *(Credit: Rodney Tolley)*

already experiencing the effects of climate chaos. The number of global natural disaster events has increased markedly since the 1970s, as has the amount of insured losses from weather-related catastrophic events (tropical cyclones, convective storms, floods, extreme temperatures, droughts and wildfires), even after controlling for inflation (Fig. 6.6). One of these weather-related catastrophic events is wildfires, or bushfires as they are commonly referred to in Australia (Box 6.1).

Globally, the number of natural catastrophe events occurring annually increased from 60 in the early 1970s to an average of 310 for the 10 years to 2018 (Moody's Investors Service, 2018). The higher insurance losses 'reflect the effects of climate change, including more frequent and severe storms, extreme weather events and the impact of rising sea levels on coastal flooding' (Moody's Investors Service, 2018, p. 5). Other effects of climate disruption include desertification and other latitudinal shifts of crop boundaries with resultant impacts on the security of food supplies, the displacement of populations, and political instability in target countries for climate refugees, relating to costs of policing, border security and housing and to concerns over issues such as national identity. Many scientists are now concerned that we are quickly approaching tipping points beyond which recovery might not be feasible. As the IPCC (2014, p. 16) says, 'The risks of abrupt or irreversible changes increase as the magnitude of the warming increases'.

These warnings were repeated and indeed amplified four years later in the IPCC (2018a) report focussing on holding warming to 1.5°C. It noted that the planet will surpass 1.5°C even if countries abide by the pledges they made in Paris in 2016 to cut emissions. By 2019, the situation had worsened, with the United Nations warning that warming of 3.2°C by the end of the century was now likely because countries had collectively failed to stop the growth in global greenhouse gas emissions (UNEP, 2019). At the same time this report was released, researchers writing in the journal *Nature* warned that the probability of

BOX 6.1 'Catastrophic' fire danger.

In Australia after the 2009 Black Saturday fires in Victoria, during which 173 people died, and 1,700 square miles (440,000 hectares) was burnt, a new category of fire danger rating was added, beyond 'Severe' and even 'Extreme'. 'Catastrophic' fire danger (Fig. 6.7) signifies that homes are not designed to withstand fires in these conditions, so the best (or only) option for residents if they wish to survive is to leave their homes and move to a location with a lower fire danger.

Catastrophic fire danger is associated with 'firestorms', the common term for 'pyrocumulonimbus bushfires – fires so intense they create their own thunderstorms, extreme winds, black hail [hail stones incorporating soot and ash], and lightning', which while they are now rare, are likely to become common (Di Virgilio, Dowdy, Evans, Sharples, & McRae, 2019). These fire-induced thunderstorms—pyroCbs—develop when fires burn hot enough to generate strong updrafts. The abundant smoke particles provide objects for water droplets to grip, resulting in suddenly developing and massive cloud formations.

A frightening video of one such event, occurring in Canberra, Australia, in 2003 has been made available by the ACT Emergency Services Agency (2019), showing how a pyrcoCb created its own devastating tornado-like vortex. These events can form clouds towering up to several km high (Fig. 6.8), driving blizzards of embers that ignite spot fires well beyond the fire front. During the Black Saturday fires in Victoria, three clearly distinct pyrcoCb storms erupted, with lightning igniting new

FIGURE 6.7 In Australia after Victoria's Black Saturday fires in 2009, a new category of fire danger was added—'Catastrophic', indicating that if a fire were to start it would be 'uncontrollable, unpredictable and very fast moving, with highly aggressive flames extending high above tree tops and buildings'. *(Credit: Paul Tranter)*

FIGURE 6.8 A pyrocumulonimbus cloud forming over the Willow Fire near Payson, Arizona in July 2004, reaching 7.6 km (4.7 miles) high. *(Credit: Eric Neitzel —Own work, CC BY-SA 3.0, https://commons.wikimedia.org/w/index.php?curid=31292202)*

fires '100km ahead of the fire front' (Dowdy, Fromm, & McCarthy, 2017, p. 7342). The human-caused climate crisis has already caused more dangerous conditions for bushfires in many areas of Australia, and 'these trends are very likely to increase due to rising greenhouse gas emissions' (Di Virgilio et al., 2019).

It is not just Australia that is experiencing increasing fire danger. In 2019 a record number of fires were burning in the Amazon rainforest, and ongoing Arctic fires have been particularly severe in Siberia and Alaska. Devastating fires have ravaged parts of California and Greece and many other nations. As Struzik (2019) summarises 'PyroCb events appear to be increasing dramatically, producing more energy, and erupting in places where they have never been seen before ... there is little doubt they will occur more frequently in parallel with the larger and hotter wildfires we are already witnessing as the world warms'.

tipping points in the earth's climate system was higher than previously assumed. The authors argued that 'the consideration of tipping points helps to define that we are in a climate emergency and strengthens this year's chorus of calls for urgent climate action—from schoolchildren to scientists, cities and countries' (Lenton et al., 2019, p. 592).

In commentary on the UNEP report the phrase 'climate emergency' began to be used to describe the unprecedented nature of the situation. For example, a Guardian newspaper editorial began with the chilling words that 'Climate change is an existential threat to the human race' (The Guardian, 2018), with 'existential' referring to a risk that poses permanent large negative consequences to humanity which can never be undone. The consequences of a 'warming of 3C, 4C or even worse ... will be globally terrible, and everywhere unavoidable. Hundreds of millions of people may die'. The editorial warned of the political and military threats, observing that 'These victims will not passively await their fates', raising the prospect of 'historically unprecedented refugee migrations as whole populations who have no choice but to starve or move set out for land where they can live. The political and indeed the military consequences are unlikely to be small' (The Guardian, 2018).

The Environment Minister of Canada (where the mining of tar sands for oil is an egregious example of accelerating GHG emissions) referred to the IPCC report as 'a call to action' (Raj, 2018) and then poignantly captured the unprecedented predicament facing the world, when she observed 'We are the first generation to feel the impacts of climate change and we are the last generation [who can] do anything about it'.

In most countries emissions from transport are a very significant (if not the largest) contributor to global heating and are frequently the fastest growing. In addition to its accelerating consumption of fossil fuels, speed affects GHG levels through other means as well. Examples found near sprawling cities include loss of forests and agricultural production, leading to reduced carbon capture and increased food miles. As Cervero, Guerra, and Al (2017, p. 44) comment, 'Urban containment can also contribute to climate change mitigation by preserving the carbon sequestration capacity of surrounding natural and agricultural areas. Urban greening and landscaping, made possible by compact development, can reduce the urban heat island effect'. Overall the effect of high-speed city transport in raising GHG levels is its most damaging environmental health impact.

We have already referred in Chapter 5 to the inequity of multi-layered levels of accessibility, with the highly mobile rich able to access services across all of the scales from local to international, in contrast to the low mobility poor, wholly dependent on local resources for their well-being. Here we see this inequality extended to climate breakdown impacts, with those who have contributed least to the problem through their transport usage most likely to suffer the worst impacts. It is those living in the Global North that are disproportionately responsible for greenhouse gas emissions. To cite just one example, a Swedish study estimates that the health impacts suffered in developing countries as a consequence of emissions of greenhouse gases from the Swedish road transport system may be three times greater than the mortality from road traffic accidents in Sweden itself (Sustainable Development Comission, 2010).

Although climate emergency effects will be most severe in low-income countries of the Global South, everywhere the urban poor will be acutely impacted, together with the elderly and children, traditional societies, subsistence farmers, and coastal populations. Poorer people are more likely to live in urban areas susceptible to higher heat stroke risks and in areas subject to weather extremes and flooding, where they will be less well protected and less likely to be insured against such risks (Sustainable Development Commission, 2011). The global consequences of the climate emergency have been grimly summarised by Smith (2008): 'The rich will find their world to be more expensive, inconvenient, uncomfortable, disrupted and colorless; in general, more unpleasant and unpredictable, perhaps greatly so. The poor will die'. Smith's blunt summary reflects an awareness of the importance of language and terminology that indicates the gravity of the climate emergency (see Box 6.2). The seriousness of this emergency also needs to be acknowledged in the way that carbon is priced in economic analyses of transport infrastructure (see Box 6.3).

In terms of mitigation, the IPCC (2014) comments that:

- 'Without additional mitigation efforts beyond those in place today, and even with adaptation, warming by the end of the 21st century will lead to high to very high risk of severe, widespread and irreversible impacts globally' (2014, p. 17);
- 'Limiting climate change would require substantial and sustained reductions in greenhouse gas emissions' (2014, p. 8); and that
- 'Implementing such reductions poses substantial technological, economic, social and institutional challenges, which increase with delays in additional mitigation' (2014, p. 20).

Given the continued acceleration of global heating, it was not surprising that the 2018 IPCC report went further. It found that 'limiting warming to 1.5°C is

BOX 6.2 Language: how terminology can affect public perception of the climate crisis.

In 2019 in response to the rapidly accumulating evidence on the danger posed to humanity by rising global temperatures, the Guardian newspaper altered its language style guide for its writers, concerned that the terms in use no longer accurately reflect the phenomena they describe. 'The phrase "climate change", for example, sounds rather passive and gentle when what scientists are talking about is a catastrophe for humanity' (Viner, quoted in Carrington, 2019). The newspaper recommended using 'climate emergency, crisis or breakdown' instead; referring to 'global heating' instead of 'warming'; and replacing 'climate sceptic' with 'climate science denier'.

These changes reflect new language being used by institutions such as the UK's Meteorological Office and the United Nations. They also follow the plea from Greta Thunberg (the Swedish teenager who began the school strikes for climate that have spread around the globe): 'It's 2019. Can we all now please stop saying "climate change" and instead call it what it is: climate breakdown, climate crisis, climate emergency, ecological breakdown, ecological crisis and ecological emergency?' (Yoder, 2019).

Within months, Oxford Dictionaries 'declared "climate emergency" the word of the year for 2019' reporting a hundred-fold increase in the usage of this term. Oxford Dictionaries' choice of 'climate emergency' reflected a 'conscious push towards language of immediacy and urgency' in the way people throughout the world are talking about climate (Zhou, 2019).

BOX 6.3 Downplaying the significance of global heating in cost benefit analysis.

The way in which speed, and how we value it, is linked to the climate crisis, is evident in the absurdity of our current mechanisms to assess new transport projects. In cost benefit analyses (CBAs) of transport projects, the value put on 'time savings' created by increasing speed (which are rarely achieved in practice) represents the majority of the 'benefits'. In contrast, the monetizing of greenhouse gas emissions is usually set at such a low value that any project's contribution to global heating is unlikely to influence the CBA results (Næss & Price, 2016). For example in Norway the price per ton of CO_2 emissions was set to US$35 in the analysis of over 100 large public works projects between 2005 and 2013 (Næss & Price, 2016). For some project analyses, a price of $5 per ton of CO_2 was set, due to a malfunctioning carbon market. Yet a recent paper in *Nature Climate Change* estimated the social cost of carbon (the economic cost associated with climate damage from emissions of an additional ton of CO_2) at a global value of over $400 (Ricke, Drouet, Caldeira, & Tavoni, 2018). However, given that the climate crisis has been described as an existential risk (which could wipe out humanity), or at least a catastrophic risk (which could kill hundreds of millions of people) (Piper, 2019), even $400 per ton seems low. Evidently, if we are serious about responding to the climate crisis, CBAs need to be seriously overhauled, in terms of their holistic assessment of time savings and likely impacts on GHGs, and in the use of a realistic price for GHGs.

possible within the laws of chemistry and physics' but would require 'rapid and far-reaching transitions in land, energy, industry, buildings, transport, and cities. Global net human-caused emissions of carbon dioxide would need to fall by about 45 per cent from 2010 levels by 2030, reaching "net zero" around 2050' (IPCC, 2018b).

The point has been made many times in this book that speed reduction is at the very least desirable and preferable for human happiness and health. When it comes to the climate emergency, however, slowing the city becomes not something that we should do, but something we have to do, because our addiction to speed is at the root of the potential destruction of life on earth. Conquering that addiction in a collective act of rehabilitation will be insufficient on its own, but we can be sure that slowing the city is absolutely essential if the catastrophic consequences of accelerating greenhouse gas emissions are to be avoided. It may be no exaggeration to say that if the city itself is to survive, all future cities must be 'slow cities'.

6.6 Consumption of space in the transport system

Roads take up a significant percentage of surface area in cities (15–20 per cent in European cities, for example, and much higher in US cities) in circumstances where land is often in short supply and expensive. Additional land take includes quarries for road building materials (such as sand, gravel and road

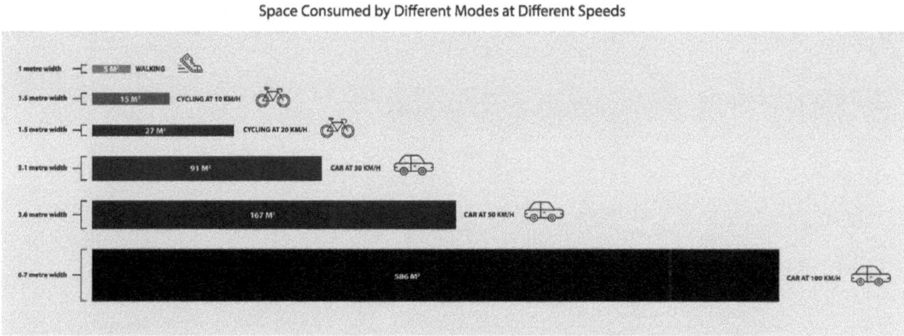

FIGURE 6.9 Total space required (m^2) for walking, cycling and cars with one occupant, at various speeds. *(Created by Jeff Steinacker)*

stone), together with land affected by hydrological changes and by run-off. It also includes changes in land use that result from transport developments. For example, the completion of new roads stimulates speculative development, which produces further volumes of traffic, fuelling demand for further transport infrastructure provision.

In addition to encouraging urban sprawl, as speeds increase the space required for each vehicle also increases: a car travelling 'at higher speeds requires more space both next to and in front of a car in order for drivers to be able to react to unexpected situations' (Peters, 2006, p. 137). Fig. 6.9 illustrates the space required by different modes at different speeds, using conservative assumptions for lane widths, shoulders and median strips for cars. The comparison shows that a car with one person at 30 km/h requires 18 times as much space as a person walking at 5 km/h (assuming that all modes need to leave a three second gap, so that a person walking needs to allow 4 metres ahead—likely far more generous than most walkers need). A car travelling at 100 km/h requires over 100 times as much space as a person walking. As speeds decrease, the space required between and beside vehicles also decreases, so a 'slower city' will use space much more efficiently. Moreover, in 'slow cities', the focus will be on moving people rather than vehicles, a distinction which is frequently misunderstood in existing car-based cities.

Cars also require space when parked. Car parking spaces are often larger than the size of an office work cubicle, meaning that 'bringing a car to work essentially doubles the amount of space that someone needs on the job' (Glaeser, 2011, p. 178). In the high-speed city, businesses and other services can only be accessed by car, and so parking areas around each facility take up large amounts of space (Fig. 6.10) an outcome frequently mandated by zoning ordinances (see Section 9.2.3). These, together with wide roads and driveways increase the area covered in impervious surfaces, which has other negative environmental health impacts. These include concentrated runoff and increased flooding, which lead to degraded surface water quality, and contaminated drinking water.

Additionally, the barrier effect of roads leads to severance and thus the splitting of natural habitats, with a consequent threat to ecological diversity.

FIGURE 6.10 One of the University of Washington's car parks in Seattle in 2001, shortly after the university initiated the U-PASS pioneering travel management plan for staff and students. *(Credit: Rodney Tolley)*

Interaction with traffic may also lead to significant animal casualties. A report by the US Federal Highway Administration estimated the number of accidents with large animals as between one and two million per year (Wollan, 2010). Another study by Guimarães (2015) estimated that of the 1.3 million animals killed every day after being struck by cars and trucks in Brazil, 9 out of 10 are small birds, frogs or snakes. John Griffin, of the Humane Society of the United States, is quoted by Kelleher (2015) as saying that this is 'one of the largest, if not the largest anthropogenic cause of death for wildlife'.

A further effect of an increase in the amount of hard-surfaced areas is enhanced urban heat island impacts, where solar energy is converted into heat by buildings and asphalt, and increased urbanisation reduces cooling provided by vegetation and water. Wouters et al. (2017, p. 8997) point out that heatwaves are now 'more intense, more frequent, and longer-lasting' in cities due to a combination of the urban heat island effect and global heating. It is possible that heat waves could be the deadliest type of natural disaster in the near future. Their study refers to combatting these growing threats through drastic reductions of greenhouse gas emissions from systems for housing and mobility, reducing motorised traffic and expansion of green open spaces.

The idea that heat stress can be reduced by slowing the city has received further support from research that argues that a person's age, the most commonly cited factor for urban heat stress risk, is actually less important than their lack of health and fitness. Schuster, Honold, Lauf, and Lakes (2017) conclude that 'The potential of health and fitness to reduce urban heat stress risk means that

FIGURE 6.11 Visual pollution: the underbelly of a Pittsburgh motorway. *(Credit: Carlos Felipe Pardo, https://www.flickr.com/photos/carlosfpardo/48809155011)*

encouraging active travel could be an effective adaptation strategy. Through reduced CO_2 emissions from urban transport, societies could reap double rewards by addressing two root causes of urban heat stress: population health and global warming'. Once again, the 'slower city' is seen as not only a precondition for environmental health, but for human health as well.

A final environmental issue with increasing land take is not so much its area, but its architectural and visual quality—or lack of it. It has traditionally been accepted that 'when a road comes to town it becomes a street', with the nomenclature referring to the differing functions, sizes and civic design language and principles of the two movement spaces. The direct and fast inter-city highway should morph at the town's edge into a space at a human scale, a place for people and local activities. But when the intention changes from facilitating human activity in a street to facilitating fast streams of traffic, the design and scale of the street changes into a road. When wide roads, flyovers and parking garages come to dominate the urban scene the results are rarely easy on the eye, because fast travel pollutes the architecture of spaces in which it takes place (Fig. 6.11).

As Jan Gehl and colleagues have observed, 'while our perception of public space depends on viewpoint and distance, the speed at which we move is crucial. Our senses are designed to perceive and process sensory impressions while moving at about 5 km/h: walking pace. Architecture that embodies 5 km/h details combines the best of two worlds: a glimpse of the town hall tower or

FIGURE 6.12 Walking amidst 60 km/h architecture, with huge billboards, high-level lighting and multiple wide lanes, Nairobi, Kenya. *(Credit: Carlos Felipe Pardo, https://www.flickr.com/photos/carlosfpardo/15712652452)*

distant hills at the end of the street and the close-up contact of ground-floor facades' (Gehl, Kaefer, & Reigstad, 2016, p. 30–31). They contrast this 'slow' architecture with the '60 km/h architecture along roads dominated by vehicles, where large spaces and signs are necessary since drivers and passengers cannot perceive detail when moving at this speed'. Whilst one could argue that these two landscapes meet the needs of their users, 'These two scales pose conflict in modern cities. Pedestrians are often forced to walk in 60 km/h urban landscapes, while new urban buildings are designed as boring and sterile 60 km/h buildings in traditional 5 km/h streets' (Gehl et al., 2016, p. 31) (Fig. 6.12).

It must be stressed that the problem of visual pollution is also affected by the huge demand for car parking. As Tolley and Turton (1995, p. 287) have argued, 'The sheer volume of cars in urban areas may spoil vistas of architectural or historical significance, as when the medieval city wall or the Renaissance square are seen across the roofs of hundreds of parked cars. Such visual intrusion undermines the quality of urban life, for cities should be places that are worth living in, not just travelling through'.

These issues are also manifested in low-density, dormitory suburbia, especially in North America, but increasingly across the world, creating landscapes where the needs of the car are paramount. The American syndicated newspaper columnist Bill Vaughan lampooned such developments in his observation that 'the suburbs are where the developer bulldozes out the trees then names the streets after them' (Vaughan (1964) quoted in Popik (2012)).

Kunstler (2004) has excoriated the landscapes that result, referring to 'The immersive ugliness of our everyday environments in America' and 'the national

FIGURE 6.13 'Auto-strip' architecture, Altoona, Pennsylvania, United States. *(Credit: Rodney Tolley)*

automobile slum'. In *The Geography of Nowhere* he connects the degradation of the public realm with a decline in civic life and the character of all the enactments that take place there, referring to 'the tragic landscape of highway strips, parking lots, housing tracts, mega-malls, junked cities, and ravaged countryside that makes up the everyday environment where most Americans live and work' (Kunstler, 1994, Book Jacket).

There is no mitigation of the land taken here except in not building the roads, car parks and 'auto-strip' architecture (see Fig. 6.13) in the first place. But if fast travel by car is sold as a legitimate aspiration to urban populations, then space-hungry facilities become essential to maintain the speed of traffic, its increased volume and its demands for parking arrangements. The result promotes sprawl so much that car use becomes essential, fuelling the process, and leaving us to cope with the ugly 60 km/h landscapes that are the inevitable consequence of being beguiled by the illusory benefits of speed.

6.7 Sprawl: the link with speed

Increased speeds feed urban sprawl, or the 'dispersed city' (Montgomery, 2013 p. 46). As explained in Chapter 3, when speeds increase, the time that transport economists expect to be saved (and hence include in their cost-benefit modelling) is rarely saved. Instead, the increased speed is used to buy more distance, which is often linked to people moving to residences further from the city. A city where 'slow' transport modes are prioritised encourages the development of denser, better connected neighbourhoods. The impact of this is evident in the lower combined housing and transport costs in these neighbourhoods (Chapter 7), compared with that in sprawling outer suburbs, and also in the much lower greenhouse gas emissions. The explanation for these differences rests not only in the regular commutes made by residents, but also in the land-use and lifestyles of adults and children in different areas of the city. In sprawling suburbs, consisting of low-density dispersed single-family houses (see Fig. 2.5), not only is the land area per house block greater, there is a greater need for more paved streets and roads, more expansive drainage systems, greater demand for water pipes, power cables, utility wiring, sewerage and other services than in denser, more walkable neighbourhoods.

Sprawling cities are also more vulnerable to global heating. The rate of increase in annual extreme heat events in the most sprawling cities in the United States between 1956 and 2005 was more than twice the rate of increase in the most compact cities (Stone, Hess, & Frumkin, 2010). Sprawling suburbs also require more support with school transport, including school buses. In the United States alone, more than 25 million children have to be bussed to school. The energy and greenhouse gas implications of these school trips would be negligible if children were able to walk or cycle to local schools.

Low-density sprawl is usually linked to a planning strategy based on the large-scale segregation of different types of land use. Residential areas are separated from commercial districts, retail parks, office parks and industrial parks, all with their own supply of paved surface car parks, and connected by high-speed roads. Not only do residents in sprawling communities spend long hours commuting, but even the trip to the gym, the closest supermarket or mall often necessitates driving at speed. Speed enables the creation of dispersed cities, and once established, the dispersed land uses force the citizens of this landscape to maintain their reliance on high-speed transport to access their destinations.

Sprawled landscapes also have a further indirect effect on energy use through the increase in consumerism associated with low-density living. More consumer items are required in low-density environments facilitated by high-speed transport, including lawnmowers, more outdoor furniture, air-conditioning and heating, landscaping, and of course, cars (sometimes several per household). In so-called 'lifestyle blocks' still further out from the city, families 'play' at being weekend farmers, with the whole gamut of devices such as quad bikes, mini-tractors, pickup trucks, and utility vehicles, plus a range of recreational vehicles such as campervans, moto-cross bikes, motor boats, jet-skis and snow-mobiles. Whilst this may seem positive for economic growth, these extreme levels of consumerism also require high levels of energy use, currently dominated by fossil fuel energy.

6.8 Rebound impacts

Much of the technological innovation in city transport over the last century has been aimed at increasing the speed of travel. Some of this innovation has also been directed towards more energy-efficient transport. Whilst any increase in energy efficiency might be assumed to have positive environmental impacts, these are by no means necessarily achieved. The reason for this relates to the phenomenon known as a 'rebound effect' (Spielmann, de Haan, & Scholz, 2008). Rebound effects refer to the reduction in the expected benefits from new technologies due to behavioural or other systemic responses.

There are multiple ways in which rebound effects from advances in transport technology may reduce, or even reverse, the environmental benefit of these advances (Berkhout, Muskens, & Velthuijsen, 2000). For example, people may purchase more cars or drive further as the efficiency of cars is increased, or they may switch to this 'faster' mode from the supposedly 'slower' modes of walking, cycling or public transport if cars become cheaper to operate. Another type of rebound occurs when increased transport efficiency leads to increased sprawl, which creates additional consumer demand (e.g. for household goods), which requires additional energy consumption. Full reversal of efficiency benefits is seen in the Jevons Paradox, where rebound effects greater than 100 per cent exceed any original efficiency gains (Sorrell, 2009). In these ways rebound impacts undermine technological advances in transport, whereas the strategy of slowing the city has clear environmental benefits.

6.9 Conclusion

This chapter has outlined some of the complexity of the environmental impacts of speed. What should be clear is that any claims that increased speed (even with improved technology) will have positive environmental benefits should be treated with great scepticism. There are multiple negative environmental impacts of higher-speed city transport, whereas slowing city transport will likely decrease all of the negative impacts of transport and promote positive impacts. As Cervero et al. (2017, p. 44) argue, 'Cities that promote shorter trips by slower modes are among the world's most sustainable places. They reduce the vehicle miles traveled (VMT) per inhabitant, the strongest correlate of environmental adversity in the transport sector: As VMT per person goes up, so do energy consumption, land takings, pavement coverage, and tailpipe emissions'.

This chapter has made clear that road transport in general—and fast travel in particular—is a growing source of pollutant emission and consumption of fossil fuels. Technological advances have led to falling pollution and energy use per kilometre travelled in individual vehicles, but these have been offset by a large rise in the number of kilometres travelled and a switch to modes of transport that consume more energy and produce more pollution per kilometre. There is increasing concern about the ability of the planet's ecosystems to cope with this growing burden, but present trends are deeply entrenched in international systems of motorisation, which conflict fundamentally with the necessity to reduce emissions.

A definition of sustainable development is that it meets the needs of the present without compromising the ability of future generations to meet their own needs, yet it is evident that current patterns and speeds of city transport do not meet this criterion. As evidence of the deterioration of planetary health mounts, so must the assumptions on which such trends are based be challenged. 'Future generations will be significantly disadvantaged by the dramatic and irreversible changes to the climate system created by the continuing growth in the use of fossil fuels required by the growing speed of movement of persons and goods in the global industrial economy' (Northcott, 2008, p. 217).

In addition to the way our global economic system is contributing to the climate emergency, there is growing concern that multiple environmental crises will coalesce to create catastrophic risks for the global economy itself. The combination of global heating, pollinator loss, soil infertility, ocean acidification and chemical leaching has been identified as creating a 'new domain of risk' that has been 'hugely underestimated by policy makers even though it may pose the greatest threat in human history' (Watts, 2019a). Most previous studies of environmental risk have focussed on specific threats in isolation, but new research is examining how the interplay of environmental crises may potentially lead to a systemic or 'runaway collapse in which economic, social and political shocks cascade through the globally linked system' similar to the 2007–08 global financial crisis (Laybourn-Langton, Rankin, & Baxter, 2019, p. 20). Given warnings such as this, the imperative of creating 'slower cities' becomes more and more urgent.

Slowing city transport will not only improve the health of present generations, but will be an invaluable strategy in promoting environmental health, including planetary health, in the long term. Moreover, 'slow cities' will bring improvements to the economic health of individuals, cities and nations, as Chapter 7 demonstrates.

References

ACT Emergency Services Agency. (2019). Fire tornado video. Available from: https://esa.act.gov.au/cbr-be-emergency-ready/bushfires/fire-tornado-video.

Agarwal, O. P., Zimmerman, S., & Kumar, A. (2018). *Emerging paradigms in urban mobility: Planning, financing and management*. Oxford, UK: Elsevier.

Andrews, C., & Urbanska, W. (2009). *Less is more: Embracing simplicity for a healthy planet, a caring economy and lasting happiness*. Gabriola Island, BC: New Society Publishers.

Appleyard, D., & Lintell, M. (1972). The environmental quality of city streets: The residents' viewpoint. *Journal of the American Institute of Planners*, *38*(2), 84–101.

Bagby, D. G. (1980). The effects of traffic flow on residential property values. *Journal of the American Planning Association*, *46*(1), 88–94.

BBC News. (2019). Millions of masks distributed to students in 'gas chamber' Delhi. *BBC News*. Available from: https://www.bbc.com/news/world-asia-india-50258947.

Bendix, A. (2019). 15 major cities around the world that are starting to ban cars. *Business Insider, Malaysia*. Available from: https://www.businessinsider.com.au/cities-going-car-free-ban-2018-12?r=US&IR=T.

Berger, M., Warsen, J., Krinke, S., Bach, V., & Finkbeiner, M. (2012). Water footprint of European cars: Potential impacts of water consumption along automobile life cycles. *Environmental Science & Technology*, *46*(7), 4091–4099.

Berkhout, P. H., Muskens, J. C., & Velthuijsen, J. W. (2000). Defining the rebound effect. *Energy Policy*, *28*(6–7), 425–432.

Buehler, R., & Pucher, J. (2011). Sustainable transport in Freiburg: Lessons from Germany's environmental capital. *International Journal of Sustainable Transportation*, *5*(1), 43–70.

Carrington, D. (2019). Why the Guardian is changing the language it uses about the environment? *The Guardian*. Available from: https://www.theguardian.com/environment/2019/may/17/why-the-guardian-is-changing-the-language-it-uses-about-the-environment.

Cervero, R., Guerra, E., & Al, S. (2017). *Beyond mobility: Planning cities for people and places*. Washington: Island Press.

Chang, M., & Herman, R. (1978). An attempt to characterize traffic in metropolitan areas. *Transportation Science*, *12*(1), 58–79.

Chu, J. (2013). Study: Air pollution causes 200,000 early deaths each year in the U.S. *MIT News*. Available from: http://news.mit.edu/2013/study-air-pollution-causes-200000-early-deaths-each-year-in-the-us-0829.

Di Virgilio, G., Dowdy, A., Evans, J., Sharples, J., & McRae, R. (2019). Climate change will make fire storms more likely in southeastern Australia. *The Conversation*. Available from: https://theconversation.com/climate-change-will-make-fire-storms-more-likely-in-southeastern-australia-127225.

Dowdy, A. J., Fromm, M. D., & McCarthy, N. (2017). Pyrocumulonimbus lightning and fire ignition on Black Saturday in southeast Australia. *Journal of Geophysical Research: Atmospheres*, *122*(14), 7342–7354.

European Environment Agency. (2017). Road traffic remains biggest source of noise pollution in Europe. Available from: https://www.eea.europa.eu/highlights/road-traffic-remains-biggest-source.

Ferguson, B., Fisher, K., Golden, J., Hair, L., Haselbach, L., Hitchcock, D., et al. (2008). *Reducing urban heat islands: Compendium of strategies: Cool pavements*. Available from: https://www.epa.gov/sites/production/files/2014-06/documents/coolpavescompendium.pdf.

Forrest, A. (2017). The death of diesel: Has the one-time wonder fuel become the new asbestos? *The Guardian*. Available from: https://www.theguardian.com/cities/2017/apr/13/death-of-diesel-wonder-fuel-new-asbestos.

Friedman, A., Naparstek, A., & Taussig-Rubbo, M. (2003). *Alarmingly useless: The case for banning car alarms in New York City*. Available from: https://www.transalt.org/sites/default/files/news/reports/2003/Alarmingly_Useless.pdf.

Gehl, J., Kaefer, L. J., & Reigstad, S. (2016). Close encounters with buildings. In H. Karssenberg, J. Laven, M. Glaser, & M. van 't Hoff (Eds.), *The city at eye level: Lessons for Street Plinths* (pp. 29–36). Delft: Eburon Academic Publishers.

Glaeser, E. (2011). *Triumph of the city*. New York: Pan Macmillan.

Grigoratos, T., & Martini, G. (2014). *Non-exhaust traffic related emissions. Brake and tyre wear PM: Literature Review*. Available from: http://publications.jrc.ec.europa.eu/repository/bitstream/JRC89231/jrc89231-online%20final%20version%202.pdf.

Guimarães, T. (2015). A principal causa da morte de animais silvestres no Brasil. Available from: https://www.bbc.com/portuguese/noticias/2015/10/150924_atropelamentos_fauna_tg.

Illich, I. (1974). *Energy and equity*. London: Calder and Boyers.

International Energy Agency. (2018). *CO_2 Emissions from fuel combustion: Overview*.

IPCC. (2014). *Climate change 2014 synthesis report: Summary for policymakers*. Available from: https://www.ipcc.ch/site/assets/uploads/2018/06/AR5_SYR_FINAL_SPM.pdf.

IPCC. (2018a). *Special report: Global warming of 1.5 °C*. Available from: https://www.ipcc.ch/sr15/.

IPCC. (2018b). *Summary for policymakers of IPCC special report on global warming of 1.5 °C approved by governments*. Available from: https://www.ipcc.ch/2018/10/08/summary-for-policymakers-of-ipcc-special-report-on-global-warming-of-1-5c-approved-by-governments/.

Kelland, K. (2012). Diesel exhaust fumes cause lung cancer, WHO says. Available from: https://uk.reuters.com/article/us-cancer-diesel-who-idUKBRE85B0ZN20120612.

Kelleher, S. (2015). More animals are killed by cars each day than we ever could have imagined. Available from: https://www.thedodo.com/road-kill-every-day-1392772624.html.

Kenworthy, J. (1986). *Driving cycles, urban form and transport energy.* PhD thesis. Murdoch University, Perth.

Kenworthy, J., Newman, P., & Lyons, T. (1989). Urban planning and traffic congestion. *Urban Policy and Research*, *7*(2), 67–80.

Kunstler, J. H. (1994). *The geography of nowhere: The rise and decline of America's man-made landscape*. New York: Free Press.

Kunstler, J.H. (2004). The ghastly tragedy of the suburbs Ted Talk. Available from: https://www.ted.com/talks/james_howard_kunstler_dissects_suburbia/transcript?language=en.

Laybourn-Langton, L., Rankin, L., & Baxter, D. (2019). *This is a crisis: Facing up to the age of environmental breakdown*. Initial Report. Available from: https://www.ippr.org/files/2019-11/this-is-a-crisis-feb19.pdf.

Lenton, T. M., Rockström, J., Gaffney, O., Hahmstorf, S., Richardson, K., Steffen, W., et al. (2019). Climate tipping points — too risky to bet against. *Nature*, *575*, 592–595.

Litman, T. (2016). *Transportation cost and benefit analysis techniques, estimates and implications*. Available from: http://www.vtpi.org/tca/.

Ma, F., Sha, A., Lin, R., Huang, Y., & Wang, C. (2016). Greenhouse gas emissions from asphalt pavement construction: A case study in China. *International Journal of Environmental Research and Public Health*, *13*(3), 351.

Monks, P. (2019). *Non-exhaust emissions from road traffic*. Available from: https://uk-air.defra.gov.uk/assets/documents/reports/cat09/1907101151_20190709_Non_Exhaust_Emissions_typeset_Final.pdf.

Montgomery, C. (2013). *Happy city: Transforming our lives through urban design*. New York: Penguin Random House.

Moody's Investors Service. (2018). *Climate change risks outweigh opportunities for property and casualty (re)insurers*. Available from: https://www.law.berkeley.edu/wp-content/uploads/2018/06/Moodys-Climate-change-risks-outweigh-opportunities-for-PC-reinsurers.pdf.

Næss, P., & Price, L. (2016). *Crisis system: A critical realist and environmental critique of economics and the economy*. Abingdon: Routledge.

Nonoise. (n.d.). Noise increases with vehicle speed. Available from: http://www.nonoise.org/resource/trans/highway/spnoise.htm.

Northcott, M. (2008). The desire for speed and the rhythm of the earth. In S. Bergmann, & T. Sager (Eds.), *The ethics of mobilities: Rethinking place, exclusion, freedom and environment* (pp. 215–232). Aldershot: Ashgate.

OECD. (2014). *The cost of air pollution: Health impacts of road transport*. Available from: http://www.oecd.org/env/the-cost-of-air-pollution-9789264210448-en.htm.

Peters, P. F. (2006). *Time, innovation and mobilities: Travels in technological cultures*. New York: Routledge.

Petit, S. (2017). World vehicle population rose 4.6% in 2016. *Wards Intelligence*. Available from: https://wardsintelligence.informa.com/WI058630/World-Vehicle-Population-Rose-46-in-2016.

Piper, K. (2019). Is climate change an "existential threat" — or just a catastrophic one? *Vox*. Available from: https://www.vox.com/future-perfect/2019/6/13/18660548/climate-change-human-civilization-existential-risk.

Popik, B. (2012). Suburbia is where the developer bulldozes out the trees, then names the streets after them. *The Big Apple*. Available from: https://www.barrypopik.com/index.php/new_york_city/comments/about_the_site_editor/.

Porritt, J. (2005). Too many, too fast. In T. Aldrich, & M. Kaiser (Eds.), *About time: Speed, society, people and the environment* (pp. 39–52). Sheffield: Greenleaf Publishing.

Raj, A. (2018). UN climate change report spurs emergency debate in house of commons. *Huffpost*. Available from: https://www.huffingtonpost.ca/2018/10/15/un-climate-change-report-emergency-debate_a_23561544/.

Ricke, K., Drouet, L., Caldeira, K., & Tavoni, M. (2018). Country-level social cost of carbon. *Nature Climate Change*, *8*(10), 895.

Sachs, W. (1996). *Why speed matters*. Paper presented at the Presentation at Doors of Perception 4: Speed, Amsterdam, November 7–8.

Sandberg, U. (2001). *Tyre/road noise – myths and realities*. Paper presented at the Proceedings of The 2001 International Congress and Exhibition on Noise Control Engineering, The Hague, The Netherlands.

Schuster, C., Honold, J., Lauf, S., & Lakes, T. (2017). Urban heat stress: Novel survey suggests health and fitness as future avenue for research and adaptation strategies. *Environmental Research Letters*, *12*(4), 044021.

Smith, K. R. (2008). Mitigating, adapting, and suffering: How much of each? *Annual Review of Public Health*, *29*, xxiii–xxv.

Sorrell, S. (2009). Jevons' Paradox revisited: The evidence for backfire from improved energy efficiency. *Energy Policy*, *37*(4), 1456–1469.

Spielmann, M., de Haan, P., & Scholz, R. W. (2008). Environmental rebound effects of high-speed transport technologies: A case study of climate change rebound effects of a future underground maglev train system. *Journal of Cleaner Production*, *16*(13), 1388–1398.

Stone, B., Hess, J.J., & Frumkin, H. (2010). Urban form and extreme heat events: Are sprawling cities more vulnerable to climate change than compact cities? *Environmental Health Perspectives*, *118*(10), 1425–1428.

Struzik, E. (2019). Fire-induced storms: A new danger from the rise in wildfires. *Yale Environment 360*. Available from: https://e360.yale.edu/features/fire-induced-storms-a-new-danger-from-the-rise-in-wildfires.

Sustainable Development Comission. (2010). *Sustainable development: The key to tackling health inequalities*. Available from: https://research-repository.st-andrews.ac.uk/bitstream/handle/10023/2417/sdc-2010-health-inequality.pdf?sequence=1&isAllowed=y.

Sustainable Development Commission. (2011). *Fairness in a car-dependent society*. Available from: https://research-repository.st-andrews.ac.uk/bitstream/handle/10023/2290/sdc-2011-car-fairness.pdf?sequence=1&isAllowed=y.

The Guardian. (2018). The Guardian view on climate change: A global emergency Editorial. *The Guardian, Australian Edition*. Available from: https://www.theguardian.com/commentisfree/2018/oct/08/the-guardian-view-on-climate-change-a-global-emergency.

Tolley, R. (1990). *The Greening of urban transport: Planning for walking and cycling in Western cities*. London: Belhaven Press.

Tolley, R., & Turton, B. J. (1995). *Transport systems, policy and planning: A geographical approach*. Harlow: Longman.

UNEP. (2019). Emissions gap report 2019, *United Nations Environment Programme*. Available from: https://wedocs.unep.org/bitstream/handle/20.500.11822/30797/EGR2019.pdf?sequence=1&isAllowed=y.

US Energy Information Administration. (2019). Energy use for transportation. *Use of Energy Explained*. Available from: https://www.eia.gov/energyexplained/use-of-energy/transportation.php.

USEPA. (2017). Research on near roadway and other near source air pollution. Available from: https://www.epa.gov/air-research/research-near-roadway-and-other-near-source-air-pollution.

USEPA. (2019). *The 2018 EPA Automotive Trends Report: Greenhouse Gas Emissions, Fuel Economy, and Technology since 1975*. Available from: https://nepis.epa.gov/Exe/ZyPDF.cgi/P100W5C2.PDF?Dockey=P100W5C2.PDF.

Vidal, J. (2016). Air pollution rising at an 'alarming rate' in world's cities. Available from: https://www.theguardian.com/environment/2016/may/12/air-pollution-rising-at-an-alarming-rate-in-worlds-cities.

Vokolkova, V. (2008). Road transport and its contribution to global warming with special regards to developing countries. In E. A. Stuhler, & S. Misra (Eds.), *Across Disciplinary boundaries towards a sustainable life: Psychodynamic reflection on human behaviour* (pp. 259–270). Munchen: Rainer Hampp Verlag.

Watts, J. (2019a). Climate and economic risks 'threaten 2008-style systemic collapse'. *The Guardian*. Available from: https://www.theguardian.com/environment/2019/feb/12/climate-and-economic-risks-threaten-2008-style-systemic-collapse.

Watts, J. (2019b). Concrete: The most destructive material on Earth. *The Guardian*. Available from: https://www.theguardian.com/cities/2019/feb/25/concrete-the-most-destructive-material-on-earth.

Wollan, M. (2010). Mapping traffic's toll on wildlife. *The New York Times*. Available from: https://www.biologicaldiversity.org/programs/population_and_sustainability/urban_wildlands/pdfs/NYT_roadkill.pdf.

World Health Organization. (2013). *Health effects of particulate matter*. Available from: http://www.euro.who.int/__data/assets/pdf_file/0006/189051/Health-effects-of-particulate-matter-final-Eng.pdf.

World Health Organization. (2015). Global Health Observatory data. Road Traffic Deaths. Available from: https://www.who.int/gho/road_safety/mortality/en/.

World Health Organization. (2016). Air pollution. Available from: http://www.who.int/airpollution/en/.

Wouters, H., De Ridder, K., Poelmans, L., Willems, P., Brouwers, J., Hosseinzadehtalaei, P., et al. (2017). Heat stress increase under climate change twice as large in cities as in rural areas: A study for a densely populated midlatitude maritime region. *Geophysical Research Letters*, *44*(17), 8997–9007.

Wu, M., & Xu, H. (2018). Consumptive water use in the production of ethanol and petroleum gasoline—2018 update. Available from: https://publications.anl.gov/anlpubs/2019/01/148043.pdf.

Yoder, K. (2019). Is it time to retire 'climate change' for 'climate crisis'? *Grist*. Available from: https://grist.org/article/is-it-time-to-retire-climate-change-for-climate-crisis/.

Zhou, N. (2019). Oxford Dictionaries declares 'climate emergency' the word of 2019. *The Guardian*. Available from: https://www.theguardian.com/environment/2019/nov/21/oxford-dictionaries-declares-climate-emergency-the-word-of-2019.

Chapter 7

Slower, richer, fairer: better economic health in 'slow cities'

'Meet the future; the future mode of transportation for this weary Western world. Now I'm not gonna make a lot of extravagant claims for this little machine. Sure, it'll change your whole life for the better, but that's all'.

Bicycle salesman in the movie *Butch Cassidy and the Sundance Kid,* 1969

Abstract

This chapter examines economic health, rather than human or environmental health. It first examines the impact of slowing city transport on individuals and families and shows that the slow-focussed, low-speed household is a clear winner in, for example, transport costs, housing equity values and medical costs. It then examines the economic health of businesses in the 'slow city', demonstrating that slowing motorised traffic makes shopping environments more attractive, increases footfall and raises spending by shoppers. Moreover, walkable places have higher GDPs and 'slower cities' are more able to attract creative people to fuel their knowledge economies. In terms of governance, the costs of operating a 'slow city' are lower, clearly evident in the reduced expenditure on crash mitigation, parking management, ameliorating traffic congestion, infrastructure provision and other municipal outlays (e.g. policing). All these issues have particular relevance for cities in the Global South, which have the choice between following the pathway to economic health in the 'slower city', or repeating the evolutionary mistakes of cities in more developed countries that have focussed on speed in city transport. In sum, the economic case for 'slow cities' is powerful, for individuals, businesses and cities themselves.

7.1 Introduction

We now turn to the consequences of the 'slower city' in terms of economic, rather than human or environmental health. 'Slowing' the city would necessarily entail people reorganising their lives to prioritise slower travel, and cities would need to re-purpose their streets and spaces to encourage a focus on places where goods and services are accessible by active travel modes. These would be dramatic changes from the status quo, and it is unlikely that they can happen unless there is a powerful economic case. Can the undoubted personal and environmental health benefits of the 'slower city' for individuals and households

Slow Cities. http://dx.doi.org/10.1016/B978-0-12-815316-1.00007-1

be supported by financial gains too? How would businesses fare in terms of access to customers and workforce, and rents, taxes and other costs? Will local governments prosper or struggle when demands on them over land use, housing, public welfare and other critical responsibilities are so different from those in the high-speed focussed city of the past? The following sections cast some light on these and related issues.

7.2 Economic health of individuals and families in the 'slow city'

7.2.1 Introduction

As we do not have fully-fledged 'slower cities' at present, it is not possible to say definitively what the economic consequences of slowing city travel would be for individuals or households. However, one way of estimating the changes would be to compare costs and benefits in different parts of existing metropolitan areas that are served by different levels of active travel. Here we will compare typical costs and benefits in a car-dependent, less walkable and cyclable area—such as a low-density suburb—with those in an area where walking, cycling and public transport use is more feasible, such as inner urban areas or transit-orientated developments. There are a number of categories of potential economic impacts—some more measurable than others—and these will be examined in this section.

7.2.2 Lower transport costs in the 'slow city'

Perhaps the most obvious issue for the economic health of individuals and families is how transport costs affect disposable incomes. Recent estimates are that the average annual cost of running a car in the United States is $10,388, rising to nearly $19,000 in New York City (INRIX, 2017). Rachele, Healy, Sallis, and Sugiyama (2017) have provided four hypothetical scenarios of varying levels of car ownership and differing transport behaviours for the city of Melbourne, Australia. At one extreme is the household that owns two cars and never uses public transport. Using cost estimates from the Australian Automobile Association for things such as servicing, tolls, fuel, insurance and loan repayments, the weekly transport expenditure for this household would be just under A$320—and this excludes a range of other costs such as parking charges and fines. At the other end of the spectrum is the slow-focussed low-speed household that owns no cars, walks and cycles everywhere locally and uses public transport to access the CBD three times a week. The weekly cost for this household is A$24.60, only 7.5 per cent of the two-car household. Even if the number of CBD public transport return trips rises to ten, the weekly saving is still nearly A$240 (Rachele et al., 2017).

Clearly, living in a slowed city where car ownership is less necessary has a major direct beneficial impact on household budgets. There are other indirect benefits too, which will be examined in the following sections.

7.2.3 Lower medical costs in the 'slow city'

The argument has been made in Chapter 5 that 'slowing the city' will bring physical and mental health benefits to individuals who shift towards health nurturing modes such as cycling and walking. By reducing pollution, noise and fear of traffic, and increasing community engagement and social capital, it will bring societal benefits for them, as well as for those who do not shift modes but who will benefit from others' changed behaviour. Moreover, there are less obvious indirect savings too, such as not having to join a gym to maintain fitness that can be acquired incidentally through daily active travel. The consequences may be reduced expenditure on medical consultations, procedures and medicines, reduced workdays lost and more workdays available in a longer working life. There would be additional savings (especially for women) in the form of reduced time spent chauffeuring vulnerable children and caring for elderly relatives who are no longer reluctant to leave their houses because of fear of traffic.

7.2.4 Contrasts in home equity between 'slow' and 'fast' cities

The implication of the consumer cost savings outlined above is that it would be logical for a family to prioritise buying or renting in a walkable/cyclable area, in order to save on transport costs. However, it is not that simple, because housing in such areas tends to be more expensive. Evidence on this matter is plentiful. In 2009 Cortright used Walk Score (a 100 point scale of walkability: see Box 7.1) to show that in a typical metropolitan area in the United States, each Walk Score point increase was associated with a \$700 to \$3,000 increase in home values (Cortright, 2009). Also in the United States, a study of sale prices and Walk Score ratings of over a million home sales across 14 major metro areas found that one Walk Score point increased the price of a home by an average of \$3,250 or 0.9 per cent (Bokhari, 2016). An Australian example shows house prices rising by an average of A\$298 per square metre for every 5-point rise in Walk Score between 60 and 100 in Melbourne (Walker & Lock, 2013). Reducing traffic volumes produces this effect too: when traffic volumes were reduced on residential streets by several hundred vehicles per day, house values increased by 18 per cent (Litman, 1999).

These differences reflect 'the value consumers attach to walkable neighbourhoods, which tend to be denser, mixed use neighbourhoods with good accessibility, including high quality public transport' (Tolley, 2011). However, such neighbourhoods in car-dependent countries are at a premium, and the demand exceeds supply. Many families are thus led into ownership on the urban fringe, where land and housing prices are lower, but as car ownership is necessary, transport costs are higher, as shown in the Melbourne example earlier.

One could argue that households are free to make whatever trade-off they wish between fringe areas with more affordable housing and higher transport costs, and denser neighbourhoods where housing is more expensive and transport

BOX 7.1 What is 'Walk Score'?

Walk Score is a web-based algorithm launched in 2007 that computes the relative walkability of an address on a scale of 1 to 100 by measuring the distance from a specific address to certain neighbourhood amenities, such as schools, restaurants, grocery stores, libraries, parks and coffee shops. Walk Score is part of a family of accessibility measures that include Transit Score and Bike Score, both of which operate in a similar way for these other active travel modes. It uses Google Maps to calculate distances between residential addresses and destinations in 13 amenity categories, and awards points that reflect proximity for each destination: maximum points are awarded if locations are less than a quarter of a mile from the residence and zero points if they are more than a mile away. Walk Scores range from zero (completely car dependent) to 100 (most walkable). Locations that have high Walk Scores are more conducive to walking and to cycling and are also likely to be served well by public transport. Such locations also enable residents to drive less, or shorter distances, if they choose to drive instead of walking.

Walk Score does not show actual walking rates, but instead shows the potential for walking to amenities. However, there are some limitations in its use. For example, it does not differentiate between different destination qualities, such as a supermarket grocery store versus a small corner store. It also does not make adjustments for the ease or comfort of walking, such as the continuity of the sidewalks and the volume or speeds of traffic. Walk Score would see no difference in walks of the same distance between locations:

a. burdened by 3-minute waits to cross wide main roads, compared to

b. where traffic is light and slow, so that the walker can cross immediately by negotiation with drivers.

'What Walk Score can't capture, and doesn't pretend to, is the on-the-ground texture of the pedestrian experience and the resulting pedestrian culture of a place ... A mile in an American suburb is a lot longer than a mile in Rome' (Goodyear, 2012). This leads to a more fundamental issue of interpretation of Walk Scores. 'Walk Score serves as a good proxy for urban design features related to walkability for neighborhoods with Walk Scores above 70 and in high-income areas, but Walk Score tends to overestimate the walkability of high access, low-income communities', primarily because 'Walk Score does not pick up on the poorer quality of the walking experience in these neighborhoods, including lower connectivity, aesthetics, and personal safety' (State of Place, 2016).

Nevertheless, despite its limitations Cortright (2016) contends that 'Walk Score works, it gets used, it has been validated independently, and it has changed real estate markets' and goes so far as to say that 'Walk Score has done more to advance interest in and awareness of walkability than any—and perhaps all—of the academic research on the subject ... What's been missing is the robust, universal and quantitative set of measures that put walking on an equal footing (sorry about the pun) with all of the quantitative measures used to promote auto mobility ... Walk Score helps level the quantitative playing field'.

The Walk Score index is available to anyone on the internet and is widely used in the real estate market. Test it out with your own address at https://www.walkscore.com/about.shtml

is cheaper (and slower). As the combined outlay on housing and transport is the same in both cases at about 45 per cent of household income, it might seem that this is an equitable outcome driven by market forces. However, there are three caveats to this view. First and most obvious are the myriad of deleterious consequences of high-speed suburban sprawled lives that this book is at pains to explore. The family choosing the suburban option will discover, and perhaps regret, that these are unexpected and unintended consequences of what seemed to be a simple geographical choice. Section 5.4.4 has discussed this issue, whereby having sustainable mobility choices and lower energy costs increases a household's ability to respond to unexpected economic shocks. These options are unavailable in sprawled, automobile-dependent areas, a key factor explaining why such districts have significantly higher mortgage foreclosure rates.

Second, there is an inbuilt systematic encouragement to sprawl, as Litman points out. 'Conventional real estate sales practices often highlight that households can obtain better value, they pay less per square foot, with urban fringe housing, and common banking practices, which only consider housing costs and ignore transport costs, tend to favor the urban fringe house' (Litman, 2017, p. 4). The result is the practice described as 'drive until you qualify' whereby purchasers have to drive further and further out from the city centre until house prices fall within their budget.

Third, the long-term equity values yielded by the two choices are very different. As vehicles tend to depreciate quickly in value, and housing tends to appreciate, choosing a 'high car-need but low-housing cost' location will produce very significant long-term equity shortfalls compared to a 'high housing cost/low car-need' location and lifestyle. Litman (2017) shows the differences in equity between the urban fringe and houses in a transit orientated development (TOD) location, using TODs as a surrogate for a walkable neighbourhood. (Transit orientated development brings people, activities, public space and buildings together within easy walking distance from high-quality public transport stations.) 'Due to its higher initial value and greater land value appreciation, after one decade the TOD home gains an additional $63,789 in equity, after 25 years it gains an additional $448,217' (Litman, 2017, p. 8). This could mean that the owners could retire at the age of 65 years, with approximately one million dollars more than the owners of the urban fringe house. Clearly, choosing the 'slow' neighbourhood is not only good for the daily wallet, but highly rewarding for the long-term bank balance too.

7.2.5 Gentrification as a potential disbenefit for economically disadvantaged people in the 'slow city'

In addition to the economic benefits outlined above of living in a slower, more accessible and multi-modal neighbourhood, there are also specific disbenefits that accrue over time to economically disadvantaged households living in sprawled areas. As Ewing, Hamidi, Grace, and Wei (2016, p. 81) point out, the principal issue is poor accessibility, which 'may be a particular problem for certain socioeconomic groups, since low income and low automobile ownership make the distances inherent in sprawl harder to overcome'. Access to employment is a key factor, as Jaffe (2016) summarises: 'there may be jobs available somewhere, but they literally can't get there'. This clearly depresses economic mobility, meaning that individuals are less likely to become economically successful. Indeed, in their US study, Ewing et al. (2016, p. 80) report that upward mobility is significantly higher in compact areas than it is in sprawling metropolitan areas/commuting zones, and that as compactness doubles, the likelihood of upward mobility increases by about 41 per cent.

This is a relevant point when we see the discussion in the literature of existing social tensions arising in many cities where walkable neighbourhoods are the exception, not the norm. Because of the increasing recognition of the benefits of slow travel in such places, they are growing in popularity—but of course, not everyone can live there because of their limited extent. The result is a process of gentrification, where deteriorated—but walkable—urban neighbourhoods are renovated by means of the influx of more affluent residents, perhaps aided by increased investments by developers, businesses and local government. Gentrification can improve the quality of a neighbourhood, but there is a risk that city investment in improving walking and cycling opportunities or public transport access may have unintended consequences of displacement of existing communities unable to afford rising rents and other prices in their existing neighbourhoods.

One example is in Atlanta, Georgia, US where the $4.8 billion BeltLine, a 22-mile mixed-use pedestrian-transit trail, is triggering sharp increases in home values in low-income and largely African-American communities, with median sale prices rising 68 per cent from 2011 to 2015 in some areas (Powers, 2017). One study (Immergluck & Balan, 2018) predicts that the success of the BeltLine could be counterbalanced by some stark negatives for Atlanta as a whole: 'In the long run, without intervention, it will lead to the economic and possibly racial resegregation of the city' (Powers, 2017).

A second controversial example is the High Line, the conversion of an elevated rail line through the meatpacking district of Manhattan, New York City into a linear park in 2009 (Fig. 7.1). Between 2009 and 2016 the sale values of properties near the High Line rose 10 percentage points faster than areas just a few blocks farther away (Barbanel, 2016). In San Francisco, some communities now see development and increased walkability as a precursor of gentrification, which will force them to leave their homes and neighbourhoods when prices inevitably rise (Barros, 2018).

The current trend of active travel opportunities improving in some areas but not others is a zero-sum game, with benefits for wealthy areas, groups and households but deleterious consequences elsewhere. In contrast, the approach recommended in this book is not about slowing some areas and ignoring others. Instead, it is about advocating for slower travel throughout the city, not just

FIGURE 7.1 The High Line, New York City, which has been implicated in rapid gentrification of the meatpacking district of Manhattan. *(Credit: Rodney Tolley)*

in some favoured neighbourhoods. This requires nothing less than treating the entire city with comprehensive strategies from which everyone benefits, such as 30 km/h speeds (or lower) in all non-arterial streets.

7.3 Economic health of businesses in the 'slow city'

7.3.1 Introduction

This section shifts the focus to businesses and their prospects in the 'slower city'. Where will people work and shop? What businesses will prosper, providing what services and what will they pay in taxes, and rent or property prices?

The initial focus in this section will be on retail, but it is important to note at the outset that slowing down travel in town centres and shopping districts can stimulate much more than shopping. Cafés, restaurants, pubs, galleries, museums, cinemas, hairdressers, doctors and dentists, banks, solicitors, estate agents and many more services and businesses will benefit too. Such places are settings for shared experiences, focal points of local identity, community pride, and common heritage and values. They are places where local people meet friends and join in community activities. Slowing the city to retain and enhance these crucial economic and social benefits has a great deal to recommend it, as we explain throughout Section 7.3 below.

7.3.2 Benefits of the 'slow city' for retailers

A considerable amount of evidence has accumulated in the past 30 years on issues of retail spending levels according to mode of access. For example, a survey of weekly spending in London by access mode showed that people walking to town centres spent on average £86 per week, compared to £73 for bus users and £62 for car drivers (Heywood, 2013) (Fig. 7.2). Another UK study has estimated that well-planned improvements to public spaces can boost footfall and trading by up to 40 per cent (Lawlor, 2013). Other surveys, such as those in Europe as a whole, in France and in individual shopping areas such as Yarra in Melbourne have produced similar evidence—that access on foot rather than car contributes disproportionately to the economic health of retail centres (Tolley, 2011). Lee, in the example of Lygon Street in Melbourne, has shown corroborative outcomes for cycling. She demonstrates that the retail spend per hour generated by one parking space allocated to cars is A$27, but if the same space were to be occupied by six bicycles the figure would be A$97.20 (Lee, 2008). 'There are much smaller financial returns that result from the investment in land for car parking compared with bike parking' (Lee & March, 2010, p. 89).

Higher spend by active transport users might at first seem counter-intuitive, but is explained by the phenomenon that although active travel users (especially people on foot) spend less per visit than car drivers, they visit much more frequently as Fig. 7.3 shows, and so cumulatively spend more. The weekly mean frequency for each mode in the London study was: car 1.8, bus 2.7, train/tube 2.3, bicycle 2.6 and walk 3.8 (Heywood, 2013, p. 18). A study in Portland, Oregon, found that 'once trip frequency is accounted for, the average

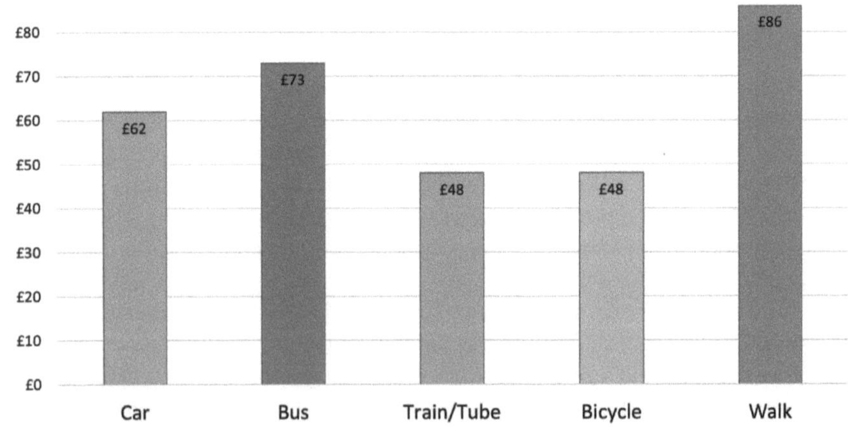

FIGURE 7.2 Weekly spend in London's town centres in 2013 by access mode. *(Source of data: Heywood (2013, p. 57))*

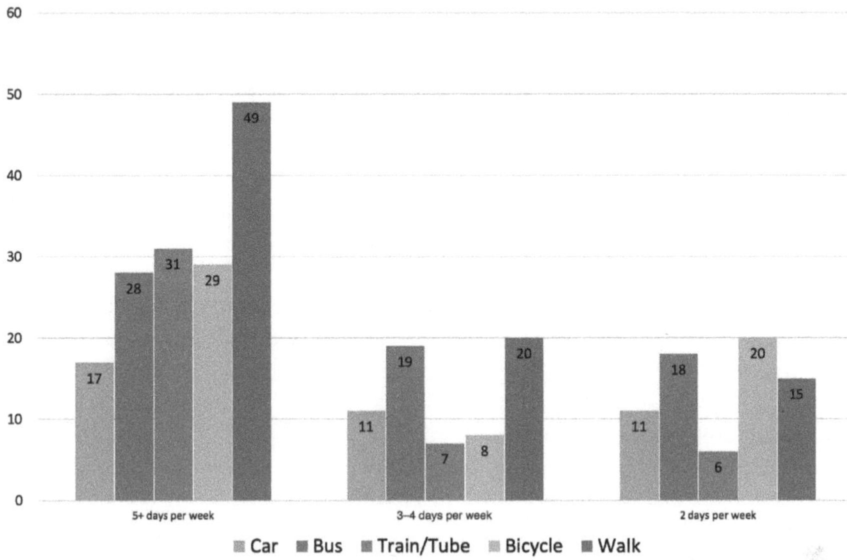

FIGURE 7.3 Frequency of visit to London Town Centres in 2013 by mode of access. *(Source of data: Heywood (2013, p. 17))*

monthly expenditures by customer modes of travel reveal that bicyclists, transit users, and pedestrians are competitive consumers and for all businesses except supermarkets, spend more, on average than those who drive' (Clifton, Muhs, et al., 2013, p. 40). Studies in the Netherlands confirm these findings: people on bicycles spend less per visit to businesses but visit the business more frequently, resulting in higher spending levels over time (Clifton, Currans, et al., 2013).

This is a triple benefit for the shopping area, because not only do active transport users spend more in aggregate, but simply by being there more often—walking around, window-shopping and having a coffee—they also contribute disproportionately to the vibrancy of the town centres and so attract others to visit too. To these two benefits we must add the local multipliers of retail spend. As David Mepham observed, 'if you spend a dollar on Amazon, it's gone. It's a one-way trip. If you spend that dollar on main street it circulates around the local economy' (Victoria Walks, 2019).

However, this evidence has for many years been misinterpreted and dismissed by retailers. The first study to draw attention to this misperception took place in Graz, Austria [Social data (1991) quoted in Sustrans (2003)], where retailers were asked to estimate the proportion of their customers that arrived by various modes. Retailers strongly over-estimated the importance of the car (estimated 58 per cent of arrivals, compared to actual 32 per cent), and conversely under-estimated the importance of walking (25 per cent estimated but 44 per cent actual), bus use (12 per cent to 16 per cent actual) and cycling (5 per cent to

8 per cent actual). Since then, similar results have been found in surveys in cities such as Bristol (UK) (Sustrans, 2002), and for restaurateurs in Brisbane, where car usage was overestimated by up to nearly 300 per cent (Yen et al., 2015). In a similar vein, there are many studies that show retailers' misperceptions of shoppers' concerns, for example in Edinburgh (Sustrans, 2003) and various cities in New Zealand (Turner, Allatt, & Tarjomi, 2011). In every case, the retailers' priority was for more parking, but this was not a priority for shoppers themselves, who put better crossing facilities and a more pleasant environment at the top of their choices.

Retailers in local shopping strips and town centres are under great pressure, struggling to attract and retain footfall in competition with out-of-town shopping and the rapid and devastating emergence of the digital economy. In these circumstances, to resort to 'more of what is familiar' (i.e. more car access) is understandable, fuelled by a number of factors. The paucity of data on active travel perpetuates myths, leading to the perception that there is much less use of these modes than we think. (Box 7.2 provides an encouraging story showing how when retailers gather their own data they discover that removing parking is something that will help their businesses.) There is also lower turnover of kerbside car parking spaces than commonly believed, and the need for kerbside parking spaces for passing trade is less important than claimed, as Turner et al. (2011) have shown. The persistence of these beliefs despite evidence to the contrary lends support to thinking of speed as an addiction, in which denial—the selective ignoring of information—plays an important role.

Disappointingly, there are also many—often anecdotal—stories of retailers disingenuously claiming that the removal of parking space from immediately outside their premises would result in serious loss of trade, when in reality the space is actually used for parking by the owner or staff themselves! (see Fig. 7.4). Cramer (2019) provides a personal anecdote illustrating this situation in Paris. In 2018 he interviewed retailers along Boulevard Jean Jaurés, Clichy, six months after the removal of parallel parking to make way for a bus/bike corridor. In answer to his question: 'Has loss of parallel parking hurt your business' 100 per cent said 'not at all', but one clothing retailer complained that it eliminated HER parking space.

A comparison of main street shopping areas with out of town shopping malls is illuminating. Malls are deliberately designed to maximise the distances that shoppers must walk to buy the goods they want, with anchor stores at the end of the structures and smaller stores arranged between. Shops selling similar goods, such as children's shoes, are kept apart so that comparison-shopping involves walking past many other shops, increasing their exposure. For Rolf Monheim—who has extensively studied pedestrianisation and shopping behaviour—the lesson for retailers is clear: 'Shopping is a collaborative effort … Retailers in main streets need to realise that shopping can only work as a team effort. Walking from shop to shop is a key element of the shopping experience' (Monheim, 2016).

FIGURE 7.4 Fully occupied kerbside parking in Devon Street, the main shopping street in New Plymouth, New Zealand. The photograph was taken at 0745, after the owners had arrived but before the shops have opened to customers. *(Credit: Rodney Tolley)*

BOX 7.2 How to bust myths about kerbside parking

In the absence of data, the myth of the indispensability of car parking will flourish. The experience of Acland Street in the Melbourne suburb of St Kilda has shown that getting the right information and using it imaginatively can go a long way to producing enlightened outcomes. Acland Street is a popular place, with its shops, restaurants, clubs, pubs and famous cake shops. Because of these varied attractions, the narrow footpaths were often overcrowded, undermining the street's attractiveness to visitors and local residents. Parking on both sides of the street, a tram track down the centre and much footpath dining limited options to find more space for people (Fig. 7.5A).

An obvious solution was to widen footpaths at the expense of losing some kerbside parking, but the Port Phillip City Council was well aware that this was likely to result in objections from retailers, based on myths about the value of adjacent parking to their business. Recognising that the success of the street remodelling would at least partly depend on the support of retailers, the Council was anxious to keep them on side from the outset. Accordingly, instead of adopting the common practice of doing their own surveys of the usage of the street and telling the retailers the results, the Council gave retailers a grant to do their own market research study.

The results showed that local residents were responsible for 85 per cent of the spend in the street; that 57 per cent of expenditure was 'walked' and a further

BOX 7.2 How to bust myths about kerbside parking (*Cont.*)

FIGURE 7.5 (A) Acland Street, St Kilda, Melbourne in 2008 before parking reduction. (B) Acland Street in 2009 after the first round of parking reduction. (C and D) Acland Street, car-free plaza with level surface from facade to facade near the tram terminus, 2019. A Walk Score at an address here is 94—a walker's paradise. *(Credit: (A) Rodney Tolley; (B) Rodney Tolley; (C and D) Nick Tranter)*

16 per cent arrived on bikes and trams. Crucially, the survey showed that only 26 per cent of the total expenditure was made by people arriving in cars. As a result of their survey, retailers petitioned for some parking removal, arguably a first for an Australian shopping street!

Subsequently 25 per cent of car parking spots were removed and replaced by widened footpaths (Fig. 7.5B). Emboldened by the success of this process, the Council has in recent years created a new tram terminus in which '"Kerb to kerb" thinking was replaced with a "façade to façade" approach', which integrates the terminus into the streetscape (Baljak, 2017). Through traffic was removed and a car-free plaza created (see Fig. 7.5C and D). Thirty per cent more space for people on foot has been reclaimed and the street has become a focal point for community activity within St Kilda, showcasing local art, culture, performances and pop-up events. It has been described by Baljak (2017) as 'a benchmark for other similar projects across Melbourne'.

The journey from concerns over kerbside parking removal in Acland Street to a thriving public space is not a victory for slow traffic over fast, because congestion meant that traffic in the street was always slow. But the significance in the context of this book is that the 'slow' modes have gained space at the expense of the fast ones, a change that has brought regeneration, economic success and a celebration of public life in public space.

FIGURE 7.6 The negative impact of drive-through shoppers on retail streets often counteracts the extra business they bring. Sidewalk parking obstructing movement for people on foot in Greymouth, New Zealand. *(Credit: Rodney Tolley)*

In such malls, the walking environment has been designed to be safe and unthreatening, with good lighting, smooth floors, seats, security personnel and no motorised traffic danger and noise. There is little perceived disutility to walking in such places: indeed this is why they are used by seniors for 'mall walking clubs' in many cities. On the other hand, in street-based shopping districts, car access produces many disutilities for walking, such as: the barriers of roads, vehicles, traffic and fences; traffic danger, pollution and noise; and parking lots forcing people to walk further. As a Sustrans report commented, 'The negative impact of drive-through shoppers on a busy retail street may be out of all proportion to the extra business they bring' (Sustrans, 2002, p. 5). (Fig. 7.6).

The conclusion for the economic health of shopping districts is clear: slowing down traffic (and reducing the space devoted to it) is essential to make the environment attractive, increase footfall and raise spending by shoppers. We may use the example of sidewalk cafés to illustrate this point. Sidewalk cafés generate street activity and interest: someone walking along a street is there only for a fleeting moment, but when they sit for a coffee or a meal, they may be there for an hour or more. Because of this, Mouzon (2015) has argued that the sidewalk café is the single most powerful tool we can use to enhance people's desire to walk in a place. The sidewalk café is, he says, 'both cause and effect of places we want to walk. It never occurs in unwalkable places, and its chance of

FIGURE 7.7 The sidewalk café is both cause and effect of places where we want to walk, adding vibrancy and in turn attracting more people on foot. Brescia, Italy. *(Credit: Rodney Tolley)*

thriving increases as the place becomes more appealing. Because it is fueled by the appeal it creates, the sidewalk café can be considered the "turbo-charger of walking"'. Mouzon also notes that 'The slower the traffic speed, the easier it is to do a good sidewalk café' (Fig. 7.7).

However, there is not always space to fit in the required tables and chairs and the parking lane constrains opportunities still further. One solution is to create a parklet, which is roadway space formerly used for parking vehicles that has been repurposed as space for people to sit (Figs 7.8 and 7.9). An economic evaluation of parklets in Philadelphia showed that they attracted up to 150 users per day in space normally occupied by just one or two parked cars (University City District, 2015). Sales at adjacent premises were up by an average of 20 per cent, so that a new parklet is likely to pay for itself after just one or two seasons. In New York City, some parklets have increased retail sales by 172 per cent (New York City, 2012) prompting one business owner to comment 'It's pretty good: I like people sitting across from us, watching what we're doing. They see the business. Maybe they don't come in today, but they come tomorrow. They know we're here' (Donohue, 2012).

Parklets are frequently outside cafés where they attract many people who linger on the sidewalk to hang out and chat with parklet users (Fig. 7.8), further enhancing the vitality of the street and creating 'places' where none existed before. In addition, parklets that reallocate road space to people on foot in places where

FIGURE 7.8 Former car parking space now occupied by a parklet outside a café in Oxford Street, Leederville, Western Australia. *(Credit: Rodney Tolley)*

FIGURE 7.9 A parklet in Lima, Peru, expanding an inadequate sidewalk. *(Credit: Carlos Felipe Pardo, Lima 2016-09, https://www.flickr.com/photos/carlosfpardo/47242568251/)*

sidewalks are narrow are valuable additions to walking and lingering space, generating opportunities to rest and increasing street activity and interest (Fig. 7.9).

The aggregate effect of the impacts of walkability on visitor spend in the city is considerable. After a meta-analysis of 70 US studies and a study of 15 walkable shopping areas, Hack (2013) concluded that business concentrations in walkable retail areas are up to three to four times as large as would be justified by the number of local residents within walking range, suggesting that walkable neighbourhoods attract drivers from surrounding areas: a 'place dividend' generated by developing a unique local identity. He also reported that 'there appears to be an unfilled demand for walkable retail uses, even in suburban areas' (Hack, 2013, p.11): the number of urban and suburban residents who express a preference for living within walking range of a diverse shopping area far exceeds the housing available, an observation corroborated by Loh, Leinberger, and Rodriguez (2016) amongst others. There are many examples of walkability-induced increases in retail spend from other parts of the world too, such as the estimate that laneway dining in Melbourne generates A$14-25,000 per square metre per annum, excluding multiplier effects of added employment (City of Melbourne, 2014).

'Slowing' the city by reducing space for vehicles and improving streets for people walking in shopping areas produces the twin effects of pedestrian propulsion (widening walking catchments) and the turbocharger effect (visiting more often and staying longer). The evidence is robust and consistent: a good walking environment is a good shopping environment, for both shoppers and retailers.

7.3.3 Enhanced commercial property values in the 'slow city'

The impact of active travel on residential property values has already been discussed in Section 7.2, and now we examine business and commercial prices and rents. Leinberger and Alfonzo (2012) divided walkability into five ascending categories from 'very poor' to 'very good' and showed that the premiums for a one category increase in Washington DC were plus $9 per square foot for office rents and plus $7 per square foot for retail rents, as well as an 80 per cent increase in retail sales. In London, improving active travel access can raise retail rents by up to 20 per cent (Lawlor, 2013) and in the United States Hack (2013) has shown that rents were up to 54 per cent higher in walkable shopping areas than in areas attracting mainly drive-to patronage. Interestingly, Hack reported a double effect of increasing walkability, whereby the presence of walkable shopping areas increases nearby housing values too.

However, it is important to stress that this is not an argument for increasing rents per se, especially for retail. Indeed, in the United Kingdom for example, recent years have seen increasing unit vacancy rates in traditional, walkable high streets, with retailers reporting on-line shopping reducing turnover and high rents and property taxes increasing costs (Brady, Owen, & Chesters, 2012). Instead, the point is being made here that in market conditions, rising rents reflect increasing demand for walkable shopping experiences and consequent greater retail trade, compared to driveable shopping areas. Higher rents for struggling retailers in the city are not an aim: that rents are diverging in existing cities with a variety of retail environments reflects the emerging demand for walkable shopping experiences, something that can be offered by all shopping districts in the future 'slower city'.

7.3.4 Boosting the knowledge economy through walkability

The knowledge economy is one in which the production, distribution and use of knowledge plays a critical role: understandably, cities all over the world are in competition for this key driver of productivity gains and economic growth. But not all places have the requisite conditions to attract such activities. As long ago as 2003 Peter Newman noted of the knowledge economy, 'This global process requires people to interact creatively "face to face" as well as to be able to use electronic communications and process information. The urban design outcome of such "face to face" requirements is the kind of human qualities expressed in the walkable environments of historic cities. The coffee shops and mixed use, dense urban environments of city centres and inner areas where cars are not dominant, is now becoming an essential component of the new global economy city' (Newman, 2003, p. 48). In short, the knowledge economy cannot function in the sprawled areas that we may call the car city and only thrives in the walking city (and to a degree in the transit city).

One of the consequences is that in the United States, Central Business Districts (CBDs) have now staunched the previous outflow of jobs to the suburbs and have begun attracting new ones instead. An examination of company relocations for the 2010–15 period noted that 'hundreds of companies across the United States are moving to and investing in walkable downtown locations' (Smart Growth America, 2015). The 500 companies studied were of many kinds and sizes, but most remarkable was that their new locations are dramatically more accessible by active travel modes than before. The average Walk Score of companies' previous locations was 51; the average Walk Score of the companies' new locations is 88. Similarly, Transit Scores went from an average of 52 to 79 and Bike Scores went from an average of 66 to 78.

Why is this happening? Amongst the major motivations for these companies to move to walkable locations, an important one was to attract and retain talented workers, whereby being located in a vibrant neighbourhood is considered a crucial selling point. Another factor was to support creative collaboration, with companies choosing locations in 'dynamic, creative, engaging neighborhoods to help inspire their employees and encourage collaboration among co-workers as well as with employees at other companies or in other industries' (Smart Growth America, 2015, p. 3). In many cases they also wished to be closer to customers and business partners, 'streamlining the process for employees who take in-person meetings with clients and partners downtown' (Smart Growth

America, 2015, p. 4). Many interviewees said they sought vibrant, walkable neighbourhoods accessible by a range of transport options, where people want to both live *and* work.

One of the first attempts at quantifying these impacts was in the Melbourne Walking Plan (City of Melbourne, 2014). It discussed the value of business agglomeration—the ability for knowledge intensive businesses to locate close together and interact with each other—and observed how ease of movement on foot was critical to this process. It calculated that reduction of walking connectivity in the CBD by 10 per cent (through adverse phasing of pedestrian crossing signals or sidewalk congestion, for example) would reduce the value of the CBD economy by up to 6.6 per cent, or A$2.1 billion. On the positive side, existing CBD through-block connections (the celebrated Melbourne 'laneways') were estimated to be worth over A$600 million to the economy. Clearly, there is a direct link between the city's economic prosperity and the safety and convenience of the walking experience.

Three years later, studies in the CBD of Auckland (New Zealand) found a strong relationship between higher productivity and connectivity on foot, with a 10 per cent increase in walking connectivity associated with a 5.3 per cent increase in productivity, worth approximately NZ$42 million. The conclusion on this 'creativity through proximity' phenomenon was bold: 'Attractive public spaces and walkable streets create a platform for business and social exchange and support the spread of knowledge' (Rohani & Lawrence, 2017, p. i). It should go without saying, that 'attractive' and 'walkable' in this context are the environments that result from 'slowing the city' (Fig. 7.10).

7.3.5 Summary of business impacts of 'slow cities'

The above sections have highlighted the economic effects on business of more active travel and by extension, slower places. In terms of local economies, there is increasing prosperity through support for local businesses (with residents shopping locally, for example) and a rise in the number of jobs available to potential workers and the pool of workers available to businesses (Levine, Grengs, Shen, & Shen, 2012). The 'slow city' has lower transport costs, and provides agglomeration efficiencies. Additionally, because housing development is more labour-intensive than vehicle and fuel production, employment and business activity rise as expenditure transfers from transport to housing. The same outcome is achieved if there is mode shift from cars to public transport, because operating and running public transport is more labour-intensive than operating a car-dependent system.

The overall impact of slowing city traffic will be positive and widely shared. Litman's (2017, p. 13) conclusions in relation to the benefits of smart growth apply with equal force to slowing the city. He explains: 'real estate and development industries, business organizations, and economic development agencies all have good reasons to encourage households to choose homes located

FIGURE 7.10 Studies in the CBD of Auckland, New Zealand have found a strong correlation between connectivity on foot and higher productivity. Here a Barnes Dance Crossing (where walkers can cross in any direction, including diagonally) in Queen Street improves connections and the walking experience. *(Credit: Rodney Tolley)*

in more accessible, multi-modal neighborhoods where they can spend less of their budget on transportation and more on housing, and support Smart Growth development policies that help create such neighborhoods'.

The aggregate impacts of a full shift to the 'slow city' would be considerable. Loh et al. (2016) reported that the per capita GDP of the three most walkable places in the United States ($62,500) was 52 per cent higher than the three least walkable ($39,700). They commented that 'For perhaps the first time in 60 years, walkable urban places in all 30 of the largest metros in the USA are gaining market share over their drivable suburban competition' and then summarise with a ringing phrase: 'The end of sprawl is in sight' (Loh et al., 2016, p. 4). The 2019 update of the report identified a pent-up demand for new walkable places which, in addition to the growth of existing ones 'would create a new economic foundation for the U.S. economy, one far more resilient than the economic foundation resulting from building drivable suburbs in the mid- to late-20th century' (Loh, Leinberger, & Chafetz, 2019, p. 5).

We can ask what all of this means for the economic resilience of individuals and businesses in the 'slowed city'. We will use the example of one US city, Portland (Oregon) to provide a partial answer. Whilst we should note at the outset that no medium-sized or large US city comes remotely close to the 'slow city' ideal that this book is advocating, Portland has made more progress than most in the right direction. It has a compact development pattern and land use planning policies which facilitate shorter trips and non-car mode choices: residents are twice as likely to use public transport to commute to work and seven times more likely to commute by bicycle than the average metropolitan resident of the United States (Cortright, 2007).

At 20.3 miles (32.7 km) per day, Portlanders drive 20 per cent less on average than other major US metro areas, saving around $1.1billion in aggregate transport costs per year. This so-called 'green dividend' amounts to about 1.5 per cent of all personal income earned in the region and is available to be spent on other things besides transport. 'The $1.1 billion Portlanders don't spend on car travel translates into $800 million that is not leaving the local region' (Cortright, 2007): citizens have $800 million per year to spend on sectors of the economy that have a much larger local multiplier effect. It is therefore not a surprise that Portlanders spend more on enjoying themselves, with above average expenditures on outdoor recreation and the third highest per capita provision of restaurants in the United States.

Finally, we should note that the issues of business benefits and individual attractions of slower movement in Portland are symbiotic, with each supporting the other. As Cortright points out 'the commitment to green policies and the prevalence of green lifestyles has attracted people and business to the region. Over the decade of the 1990s, the number of college-educated 25 to 34 year-olds increased 50 per cent in the Portland metropolitan area—five times faster than in the nation as a whole' (Cortright, 2007). This is the 'creative class' sought by cities across the world to fuel their knowledge economies. This example illustrates how a life of more active travel at the individual level yields not only strong personal benefits, but rich economic dividends for local regions too.

7.4 Governance: the economic health of 'slow cities'

7.4.1 Introduction

Having examined slowing city benefits at the level of households and businesses, we now examine the fiscal and economic impacts on governing and operating the city. An obvious way of appreciating the economic benefits for government in the 'slow' city is to compare nations with different shares of urban trips by foot, bicycle and public transport. In Germany, these modes account for around 40 per cent of all trips, while in the United States they account for only around 10 per cent. This difference is associated with significant economic cost. Bassett, Pucher, Buehler, Thompson, and Crouter (2008) showed that in 2006, per-capita government spending on transport was lower in Germany, by about 25 per cent. Government subsidies for public transport were much lower, accounting, for only 30 per cent of operating budgets, versus almost 70 per cent in the United States. (They also compared the spending on transport of households in Germany and the United States, showing that in 2003 American households spent US$2,712 more each year on transport than German households, and a larger share of their disposable income—19 per cent versus 14 per cent.)

Within Germany, cities with high-mode shares for the 'slow' modes spend even less on transport. Freiburg for example, is one of the world's best examples of slower city transport. Between 1982 and 2007 the share of trips by car in Freiburg fell from 38 per cent to 32 per cent, and this in a period when the mode share for car trips rapidly increased in most other cities throughout the world. 'At the same time, the bike share of trips in Freiburg almost doubled, from 15% to 27%, and public transport's share of trips rose from 11% to 18%' (Buehler & Pucher, 2011, p. 49). These impressive results for slowing city transport are accompanied by savings for the city government: Freiburg requires only 10 per cent of its public transport operating costs to be subsidised (Buehler & Pucher, 2011).

7.4.2 Reduced transport externalities

Introduction

The use of vehicles imposes various public costs and this section will focus on those that fall on municipalities. Much of this discussion will be around externalities, the costs or benefits that affect a party who did not choose to incur those costs or benefits (Buchanan & Stubblebine, 1962). It will comment in particular on how externalities are generated or exacerbated by rising vehicle speeds. It relies heavily on Litman (2016), *Transportation Cost and Benefit Analysis*. Litman has developed and extended this definitive work over a number of years and his analysis incorporates the results of hundreds of specific studies from many countries.

Fig. 7.11 compares the estimated external costs of driving compared to walking. Shifting from driving to walking provides savings averaging 'approximately 25¢ per vehicle-mile reduced, and 50¢ per vehicle-mile reduced under urban-peak conditions' (Litman, 2018, p. 10). Environmental consequences of rising speeds have already been examined in Chapter 6 and so the analysis here will focus on non-environmental costs, in order to indicate the potential reduction in external costs that might result from slowing the city. We discuss the external costs of: crashes, parking, congestion, roadway land and facilities, and barrier effects on active travel users.

Crashes

Many crash costs are borne directly by travellers, such as pain and suffering, lost quality of life, as well as grief and lost companionship to crash victims' family and friends. However, there will be external costs too, and many of these will be paid by government in some form. These include property damage, emergency response services and crash prevention and protection expenditures. Walking and cycling have relatively high crash risks per km, but compared with motorised travel there is reduced risk to other road users and shorter trips. There

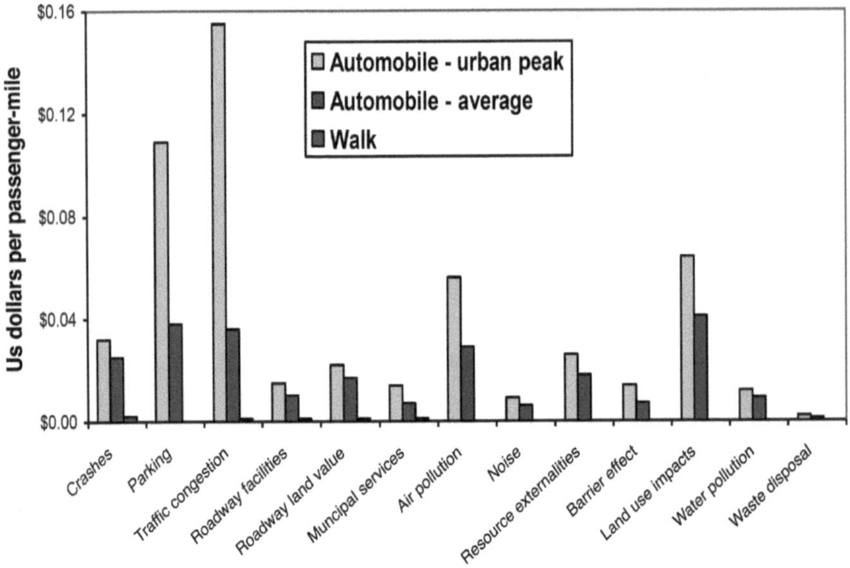

FIGURE 7.11 Estimated external costs of automobile travel and walking (Litman, 2018). *(Reproduced with permission from Todd Litman)*

is evidence that US neighbourhoods with connected street grids and more compact, multi-modal communities have significantly lower per capita fatality rates than car dependent, sprawled districts (Dumbaugh & Rae, 2009). In the 'slower city', where most trips involve active travel, the primary causes of danger (cars travelling at speed) have been largely removed. There would still be trips and falls, and danger from delivery vehicles and public transport, but the system would be much safer, and costs for individuals and society would be extremely low, as Fig. 7.11 indicates.

Parking

Parking costs include parking facility, land, and construction costs, which in the case of car parking spaces in structured garages 'cost more than the cars that occupy them' (Litman, 2016, p. 8). They also include operating costs, such as cleaning, lighting, maintenance, security, snow ploughing, insurance, labour and administration, plus indirect costs such as storm water management. Litman estimates that typical annualised costs per space in 2007 ranged from $765 (suburban on-street) to over $4,000 for a CBD underground parking garage, with bicycle parking 95 per cent cheaper. Of course, people on foot require no parking at all, unless the cost of providing places to sit is included.

Each vehicle requires at least two parking spaces (for the start and end of a trip), but there are often many more than that. A recent survey shows that in the United States 'car storage has become the primary land use in many city areas'

(Scharnhorst, 2018, p. 6). In Des Moines, Iowa, for example there are 18 times as many parking spaces per acre as households—1.6 million parking spaces for about 81,000 homes.

In some cities, parking and fines are important sources of revenue, which administrations are reluctant to forego: for example, Melbourne City Council collected more than A$85 million in parking fines in 2013–14 (Masanauskas, 2014). However Donald Shoup estimates that drivers in the United States park free at the end of 99 per cent of their trips (Shoup, 2018, p. 21). Because of its high cost to the municipality, this represents an enormous public subsidy, skewing travel choices towards high-speed transport and resulting in extra air pollution, higher oil consumption, traffic congestion and sprawl, and it also increases the cost of housing, goods and services. Quoting Mumford (1963), Shoup argues that: 'The right to have access to every building in the city by private motorcar in an age when everyone possesses such a vehicle, is actually the right to destroy the city' (Shoup, 2018, p. 16). In the 'slowed city', there would be an opportunity to reclaim and re-purpose the enormous amounts of space devoted to parking, and to end the public subsidy that encourages ever more car use.

Traffic congestion

Traffic congestion costs—such as incremental delay, vehicle operating costs, pollution emissions and stress—are those imposed on other road users, particularly as traffic volumes approach a road's capacity. Costs are large, (averaging about 13¢ per mile in peak periods in the United States) and frequently measured and discussed, but reducing them is complicated by the way that urban congestion tends to maintain equilibrium, because traffic volumes increase until delays discourage additional trips. Any attempt to expand road capacity generates (induces) traffic attracted by free roadway space and the illusion of higher speeds, until congestion reaches a new equilibrium, with higher levels of external costs.

More active travel will of course reduce these costs. In a tabulation allocating congestion costs by mode, Litman (2016, p. 5.5–25) estimates that bicycles cause only five per cent of the congestion of an average car. Walking causes virtually no congestion costs for vehicle users, but of course there are delays imposed on other walkers at peak times in city centres. For some people walking in a hurry this may seem an annoyance, but for others it simply adds to the vibrancy of the street scene.

Roadway land and facility external costs

These are construction and operating expenses not paid by user fees. Roadway costs include public expenditures to build and maintain roadway facilities, including land, road construction, maintenance and operations. They are affected not only by strength required (e.g. for heavy trucks) but also by design

FIGURE 7.12 Cycling in safety in a local street in Brooklyn, New York City, where many streets now have a 20 mph limit. *(Credit: Paul Tranter)*

specifications, with higher intended speeds requiring wider lanes and more clearance around each lane.

There is a widespread view that these costs are covered by motorists, but this is incorrect. Private motor cars are the most heavily subsidised modes of city transport, particularly in the United States (Delucchi, 2007; Dutzik, Davis, & Baxandall, 2011). For example, Litman (2016) reports that, in 2007, only 51 per cent of US highway expenditures were financed by user fees (fuel taxes, vehicle registration fees and tolls) with the rest coming from general taxation revenue and bonds. Expenditure on active travel facilities is very low by comparison—and indeed most of that is for protection from vehicles (e.g. sidewalks and bike lanes), because where motorised traffic is slight and slow, people walking and cycling simply use the street (see Fig. 7.12). Walking and cycling require relatively little space and cause virtually no pavement wear, so their operating costs are extremely low.

In the European Union motor vehicles are also heavily subsidised. As Gössling, Choi, Dekker, and Metzler (2019, p. 65) explain, in the European Union, 'each kilometer driven by car incurs an external cost of €0.11 [US$ .12], while cycling and walking represent benefits of €0.18 [US$ .2] and €0.37 [US$ .4] per kilometer. Extrapolated to the total number of passenger kilometers driven, cycled or walked in the European Union, the external disbenefit of automobility is about €500 [US$547] billion per year. Due to positive health effects, cycling provides

FIGURE 7.13 Fencing erected to force people to cross at the traffic lights reduces shopping opportunities, encourages higher motorised traffic speeds and detracts from the visual quality of the urban scene. Charlestown, Lake Macquarie, New South Wales, Australia. *(Credit: Rodney Tolley)*

an external benefit worth €24 [US$26] billion per year and walking €66 [US$72] billion per year'. It is clear that cities with a high proportion of trips made by 'slower' modes are also cities where city governments devote a lower percentage of their budget to transport. Kenworthy and Laube (1999) show that the percentage of gross regional product (GRP) devoted to transport in Australian cities was 13.2 per cent compared to only 8.1 per cent in European cities.

Barrier and severance effects on active travel users

The barrier effect refers to delays, discomfort and lack of access that vehicle traffic imposes on people walking and cycling (Fig. 7.13), while severance usually focusses on the impacts of new or wider highways. These impacts are inequitable because they are imposed on people walking and cycling by vehicles travelling at speed, but virtually never the other way around. They also disproportionately impact disadvantaged populations, as these depend more on active modes of movement. The aggregate effect is to reduce accessibility on foot and by bike and to stimulate a modal shift towards cars, which increases external costs still further.

There are many cases where people would like to walk and cycle more, but are discouraged by these barrier effects. Some population groups are particularly affected by high speed traffic on wide roads, such as children (who are less

FIGURE 7.14 Children trying to judge gaps in the traffic while crossing a road in Dhaka, Bangladesh. *(Credit: Sudipta Arka Das, https://www.flickr.com/photos/sudiptadas/16486890923/)*

able to judge crossing gaps) (Fig. 7.14) and people with physical disabilities and the elderly who tend to need more time than is normally allowed at signalised crossings (see Box 8.2). Another obvious example is when school children who want to use active travel to school, are instead chauffeured by their parents due to their concerns for the safety of children crossing busy roads. The economic impact for municipalities in this case would include paying for school crossing guards and enforcing speed limits, amongst other costs.

Summary

It is very clear from Fig. 7.11 that the low-speed mode of walking produces negligible externalities, whereas driving impacts occur in all categories and are sometimes very large. Many externalities have impacts on non-drivers, but in addition all of the ones that have been examined here impose substantial costs on municipal governments, although drivers themselves should have paid them if they were to pay the full cost of their travel. Residents and local businesses are thus burdened with higher local taxes than otherwise would have been the case. Many of these externalities reduce with lower speeds, so the 'slower city' would yield financial benefits irrespective of the amount of modal switching to active travel that would almost certainly take place. It is important to stress that more walking would replace mostly short vehicle trips, which have high costs per vehicle-mile, especially due to high fuel consumption and pollution from cold vehicle engines.

Moreover, as well as reducing costs, there would be an opportunity to increase municipal revenues in the 'slow city'. Households would spend less on transport and—since there is an inverse relationship between money spent on transport and housing—homes would be more valuable and generate higher property taxes. Additionally, since development would be more compact, tax revenues per unit of land would also rise. One study by Public Interest Projects (PIP, 2009) (quoted in Litman, 2017, p. 15) found that 3.4 acres of mixed urban development in Sarasota County, Florida provides the same number of housing units as 30.6 acres of suburban housing, has only 57 per cent of the infrastructure costs, and provides 8.3 times as much tax revenue. Litman (2017, p. 15) summarises: 'Because Smart Growth residents tend to impose lower public service costs and pay more property taxes per capita … municipal governments have good economic reasons to implement policies that support more compact and multi-modal development where residents can spend less on transport and more on housing'. Clearly, there is thus huge potential for local governments to find legitimate cost savings without compromising service quality, by taking steps towards the 'slower city' ideal.

7.5 Pathways to slower cities in the Global South

With lower levels of motorisation, many cities in the Global South already have 'slow city' characteristics, with strong reliance on active travel modes, especially walking. However unfettered growth of car ownership and use is creating cities of extreme inequality in terms of transport access, with negative consequences in terms of delays to people walking and cycling (Fig. 7.15). Pursuit of economic growth often leads to assumptions about motorisation that this book has argued are false: that faster movement is an inevitable accompaniment to economic transition. The danger of course is that such cities will continue to pursue high-speed movement, at just the same time as cities in economically advanced countries are renouncing their addiction to speed and developing sustainable, slow, place-based characteristics.

The question thus arises as to whether Global South cities have to proceed linearly and sequentially through the stages that have typically been followed in wealthier cities. 'Cities in developing countries are faced with a choice of repeating the evolutionary mistakes of many of the cities in more developed countries, or "leapfrogging" car-oriented mobility to directly develop more sustainable and liveable cities' (T-SUM, 2019). The T-SUM project (Transitions to Sustainable Urban Mobility in Sub-Saharan Africa) aims to 'identify the conditions under which pathways to sustainable and inclusive transport and land use development can be accelerated in growing cities in the Global South' (T-SUM, 2019). It has a particular focus on alternative city trajectories, because poorer cities have the opportunity to shape their future mobility patterns as their

FIGURE 7.15 Heavy motorised traffic in Cairo. In these conditions, delays for people on foot are likely to have negative consequences, as a result of disruption to economic exchanges. *(Credit: David Evers, Midan Tahrir, Flickr, https://www.flickr.com/photos/31216636@N00/2889283497)*

wealth increases. The key will be 'the formulation and implementation of policies, practices and partnerships that can support an accelerated implementation of sustainable mobility structures' (T-SUM, 2019). An attempt will be made in the project to answer questions as to what visions will be required; what are the triggers, conditions and success factors for policy evolution; and fundamentally whether it is actually possible for cities in the Global South to by-pass the car-mobility phase and directly achieve equality, safety and economic success in future 'slow cities'. A promising example of what might be achieved can be found in La Paz, Bolivia (see Box 7.3).

BOX 7.3 Encouraging 'slow' transport modes in La Paz, Bolivia.

La Paz provides a case study of how to encourage the slower modes of walking, cycling and public transport (Cramer, 2019). A significant economic issue for low-income residents in La Paz has been the inconvenience of transport, particularly from mountainous sections of the city, which are difficult to reach. Perhaps the most impressive aspects of La Paz's recent transport innovations, are the addition of state-owned teleféricos (cable cars) (see Fig. 7.16), and the new Pumakatari public bus system, both of which are bicycle friendly. Activist bicycle organisations played a partnering role with city authorities in planning these innovations. The first teleférico line dates from 2014, and a further nine lines have been opened. Even though it travels at a low speed, travelling by cable car cuts commute times on average from 1 hour by bus to 10 minutes.

BOX 7.3 Encouraging 'slow' transport modes in La Paz, Bolivia. (*Cont.*)

FIGURE 7.16 Bicycle transport on the teleférico (cable car) in La Paz, Bolivia. *(Credit: Mark Cramer)*

The popular Pumakatari bus system is specifically designed to reach low income areas that are underserved by the privatised bus system, particularly outlying neighbourhoods and those in hilly terrain. When travelling on the Pumakatari buses, both children and seniors are given priority. Aside from the driver, there is a fare-taker, who not only collects fares but intervenes to ask younger or stronger passengers to cede their seat to a senior or child. In addition to making travel easier (or indeed, viable) via public transport, planners have also developed 19 self-sufficient walkable municipal districts that would eliminate the need for a significant proportion of commuting, with hundreds of refurbished, distance-shortening public stairways which are obligatory in the canyon context.

7.6 Conclusion

The aim of this chapter was to shed light on the economic realities of life in the future 'slower city', for families, businesses and the city itself. It set out to ask if this would be an economically beneficial change and if so, by how much and for whom. In this concluding summary, we can now say that the evidence is clear that the benefits for economic health of the 'slower city' are significant, and that these benefits are spread across all of the sectors we examined. Households and individuals will reap rewards from lower transport costs, higher levels of disposable income, greater resilience to economic shocks, lower medical costs, increased accessibility and increased modal choice and of course amenity benefits from greater enjoyment from walking and cycling. Businesses will benefit from more local customers, a more accessible labour force, lower transport and parking costs, less congestion, and increased agglomeration efficiencies. City administrations will find that the many vehicle and municipal externalities that fall on the public purse will be reduced or eliminated, tax yield per unit of land will rise, and agglomeration economies will support city competitiveness. Finally, we must recognise that in a world where over 55 per cent of the population live in urban areas, the slower city will make a very large and essential contribution to reducing the global financial burden of decarbonising transport, which is necessary to prevent climate catastrophe.

Moreover, the health benefits of physical activity are also an important issue for the assessment of the economic benefits of slower city transport. Typically, few of the health disbenefits of driving are included in cost-benefit analyses: if health is examined, the usual focus is on road trauma (injury and deaths), but rarely on the negative health impacts of sedentarism. As sitting is fast becoming 'the new smoking' (Baddeley, Sornalingam, & Cooper, 2016), any economic assessment of the costs of speed should ideally consider lack of physical activity in addition to the individual, business and municipal considerations examined in this chapter.

In sum, the economic health case for 'slow cities' is very powerful indeed. Individuals, businesses and cities themselves will benefit hugely from the boost to individual city attractiveness through enhancing city branding and identity, promoting tourism, encouraging inward investments and attracting the creative class. Because the economic health case for the 'slow city' is strong (just as is the human and the environmental health case), a variety of strategies are needed to achieve a slowing of city transport—and these strategies will be examined in the following chapters.

References

Baddeley, B., Sornalingam, S., & Cooper, M. (2016). Sitting is the new smoking: Where do we stand? *British Journal of General Practice*, *66*(646), 258.

Baljak, M. (2017). Concept to reality: Acland Street's rejuvenation in review. Available from: https://www.urban.com.au/news/concept-to-reality-acland-streets-rejuvenation-in-review.

Barbanel, J. (2016). *The High Line's 'Halo Effect' on Property*. Available from: https://www.mansionglobal.com/articles/the-high-line-s-halo-effect-on-property-36023.

Barros, J.R. (2018). Displacement and gentrification: San Francisco's new vision for SoMa. Available from: http://www.sfexaminer.com/displacement-gentrification-san-franciscos-new-vision-soma/. *San Francisco Examiner*.

Bassett, D. R., Pucher, J., Buehler, R., Thompson, D. L., & Crouter, S. E. (2008). Walking, cycling, and obesity rates in Europe, North America, and Australia. *Journal of Physical Activity and Health*, *5*(6), 795–814.

Bokhari, S. (2016). How much is a point of walk score worth? Available from: https://www.redfin.com/blog/2016/08/how-much-is-a-point-of-walk-score-worth.html.

Brady, B., Owen, J., & Chesters, L. (2012). Rent day spells D-day: The crisis on our high streets. *The Independent*. Available from: https://www.independent.co.uk/news/uk/home-news/rent-day-spells-d-day-the-crisis-on-our-high-streets-7584575.html.

Buchanan, J., & Stubblebine, W. C. (1962). Externality. *Economica*, *29*(116), 371–384.

Buehler, R., & Pucher, J. (2011). Sustainable transport in Freiburg: Lessons from Germany's environmental capital. *International Journal of Sustainable Transportation*, *5*(1), 43–70.

City of Melbourne (2014). *Walking plan 2014-17*. Available from: https://www.melbourne.vic.gov.au/parking-and-transport/streets-and-pedestrians/Pages/walking-plan-2014-17.aspx.

Clifton, K.J., Currans, K.M., Muhs, C.D., Ritter, C., Morrissey, S., & Roughton, C. (2013). *Examining consumer behavior and travel choices*. Paper presented at the 92nd Annual Meeting of the Transportation Research Board, Washington, DC. Available from: https://nacto.org/docs/usdg/consumer_behavior_and_travel_choices_clifton.pdf.

Clifton, K.J., Muhs, C.D., Morrissey, S., Morrissey, T., Currans, K.M., & Ritter, C. (2013). *Examining consumer behavior and travel choices*. Available from: http://dx.doi.org/10.15760/trec.114.

Cortright, J. (2007). *Portland's green dividend: A white paper from CEOs for cities*. Available from: https://www.dropbox.com/s/oxhftrtm3cisjmv/Cortright_Green_Dividend_2007.pdf?dl=0.

Cortright, J. (2009). *Walking the walk: How walkability raises home values in U.S. cities*. Available from: http://blog.walkscore.com/wp-content/uploads/2009/08/WalkingTheWalk_CEOsforCities.pdf.

Cortright, J. (2016). Walk on by: How not to improve walkability measures. *CityCommentary*. Available from: http://cityobservatory.org/walk-this-back-please/.

Cramer, M. (2019). *Old man on a green bike: Chronicles of a self-serving environmentalist*. Greenfield, MA: Wordbound Media.

Delucchi, M. A. (2007). Do motor-vehicle users in the US pay their way? *Transportation Research Part A: Policy and Practice*, *41*(10), 982–1003.

Donohue, P. (2012). Improved New York streetscapes give businesses a boost, mayor's office says. *New York Daily News*. Available from: http://www.nydailynews.com/new-york/-article-1.1190648.

Dumbaugh, E., & Rae, R. (2009). Safe urban form: Revisiting the relationship between community design and traffic safety. *Journal of the American Planning Association*, *75*(3), 309–329.

Dutzik, T., Davis, B., & Baxandall, P. (2011). *Do roads pay for themselves? Setting the record straight on transportation funding*. Available from: http://cdn.publicinterestnetwork.org/assets/28b773b9f18cdb23da3e48a8d7884854/Do-Roads-Pay-for-Themselves_-wUS.pdf.

Ewing, R., Hamidi, S., Grace, J. B., & Wei, Y. D. (2016). Does urban sprawl hold down upward mobility? *Landscape and Urban Planning*, *148*, 80–88.

Goodyear, S. (2012). 'Walk score' is great, but it still doesn't capture 'walk appeal'. *CityLab*. Available from: https://www.citylab.com/transportation/2012/08/walk-score-great-it-still-doesnt-capture-walk-appeal/2858/.

Gössling, S., Choi, A., Dekker, K., & Metzler, D. (2019). The social cost of automobility, cycling and walking in the European Union. *Ecological Economics, 158*, 65–74.

Hack, G. (2013). *Business performance in walkable shopping areas, Active Living Research Technical Report, San Diego, CA*. Available from: https://activelivingresearch.org/sites/default/files/BusinessPerformanceWalkableShoppingAreas_Nov2013.pdf.

Heywood, C. (2013). *Town centres 2013, prepared for Transport for London*. Available from: http://content.tfl.gov.uk/town-centres-report-13.pdf.

Immergluck, D., & Balan, T. (2018). Sustainable for whom? Green urban development, environmental gentrification, and the Atlanta Beltline. *Urban Geography, 39*(4), 546–562.

INRIX. (2017). New INRIX study finds parking is the largest cost of driving. Available from: http://inrix.com/press-releases/cod-us/.

Jaffe, E. (2016). Where sprawl makes it tougher to rise up the social ranks. *City Lab*. Available from: https://www.citylab.com/transportation/2016/01/sprawl-social-mobility-ewing-chetty-krugman/431535/.

Kenworthy, J., & Laube, F. (1999). *An international sourcebook of automobile dependence in cities, 1960-1990*. Colorado: University Press of Colorado.

Lawlor, E. (2013). *The pedestrian pound: The business case for better streets and places*. Available from: https://www.livingstreets.org.uk/media/1391/pedestrianpound_fullreport_web.pdf.

Lee, A. (2008). *What is the economic contribution of cyclists compared to car drivers in inner suburban Melbourne's shopping strips?* (Masters of Urban Planning). University of Melbourne, Melbourne. Available from: http://colabradio.mit.edu/wp-content/uploads/2010/12/Final_Thesis_Alison_Lee.pdf.

Lee, A., & March, A. (2010). Recognising the economic role of bikes: Sharing parking in Lygon Street Carlton. *Australian Planner, 47*(2), 85–93.

Leinberger, C.B., & Alfonzo, M. (2012). *Walk this way: The economic promise of walkable places in metropolitan Washington, DC*. Available from: https://www.brookings.edu/wp-content/uploads/2016/06/25-walkable-places-leinberger.pdf.

Levine, J., Grengs, J., Shen, Q., & Shen, Q. (2012). Does accessibility require density or speed? A comparison of fast versus close in getting where you want to go in US metropolitan regions. *Journal of the American Planning Association, 78*(2), 157–172.

Litman, T. (1999). *Traffic calming benefits, costs and equity impacts*. Available from: http://www.vtpi.org/calming.pdf.

Litman, T. (2016). *Transportation cost and benefit analysis techniques, estimates and implications*. Available from: http://www.vtpi.org/tca/.

Litman, T. (2017). *Selling smart growth: communicating the direct benefits of more accessible, multi-modal locations to households*. Available from: http://www.vtpi.org/ssg.pdf.

Litman, T. (2018). *Economic value of walkability*. Available from: http://www.vtpi.org/walkability.pdf.

Loh, T.H., Leinberger, C.B., & Rodriguez, M., P. (2016). *Foot traffic ahead: ranking walkable urbanism in America's largest metros*. Available from: https://www.smartgrowthamerica.org/app/legacy/documents/foot-traffic-ahead-2016.pdf.

Loh, T. H., Leinberger, C. B., & Chafetz, J. (2019). *Foot traffic ahead: Ranking walkable urbanism in America's largest metros*. Available from: https://smartgrowthamerica.org/resources/foot-traffic-ahead-2019/.

Masanauskas, J. (2014). Councils rake in $200m in parking fines over 12 months. Available from: https://www.heraldsun.com.au/news/victoria/councils-rake-in-200m-in-parking-fines-over-12-months/news-story/109fe9a8ca2f41be9420201907c6e343.

Monheim, R. (2016). *Presentation to the Walk the City International Conference, Stavanger, Norway, 26th October.*

Mouzon, S. (2015). Sidewalk cafes - silver bullets of walkable places. Available from: http://www.originalgreen.org/blog/2015/sidewalk-cafes---silver.html.

Mumford, L. (1963). *The highway and the city*. New York: Harcourt, Brace and World.

New York City. (2012). *Measuring the street: New metrics for 21st Century streets*. Available from: http://www.nyc.gov/html/dot/downloads/pdf/2012-10-measuring-the-street.pdf.

Newman, P. (2003). Walking in a historical, international and contemporary context. In R. Tolley (Ed.), *Sustainable trasnport: Planning for walking and cycling in urban environments* (pp. 48–58). Cambridge: Woodhead Publishing Limited.

PIP. (2009). *Smart growth: Making the financial case*. Available from: https://app.box.com/s/o4a47iy5th.

Powers, B. (2017). *Putting the brakes on runaway gentrification in Atlanta*. Available from: https://www.citylab.com/equity/2017/11/putting-the-brakes-on-runaway-gentrification-in-atlanta/545555/.

Rachele, J., Healy, A., Sallis, J.F., & Sugiyama, T. (2017). Designing suburbs to cut car use closes gaps in health and wealth. *The Conversation*. Available from: https://theconversation.com/designing-suburbs-to-cut-car-use-closes-gaps-in-health-and-wealth-83961.

Rohani, M., & Lawrence, G. (2017). *The relationship between pedestrian connectivity and economic productivity in Auckland's city centre, Auckland Council technical report, TR2017/007*. Available from: https://static1.squarespace.com/static/58e441d2f7e0abde3be51110/t/5a559d50085229d58dfed85b/1515560335402/TR2017-007-2-Pedestrian-connectivity-economic-productivity-Auckland-city-centre-scenarios.pdf.

Scharnhorst, E. (2018). *Quantified parking: Comprehensive parking inventories for five U.S. cities, Research Institute for Housing America Special Report*. Available from: https://www.mba.org/Documents/18806_Research_RIHA_Parking_Report%20(1).pdf.

Shoup, D. C. (2018). Truth in transportation planning. In D. Shoup (Ed.), *Parking and the city*. New York: Routledge.

Smart Growth America (2015). *Core values: Why American companies are moving downtown*. Available from: http://old.smartgrowthamerica.org/documents/core-values.pdf.

State of Place. (2016). Does walk score walk the walk? Available from: http://www.stateofplace.co/our-blog/2016/10/does-walk-score-walk-the-walk.

Sustrans. (2002). *Shoppers and how they travel, liveable neighbourhoods information note LN02*. Available from: http://www.tut.fi/vernc/aineisto/Shoppers-and-how-they-travel.pdf.

Sustrans. (2003). *Traffic restraint and retail vitality, Information Sheet FF39*. Available from: http://cidadanialxmob.tripod.com/trafficrestraint.pdf.

T-SUM. (2019). Transitions to sustainable urban mobility in sub-Saharan Africa. Available from: https://www.t-sum.org/.

Tolley, R. (2011). *Good for busine$$ - the benefits of making streets more walking and cycling friendly, Heart Foundation South Australia*. Available from: https://www.heartfoundation.org.au/images/uploads/publications/Good-for-business.pdf.

Turner, S., Allatt, T., & Tarjomi, L. (2011). *What shoppers want - the reallocation of road space*. Paper presented at the Asia Pacific Cycle Congress, Brisbane, 19–21 September.

University City District. (2015). *The case for parklets: measuring the impact on sidewalk vitality and neighborhood businesses*. Available from: https://issuu.com/universitycity/docs/the_case_for_parklets_2015?e=4547788/11667837.

Victoria Walks (2019). Smart urban futures conference wrap. Available from: http://www.victoriawalks.org.au/news/1650.

Walker, J., & Lock, O. (2013). *Wonderful walkability*. Available from: http://secretagent.com.au/wp-content/uploads/2013/08/The-Secret-Agent-Report-August-2013-Wonderful-Walkability.pdf.

Yen, B.T., Burke, M., Tseng, W., Ghafoor, M., Mulley, C., & Moutou, C. (2015). *Do restaurant precincts need more parking? Differences in business perceptions and customer travel behaviour in Brisbane, Queensland, Australia*. Paper presented at the Australasian Transport Research Forum (ATRF), 37th, 2015, Sydney, New South Wales, Australia.

Part III

Strategies

Chapter 8

Hit the brakes: slowing existing motorised traffic

'... much of what is wrong with our current transportation arrangements in cities could be greatly alleviated if we can find ways just to slow down'.

Eric Britton, 2011

Abstract

This chapter explains the importance of reducing the speed of motorised traffic as an alternative to policies that have sought to adapt the city and its citizens to speed. The chapter examines various approaches to reducing speed, including posted speed limits of 30 km/h (or 20 mph) or lower (either alone or in combination with other measures), and physical traffic calming involving changes to street widths, alignments and vertical profiles. An alternative to physical traffic calming is psychological traffic calming, which involves using non-physical cues to encourage drivers to slow down. The concept of 'self-explaining roads', in which the road design tells the story of how drivers should behave, is outlined. The chapter also examines holistic approaches to reducing danger, such as Vision Zero, which has an aim of zero deaths through road crashes. Finally, we consider the safety implications of the potential implementation of autonomous vehicles and emphasise again, that whether the vehicle has a driver or not, the critical issue for active travel users is to slow motorised vehicles down.

8.1 Introduction

Previous chapters demonstrated the futility of policies, developed over the last 100 years, designed to increase the speed of city transport. These policies left a damaging legacy of road deaths and injury, growing health costs associated with physical inactivity and pollution, unsustainable demands on energy, continually growing requirements for infrastructure, and a significant contribution to the global climate emergency. Slowing city transport helps to alleviate all these damaging effects of current transport systems. Our focus now shifts to potential solutions to our collective addiction to high-speed cities.

The three chapters in this third part of the book (Chapters 8, 9 and 10) explain the range of strategies that can be (and have been) employed to slow city transport. We recognise that every city has unique challenges and consequently each

Slow Cities. http://dx.doi.org/10.1016/B978-0-12-815316-1.00008-3

city needs to find its own combination of strategies to slow the city. These three chapters provide evidence about the tools and practices that exist already, as well as observations about emerging opportunities and challenges for city transport (e.g. autonomous vehicles and micromobility modes such as electric scooters). Chapter 9 examines the role of planning for future 'slow cities'. This includes changing land uses, reducing road and parking space, reducing motorised traffic volumes, and changing densities and zoning. Chapter 10 addresses the broader behavioural and cultural changes that are required, which is a more challenging task. Recognising the need for a change in planning and in culture in the longer term, there is first a need to slow the existing motorised traffic—and it is to this issue that we now turn in this chapter.

Reducing the speed of motorised traffic is arguably the most effective road-safety strategy available to policy makers. Yet, whilst there is widespread consensus that lowering motorised traffic speed is effective in reducing the frequency and severity of road crashes (Aarts & Schagen, 2006), there is less agreement on the most effective ways to achieve this. In this chapter we review several approaches to reducing speed, each of which has advantages and limitations.

8.2 What interventions?

Without doubt, lower speeds produce safer streets for car occupants, but especially for vulnerable road users. Several approaches have been employed to achieve lower motorised traffic speeds, the simplest of which is to lower the posted speed limit (PSL), which can be cost-effective over large areas. Physical traffic calming is another type of intervention, and this may sometimes be applied in combination with lower PSLs, as in Britain's 'low speed zones'. Speed limits may be 30 km/h or even 20 km/h or less, as in the Dutch woonerven or British home zones (see Section 8.7). An alternative approach, which provides a temporary respite from speed, involves closing particular streets to cars for certain periods. Examples of this approach include play streets and school streets. A different approach again is to calm streets using psychological cues to change the perception of streets in a way that leads to reduced speeds. In all speed reduction schemes, compliance is increased if the road is designed in such a way as to 'tell the story' to users to guide their behaviour—and this is discussed under the heading of 'self-explaining roads'. Transformational systems-based approaches under the name Vision Zero are explained and evaluated, followed by a discussion of some of the many imponderables related to safety for active travel users in future cities potentially dominated by autonomous vehicles.

8.3 Lower posted speed limits

The United Kingdom Stage Carriage Act 1832 first introduced the offence of endangering the safety of a passenger or person by 'furious driving' (Willett, 1964). The first numeric speed limit of 10 mph was created in the

United Kingdom in 1861, and was lifted to 20 mph in 1903, and then to 30 mph on built-up roads in 1935 (Box & Bayliss, 2012). Now in most countries speed limits set the maximum speed at which road vehicles may legally travel on particular stretches of road. This limit is often set at the 85th percentile operating speed, that is the speed that no more than 15 per cent of traffic is exceeding. In cities, this is commonly 20, 30 or 40 mph, (or 30, 50 or 70 km/h) depending on the road hierarchy and the road environment, though frequently actual speeds are limited by traffic congestion, traffic light phasing and junction capacity.

Speed limit reductions are now the standard recommendation of road safety researchers and practitioners, and implementation is commonplace throughout the world. The accepted view is that speeds of 50 or 60 km/h (31–37 mph) are not appropriate in residential streets, considering the speed differential between motor vehicles and children playing and people walking, cycling or crossing the street (Islam, El-Basyouny, & Ibrahim, 2014). Setting speed limits below 50 km/h is strongly supported by safety agencies. The World Health Organisation reports that excessive or inappropriate speed contributes to one in three of the 1.35 million road crash fatalities on the world's roads. 'Measures to address speed prevent road traffic deaths and injuries, make populations healthier, and cities more sustainable' (World Health Organization, 2017).

How effective are these interventions? Studies 'consistently show that crash incidence or crash severity decline whenever speed limits have been reduced' (Oxley, Corben, Fildes, O'Hare, & Rothengatter, 2004, p. 57). For example, in France, when the basic speed limit was reduced from 60 to 50 km/h in November 1990, this produced significant safety benefits. Even though actual speeds decreased only slightly (by 2–5 km/h), for the entire nation, injury crashes in urban areas fell by 14.5 per cent from the two years before the speed reduction to the two years after, while in rural areas, where speed limits were unchanged, the decrease was only nine per cent (Leaf & Preusser, 1999, p. 18).

Good practice, according to WHO, is 'implementing an urban speed limit of 50 km/h or less and allowing local authorities to reduce these limits further on roads around schools, residences and businesses' (World Health Organization, 2017). A growing number of cities, particularly in Germany, the Netherlands, Denmark and Britain are doing just this, with speed limits of 30 km/h introduced across large areas. As early as 1976, the Danish government introduced legislation requiring local governments to reduce speeds to 30 km/h and to develop infrastructure to encourage walking and cycling. Denmark now has much lower casualty rates than the United Kingdom (Whitzman et al., 2010, p. 108). However, lowering speed limits to 30 km/h can trigger opposition from community groups, at least when first proposed. This was so in Graz, Austria, which was the first city to introduce lower speed limits across an entire urban area.

In 1992, experimental city-wide 30 km/h speed limits were applied to all streets in Graz except some priority roads, where the limit was 50 km/h. When they were first proposed, most citizens opposed the lower limits. 'Using the

FIGURE 8.1 Bicycle parking in Keplerstraße, a street in Graz, Austria, where 30 km/h speeds have boosted the numbers of people cycling. *(Credit: thisisbossi Flickr, https://www.flickr.com/photos/thisisbossi/2933422496)*

argument that people could not effectively judge a situation that they had not experienced, the government introduced the lower speed limits despite low-public approval' (Tranter, 2018, pp. 232–233). Within 18 months of their introduction there was majority support for the 30 km/h limits, including even from private car drivers (Leaf & Preusser, 1999) who appreciated the increased liveability of the city and were reported to be showing greater consideration to one another on 30 km/h streets. The lower-traffic speeds made streets safer and more convenient for people on bicycles (Hoenig, 2000) (Fig. 8.1). The reduced speed limits were combined with signs and roadway markings, extensive public information and awareness campaigns and enforcement. The limits were made permanent in 1994 and resulted in a 12 per cent reduction of crashes causing minor injury, a 24 per cent reduction in serious injury crashes, a 17 per cent fall in pedestrian injuries and a strong increase in cycling from the year before the change to the year after (Hoenig, 2000; Leaf & Preusser, 1999).

The story of lower speed limits in Graz shows how community attitudes to speed can change when people are given the experience of living in low-speed environments. It also shows the importance of strong leadership, when politicians demonstrate the courage to implement new ideas. The Graz example shows that while new visions may not start with widespread support, if politicians are willing to implement ideas to slow the city, then majority support may soon follow.

We now see a growing acceptance of lower speed limits across the world (Islam et al., 2014) and a notable spread of area-wide and even city-wide 20 mph/30 km/h limits. For example, 13 million people live in default 20 mph zones in the United Kingdom, which are publicised using the slogan '20's Plenty for Us'; 38 per cent of the Swiss population live in 30 km/h zones; and Spain's new general road law envisages 30 km/h limits on most city streets (European Transport Safety Council, 2015). As far as particular cities are concerned, Edinburgh's 20 mph zones cover 80 per cent of the city's streets; Paris has announced plans for lower speed zones across the whole city; and in the United States, Boston and Seattle are developing lower speed zones and Portland had a default 20 mph speed limit on 70 per cent of its street mileage by 2018.

8.4 Speed enforcement measures and techniques

Despite these positive outcomes from lower PSLs, many drivers ignore these limits. In 2012 it was reported that in the United Kingdom, 30 per cent of drivers did not comply with speed limits; and that in Europe, between 2009 and 2012, 20 per cent of drivers were fined for speeding (Box & Bayliss, 2012). As a result, police enforcement is being increasingly supplemented by automated speed enforcement ('safety cameras'), which can lead to long-term benefits, reducing crashes between eight per cent and 49 per cent in one US study (Ferrier, 2017). Enforcement is more effective when linked to extensive publicity (Box & Bayliss, 2012).

The technology to enforce speed limits is constantly evolving, such as using 'average speed cameras' around a low-speed zone, but one has to be careful that the impression is not given that limits are only enforced in such zones and that drivers can speed elsewhere with impunity. Speed-limiting devices are also now available to fit to vehicles and these could be activated by roadside responders. However, whilst such technology is available, political will is the problem; such measures, in isolation, can generate considerable opposition. As Box and Bayliss (2012, p. 36) observe, 'It is vitally important that any implementation of automatic enforcement includes adequate provision of information to the media, interest groups and the public'.

8.5 Physical traffic calming

Many cities across the world have implemented various design interventions such as changes to street widths, alignments, and vertical profiles. These changes are intended to lower travel speeds, reduce environmental and safety problems, alter driver behaviour and improve conditions for slower and more vulnerable road users. These are commonly applied to entire residential neighbourhoods as area-wide traffic-calming schemes, sometimes together with a clear road hierarchy to direct through traffic away from residential streets and with selected road closures to through traffic.

Research on the impacts of area-wide traffic calming has consistently shown effective reductions in injury accidents (Elvik, 2001). In Britain, 20 mph low-speed zones led to significant decreases in casualties (Grundy et al., 2009; Jones & Brunt, 2017). These zones reduced traffic speed and volume leading to a 40 per cent reduction in casualties and collisions from 1986 to 2006 (Grundy et al., 2009). There was no increase in casualties in adjacent areas. The reduction in casualties was highest for younger children (48.5 per cent) (Grundy et al., 2009). These findings are also reflected in other studies (Ameratunga, 2009) demonstrating that 'twenty mile per hour zones and limits are effective means of improving public health via reduced accidents and injuries' (Cairns, Warren, Garthwaite, Greig, & Bambra, 2014).

The Netherlands has been a leader in Europe in traffic calming since the 1970s, and now has over 75 per cent of its urban roads traffic-calmed at 30 km/h or less (SWOV Institute for Road Safety Research, 2017), and as Buehler, Pucher, Gerike, and Götschi (2017) note, traffic calming has spread to many other cities in Europe as well: for example, 85 per cent of streets in Munich are calmed, 78 per cent in Berlin, 75 per cent in Vienna, 50 per cent in Zurich and 50 per cent in Hamburg. All these cities have plans to traffic-calm almost all residential streets in future years.

In many cities in the Global South, whilst traffic calming has not been implemented on the scale it has in European cities, there are increasing efforts by city governments and global road safety non-profit organisations to calm traffic. A notable example is the 'School Areas Road Safety Assessments and Improvements (SARSAI) program' in Tanzania, run by the charitable not-for-profit organisation, *Amend* (Galvin & Maassen, 2019). This focusses on schools with high rates of student injuries, aiming to improve safety in corridors between the schools and children's homes. *Amend* works with local authorities to install speed bumps and other traffic calming measures, and sometimes new entrances to schools to reduce traffic danger. These strategies typically cost only US$25,000 per school, and are already having a positive impact in cities such as Dar es Salaam, Tanzania, where danger from motor vehicles is linked with high-injury rates for people walking and cycling (Fig. 8.2).

8.6 Lower speed limits alone compared with a combination of signs and calming

It is useful to discuss the relative merits of limiting speeds through signs alone, compared with signs used in combination with physical traffic calming. If 20 mph limits replace 30 mph limits, reductions of around two mph or less can be expected (Calvert, 2015; Islam et al., 2014). In contrast, the introduction of 'low speed zones' (lower-speed limits accompanied by physical changes to streets such as speed humps and chicanes) could lead to reductions in speed as large as 10 mph (Mackie, 1998).

FIGURE 8.2 Though limited in extent, some traffic calming exists in Dar es Salaam, Tanzania, and more is being introduced with the support of organisations such as *Amend*. Here a speed table near Mkwajuni Bus Rapid Transit station improves safety for children and adults. *(Credit: Carlos Felipe Pardo, Dar es Salaam 201806, https://www.flickr.com/photos/carlosfpardo/41191913210)*

When applied at an area-wide level, lower-speed limits are much cheaper to implement than physical traffic calming, so that even if they are less effective than low-speed zones in particular streets, lower PSLs can be cost-effective overall. King and Semlyen (2016) estimate that each one mph reduction in average speed leads to five per cent to six per cent fewer casualties, and that a fall of one to two mph over a whole network leads to 'much more benefit to more residents than a large reduction on a few streets in a zone' (King & Semlyen, 2016, p. 66). These arguments are supported by Richter, Berman, Friedman, and Ben-David (2006, p. 140) who observe that 'it is a fundamental principle of epidemiology that small reductions in risk in the entire population save more lives than do big reductions in risk in the small number of high-risk individuals'.

Consistent application of speed limits over large areas 'conveys the message that 20 mph is a suitable, normal speed in residential areas' (Calvert, 2015), whereas isolated physically calmed zones can imply that drivers should speed up as they exit the zones (King & Semlyen, 2016). Therefore to effectively employ lower-speed limits, it is important that 20 mph limits are seen 'as the new norm for urban areas' (Toy, Tapp, Musselwhite, & Davis, 2014, p. 165). Moreover Atkins Limited, AECOM, and Maher (2018) observed that driving speeds in 20 mph areas in the United Kingdom are influenced more by the 'look and feel of the road' than the posted speed limits. Their research

TABLE 8.1 Advantages of calming residential areas.

Less cut-through driving in side streets	More social use of the street by adults
Fewer crashes	More play use of the street by children
Less severe crashes	Safer routes to school
More protection for the elderly and disabled	Greater safety and mobility for women
Better facilities for people walking	Less anxiety
Less air and noise pollution	Greater equality between street users
Less contribution to global heating	Enhanced community spirit
Safer cycling	More attractive residential environment
A healthier population	Safety for children

(Adapted from Tolley, 1990, p. 126)

noted the need for higher levels of police enforcement, combined with more effective community consultation and education: 'the most effective schemes are likely to be those which are based on a broad integrated policy agenda (involving health, environment, urban planning, emergency services, education, community representatives, etc.)' (Atkins Limited, AECOM, & Maher, 2018, p. 198).

Implementing physical design changes (rather than simply reducing PSLs) would bring aesthetic and other benefits to the street. We need to remember that 'traffic calming has wider objectives than road safety alone, so that if residential area calming is to be successful attention must be paid to issues other than just road safety' (Tolley, 1990, p. 127). For example, Table 8.1 lists advantages of calming residential areas, only some of which would be achieved by speed limits and enforcement alone. It is important to stress that modern traffic calming is much more subtle and attractive than the original approach of simply installing speed bumps.

8.7 The woonerf and the home zone

The woonerf (plural woonerven) represents a unique type of physical traffic calming. Tolley (1990, p. 19) has discussed how in the 1970s, a new residential street layout emerged in the Dutch city of Delft, incorporating what was (at the time) a 'startling and revolutionary notion that in residential areas traffic and people ... should be integrated. Cars should not be banned but instead should be admitted on the residents' terms – that is, slowly and without superior rights ... Playing, walking, recreation and social events would be restored to their historical position as focal points of street life'. Such a 'living yard' or 'woonerf'

FIGURE 8.3 A woonerf in Malmo, Sweden. *(Credit: La Citta Vita, https://flickr.com/photos/la-citta-vita/4749149701)*

could be facilitated by the construction of a new residential environment, with the street rebuilt without sidewalks and used for both motorised and foot traffic, with space shared, and users mingling. All users have equal rights, though 'the pedestrian is a bit more equal than the others' (Grotenhuis, 1979) quoted in Tolley (1990, p. 19).

In the woonerf, in order to reduce speeds to no more than 20 km/h, the distinction between space for vehicles and people on foot and bicycle was removed. This was augmented by the installation of combinations of infrastructural measures, such as chicanes, ramps, gateways, pinch-points, garden beds and textured paving (Fig. 8.3). Similar interventions can now be seen in many countries including Denmark, Britain, Japan, Australia, New Zealand and Israel. In Denmark, the significance of 15 km/h streets for children's play is indicated in their name: 'Rest and Play' streets (Karndacharuk, Wilson, & Dunn, 2014). Britain's 'home zones' are similar, often embellished with tree planting, better lighting, textured surfaces and symbolic gateway entrances (Whitzman et al., 2010).

Studies of such streets in several nations have found considerable reductions in traffic accidents (Ben-Joseph, 1995), but they have drawbacks. 'Woonerven were almost totally successful in reducing the speed and dominance of the automobile, but they were, in view of the need to completely rebuild the street, very expensive' (Tolley & Turton, 1995, p. 220). As King and Semlyen (2016) pointed out, the cost of physical traffic calming is about £60,000 per km compared to £1,100 per km for speed limits alone. For the cost of one km of physical calming, 50 km of roads could have 20 mph limits. For this cost, physical traffic calming might make the roads safer for about 250 people, compared to around 12,500 people with 20 mph limits only. In these circumstances, it is not surprising that 'The woonerf, though without doubt a valuable contribution to safe living areas, has not proved to be a universal solution' (Tolley, 1990, p. 26).

On the other hand, new residential developments designed with woonerf concepts in mind have advantages over traditional layouts, in that less space is allocated to streets, thus reducing costs, allowing density increases without compromising privacy and allowing for more green space. Moreover, though the woonerf was a specific residential area treatment originally, its traffic calming elements have since been successfully applied in many different low-volume street environments around the world.

8.8 Play streets and school streets

Whilst home zones and woonerven restrict motor vehicles to very low speeds at all times, another approach restricts their access temporarily. In play streets and school streets, rather than reducing the speed of motorised traffic, traffic is restricted at certain times. Play streets serve to formalise the long-standing practice of children using their residential streets for play (Tranter, 2016).

The use of officially sanctioned 'play streets' to provide for children's play first appeared over 100 years ago (Fig. 8.4). In New York City, in the 1920s, around 60 streets were closed to motorised traffic during limited hours to provide a place for children to play, an idea that was regarded as necessary for the 'rights of play and child welfare' (Gaster, 1992, p. 41). Britain enacted play street legislation in 1938, and in the 1950s there were 700 play streets in Wales and England. Whilst play streets lost favour by the 1980s, they experienced a resurgence from 2008. Play streets in the United Kingdom are now actively supported by the organisation 'London Play' (Fig. 8.5). Many parents appreciate the considerable benefits of play streets, which can be seen as 'A little bit inconvenient for motorists, but a very small price for kids to be able to come out and play' (Gilbert, 2014). In the USA, New York City now has its own 'play streets' programme, which aims to provide a low-cost way to create active play space for children. Similar schemes are now being developed in other nations, including Australia, New Zealand, Germany and Belgium.

Whilst play streets may help challenge the dominant culture of speed in city streets, there is a risk that restricting children's play to certain times reinforces a view that children playing on streets is something that should only be permitted under very specific and regimented conditions. In truly child-friendly,

FIGURE 8.4 Children playing stickball in a play street in New York City in 1916. *(Credit: NYPD Collection, NYC Municipal Archives. https://www.archives.nyc/blog/2018/6/21/summer-in-the-city)*

FIGURE 8.5 Children lining up for a bicycle race in a play street in Kynaston Road, in the London Borough of Enfield. *(Credit: Kate Faxen, via London Play)*

'slow cities', residential streets would be seen as places where children and adults could legitimately and safely play, walk, cycle or socialise at any time. The children's advocacy organisation 'Playing Out' understands this critique, yet argues:

> *'We are aware that the current model is not the long-term answer ... but until a real culture of playing out is restored it is good to feel that there is a way to realize some of the benefits of street play right now' (Playing Out, 2014).*

Tim Gill, a prominent advocate for child-friendly environments, sees resident-led play streets as 'the most promising child-friendly idea to have emerged in the last 20 years' (Gill, 2017). Gill accepts that play streets are not a silver bullet, and that other strategies are needed to create child-friendly cities, including smarter ways to tame traffic. Yet he argues that play streets are affordable, sustainable and applicable in a wide range of areas, and they have a hugely beneficial impact on children as well as the wider community.

Play streets can be of profound importance for slowing city transport. They show 'people how their lives would be improved if their neighbourhoods were less car-dominated' (Gill, 2017). That play streets can change the attitudes and behaviours of residents is indicated in comments made in a survey by Playing Out (2017), of people directly involved in street play sessions, such as: 'I feel more empowered to make positive change in my community and feel I can positively impact the street where I live'; 'I feel more confident at giving my daughter independence'; and 'I feel inspired that there are things that can be done to help not just kids play outside but everyone to experience the city without fear of traffic'.

A variation of the play streets idea is the 'school streets' movement (Sanderson, 2019). In Europe, growing numbers of cities are banning cars from streets outside schools during the morning and afternoon drop-off and pick-up periods for between 15 minutes and an hour. Instead of car engines, the sounds in the street are of children and adults talking. 'Families get respite from the traffic that dominates every other street in their cities' (Sanderson, 2019). The school streets idea grows out of a long history of closing streets for play, parties or Ciclovías (see Chapter 1). Compared to traffic calming, the school street closures are relatively simple to instigate, though their success does depend on support from local government (Fig. 8.6), and enforcement, ranging from police patrols to using automatic number plate recognition cameras to fine drivers. Successful school streets have generated broad community support, cultivating close relationships between schools and local authorities, including the police. Before they are implemented 'a wealth of promotion happens to help drivers adjust and think about their journeys' (Sanderson, 2019), which is an important part of psychological traffic calming, discussed in the following section.

FIGURE 8.6 Councillor Feryal Demirci, Deputy Mayor of the London Borough of Hackney, at the Gayhurst Community School with the toolkit developed to help local authorities establish school streets. *(Credit: Gary Manhine/Hackney Council)*

8.9 Shared streets and psychological traffic calming

'Slow cities' promote the sharing of transport. This can apply to the sharing of space on public transport, the sharing of autonomous vehicles, or the sharing of scarce road space, all of which have significant potential as a way of slowing city transport.

Although physical traffic calming can effectively reduce speed and crashes and their severity, it is sometimes unpopular and can be expensive. Alternative calming techniques have been developed using psychological signals that indicate to drivers that the street has other functions and is shared by multiple users, who deserve respect. That this can significantly reduce driving speeds was first demonstrated by Hans Monderman, the head of road safety for Friesland in the Netherlands in the 1980s, who 'pioneered an approach that respected the driver's common sense and intelligence instead of reliance on signs, road markings, traffic signals and physical barriers' (Hamilton-Baillie, 2008a). 'He made roads safer by making them seem more dangerous. Removing safety barriers and signs made streets more like a village' (Tranter, 2018, p. 235). Even Monderman was surprised when after familiar safety treatments had been removed, speeds dropped dramatically, much more than with traditional traffic calming (Hamilton-Baillie, 2008b).

The terminology in use to describe these approaches can be confusing, not least because shared space can have varying levels of demarcation and segregation between different street users. Though there are many overlaps, broadly speaking there are two principal variants embedded within the shared space concept, those of 'naked streets' and 'shared surfaces'. The first of these variants, the naked street, is used to describe one where traffic engineering devices designed to make roads 'safer' (e.g. traffic signals, guard rails, road signs) have been removed in an attempt to make the road more attractive and, counterintuitively, safer. A well-known example is Kensington High Street in London, a busy arterial and shopping street, where danger was reduced by simplifying the design and removing guard railings (Figs 8.7 and 8.8). The new design is a naked street (less clutter and regulation) and also a shared street (but not a shared surface), as it is less focussed on the motion of vehicles and more on the fact that this is a multi-functional street with a variety of users. Consequently, motorists have to pay more attention to their surroundings, which automatically slows them down, which in turn produces an environment that is extremely safe for people on foot or bicycles.

Another naked street strategy led to 'a statistically significant reduction in vehicle speeds as a result of removing central markings on the carriageway', which seems to be because it 'introduces an element of uncertainty which is reflected in lower speeds' (Cooper & Wright, 2014, p. 8). Drivers on the reconfigured streets slowed down about seven mph (11 km/h) on average, which as

FIGURE 8.7 Kensington High Street in West London as a motorised traffic thoroughfare before it was re-designed as a 'naked street'. *(Credit: Rodney Tolley)*

FIGURE 8.8 Kensington high street as a 'naked street' after removal of guard railings, traffic signs and clutter (though crossing signals still remain). *(Credit: Rodney Tolley)*

Speck (2018) observes: 'in the context of danger to people walking, 7 mph is a huge margin'.

A second variety of shared space interventions is that of the shared surface. In such spaces, slow vehicle speeds are achieved by 'removing the formal distinction between spaces dedicated to pedestrians, cyclists and motorised vehicles, the street is shared by everyone' (NACTO, 2016, p. 216). Removing kerbs produces places that look much less like roads and more like shared spaces that the community can use for its own benefit. Lower speeds result, and are frequently reinforced by, for example: block paving surfacing; reduced use of signs; visual narrowing of the street; reduced forward visibility; tighter geometry; and unconventionally placed street furniture or public art. The 'shared surface' that results redefines the public realm to ensure that the car does not own it, but is the guest, a concept that allows for a new design of urban space (Fig. 8.9).

In the 19th and early 20th century the sharing of surfaces between people walking and cycling, horse-drawn carriages, and streetcars was the norm (Fig. 8.10). However, as motorised traffic increased in speed and volume in the 20th century, physical separation of people on foot from cars was gradually imposed in order to allow increased motor vehicle speeds and reduce casualties. Such segregation of modes from each other may have increased feelings of safety, but in practice it appears now to be counterproductive: it blinkers people

FIGURE 8.9 A shared surface in Bendigo, Victoria, Australia in 2009. *(Credit: Rodney Tolley)*

FIGURE 8.10 People walking, electric trams and horse-drawn carriages sharing the street, King Street, Sydney, Australia, 1900. *(Credit: Tyrrell Photographic Collection, Powerhouse Museum. https://commons.wikimedia.org/wiki/File:Electric_trams,_King_Street,_Sydney,_1900.jpg)*

and causes an increase in speed, and because everyone has their own lane, people take less account of other road users. These effects are largely eliminated in shared surface areas where behaviour is moderated by informal social protocols and negotiation.

The schemes described earlier deliberately create ambivalence in public spaces through design solutions rather than formal regulations and controls, thus making users more aware of other users and more responsive to their needs. However, there need not necessarily be permanent physical changes to the street to achieve similar outcomes, a concept that may be referred to as 'psychological traffic calming'. Engwicht (2005) describes approaches that focus on interventions by the community in residential areas that may create what he called 'mental speed bumps'. He argues that motorists will drive more slowly when they are 'uncertain' about whether people will be on the street, and when they are 'intrigued' enough by the street environment to slow down to take a closer look. He also advocates the use of humour to encourage motorists to relate to others as humans, as 'an effective strategy to diffuse road rage and calm traffic in a way that contributes life and magic to the public realm' (Raphael, 2009). These experiences contribute to the reclaiming of streets for community-building activities such as play, socialising and simply walking around the neighbourhood. This automatically leads to slower traffic, because, as Engwicht (2005) explains: the speed on streets is largely determined by the extent to which residents have psychologically retreated from their street.

Engwicht's view is that it is more effective to use community visions, rather than design criteria, to determine the amount of intrigue and uncertainty achieved in a space. For example, psychological traffic calming can be instigated by residents making subtle changes to their behaviour that can influence the way streets are used, such as parents supporting their children to walk to school. This is because, as Tranter (2018, p. 235) points out, 'drivers are more careful when driving past groups of children walking, especially if the drivers know the people who are walking'. Even something as simple as sitting on the front steps of houses can help to change the psychological feel of streets (Tranter, 2016). Another idea involves moving as much domestic activity as possible to near the kerbside (e.g. using tables and chairs at the front of housing) (Fig. 8.11). This creates ever-changing streetscapes where human activity becomes a major source of intrigue and uncertainty, which causes drivers to slow down. How realistic it is to expect large numbers of communities to act in this counter-intuitive way is not clear, but it is certainly an interesting take on shifting the cultural perspectives relating to speed.

Although most shared streets are residential, the concept is increasingly being applied in commercial areas, for example in Auckland's CBD, where several streets have been converted to shared surfaces with positive results. After Fort Street was rebuilt as a shared surface (Fig. 8.12), footfall increased by 54 per cent, spending by 47 per cent, and 80 per cent of visitors felt safer than before (NACTO, 2016, p. 225).

FIGURE 8.11 The presence of a mother and child, along with tables and chairs and children's bikes and toys on the side of this street in Copenhagen provides a form of psychological traffic calming, creating intrigue and uncertainty for passing motorists. *(Credit: Elliot Fishman)*

FIGURE 8.12 Fort Street, Auckland, New Zealand in 2011, where creation of a shared surface has led to substantial economic uplift. *(Credit: Rodney Tolley)*

However, shared space is not just a speed management issue or a safety issue: it also offers the opportunity to reorganise space to make it more attractive and comfortable by removing signs and other traffic-related clutter and providing seating, lighting, public art and other aesthetic benefits. In other words, shared space areas can be both safe and beautiful, thus attracting new users and more slow uses. For example, the rebuilding of New Road, Brighton, United Kingdom as a shared space resulted in a 62 per cent increase in people walking and a 600 per cent increase in lingering activities such as people gathering and socialising (Dutoit, Søholt, Risom, & Gagner, 2017).

The operation of shared space schemes in continental European countries has in no case resulted in casualty increases, and given the increase in usage of such places by people walking and cycling, this represents a real reduction in risk. There remains a problem, however. No matter that there is a convincing evidence base for speed and crash reduction in psychologically reclaimed streets and shared spaces, they have been adopted more slowly than they deserve, for one major reason. Whilst Monderman's ideas gained credence amongst local communities, which benefited from fewer crashes and traffic delays and greater quality of public space, they also caused some discomfort amongst governments and engineers (Hamilton-Baillie, 2008a), trained to believe that segregation and certainty were essential components of safety.

An example of this discomfort was experienced by one of this book's authors in 2007, prior to giving a presentation in an Australian city. He was told by the meeting convenor that 'You may have noticed I have deleted reference to Hans Monderman's work in the draft programme ... the more conservative professionals in our midst may be immediately "off-side" and stop listening if his name is mentioned to introduce "go slower to move quicker". There is a school of thought that says this type of traffic and pedestrian movement planning is too radical'. It is heartening to report that, despite those troubling beginnings, the community concerned now has a safe, successful and popular shared space, connecting civic buildings to the retail core, but only after a protracted and wearying battle to overcome entrenched resistance from within the local government itself.

8.10 Self-explaining roads

We have seen above that reducing the posted speed limit (PSL) is a widely adopted strategy in managing speed. However, if road conditions suggest that the PSL is too low, drivers may simply ignore it. Ideally, to maximise the effect of any new speed limit, streets should be designed to match the designated speed. Current road designs often perversely lead to higher speeds than the legal limit. The Global Street Design Guide comments that 'Conventional practice designates a design speed higher than the posted speed limit to accommodate driver errors. But, in fact, this practice only encourages speeding and increases the likelihood of traffic crashes, fatalities and injuries' (NACTO, 2016, p. 178). The Guide emphasises that 'Designers must not use highway-based design speed practices in urban areas' (NACTO, 2016, p. 178). These highway-based design speed practices have led to American cities being dominated by city streets that are actually high-speed roads. The Strong Towns Organisation refers to these environments as 'Stroads'. It says that whereas successful streets are environments where humans, and human interaction, flourish, in contrast a road is a high-speed connection between two productive places. 'Stroads are a mash-up of these two types of paths ... Besides being a very dangerous environment … they are enormously expensive to build and, ultimately, financially unproductive' (Marohn, 2017).

Instead of the highway-design approach of setting the limit at the 85th percentile operating speed, it is better to have an approach which considers vulnerable road users, and uses design to achieve a target speed, thereby guiding drivers with physical and perceptual cues. These cues include narrower lanes, tighter corner radii, gateway treatments, changed roadway surface materials and appearance, mini roundabouts and other speed management techniques (NACTO, 2016, p. 178). These ideas are the basis of 'self-explaining roads' (Charlton et al., 2010) where, even in the absence of speed signs, drivers can guess the speed limit and travel at speeds appropriate to the class of road they are on. Drivers react to the story being told by the road, so it is important to get the design right in the first place (Fig. 8.13).

FIGURE 8.13 What is a driver to do? The 'story' told by this road in Canberra, Australia is 'to drive fast'—and the sign warns him or her of official disapproval (and dire consequences) if he or she does so. Better to get the design right from the outset. *(Credit: Rodney Tolley)*

Munich's traffic calming polices are founded on the principles of self-explaining roads. Munich established its first 30 km/h zone in 1988, and in 2019 more than 80 per cent of its 2,300 km road network had this limit. The default limit on major roads is 50 km/h. An important aspect of Munich's approach is that when streets are redesigned and speed limits reduced, existing cycle paths and lanes (if present) are removed. An official responsible for implementing the cycle routes explained: 'The best and safest cycle path is, ultimately, the one that is not needed because of the traffic structure and the traffic proficiency of the users' (McKibbin, 2014, p. 4).

8.11 The 'safe systems approach' and Vision Zero

8.11.1 Introduction

In October 1997 the Swedish Parliament adopted its Vision Zero road safety policy, with a goal of zero deaths and zero serious injuries in the road traffic environment. This approach has been described as 'transformational', with the Vision Zero target being 'both an ethical and a practical necessity. It is unarguable that we should do as much as possible to … harness the full potential of safe systems and system design to reach zero … Doing more of the same is not good enough and system designers have a shared responsibility with users to contribute to the achievement of zero' (Vision Zero UK, n.d.).

Reaching this target depends on all of those responsible for the total road safety system. In practice this means that road design, vehicle design and driving behaviour must be tackled using a 'safe systems approach'. As the World Health Organisation has said, 'Road traffic crashes are predictable and therefore preventable. In order to combat the problem, though, there needs to be close coordination and collaboration, using a holistic and integrated approach, across many sectors and many disciplines' (Peden et al., 2004, p. 164).

8.11.2 What is the safe systems approach?

Underpinning the safe systems approach is the belief that human life and health is paramount, and this should be the foremost consideration in designing and operating a road network. The principles behind the safe system have been outlined by the Towards Zero Foundation (n.d.) as follows:

- People make mistakes that can lead to crashes; however, no one should die or be seriously injured on the road as a result of these mistakes;
- To build a safe road system the human body's tolerance to impact forces should be the guiding tool;
- Road safety is a shared responsibility amongst everyone, including those that design, build, operate and use the road system;
- All parts of the road system must be strengthened in combination to multiply the protective effects. If one part fails, the others must still protect people.

The safe systems approach signals a shift in focus from expecting citizens (and children) to take individual responsibility for their own safety, to a realisation that governments need to take collective action to keep people safe. This shift is evident in a Vision Zero poster that contrasts the dominant road safety philosophy in 1959 and 2019, using the two phrases below (Vision Zero Canada, 2019):

1959: Look twice before you cross the street
2019: Think twice before you build the street

The '2019 philosophy' is beginning to be evident in the consideration of the time allowed to cross roads at controlled crossings. Traffic engineers for many years set the crossing times without consideration of the walking speeds of children or elderly. In a study of signal crossings in Melbourne, Selman (2008) found that at one intersection the time allowed to make a crossing was ten seconds less than the time taken by children in a walking school bus. New approaches are now being considered to help some vulnerable groups cross roads safely, but the traffic engineering mindset still needs to change (Box 8.1).

BOX 8.1 How fast is your granny? Ethical dilemmas in setting crossing speeds acceptable to elderly people.

On Feb 15th 2006, 82-year-old Mavis Coyle was walking home in Los Angeles, cane in one hand and grocery bag in the other. She was half way across an intersection when the 'Walk' signal changed to 'Don't Walk'—and a motorcycle police officer began shouting at her that she was obstructing the flow of traffic. 'Coyle tried to explain to him that she couldn't make it across in time because of her age but he refused to listen' (Covarrubias & Cho, 2006). She was ticketed, prosecuted and found guilty of jaywalking—but in view of the negative publicity the case generated, her $114 fine was waived.

Though this is an egregious example, it is not just a problem in the United States. In the United Kingdom 80 per cent of people over 65 cannot walk at the speed required to use a light-controlled crossing, set at 1.2 metres per second (Asher, Aresu, Falaschetti, & Mindell, 2012), an issue lampooned in a funny (but sad) video featuring elderly Londoners: *Hey Mr Boris* (Loud Minority, 2013).

There are a number of 'solutions' to this problem. One scarcely credible response was mooted by the authors of a Swiss study, which on finding that 74 per cent of elderly pedestrians couldn't reach 1.2 m/sec crossing speeds, concluded that 'training measures to improve the older population's cognitive and physical fitness should be promoted to enhance walking speed and safety of older pedestrians' (Eggenberger, Tomovic, Münzer, & de Bruin, 2017).

Thankfully, more enlightened approaches than training older people to walk faster are being tested in many cities. In Singapore the 'Green Man Plus' Programme allows over 60s to swipe their transit fare card at a sensor at the intersections, which gives them an extra 6 to 13 seconds to cross (Sim, 2013). In Tilburg, The Netherlands, the 'Crosswalk' App gives walkers with restricted mobility extra crossing time through a sensor that changes light settings if it sees an app holder waiting (Darroch, 2017). In many other cities (including New York) lights have a Pedestrian Lead Interval where walkers are given a head start over turning traffic, which benefits everyone, but especially the slower walkers.

These are helpful steps, but they are not dealing with root causes. Crossing speeds are set by traffic engineers using a similar algorithm to that used to set urban speed limits. The problem is thus an ethical one, in that a decision is made on how many people get left behind. Usually in the past the 85th percentile has been used, which in practice means that the crossing has been designed to leave 15 per cent of pedestrians still in the street when the lights change. This is not only too favourable to motorised traffic but is becoming more and more unacceptable as the population ages. Instead, there is a need for a combination of slowing traffic in general (to reduce the severity of crashes if they do occur) and changing the default so that traffic lights are set to be normally on green for people on foot. This is a safer, more equitable policy, befitting the goals of future 'slow cities'.

Investment is thus required in creating safe roads, safe speeds, safe vehicles, safe people and post-crash care in order to fold layers of protection around people. 'Safe roads' are required because roads and road features play a vital role in reducing crashes and/or the injury outcomes in the event of a crash (Fig. 8.14), whilst well-designed 'safe vehicles' can either help prevent a crash or reduce some of the impact forces to help decrease the risk of death and serious injury. 'Safe speeds' are required to build a safe road system, so speed limits should acknowledge the human body's tolerance to external forces (Fig. 8.15). These measures are synergistic, as 'Appropriate speed limit setting and compliance can also enhance the effectiveness of initiatives implemented in the road or vehicle space' (Towards Zero Foundation, n.d.). The 'safe people' criterion refers to the need for road users to operate within the boundaries set by the road system designers, whilst 'post crash care' can help reduce the risk of death and serious injuries as a result of the best possible emergency treatment, trauma care and rehabilitation.

8.11.3 Vision Zero: achievements and challenges

Sweden, the original country adopting Vision Zero, has had considerable success in reducing road fatalities. Between the year 2000 and 2018, the number of these fatalities halved. Sweden now has one of the world's lowest number of traffic fatalities per capita (Rothschild, 2018). Policymakers and practitioners in many countries such as Finland, Norway, Germany, the Netherlands, Switzerland and Austria, or states such as Victoria in Australia, have been impressed by this remarkable achievement and are in varying stages of either adopting Vision Zero or embedding safe system approaches into road safety policies (Pucher & Buehler, 2016; VicRoads, 2016). Many cities have been

FIGURE 8.14 Vision Zero requires safe roads, but this design would not qualify: there is no safe way to walk across this junction in the Gold Coast, Australia. There are missing sidewalks and the dirt track desire line on the right leads people to cross two dangerous slip lanes unaided. The purpose of the sidewalk on the central green island is hard to fathom.

FIGURE 8.15 A Vision Zero principle is that to build a safe road system the human body's tolerance to impact forces should be the guiding tool. Oslo, Norway, is planning 30 km/h speed limits—'Sone 30'—on all local roads. *(Credit: David Hall, Facit, https://www.flickr.com/photos/moonhouse/2663938840)*

remarkably effective in applying Vision Zero principles: Helsinki and Oslo being exemplars. After many years of action, applying the sorts of strategies advocated in this book, (e.g. reducing speed limits, changing street design and removing space for cars) 'neither city recorded a single pedestrian fatality in 2019' (Murray, 2020).

However, progress in countries around the world in reducing road danger is very uneven. In the United States the pedestrian death rate per million people is now 75 per cent higher than in Europe (Cortright, 2019). When US road safety experts were asked to explain this, they answered:

- 'Americans are driving more than ever, more than residents of any other country;
- 'More of them than ever are living … in urban sprawl;
- 'A growing number of pedestrian fatalities occur on the fringes of cities, where high-volume, high-speed roads exist in close proximity to the places where people live, work, and shop;
- 'Speed limits have increased across the country over the past 20 years, despite robust evidence that even slight increases in speed dramatically increase the likelihood of killing pedestrians;
- 'American road engineers tend to assume people will speed, and so design roads to accommodate speeding; this, in turn, facilitates more speeding, which soon enough makes higher speed limits feel reasonable' (Baker, 2019).

Not only is the problem for vulnerable road users more severe in the United States, but recent trends show that it is worsening. Through the 1990s and 2000s, the pedestrian death count had declined in almost every year and there was a general presumption that decreasing deaths and injuries were part of a trajectory of development. However, over the last decade, trends have reversed, with deaths of people on foot rising by 35 per cent between 2008 and 2017, to the highest level in nearly 30 years, whilst the combined number of all other traffic deaths decreased by six per cent (Retting & Schwartz, 2019). In the United States 'For drivers, roads are as safe as they have ever been; for people on foot, roads keep getting deadlier', and nor are things better for people on bicycles, with fatalities increasing by 25 per cent between 2010 and 2017 (Baker, 2019).

The biggest challenge for the application of Vision Zero in the United States is not technical, but political. One activist has observed that 'The fundamental issue in America is that almost anywhere they try to implement Vision Zero, almost everyone in those cities drives. They aren't willing to be slowed down, they object, and the politicians refuse to do anything that's going to make drivers angry' [quoted in Laker (2017)]. Any city can call itself or its safety programmes Vision Zero (and over 30 cities in the United States had done so by 2018). However, it seems that what many are doing is cherry picking those 'Vision Zero policies' that they can implement without confrontation with powerful motorist lobbies. The holistic and synergistic benefits of the safe system approach have been undermined. Los Angeles, for example, announced its first Vision Zero strategy in 2017, with a goal of eliminating traffic deaths by 2025. Work was to focus first on reducing vehicle lanes on 40 High-Injury Network streets, but faced with pushback from residents and drivers 'Local city leaders downgraded lane removals to things that wouldn't interfere with motor traffic: sidewalk repairs, new traffic signals and crosswalks ... Road deaths rose rather than falling, increasing 80% in two years' (Laker, 2017).

Vision Zero is now being described as 'a term that's increasingly being used and misused around the world' (Vision Zero Canada, 2019). 'Throughout North America politicians, transport engineers, police and professional advocates are now piously declaring that "no loss of life is acceptable" on our streets and highways. Many would have us think that by saying this, and that by setting zero or interim "moving towards zero" targets, they are "committing" to "Vision Zero". But in most cases they are not doing anything worthy of the name' (Vision Zero Canada, 2019). It appears that our speed addiction has proven too challenging to confront for many politicians, policy makers and 'experts'.

The political challenge for Vision Zero in cities is that one of its criteria, 'safe people', not only requires a full understanding of behavioural factors in crash causation, but also application of this knowledge in the political realm to achieve safer outcomes. We have already seen in the motordom story how perceptions may be distorted by powerful lobbies—and unfortunately it seems as though this is now happening with renewed force.

The myth of the 'distracted pedestrian' has taken hold in the past decade. In Sydney a motoring organisation study identified that 3.4 per cent of pedestrians crossed illegally whilst using their smartphones (NRMA, 2019) and based on these data, referred to the need to 'crack down on this behaviour'(Sydney Morning Herald, 2019). Compounding the bias, the newspaper that reported this study used a photograph of people on foot legally using a crosswalk, with the caption 'Smartphones and pedestrians: how we're texting our lives away'. Admittedly, walking across a crosswalk using a phone may not the best idea, but it is important to remember that a crosswalk is a right of way for people on foot so it is not illegal, any more than is being distracted by chatting to a companion whilst crossing, an activity which many of us do as a matter of course.

The distracted pedestrian has also been targeted in China. In the Chinese city of Wenzhou, a woman was fined for being a 'smartphone zombie'. The fine of 10 yuan (about US$1.50) was for using her phone whilst crossing the road. Social media users are reported as supporting the fine (Pierpoint & Allen, 2019), not surprising when there is substantial media coverage and motor car industry promotion of the problems allegedly caused by 'petextrians'. An example is the Ford Motor Company claim that its Pre-Collision Assist system 'helps predict distracted "petextrians"'; Ford justifies the need for such a system by referring to 'a global influx of "petextrians"' (Ford, 2019).

Whilst the motoring lobby would like city residents to believe that distracted pedestrians are causing havoc on the streets, there is little evidence to support this belief—from 2010 to 2014 in the United States, 'electronic devices in the hands of walkers were a factor in just 25 of 23,240 pedestrian deaths' (The Globe and Mail, 2017), only one in 930 cases. Moreover, there is evidence that distracted driving is a more serious issue than distracted walking, and drivers do not have to be holding a mobile phone to be distracted by using the phone (Box 8.2).

The reasons for blaming road crashes on people being distracted whilst walking are complex. One possible reason is related to what is known as a 'windshield perspective', especially in car-dominated societies like North America, where most adults drive and relatively few walk daily. Moreover, in crashes

BOX 8.2 In-car phone use: and speeding: what's the connection?

Many countries have laws prohibiting drivers from texting or talking on hand-held devices, yet such regulations are commonly ignored. In one study when drivers were asked about the past month, more than 2 in 3 drivers reported talking on their cell phone while driving, and nearly 1 in 3 admitted sending a text message or email (AAA Foundation for Traffic Safety, 2017).

Whilst the danger of *hand-held* phone use at the wheel is widely understood, it is generally assumed that *hands-free* devices are safe because they eliminate the twin risks of taking the eyes from the road and taking hands off the steering wheel. However, a third type of distraction involves 'inattention blindness ... drivers using cell phones look at but fail to see up to 50 per cent of the information in their driving environment' (National Safety Council, 2012, p. 2). Drivers using hand-held or hands-free devices are equally subject to such 'cognitive distraction'. A review of over 30 studies from several countries showed that 'hands-free phones offer no safety benefit when driving' (National Safety Council, 2012, p. 4). Driving while talking on cell phones—hand-held or hands-free—increases risk of injury and property damage crashes fourfold.

Drivers travelling apparently 'safely' below the speed limit compromise their law-abiding behaviour as soon as they start talking on a phone, even if they have both hands on the wheel and believe that they are concentrating hard on the road ahead. Inattention blindness causes the field of view of distracted drivers to narrow. One study tracked the eye movements of drivers using hands-free phones, and repeated the measurement when these drivers were not on the phone. The results showed that drivers looked less at the periphery. In Chapter 5 of this book, Fig. 5.10 showed how as speeds increase, the field of vision narrows. The view of the road environment experienced by mobile phone users closely mirrors the tunnel vision of higher-speed drivers depicted in Fig. 5.10. Whether they are driving at speeds over 30 km/h or driving while talking on the phone, drivers become unaware of the presence of people on the side of the street—and thus are unable to compute likely scenarios or anticipate movements of perhaps unpredictable, vulnerable road users.

where both parties survive, it is normal for each to blame the other for being at fault, but when a pedestrian is killed, frequently the only witness to whom the police speak is the driver. Media reportage is by no means blameless. In an analysis of 200 articles covering bike and pedestrian deaths, Ralph, Iacobucci, Thigpen, and Goddard (2019, p. 669) note that:

> *'local news coverage subtly, but consistently, blames VRUs [vulnerable road users] for crashes ... rather than addressing commonalities between crashes, coverage almost always treated crashes as isolated incidents ... journalists should be aware of how grammatical choices shape perceived blameworthiness and they should consciously counteract the natural tendency to blame the victim ... "accident" was the most commonly used term for referring to crashes ... The term obscures the preventable nature of crashes. The use of the term "accident" was particularly jarring when the driver was charged with one or more crimes or was arrested'.*

It is not possible to achieve 'safe people' in the Vision Zero system by shifting blame and responsibility on to vulnerable users. Instead there needs to be a profound reform of legal procedures and road safety policies, basing them on 'a presumption that there is a duty of care on drivers to pedestrians and cyclists' and a recognition that 'all drivers have duties and responsibilities but no rights beyond the "right to life" that all users of the system have' (Vision Zero UK, n.d.).

But though that is necessary, it is insufficient. Reducing road deaths in the long term means redesigning roads to restrict motor traffic speeds—and without a culture change, that becomes deeply problematic in car-dominated societies. Baker has observed that in the United States, whilst safety experts tend to focus on the broader issues related to the road environment, 'America's cultural discourse on road safety tends to go in the opposite direction, zooming in on that most American of variables: the individual ... making bad choices about how to use the roads'. Dumbaugh points out that 'you have to design streets differently ... You have to slow the cars down. You have to recognise the reality of road users who aren't in cars ... But these basic realisations aren't things the US transportation system knows or integrates into practice. And so people keep getting killed' [quoted in Baker (2019)].

Schmitt (2017) summarises the misperceptions in saying that 'cell phones don't make walking dangerous — car-based cities do'. She cites Schneider, Vargo, and Sanatizadeh (2017), who find that the likelihood of pedestrian death is five times higher in the most dangerous US cities as in the safest ones, with the most dangerous being those cities that were shaped during the heyday of auto-sprawl. For example, Orlando, Florida (Fig. 8.16) has the highest Pedestrian Danger Index (PDI) in the United States. The PDI indicates how deadly it is for walkers in a city based on the numbers of people killed whilst walking, controlling for the numbers of people living in that city, and the numbers who walk to work: Orlando's 'streets were never designed for anything other than traveling at ludicrous speeds in a steel cage' (Wolf, 2019). Ironically, Orlando also rates as one of the worst cities in the world for traffic congestion (LeBar, 1017).

FIGURE 8.16 The city of Orlando, Florida, which ranks as the USA's deadliest city for people on foot. Unsurprisingly, there is no one on foot in this image. *(Credit: Formulanone, FL50 East US17 North US92 East – Orlando, https://www.flickr.com/photos/formulanone/43720081875)*

As a Canadian newspaper editorial puts it 'All those pedestrian deaths? It's the cars, stupid'. It continued: 'Our car-centric cities and suburbs too easily become killing fields for those navigating them on foot, especially the elderly. The problem is cars, not people negligently walking into them. If you want to save pedestrian lives, slow down the vehicles. Install more crosswalks. Add speed bumps. Lower speed limits. Widen sidewalks. Narrow roads' (The Globe and Mail, 2017).

In general, progress in reducing danger from speeding vehicles in European countries has been greater and longer lasting than in the United States. From 2007 to 2016, pedestrian deaths decreased by 36 per cent. However, there is concern that other fatalities fell faster, so that there was a rise in the percentage of deaths comprising people on foot (European Commission, 2018).

It is hard to know why this is happening. One possibility is that a lot of the low-hanging fruit has been picked, so that 'now it's the difficult decisions that need to be made, decisions about whether we're going to fundamentally reshape the landscape to be a place where everyone can travel in a safe and healthy way' [the UK road safety charity Brake, quoted in Baker (2019)]. Maintaining the momentum—politically and technically—may be more difficult when crash reduction efforts become less effective through time and consequently more expensive.

Despite this slowdown, it is important to make a distinction between Europe and the United States in terms of the application of many of the speed-reducing tools and practices discussed in this chapter. In general, European cities have had longer and deeper engagement with these approaches than US cities, and whilst it would be naïve to imply that this wholly explains the lower casualty rates, the sheer number of interventions with safer outcomes has likely had a cumulative effect. Commenting on the fact that the US pedestrian death rate per million population is now 75 per cent higher than in Europe, Joe Cortright has noted that Americans 'walk less, but we die more'. He concludes that these data 'should be at once heartening and discouraging to advocates of Vision Zero. On the one hand, they show that it is entirely possible to have a modern economy, with technology and with lots of cars, that doesn't kill so many pedestrians. On the other hand, they show us that the U.S. is very much on the wrong track' (Cortright, 2019).

8.12 Safer vehicles and safer roads through technology: the allure of autonomous vehicles

An emerging theme that needs to be examined in relation to Vision Zero approaches is the potential safety benefit of new technologies. For example, the policies which accompany the introduction of autonomous vehicles (AVs) will affect whether or not such vehicles will make cities safer for drivers and their passengers, and for vulnerable road users such as those on foot or bike. An important consideration is the speeds at which AVs will operate in cities.

Though the implementation of AVs is highly controversial and uncertain, it is essential to consider the issues around them in a safety and speed context. Many of the measures and approaches discussed earlier, such as speed limits, enforcement and psychological traffic calming are predicated on there being a driver in the car. These measures are of dubious value if there is no driver. What is the relevance of a self-explaining road to a computer on wheels? Even if the road is 'dangerous by design', the programming in the car should be able to overcome that problem.

A tenet of Vision Zero is that mistakes by drivers on the road should not result in a death sentence to themselves or others. The attraction of AVs in this context is clear. The computers that underpin AVs do not get tired, drunk, drugged or distracted and do not make the kind of human misjudgements that can be so dangerous to all road users. The relevance of AV technology is that—as its proponents argue—AVs will remove the risk posed by fallible drivers, leading to an elimination of fatalities and casualties.

However, there are tremendous obstacles to overcome for this vision to come to fruition—and many researchers doubt that this is going to be possible. The road driving environment is so diverse and unpredictable that it poses an immense problem for software developers. Singer (2018) has noted that: 'Pedestrians are detected simply as moving, column-shaped blurs of pixels ... the car wouldn't be able to spot a police officer at the side of the road frantically waving for traffic to stop'. The complexities are formidable: AVs will need a database that can distinguish between wild animals and party-goers, perhaps the worse for wear, in wild animal costumes. It would be hoped that the AV would stop in either eventuality, but in a dynamic road environment with other lethal moving vehicles, the programmed ethical choices of hitting what might or might not be a giant rabbit or killing the AV driver herself start to get very difficult.

In these circumstances, it is important to consider the question of who is in charge of the programming. As Litman (2019, p. 3) observes, 'autonomous vehicles can be programmed based on user preferences (maximizing traffic speeds and occupant safety) or community goals (limiting speeds and protecting other road users)'. The experience of motordom tells us that the car industry will not relinquish control easily and will want to be at the forefront of programming the necessary moral decisions into the computers that will run AVs. Should the car swerve into oncoming traffic to avoid a person walking or cycling? Or to put it another way, 'will your driverless car be willing to kill you to save the lives of others?' (Sample, 2016). Without regulation, the motorcar industry will be able to choose between selling cars that are either 'altruistic' or 'selfish', and we might speculate what the outcome might be. There is a limit to the number of people who will buy a car knowing that it is programmed to kill them in some circumstances.

A further road danger problem is that many of the predicted benefits of AVs, such as congestion reductions, require dedicated lanes to allow vehicles to travel close together at high speeds. How would vulnerable users get across such dedicated lanes of 'platooning', or 'swarming' AVs? Depending on who was in charge of the programming, two outcomes are possible: pedestrian fatalities on an unimaginable scale or, if the default is to avoid crashes at all costs, stationary traffic every time someone on foot attempted to cross. Neither outcome would be acceptable and so the strong probability is that the mixing of 'soft' road users with swarming AVs would be prevented, either by draconian enforcement of jaywalking ordinances or the erection of formidable barrier fences along street edges. We have been here before: it is not likely that society would accept these outcomes either.

These issues can be addressed by one crucial intervention, that of limiting the speed of AVs. Slower vehicles of any type are less likely to kill people. A simple strategy to reduce the likelihood of ethical dilemmas is to reduce motor vehicle speeds to 30 km/h or less. NACTO (2019, p. 94), in its detailed principles for street design and management if AVs are implemented in cities, stresses that safety is the top priority: 'To ensure a safe environment for active transportation modes, cities must actively manage speeds. Speeds should be limited to 25 mph citywide and lower (typically 15 to 20 mph) in city centers, residential areas, and near schools and other sensitive locations'.

These outcomes may be what society wants, but we have seen in the motordom example earlier that these may be subverted by different agendas provided by powerful vested interests. Peter Norton—the historian of traffic in US cities—has argued that 'There is simply a very good business reason for car companies to sell people a future where everything is better, especially when the way to get there is by purchasing a lot of cars … I don't think there's any chance that autonomous vehicles will deliver us a safe future, and I don't necessarily think the companies think so either. I think they think we'll buy a lot of stuff. The safe future will recede before our eyes like a desert mirage' [quoted in Baker (2019)]. Similarly, Etienne Krug, Chair of the UN Road Safety Collaboration, argues that it is naïve to think that autonomous vehicles will be a 'miracle solution … Even if they were ready tomorrow: it takes a long time for the fleet of vehicles on the road to get totally replaced. Let's say it takes 10 years. What are we supposed to do in the meantime? Let millions of people die on the road? And then what if the miracle solution never comes? We need to assume it won't' (Baker, 2019).

In summary, AV technologies are being promoted as solutions to road danger and other city transport issues, whereby cars of the future will allegedly provide solutions to the problems created by cars of the present. However, this is making the assumption that the future is going to revolve around the car. If we wish to slow the city effectively, we have to question this view, and apply new technology in ways that will benefit the 'slower' modes and thus the health of cities, their inhabitants and the global environment.

Speck (2017) reinforces this view by positing that: 'Autonomous vehicles are the right answer to the wrong question. Why do MIT's Media Lab, and Google keep asking how we can make cars better? Where has that question ever gotten us? A better question is how can we provide the most useful mobility to the most people with the most positive outcomes for society?' To answer that question Speck sets out ten rules for AVs, the last of which is to 'Invest in the current technological revolution'. He observes that 'A transportation technology available now has outperformed AVs by almost every measure. It travels 50 to 80 times further per calorie expended than the automobile, requires very little space, works on existing infrastructure with minimal modification, doesn't pollute, and makes its users healthier, happier, and skinnier. That technology is called a bicycle'. (He might have added that it saves us time too.)

8.13 Conclusion

Restricting the speeds of private motorised traffic, particularly in residential streets or any streets where vulnerable road users are present (e.g. near shops) is a logical and necessary first step towards slowing the city. Not only will this provide benefits in terms of reductions in road danger, it will also produce more attractive streetscapes and provide a range of health benefits for individuals, for communities, for local and city economies, and ultimately for planetary health. In this chapter we have explained many of the various ways in which the slowing of private motorised traffic can be successfully achieved. The most widely implemented technique for reducing speeds—lower posted speed limits—is likely to be much less successful by itself than when combined with strategies such as physical and/or psychological traffic calming, speed enforcement and education, self-explaining roads and Vision Zero.

The critique of the application of Vision Zero presented in this chapter is not in any way written to undermine the substantial gains already made by the safe systems approach and the prospects for its successful adoption in more cities around the world. When judged against traditional road safety policies, that put a value on a life and determined how many lives lost were 'worth' gains in speed or mobility, it is an enormous leap forward. Traditionally, the responsibility for staying safe on the road fell on individual road users and there was an unspoken presumption that death on the road is the price we had to pay for progress ('as long as it is not *my* life that paid for the progress'). This has been replaced by an ethical approach in which road safety is a shared responsibility amongst everyone. However, Vision Zero remains a tool, and like all tools, can be misused. Taking individual elements from a system and expecting them to work on their own is an approach that is, by definition, doomed to failure. Once again, when dealing with speed reduction, it emphasises the need to replace former opportunistic problem-solving through piecemeal actions with holistic, synergistic approaches.

We have argued here that lowering the speed of existing motorised traffic is a critical aspect of future 'slow cities'. However, by itself, it is unlikely to produce the changes necessary to realise the benefits for health (individual, environmental and economic) that are potentially achievable. Policies to bring about lower traffic speeds need to be supported by broader changes in city land use and transport planning. There is limited value in reducing the speed of traffic in residential streets if the planning ethos continues to prioritise the speed and dominance of motor cars throughout the city. Importantly, the space provided for the motor car (which is greater when speeds are increased) needs to be considered in city planning. Even more fundamental is recognition of the cultural contexts in which the speed of city transport is considered. These are the issues for discussion in the following two chapters. Chapter 9 examines the potential for transport and land use planning to support the transition to a slower city, and Chapter 10 addresses the issue of how to change the behavioural and cultural context of speed. All three approaches—slowing existing traffic, designing land uses for lower speeds and changing behaviour—are needed if our addiction to speed is to be overcome and health and sustainability achieved in the future 'slow city'.

References

AAA Foundation for Traffic Safety. (2017). *2016 Traffic Safety Culture Index*. Available from: https://aaafoundation.org/wp-content/uploads/2017/11/2016TrafficSafetyCultureIndexReport.pdf.

Aarts, L., & Schagen, I. (2006). Driving speed and the risk of road crashes. *Accident Analysis and Prevention*, *38*(2), 215–224.

Ameratunga, S. (2009). Traffic speed zones and road injuries. *BMJ*, 339, b4743.

Asher, L., Aresu, M., Falaschetti, E., & Mindell, J. (2012). Most older pedestrians are unable to cross the road in time: a cross-sectional study. *Age and Ageing*, *41*(5), 690–694.

Atkins Limited, AECOM, & Maher, M. (2018). *20mph research study: Process and impact evaluation: technical report.* Available from: https://assets.publishing.service.gov.uk/government/uploads/system/uploads/attachment_data/file/757302/20mph-technical-report.pdf.

Baker, P., C. (2019). Collision course: why are cars killing more and more pedestrians? *The Guardian.* Available from: https://www.theguardian.com/technology/2019/oct/03/collision-course-pedestrian-deaths-rising-driverless-cars.

Ben-Joseph, E. (1995). Changing the residential street scene: Adapting the shared street (woonerf) concept to the suburban environment. *Journal of the American Planning Association*, *61*(4), 504–515.

Box, E., & Bayliss, D. (2012). *Speed limits: A review of evidence.* Available from: https://www.racfoundation.org/assets/rac_foundation/content/downloadables/speed_limits-box_bayliss-aug2012.pdf.

Britton, E. (2011). Slowth: Or why it is so very important (and so very easy) to slow down traffic in cities. *World Streets Emergency Climate/Mobility Action/Plan* Available from: https://worldstreets.wordpress.com/2011/07/08/slowth-or-why-it-is-so-very-important-and-so-very-easy-to-slow-down-traffic-in-cities/.

Buehler, R., Pucher, J., Gerike, R., & Götschi, T. (2017). Reducing car dependence in the heart of Europe: Lessons from Germany, Austria, and Switzerland. *Transport Reviews*, *37*(1), 4–28.

Cairns, J., Warren, J., Garthwaite, K., Greig, G., & Bambra, C. (2014). Go slow: An umbrella review of the effects of 20 mph zones and limits on health and health inequalities. *Journal of Public Health*, *37*(3), 515–520.

Calvert, T. (2015). Evidence Measure Review No.6: Environmental Zones. *European Platform on Sustainable Urban Mobility Plans.* Available from http://www.uemi.net/uploads/4/8/9/5/48950199/environmental_zones_in_depth_review.pdf.

Charlton, S. G., Mackie, H. W., Baas, P. H., Hay, K., Menezes, M., & Dixon, C. (2010). Using endemic road features to create self-explaining roads and reduce vehicle speeds. *Accident Analysis & Prevention*, *42*(6), 1989–1998.

Cooper, R., & Wright, S. (2014). *Centerline Removal Trial.* Available from: https://velobuscotedopale.files.wordpress.com/2017/07/tfl-2014-centreline-removal-trial.pdf.

Cortright, J. (2019). Why are US drivers killing so many pedestrians. *Strong Towns.* Available from: https://www.strongtowns.org/journal/2019/7/2/why-are-us-drivers-killing-so-many-pedestrians.

Covarrubias, A., & Cho, C.H. (2006). She Has World at Her Not-So-Fleet Feet. *Los Angeles Times.* Available from: https://www.latimes.com/archives/la-xpm-2006-apr-14-me-mayvis14-story.html.

Darroch, G. (2017). The slow lane: Dutch app allows elderly to 'hack' traffic lights. *The Guardian.* Available from: https://www.theguardian.com/cities/2017/jul/12/dutch-app-elderly-hack-pedestrian-crossings.

Dutoit, A., Søholt, H., Risom, J., & Gagner L. J. (2017). Paving the Way for City Change. *Gehl/Making Cities for People.* Available from: https://gehlpeople.com/cases/new-road-brighton-uk/.

Eggenberger, P., Tomovic, S., Münzer, T., & de Bruin, E. D. (2017). Older adults must hurry at pedestrian lights! A cross-sectional analysis of preferred and fast walking speed under single- and dual-task conditions. *PLoS one*, *12*(7), e0182180.

Elvik, R. (2001). Area-wide urban traffic calming schemes: A meta-analysis of safety effects. *Accident Analysis & Prevention*, *33*, 327–336.

Engwicht, D. (2005). *Mental Speed Bumps: The Smarter Way to Tame Traffic*. Sydney: Envirobook.

European Commission. (2018). *Traffic Safety Basic Facts 2018, Pedestrians.* Available from https://ec.europa.eu/transport/road_safety/sites/roadsafety/files/pdf/statistics/dacota/bfs2018_main_figures.pdf.

European Transport Safety Council. (2015). *30 km/h limits gaining rapid acceptance across Europe*. Available from: https://etsc.eu/30-kmh-limits-gaining-rapid-acceptance-across-europe/.

Ferrier, K. (2017). Landmark National Study Urges Safety Over Speed. https://visionzeronetwork.org/safety-over-speed/.

Ford. (2019). One Step Ahead of Pedestrians: Ford's Pre-Collision Assist helps predict distracted "petextrians" movement. Available from: https://corporate.ford.com/articles/winning-portfolio/petextrian.html.

Galvin, M., & Maassen, A. (2019). Urban Transformations: In Tanzania's Capital, Safer Children Mean Better Neighborhoods. *World Resources Institute*. Available from: https://www.wri.org/blog/2019/04/urban-transformations-tanzania-s-capital-safer-children-mean-better-neighborhoods

Gaster, S. (1992). Historical changes in children's access to US cities: A critical review. *Children's environments*, *9*(2), 23–36.

Gilbert, P. (2014). Playing Out - Video. Available from: http://vimeo.com/13512080.

Gill, T. (2017). Could street play hold the key to creating more sustainable, livable cities? *Rethinking Childhood*. Available from: https://rethinkingchildhood.com/2017/08/02/reports-street-play-key-sustainable-livable-cities/.

Grundy, C., Steinbach, R., Edwards, P., Green, J., Armstrong, B., & Wilkinson, P. (2009). Effect of 20 mph traffic speed zones on road injuries in London, 1986-2006: Controlled interrupted time series analysis. *BMJ: British Medical Journal*, *339*, b4469.

Hamilton-Baillie, B. (2008a). Hans Monderman. *The Guardian, Road Safety*. Available from: https://www.theguardian.com/news/2008/feb/02/mainsection.obituaries.

Hamilton-Baillie, B. (2008b). Shared Space: Reconciling People, Places and Traffic. *Built Environment*, *34*(2), 161–181.

Hoenig, M. (2000). *The Graz traffic calming model and its consequences for cyclists*. Paper presented at the Fourteenth Velo-city International Conference Proceedings. Munich.

Islam, M. T., El-Basyouny, K., & Ibrahim, S. E. (2014). The impact of lowered residential speed limits on vehicle speed behavior. *Safety Science*, *62*, 483–494.

Jones, S. J., & Brunt, H. (2017). Twenty miles per hour speed limits: A sustainable solution to public health problems in Wales. *Journal of Epidemiology and Community Health*, *71*(7), 699–706.

Karndacharuk, A., Wilson, D. J., & Dunn, R. (2014). A review of the evolution of shared (street) space concepts in urban environments. *Transport Reviews*, *34*(2), 190–220.

King, R., & Semlyen, A. (2016). Some comments on measure review number 6 specifically relating to 20mph/30kph policies and interventions. *World Transport Policy & Practice*, *22*(1/2), 66–68.

Laker, L. (2017). Vision Zero: Has the drive to eliminate road deaths lost its way? *The Guardian, 17 September*. Available from: https://www.theguardian.com/cities/2018/sep/17/vision-zero-has-the-drive-to-eliminate-road-deaths-lost-its-way.

Leaf, W. A., & Preusser, D. F. (1999). *Literature review on vehicle travel speeds and pedestrian injuries*. Springfield, Virginia: US Department of Transportation, National Highway Traffic Safety Administration.

LeBar, R. (1017). New study says Orlando's traffic is one of the world's worst, *Orlando Weekly*. Available from: https://www.orlandoweekly.com/Blogs/archives/2017/02/22/new-study-says-orlandos-traffic-is-one-of-the-worlds-worst.

Litman, T. (2019). *Autonomous vehicle implementation predictions: implications for transport planning*. Available from: https://www.vtpi.org/avip.pdf.

Loud Minority. (2013). Bolder Voices - Hey Mr Boris. *Vimeo*. Available from: https://vimeo.com/76412666.

Mackie, A. (1998). *Urban speed management methods, TRL report 363*. Crowthorne: Transport Research Laboratory.

Marohn, C. (2017). The Stroad. *Strong Towns*. Available from: https://www.strongtowns.org/journal/2017/10/30/the-stroad.

McKibbin, D. (2014). *Speed limit compliance and enforcement*. Available from: http://www.niassembly.gov.uk/globalassets/documents/raise/publications/2015/regdev/1415.pdf.

Murray, J. (2020). How Helsinki and Oslo cut pedestrian deaths to zero. *The Guardian*. Available from: https://www.theguardian.com/world/2020/mar/16/how-helsinki-and-oslo-cut-pedestrian-deaths-to-zero.

NACTO. (2016). *Global Street Design*. Available from: https://globaldesigningcities.org/publication/global-street-design-guide/.

NACTO. (2019). *Blueprint for autonomous urbanism: Second Edition*. Available from: https://nacto.org/publication/bau2/.

National Safety Council. (2012). *Understanding the distracted brain: Why driving while using hands-free cell phones is risky behavior*. Available from: https://www.nsc.org/Portals/0/Documents/DistractedDrivingDocuments/Cognitive-Distraction-White-Paper.pdf.

NRMA. (2019). *Look up: Keeping pedestrians safe*. Available from: https://www.mynrma.com.au/-/media/documents/advocacy/look-up-keeping-pedestrians-safe.

Oxley, J., Corben, B., Fildes, B., O'Hare, M., & Rothengatter, T. (2004). Older vulnerable road users measures to reduce crash and injury risk. *Monash University Accident Research Centre Reports*, *218*, 162.

Peden, M., Scurfield, R., Sleet, D., Mohan, D., Hyder, A.A., Jarawan, E., et al. (2004). *World report on road traffic injury prevention*. Available from: https://www.researchgate.net/publication/237554619_World_Report_on_Road_Traffic_Injury.

Pierpoint, G., & Allen, J. (2019). 'Smartphone zombie' fine cheered on Chinese social media. *BBC News*. Available from: https://www.bbc.com/news/blogs-trending-46902965

Playing Out. (2014). Why play out? Ten good reasons for street play. *Childhood*. Available from: http://playingout.net/play-ten-good-reasons-street-play/.

Playing Out. (2017). *Survey of 'playing out' streets: Summary and Report*. Available from: https://playingout.net/wp-content/uploads/2017/07/Playing-Out-Survey-Report-2017.pdf.

Pucher, J., & Buehler, R. (2016). Safer cycling through improved infrastructure. *American Journal of Public Health*, *106*, 2089–2091.

Ralph, K., Iacobucci, E., Thigpen, C. G., & Goddard, T. (2019). Editorial patterns in bicyclist and pedestrian crash reporting. *Transportation Research Record*, 2673(2), 663-671.

Raphael, C. (2009). David Engwicht: Project for Public Spaces. Available from: https://www.pps.org/article/david-engwicht.

Retting, R., & Schwartz, S. (2019). *Pedestrian Traffic Fatalities by State: 2018 PRELIMINARY DATA, Governors Highway Safety Association (GHSA)*. Available from: https://www.ghsa.org/sites/default/files/2019-02/FINAL_Pedestrians19.pdf.

Richter, E. D., Berman, T., Friedman, L., & Ben-David, G. (2006). Speed, road injury, and public health. *Annual Reviews on Public Health*, *27*, 125–152.

Rothschild, N. (2018). How Sweden became the EU's road safety champion. *Euronews*. Available from: https://www.euronews.com/2018/02/20/how-sweden-became-the-eu-s-road-safety-champion.

Sample, I. (2016). Will your driverless car be willing to kill you to save the lives of others? *The Guardian, Science*. Available from: https://www.theguardian.com/science/2016/jun/23/will-your-driverless-car-be-willing-to-kill-you-to-save-the-lives-of-others.

Sanderson, N. (2019). What are school streets? Available from: https://www.880cities.org/what-are-school-streets/.

Schmitt, A. (2017). Cell Phones Don't Make Walking Dangerous — Car-Based Cities Do. *Streetsblog USA.* Available from: https://usa.streetsblog.org/2017/08/01/cell-phones-dont-make-walking-dangerous-car-based-cities-do/comment-page-1/.

Schneider, R. J., Vargo, J., & Sanatizadeh, A. (2017). Comparison of US metropolitan region pedestrian and bicyclist fatality rates. *Accident Analysis & Prevention, 106*, 82–98.

Selman, M. (2008). The 50 metre dash – trials and tribulations of the walking journey to school. *World Transport Policy and Practice, 14*(1), 48–55.

Sim, R. (2013). More locations for scheme that gives elderly extra time to cross the road. *The Straits Times.* Available from: https://www.straitstimes.com/singapore/more-locations-for-scheme-that-gives-elderly-extra-time-to-cross-the-road.

Singer, A. (2018). Driverless cars and the cult of technology. *Strong Towns.* Available from: https://www.strongtowns.org/journal/2018/9/12/driverless-cars-and-the-cult-of-technology.

Speck, J. (2017). Ten rules for cities about automated vehicles. *Public Square, A CNU Journal.* Available from: https://www.cnu.org/publicsquare/2020/02/27/ten-rules-cities-about-automated-vehicles.

Speck, J. (2018). For a Walkable City, Remove Centerlines on Local Streets. *Streetsblog USA.* Available from: https://usa.streetsblog.org/2018/10/15/jeff-speck-for-a-walkable-city-remove-centerlines-on-local-streets/.

SWOV Institute for Road Safety Research (2017). Stichting Wetenschappelijk Onderzoek Verkeersveiligheid [Dutch Institute for Road Safety Research]. Personal Communication with authors.

Sydney Morning Herald. (2019). 'Smartphone zombies' at risk on Sydney streets, NRMA warns. Available from: https://www.smh.com.au/national/nsw/smartphone-zombies-at-risk-on-sydney-streets-nrma-warns-20190613-p51xbc.html.

The Globe and Mail. (2017). Globe editorial: All those pedestrian deaths? It's the cars, stupid. Available from: https://www.theglobeandmail.com/opinion/editorials/globe-editorial-all-those-pedestrian-deaths-its-the-cars-stupid/article36898698/.

Tolley, R. (1990). *Calming traffic in residential areas.* Tregaron: Brefi Press.

Tolley, R., & Turton, B.J. (1995). *Transport systems, policy and planning: A geographical approach*: Harlow: Longman.

Towards Zero Foundation. (n.d.). The Safe System. Available from: http://www.towardszerofoundation.org/thesafesystem/.

Toy, S., Tapp, A., Musselwhite, C., & Davis, A. (2014). Can social marketing make 20mph the new norm? *Journal of Transport & Health, 1*(3), 165–173.

Tranter, P. (2016). Children's Play in their Local Neighborhoods: Rediscovering the Value of Residential Streets, Living Reference Work Entry. In B. Evans, J. Horton, & T. Skelton (Eds.), *Play, Recreation, Health and Well Being, Geographies of Children and Young People* (pp. 211–236). (Vol. 9). Singapore: Springer.

Tranter, P. (2018). Taming traffic to encourage children's active transportation. In R. Larouche (Ed.), *Children's Active Transportation* (pp. 229–242). Oxford: Elsevier.

VicRoads. (2016). Towards Zero 2016-2020. Available from: https://www.vicroads.vic.gov.au/about-vicroads/our-strategy/road-safety-strategy.

Vision Zero Canada. (2019). Vision Zero Principles, The right to safe mobility. Available from: https://visionzero.ca/#right.

Vision Zero UK. (n.d.). Vision Zero Charter. Available from: https://visionzerouk.wordpress.com/vision-zero-charter/.

Whitzman, C., Romero, V., Duncan, M., Curtis, C., Tranter, P., & Burke, M. (2010). Links between children's independent mobility, active transport, physical activity and obesity. In E. Waters, B. Swinburn, J. Seidell, & R. Uauy (Eds.), *Preventing Childhood Obesity: Evidence Policy and Practice*. Sydney: Wiley-Blackwell.

Willett, T. C. (1964). *Criminal on the road: A study of serious motoring offences and those who commit them*. London: Routledge.

Wolf, C. (2019). Once again, Orlando ranks as the country's deadliest city for pedestrians. *Orlando Weekly*. Available from: https://www.orlandoweekly.com/Blogs/archives/2019/01/24/once-again-orlando-ranks-as-the-countrys-deadliest-city-for-pedestrians-says-new-study.

World Health Organization. (2017). Speed management key to saving lives, making cities more liveable. Available from: https://www.who.int/news-room/detail/05-05-2017-speed-management-key-to-saving-lives-making-cities-more-liveable.

Chapter 9

Slow modes, slow design, slow spaces: new goals for traffic management and planning

'By far the greatest and most admirable form of wisdom is that needed to plan and beautify cities and human communities'.

Socrates

Abstract

A critical component of planning for the 'slower city' involves rearranging land uses to shorten trips. In this chapter we outline seven 'Ds' that make this possible, along with the 'P' of Placemaking. The seven 'Ds' are: density, diversity, design, destination accessibility, distance to public transport, demand management and distribution of employment. Other critical factors to consider include ensuring the zoning ordinances and regulations are not biased in favour of high-speed transport, and that traffic management approaches positively encourage integrated networks of active travel. Planning also needs to be proactive in terms of winning back space for walking and cycling, which includes restricting road capacity through a variety of interventions. While much of the chapter focuses on planning approaches that have been demonstrated to be effective for slowing city transport, we also explore the implications of autonomous vehicles (AVs) and micromobility modes for planning.

9.1 Introduction

This chapter continues the discussion of potential solutions to the problems of the fast city—and as such examines ways to conquer our addiction to speed. Whilst Chapter 8 focussed on reducing the speed of motorised traffic through targeted strategies, this chapter examines planning approaches that encourage a reduction in private motorised traffic, as well as a shift to 'slower' modes of transport through changes in land use and traffic management. Chapter 10 focusses on changing societal values, attitudes and behaviour to slow city

Slow Cities. http://dx.doi.org/10.1016/B978-0-12-815316-1.00009-5

transport. Unavoidably, there is overlap between all three chapters in Part 3 of the book, because, as Gordon (2018, p. 44) observes, 'In a broad sense, any intervention is about changing behavior'.

We begin this chapter by making a distinction between land-use planning (Section 9.2) and traffic planning and management (Section 9.3), although it is important to grasp that these issues are intertwined in cause-and-effect feedback loops. As Tolley and Turton (1995, p. 229) summarise, 'just as the promotion of new transport infrastructure changes land uses, so can the planning of land uses influence the demand for transport. Rather than the transport planner providing facilities to attempt to meet the demand, it is vital that the land use planner places facilities in locations where they will minimise the need for movement'.

9.2 Land use and street organisation in the 'slower city'

9.2.1 Relationships between land use and traffic

During the 20th century, as car use became widespread and speeds increased, virtually all cities experienced reductions in density, with journeys becoming longer as distance between necessary functions increased. By manipulating land uses, accessibility can be enhanced through shorter trips, producing more favourable conditions for 'slower' modes. Levine, Grengs, Shen, and Shen (2012) have pointed out that, contrary to what many planners and citizens believe, even in car-dominated US metropolitan areas, 'having destinations nearby, as when densities are high, offers benefits even when the associated congestion slows traffic' (Levine et al., 2012, p. 157). Access is improved more by increasing density than increasing speed. These benefits apply to car users and are strongly magnified for public transport users and people walking and cycling.

We discuss strategies that reduce the space available for speed, encouraging motorised traffic volume to shrink to fit this space. Coordinated land use and transport planning also produces shorter trips more amenable to walking, cycling or using public transport, so that a higher proportion of the reduced overall amount of traffic will be by active travel modes. The result is a slowing of city transport systems.

9.2.2 Land use and street organisation in the 'slower city': seven Ds and a P

Introduction

Whilst many cities have focussed on increasing densities as the main strategy in promoting sustainability, Ewing and Cervero (2010) argue that it is not density per se that matters, as it seems inadvertently to act as a proxy for other significant land use features. They categorised these related features that encourage more walking, cycling and public transport usage into what they referred to as the 'six Ds': Density, Diversity, Design, Destination accessibility, Distance to public transport and Demand management (cost and availability of parking). The six Ds make the biggest impact when they work together. As Udell, Daley, Johnson, and Tolley (2014, p. 19) comment in relation to walking, 'When density, a connected mix of land uses, and enhanced public transport are put together, their synergistic outcomes are much greater than their individual contributions to improved walkability'. In addition to the six Ds, Udell et al. identified the concept of 'Placemaking' as also critical in strategies for creating 'slow cities'; hence we identify six Ds and a P. Other researchers have identified slightly different categorisations in a list of important Ds. For example Giles-Corti et al. (2016, p. 2913) expand on the six Ds by adding two more—Distribution of employment and Desirability in their list of eight Ds, 'integrated interventions that are needed to create cities that promote health'. In this chapter, we use Ewing and Cervero's six Ds and a P, and add a seventh D—'Distribution of employment' to the list of interventions we discuss, making seven Ds and a P, on the basis that 'Desirability' is encapsulated in the concept of 'placemaking' (the P).

Density

Density is a key element affecting the functioning of a city. Higher density development brings activities closer together, reducing the need to travel and thus reducing the reliance on high-speed transport. Higher population thresholds within a given area improve the viability of shops and services, allowing destinations to cluster, increasing convenience for residents to access a variety of needs, and permitting chaining of trip purposes. Importantly for walking and cycling, greater densities also put more eyes on the street, contributing to perceived and actual street safety.

However, increasing residential density alone will not always and necessarily lead to the slowing of the city: it is not difficult to find urban neighbourhoods where densities are high, but levels of walking and cycling are not commensurate with this. What is needed in addition is the mixing and connecting of land uses to reduce distances to destinations.

It is important to note here that whilst there are potential benefits in increased density, we also appreciate that density is not the magic answer to all city transport problems, and transforming huge tracts of low-density suburbia into high-density development is a challenging task. There are strategies that can be employed, even in low-density suburbs, that will encourage a 'slowing' of transport as well as improve the liveability of these areas (see Section 9.2.3). Indeed it is also possible to identify current examples where suburbia works in a 'slow city' way: where there are reasonably high levels of walking, cycling and public transport, and where car speeds are kept under some control. For example, post-war suburbs of Tokyo and Osaka have modest to low densities in many neighbourhoods. Yet they also have low-speed streets, civil-driving behaviours, local destinations, a mix of land uses, good public transport provision and high rates of children walking to school. Whilst we are not arguing that the pace of life in Tokyo is slow, many suburban locations in these cities demonstrate that suburbia can provide a 'slow city transport' environment. This is an important point for this book, as it indicates that planning 'slow cities' does not mean turning our backs on suburbia.

Diversity

A second 'D' is diversity, which refers to the degree of representation of different land uses and includes the balance between jobs and housing (Ewing & Cervero, 2010). Additionally, there needs to be a diversity of housing choice itself, through varied parcel size and housing type, such as apartments and single-family homes, all with services and shops interspersed. Mixed land uses typically result in shorter distances between origins and destinations, which tends to reduce car driving and increase use of alternative modes, particularly walking (Litman, 2018).

Design (intersection density)

The next 'D', design, is more accurately referred to as the combination of street connectivity and intersection density. Street connectivity refers to the layout of the street network. Cities with grid-pattern street networks typically have greater connectivity than those with curvilinear layouts, where close-by places may still involve a circuitous journey. However, density of intersections is important too, as neighbourhoods with smaller blocks have more intersecting streets than places with large blocks—and so distances on the ground tend to be shorter. Grid patterns favour walking and cycling, and grid patterns with small blocks are more favourable still. As far as walking is concerned, it is intersection density, rather than street connectivity that is most important. Indeed, mode share and likelihood of walking trips are more strongly related to intersection density than any other of the Ds (Ewing & Cervero, 2010) and a doubling of intersection density results in about a 44 per cent increase in walking (Campoli, 2012). This is because 'an interconnected street system gives pedestrians what they want – a more direct path and a choice of routes' (Campoli, 2012).

Jane Jacobs' ideas for encouraging the 'slower' modes were introduced in Chapter 3. Recent research in Italian cities has found strong support for her approach. Jacobs favoured short streets and city blocks with lots of corners (see Fig. 9.1). Using data from mobile phone usage, Italian researchers demonstrated that those parts of Italian cities that meet the criteria for Jacobs' ideal city streets are also the ones that promote vibrant city life and walking. Those areas with 'dense streets which, in fact, slow down cars … make it easier for pedestrians to cross, creating what Jane Jacobs called the "sidewalk ballet"' (De Nadai et al., 2016, p. 420). For Jacobs, this 'ballet' was critical to the liveability of a city, helping to promote informal contacts and public trust.

Destination accessibility

Destination accessibility is the fourth 'D' and is the main environmental influence on trip length and thus on mode choice: people will only choose to travel

FIGURE 9.1 Short blocks with lots of corners promote vibrant city life and walking in Rome, Italy. *(Credit: Peter Carr, Rome 2012, View from the Spanish Steps. https://www.flickr.com/photos/peterdcr/7392541594)*

on foot or by bike if their destination is close by and within reach by that mode. As outlined in Chapter 7, Walk Score, Transit Score and Bike Score are well-known tools that use destination accessibility for calculating the accessibility of a place by non-car modes. In addition to the distances to destinations, quality is important too: the more desirable the destination (and the route), the further people are willing to walk (or ride) (Kent, Thompson, & Jalaludin, 2011) as discussed in Section 9.3.5.

Distance to public transport

Distance to public transport is the fifth 'D'. Ewing and Cervero (2010) showed how having public transport stops nearby might stimulate walking, as well as encourage people to use public transport. If 'nearness to public transport' is associated with other variables discussed in this section, its power is enhanced. For example, access distances to stops and stations are reduced by high intersection densities, whilst diversity of land uses makes trip chaining—such as picking up some groceries on the way home from the train station—more feasible. Moreover, Campoli (2012, p. 16) has referred to 'the virtuous cycle of density and transit', whereby concentrating people and jobs next to public transport increases ridership, which facilitates enhanced frequencies, which in turn make public transport more attractive and driving less necessary.

Demand management

A variety of interventions fit under the heading of this 'D', demand management, and some will be examined in more detail in Chapter 10. Here we deal with the original focus of Ewing and Cervero (2010): the availability and cost of car parking, which have significant effects on travel behaviour, mode choice and speed. Plentiful parking encourages car journeys that would not be made if no parking were available at the end of the trip. Low parking costs, which are heavily subsidised by municipalities (as detailed in Chapter 7) encourage greater car use, with a myriad of deleterious consequences for the 'slower' modes. Less space for parking would allow more housing and other activities, thus raising densities, which would increase ridership on public transport, making more frequent service possible and reducing the demand for parking. As Udell et al. (2014, p. 27) summarise, 'replacing surface lots and street level garages and parking with homes or businesses improves the quality of the street; makes public transport more attractive; and encourages trips by bike or on foot'.

Distribution of employment

One of the consequences of a sprawling city designed around high-speed roads is that new dormitory suburbs are often created. Whilst this provides space for people and their cars, it usually also means that the only choice for people to get to their jobs is to drive long distances. To facilitate access to employment, one useful strategy is known as 'sprawl repair', discussed in Section (9.2.3). An important part of sprawl repair is the move away from a monoculture of land use where specific land uses dominate large areas, creating a reliance on high-speed modes. Introducing new employment centres, linked with public transport and aiming to increase the percentage of the population with access to employment within 20 to 30 minutes of their home by walking, cycling or public transport supports the creation of 'slow cities'. However, not only is it important that local employment be created, but employment centres should also be designed as 'places' that people want to be in.

Placemaking

If the seven Ds are enhanced in a city, it follows that more people could spend more time in the streets travelling by the active modes. But though the seven Ds are necessary, they are not sufficient, for they do not deal with the quality of the public environment. To maximise the use of feet and bicycles, streets, public transport stations and public squares also need to be attractive places for people to move through and gather and linger. As densities rise, so does the importance of public space for relaxation and socialising. This requires conscious 'placemaking', because many existing spaces in car-dominated cities have been designed and managed to maximise the speed of motorised vehicles, with the space set aside for people often an afterthought. Placemaking transforms a place into a desirable, vibrant community place, a place to *be* somewhere, not

(A)

(B)

FIGURE 9.2 Photo A: Campus Martius Park in Detroit, a striking example of the power of successful placemaking. It attracts people throughout the day by offering activities for all ages and social backgrounds and has helped bring new investment into downtown. Photo B: Placemaking in Commercial Drive, Vancouver, Canada. A local 'street library' and kerbside garden provides a focal point for social interaction. *(Credit: Photo A, jodelli, Campus Martius. https://www.flickr.com/photos/23056733@N05/2655748043/; Photo B, Paul Tranter)*

just to *get* somewhere (Fig. 9.2). The Project for Public Spaces (PPS) explains that placemaking is about 'more than just promoting better urban design'; it 'facilitates creative patterns of use, paying particular attention to the physical, cultural, and social identities that define a place and support its ongoing evolution' (Project for Public Spaces, n.d.). As Udell et al. (2014, p. 22) comment, 'Creating attractive, quiet spaces for people, at a human scale, designed specifically for people to meet and interact on foot, dramatically increases the time people spend in the street, not so much travelling, but sojourning. Vibrant streets need people on foot to be there – and in turn this creates more vibrancy'. Fig. 9.2 provides illustrations of two different types of placemaking: large-scale placemaking helping to rejuvenate an inner-city location; and small-scale placemaking in a suburban neighbourhood.

9.2.3 Zoning for a 'slower city'

Many practical ways of achieving these seven Ds and a P outcomes can be obstructed by an enormously influential and pervasive 'hidden hand' in city planning, that of zoning ordinances. This is often the case when parking management is considered, because zoning ordinances often specify a minimum number of off-street parking places to be provided with each new development. This is the case in the United States and Canada, but other countries as diverse as Australia, India and Malaysia have adopted the same approach. For each increment of square footage to be developed, more off-street parking must be added.

Graña (2018) provides the example of Marietta, Georgia where 'Zoning ordinances mandating parking, and the public works practice of increasing road capacity in tandem with new development, make it impossible to build new compact development. And over time they have even transformed a critical area for potential value—the downtown business district—into what is predominantly a parking lot'.

Many cities in Europe have removed minimum parking requirements and some, such as London, have replaced them with a maximum standard (Guo & Ren, 2013). There is now a nascent movement to do so in the United States, exemplified by Buffalo, New York, where minimum codes were adopted in the 1950s as the city tried to compete with new workplaces emerging in the suburbs by providing cheap or free parking in the central business district (Hess, 2017). After 70 years of sprawl the CBD was left cratered by surface parking lots. However, in 2017 a new 'green code' was adopted, which removes minimum parking requirements and reduces barriers to infill development and adaptive reuse (Hess, 2017). The city and its waterfront are now undergoing rapid, and partially walkable, regeneration. It is a classic example of the aphorism that 'no-one ever goes to a place because it has great parking'.

What Buffalo is doing (along with many other cities) is overhauling its conventional zoning ordinances, which typically micromanage and segregate land uses, controlling development intensity through abstract parameters (e.g. parking ratios), but ignore the liveability of neighbourhoods. These ordinances are being replaced by 'form-based codes', which consider the importance of building facades to people's experience of place, as well as the scale and types of streets and intersections. This fosters a high-quality public realm 'using physical form (rather than separation of uses) as the organising principle for the code' to 'achieve a community vision based on time-tested forms of urbanism' (Form Based Codes Institute, 2018).

Of course, zoning changes are medium to long term in impact, and do not have the immediacy of some of the 'lighter, quicker, cheaper' interventions described in Chapter 10, but they are an essential building block for a lasting shift towards the 'slower city'. They may have a profound impact, by arresting current inappropriate developments and creating the conditions for radically different 'slower cities' of the future.

Rezoning for walkable city centres and building transit-orientated developments are vital tasks, but in car-dominated societies most residents live in the suburbs and many are currently denied the opportunity to access health-nurturing 'slower' modes of movement. There will be no quick fixes for this, so strategies for incremental and opportunistic redevelopment need to be adopted for so-called 'sprawl repair' or suburban transformations. Useful examples of how this can be achieved are provided by Montgomery (2013), Tachieva (2010a) and Cervero, Guerra, and Al (2017). Tachieva (2010b) has argued that such sprawl repair should be pursued using 'the same instruments that made sprawl the prevalent form of development … a comprehensive method based on urban design, regulation, and strategies for funding and incentives'. In her *Sprawl Repair Manual* Tachieva (2010a) shows how business parks can be transformed into vibrant commercial centres by building streets and shops on tarmac formerly used for parking. Wide roads can be put on diets and turned into 'main streets', with slower traffic in narrower lanes, with more streetlights and sidewalks. Walkability in poorly connected networks of culs-de-sac can be improved by strategic insertion of connecting roads and lanes.

Montgomery (2013, pp. 283–285) illustrates the success of such sprawl repair in the example of a retrofit of a vast, dying mid-century shopping mall and parking lots on a 104-acre (42 hectare) site in Lakewood, near Denver, that had lost business to newer malls. The original superblock was transformed into what is now known as the Belmar Town Center redevelopment, with 23 smaller blocks and streets connecting to surrounding residential areas. Small retail shops line the streets, keeping them slow and walkable. The new development also has a central town green and plaza, encouraging people to visit and linger without needing a purpose such as shopping (Fig. 9.3). There are also new residential developments on the site, with people living in townhouses, apartments above stores, and lofts (Montgomery, 2013).

Although it is possible to find successful examples of sprawl repair, it is important to recognise that rebuilding the suburbs will require 'strong leadership, extensive community engagement, and willing development partners – any of which may be lacking in particular suburbs' (Steuteville, 2018). This will be an immense challenge, but one that cannot be shirked. In order to win back health and sustainability, the 'slow city' cannot be just the inner districts, but must encompass entire suburban areas too where many people now live their lives.

FIGURE 9.3 Sprawl repair: a plaza encouraging people to linger in the new Belmar Shopping Center, built on the site of a dying former shopping mall in Lakewood, Colorado. *(Credit: Amy Aletheia Cahill, Plaza 3, Belmar Shopping Center. https://www.flickr.com/photos/themeowverlord/15453438595)*

9.3 Traffic management approaches to slowing the city

9.3.1 Introduction

The case for more cycling, walking and public transport use underpins the purpose of this book. Recent research clearly demonstrates that investment in walking and cycling is a far more effective investment than any project that supports car use, even using benefit-cost analysis that (wrongly) assumes that time savings occur with projects that increase speeds. Whilst benefit-cost ratios of only 2:1 are regarded as high value for money in road projects, the economic benefits of interventions to promote walking and cycling have average benefit cost ratios of 13:1, and for the United Kingdom alone, the median figure is even higher, at 19:1 (Davis, 2010). Despite clear evidence of the economic benefit of support for walking and cycling, this investment is not happening in the majority of the world's cities (for reasons explored in Chapter 10). For example, at present rates of investment, it is likely to take more than 50 years to get a bare-bones, low-risk, trunk cycling network across the suburbs of most Australian, US or Canadian cities.

In the following sections we discuss the specific methods required for improving the opportunities for the 'slower' modes of walking and cycling, outlining them individually, but always being cognisant of their synergistic characteristics and thus the need for integrated planning for networks of active travel. We deal with cycling first, followed by walking, micromobility modes and lastly, public transport.

9.3.2 Promote and encourage cycling

The two principal 'slower modes', cycling and walking, are dealt with separately here, and this is quite deliberate. It was unfortunate that as planning for these modes accelerated early in this century, cycling frequently dominated, with walking sometimes included almost as an afterthought. Many 'walking and cycling plans' are mostly about cycling, and they commonly display a misunderstanding of the very different characteristics and requirements of the two modes. 'Fast cities' have planned for cars first and then allocated the left over space to people on foot or bicycles. This is frequently justified by the argument that there is not enough space to provide separate facilities for the two modes, whereas in reality there is space—but the city has filled it up with cars. Paths shared between people cycling and others walking meet the specific needs of neither people on foot nor bikes. People riding bicycles have their clear path obstructed by dogs, children and slow walkers, whilst those on foot are often intimidated by inconsiderate or fast riding. For example, in Australia a Victoria Walks survey of seniors walking on Victorian shared paths reported considerable fear of people on bicycles (Garrard, 2013). We should be clear, as Forsyth and Krizek (2010, p. 440) concluded, that walking and cycling warrant separate consideration and that 'hard and soft interventions to promote one do not necessarily work to promote another'. As a result, with rare exceptions, separate facilities are warranted.

In order to stimulate more use of bicycles, there are key design criteria for the provision of successful and effective cycling infrastructure. Here they are adapted from the Greater Manchester Cycling Design Guidance and Standards (Greater Manchester District Authority Partners, 2014).

- **Safety**: cycling infrastructure must cater for all age groups and the full range of cycling abilities, achieved through largely segregated cycle facilities whereby people on bikes are separated from other road users;
- **Coherence**: the cycle route must be easy to find and intuitive to navigate; be consistent in quality; and offer route continuity and completeness;
- **Directness**: the cycle facilities must be direct in terms of both distance and time. Cycle routes need to serve key desire lines, connecting origins to destinations end-to-end without significant detour or delay;
- **Attractiveness**: the cycling environment along a route should be pleasant and interesting to encourage the full range of people on bikes including beginners, and those cycling for recreation and commuting. There should be good levels of natural surveillance and street lighting in order to promote personal safety;
- **Comfort**: cycling infrastructure should be designed, built and maintained for ease of use and for comfort. This means application of high-quality surface treatment and seeking to minimise the number of times it is necessary to stop or conflict with other road users.

As a result of the application of these principles, a large variety of cycle facilities can be envisaged which may be protected, buffered, raised, uni- or bi-directional, contraflow or entire cycle streets (NACTO, 2016a). Increasingly popular are kerbside lanes, known as 'Copenhagen style' lanes, which are aligned between the sidewalk and a parking lane, thus largely removing danger from car doors being opened and from moving vehicles.

Aside from these specific design criteria, there is also a recognised hierarchy of provision of cycle link facilities, whereby planners should consider first, motorised traffic volume reduction and then successively: motorised traffic speed reduction; junction treatment; reallocation of carriageway space; and last, cycle tracks away from roads. Routes will need improved signage, wayfinding and dedicated traffic lights. Nor should we forget that provision for cycling is not just about routes, but about end of trip facilities too. Secure cycle parking (carefully located and tailored to destination and function), showers, repair facilities, and sharing and docking options may all be needed.

In applying these criteria and priorities, conflicts will likely arise—as when, for example, the safest route planned may not be the most convenient. Flexibility and judgment are required, together with the recognition that people on bikes are not a homogeneous group. This is not an exercise in catering only for the fearless and fast, as many Australian cities have done in prioritising the so-called MAMILs (Middle Aged Men In Lycra). Such an approach is never adopted in cities and countries where cycling is seen and planned as a mainstream modal choice, used for practical purposes by all population groups (and ages from at least 8 to 80 years) as part of normal everyday activity (Pucher & Buehler, 2008).

One of the key issues in planning routes concerns whether people cycling will have their own space or whether they will share space on the road with cars. The classic Dutch design manual (CROW, 1993) says that the speed and intensity of motorised traffic are the main factors to be considered, and it provides detailed technical advice on how best to respond to various combinations of motor traffic volume and speed. In recent years this debate has swung decisively towards segregation, with (NACTO, 2014) design guidance indicating that separated bike lanes improve perceived comfort and safety, and as a result are more attractive to a wide range of people on bikes at all levels and ages. This trend has led to a strong push for segregated cycle lanes, such as the 100 miles of protected bike lanes in New York City (New York City Department of Transportation, 2017); the cycling superhighways in London (Buczynski, 2018); and the 75 miles of segregated tracks planned for Manchester in Britain's largest cycling network (Cox, 2018).

However, though these lanes take some space from the car, in the context of this book they are a partial solution at best. The CROW manual was prescient in pointing out that just because an integrated solution is not appropriate, it does not mean that segregation is necessarily the answer, because 'The other possibility is to take away the source of the incompatibility by changing the composition of the traffic flow' (Godefrooij, 1997, p. 235). In the 'slow city', cycling (and public transport) would be the dominant use of road space and should have priority because 'Whenever integrated solutions are chosen, the quality for cyclists will be improved by reducing speed and flow of the motor traffic'

(Godefrooij, 1997, p. 236). Thus, the holistic view is that a central tenet of promoting cycling is restraining faster—and more dangerous—traffic. Reducing speeds in all residential streets to 30 km/h or lower will make it safer for people on bikes throughout the city (see Fig. 7.12), whereas separated cycling lanes cannot be built for every street. This is already happening in many European cities. For example, many streets in Norwegian cities have been designated 'Sone 30', and Oslo is planning 30 km/h speed limits on all local streets (see Fig. 8.15), making cycling on these streets safer and hence more appealing.

9.3.3 Promote and encourage walking

Though—or perhaps because—walking is the oldest form of travel, planning for it is the youngest. Until this century, the prevailing (if implicit) view was 'Why would we need to plan for something that everybody does, something that is just a part of life?' It was not until the late 20th century that the decline in walking became apparent, at the same time as the realisation that catering for the speed demands of motor cars was causing difficulties for city life, such as congestion, pollution, sprawl and ill-health. Such planning as there was for walking was usually focussed on trying to protect people on foot from the worst impacts of vehicular traffic.

In 2000, the London Walking Forum reflected that 'Walking is one of the first things a child wants to do, and one of the last things an adult wants to give up' (London Walking Forum, 2000, p. 3), and yet as a society we have been taking walking for granted. In the words of the London Planning Advisory Committee (1996) walking is 'so basic to all planning and transport activities, and so undemanding in terms of government finance, that it somehow slips through the net in strategy formulation'.

A key issue for this (past) lack of appreciation of the importance of walking was the lack of data. On the principle that what is not counted, does not count, John Adams wryly observed that the UK Department of Transport's statisticians 'did not consider walking to be a form of transport and did not collect information about it' (Adams, 1993, p. 74). In turn this justified the dismissal of walking at policy level: though walking accounted for nearly one-third of trips in the United Kingdom, only *two* staff were in post nationally in 2001 to plan for it. The relevant Minister extraordinarily thought this to be 'about right … because most of us know how to do it' (Tolley, 2008, p. 128).

At the practical level, walking projects were small scale, inexpensive and unglamorous, a far cry from the big-ticket investments (or 'boys' toys'), association with which was expected to further planners' careers. Equity and gender issues were evident in the lack of planning for walking, as the majority of transport planners were middle class men, precisely the group who walked the least and drove the most. It would be interesting to speculate on how government advice and policy might have been different if delivered by women, especially mothers of young children, or from a pushchair perspective rather than from through a windscreen (Matchett, 2018). There was no organised constituency

TABLE 9.1 Primary characteristics of walkable communities and routes: the 'five Cs'.

Characteristics	Definition	Benefits
Connected	The extent to which the pedestrian network or route links to key destinations and to other routes	People can walk from one place to another without encountering major obstacles or severance
Convivial	The extent to which walking is a pleasant activity, in terms of interaction with the built and natural environment, and other road users	Pedestrian routes are friendly and attractive, and are perceived as such by pedestrians
Conspicuous	The extent to which walking routes and public spaces feel safe and inviting for people on foot	Suitable levels of lighting, visibility, surveillance, delineation and signage
Comfortable	The extent to which walking is accommodated for all types of people within the transport corridor	High quality and well-maintained footpaths of suitable widths, attractive landscaping and architecture, shelter and rest places and a suitable allocation of roadspace
Convenient	The extent to which walking is able to compete with other modes of transport in terms of efficiency (in time, money and space)	Walking is a realistic travel choice, because walking routes are of a suitable length as a result of land use planning, with minimal delays

(Sources: Grant & Tolley, 2005; Transport for London, 2004)

for such views, because few people self-identify as pedestrians (unlike drivers, for example). This lack of powerful lobby or advocacy groups compounded the problem of the invisibility of walking, and not just in the United Kingdom.

The importance of planning for walking is now obvious and widely supported, but it bears re-stating. Clearly, for people to decide to walk, there must be individual factors in place, such as awareness of neighbourhood opportunities, support of family and friends, and seeing other people out and about walking. But such personal motivation—'willingness to walk' factors—must be supported by conducive environments, which requires conscious appreciation of the many real or perceived deterrents to going out on foot. These include personal safety and fear of crime, speeding traffic, noise and pollution, lack of seating and toilets and inadequate sidewalks (made worse by traffic-related paraphernalia such as guard rails, traffic signs and insensitively parked cars). Above all, walking must be a feasible option in terms of distance and connectivity. A structure for dealing with these issues is provided by the widely used 'five Cs of walkability' (Pharoah, n.d.) (Table 9.1).

FIGURE 9.4 A high quality walking environment meeting all of the 'five Cs of walkability' criteria, in Brisbane, Australia. *(Credit: Rodney Tolley)*

Applying the 'five Cs' is not a case of an upgraded sidewalk here, or a better road crossing there, but instead requires a holistic approach that provides for all kinds of walking, by all inhabitants, within the whole urban area. The outcome should be complete networks for walking, which are connected to key destinations, and are permeable, accessible, comfortable, safe, and relevant to context, recognising character, identity, topography, nature, human scale and complexity (Fig. 9.4). However, the reality in many cities is a range of network discontinuities for people on foot, particularly focussed on the intersection of walking routes and routes for motorised traffic (Fig. 9.5).

It is particularly relevant to comment on Photos E and F in Fig. 9.5. To some it may seem counter-intuitive to describe a footbridge over a road as a 'discontinuity'. However, crossing this bridge will involve walking an extra 120 metres, adding about 1.5 minutes at typical walking speeds of 80 m/minute. This time delay can comprise a high proportion of a short-range walking trip, to the shops or friends' houses for example. Moreover, the gradients involved will slow wheelchair users and those with children, strollers or baggage, and perhaps be insurmountable to physically impaired or elderly individuals.

It would be claimed that this bridge makes walking 'safer'—and so it does on the drawing board. But humans are effort minimisers and they may not behave predictably if obstacles are put in their way. The reality is that such foot overbridges present such a barrier to many people that they depress the number of

FIGURE 9.5 Network discontinuities for people on foot. (A) The sidewalk ends and a desire line avoids a tree, Australian National University, Canberra; (B) The onus placed on people walking to 'look out for traffic' in the Gold Coast, Australia; (C) A wheelchair user struggles to reach the button at traffic control lights, Bundaberg, Australia; (D) People on foot making a dash from their 'cage', York, United Kingdom; (E) Youths crossing an 80 km/h road in Melbourne, Australia, to avoid using the footbridge; (F) A urine-scented and tagged road underpass entrance in Melbourne, Australia. *(Credit: Photos A to D, and F, Rodney Tolley; Photo E, Paul Tranter)*

walking trips in the neighbourhood. The result is that people make fewer walking trips, or—if they feel brave and are fleet of foot—they can make a run for it across the 80 km/h road, as the young men in the picture are doing. In a holistic sense it cannot conceivably be argued that depressing the number of walking trips or expecting people to refrain from running across the road constitute making people 'safer'. The very existence of the bridge will encourage drivers to go faster and pay less attention, (as the expectation will be that there will be no

FIGURE 9.6 Continuous sidewalks make people on foot feel empowered, respected, valued and welcomed in Boroondara, Melbourne, Australia. *(Credit: Rodney Tolley)*

people close to the road) thus making the situation more dangerous still. Similar arguments apply to the use of foot underpasses, such as pictured in Photo F in Fig. 9.5. This is clearly a discontinuity for people in wheelchairs, and is unlikely to be used by anyone because of the perceived risks of walking in an area with no passive surveillance, in addition to the visual and olfactory unpleasantness.

One way to avoid these network interruptions is to design walking routes using the principle of continuous sidewalks, which recognises the drawbacks of crossing roads using footbridges, underpasses and marked pedestrian crossings (or pedestrian crosswalk lines). A street with a marked crossing provides a message to all road users—including drivers and people walking—that when crossing the street walkers are entering the domain of motorised traffic and vulnerable road users need to 'watch their step'. On the other hand, continuing sidewalks across side streets (Fig. 9.6) reduces road danger and sends a message to motorists that they are crossing an area designed for walkers, and hence it is their responsibility to look out for—and give way to—people on foot. This is an important physical and psychological distinction that not only makes walking more comfortable, but in addition empowers walkers, making them feel respected, valued and welcomed.

Signage and wayfinding are essential if we are to promote walking, using a 'clear visual language that can be universally understood' (NACTO, 2016a, p. 76). The Vienna 'strolling promenades' are a good example of this approach, designed to form a network of walking routes across different districts. These promenades encourage longer distance walking, with signage systems, resting areas and seats, and broader sidewalks, with the intention to improve the quality of time spent along the routes so people on foot can get from A to B comfortably, safely and in an attractive environment.

This approach can be hard to grasp for those cities that have not normally taken a strategic view of the importance of providing for high quality walking conditions. Recognising this, the access charity Walk21 launched the International Charter for Walking in 2006, which identifies the needs of people on foot and provides a common framework to help authorities focus their policies, activities and relationships to create a culture where people choose to walk. To date the Charter has been signed by more than 500 Mayors worldwide (see Fig. 1.6), committing their authorities to adhere to its eight principles: supportive land use and spatial planning; reduced road danger; less crime and fear of crime; improved integration of networks; well-designed and managed spaces and places for people; increased inclusive mobility; more supportive municipalities; and a culture of walking (Walk21, 2019). Supporting each principle, the Charter suggests examples of more specific interventions that may be adopted as local circumstances permit.

The Charter has proved to be a very successful device to change the culture at local government level and to assist planners, politicians and practitioners to appreciate that walking is a fundamental human right. It has raised the level of recognition that 'walking' is not just about 'pedestrians', using 'routes' to be provided by 'the traffic engineers' 'so long as vehicular traffic is not interrupted'. Instead it is about creating attractive, safe places for people to stroll, linger, sit and socialise. The presence of such places encourages people to walk to them and through them, and has a major impact on the liveability of our cities. It is no exaggeration to state that walkers are an indicator species for quality of life in the city.

9.3.4 Micromobility devices

Walking has always defined us as humans, and cycling has been with us for over 130 years, but a new phenomenon is now poised to fundamentally change short-distance movement in cities. Micromobility share companies that did not exist a couple of years ago are now attracting enormous sums of investment and popping up unannounced in cities all over the world. For example, in 2018, US users took more than double the number of trips taken in 2017, nearly half of them on shared e-scooters, 'the newest vehicle type in the shared micromobility marketplace' (NACTO, 2019b, p. 5). The diversity is astonishing—electric scooters (Fig. 9.7), hoverboards, segways, solowheels, roller-skates and other micro-vehicles—most of them dockless (i.e. do not have a fixed location and can be dropped off and picked up at different locations) and shared and rented through smartphone apps.

FIGURE 9.7 E-Scooter riders in central Bogotá, Colombia. *(Credit: Carlos Felipe Pardo, BOG scooters 2019-04-03, https://www.flickr.com/photos/carlosfpardo/40592718893/)*

City administrations are reeling from the onslaught of micromobility modes, unsure of how to deal with them. Yet the potential of micromobility to support a move towards slower city transport may be huge:

> *'The micromobility revolution not only highlights a burgeoning need for more slow lanes: It can vividly illustrate the people-moving power of very modest speeds. When a dude on an electric scooter that rarely goes over 10 mph handily beats a BMW across town at rush hour, it's easier to see how the scale of cities supports more-but-slower vehicles' (Small, 2019).*

The micromobility field is changing so fast that it is impossible to write about it without risking being out of date within months. New studies keep appearing, new regulations enacted, new social, practical and ethical concerns voiced. It makes little sense to speculate on the future of micromobility: all we can do at this stage is to raise some of the questions that these new technologies and ownership models might (or might not) raise for the 'slow city' of the future.

- **Sharing.** Are new ownership models a temporary disruption or are they a more profound upheaval of business-as-usual in how we own and operate vehicles in the city?
- **Health.** Will micromobility make health worse by diverting trips from walking and by increasing crashes? Will it depress walking numbers by endangering people walking on footpaths? Or could it improve health by putting the power of the rideable startups behind the provision of better, shared bike facilities?
- **Equity.** Will micromobility devices increase 'transport fairness' by offering safe and inexpensive movement opportunities for seniors, women, children, and those with disabilities? Or will they continue to be predominantly rich, white, boys' toys?
- **Environmental impact.** Will electric rideables benefit the environment by replacing trips by car? Or on the other hand, how can their environmental footprint be minimised, when they continue to be discarded at astonishing rates, exemplified by the scrapping of millions of shared bikes already and scooters lasting only a few months or even weeks before being replaced?
- **Safety.** Micromobility may not qualify as active transport but does qualify as vulnerable. How can the safety of users and others be guaranteed when they are not regulated or licensed? Should helmet use be mandated? Must rider responsibilities be the same as for car drivers, for example regarding alcohol or drug use, especially amongst young males at night? How can the speed differentials between micromobility and walking be managed? Should they be subject to low-speed limits, such as 15 km/h or 10 mph?
- **Public transport.** What are the implications for public transport of widespread use of micromobility devices? Will there be a reduction of trips using public transport for short distances, or a supportive role by allowing penetration of the 'last mile' that public transport struggles to reach?
- **Urban design and public space issues.** A fundamental issue for micromobility modes is the way in which these vehicles make use of public space, particularly sidewalks, but also cycle lanes and roads (Zarif, Pankratz, & Kelman, 2019). Should vulnerable micromobility users be required to share a street with fast, heavy vehicles or should they be allowed to use sidewalks? How should we deal with the current imbalance between the growing mode split for these modes and the actual share of public space they have? Could we hand over 10 to 20 per cent of the road network in city centres to active and micromobility modes?

Micromobility will bring new layers of speeds with very different space needs, which are likely to bring profound disruption to 100-year notions of how space is shared between different users of the urban realm, thus 'requiring cities to establish and adapt new oversight tools, metrics, and practices. E-scooters, in particular, pose unique challenges and opportunities as a new vehicle type, with emerging regulatory standards' (NACTO, 2019b, p. 5). Indeed, we may need to question fundamental concepts, such as who and what we think streets, cycle lanes or sidewalks are actually for.

Adoption rates may vary, but eventually all citizens, of large and small cities in the Global North and South, will be affected. It is vital that a widespread introduction of these new technologies should be used in ways that slow the city, rather than speed it up. In light of that, it is evident that we are going to need very careful thought to ensure that application of this technology supports healthy, happy and sustainable cities and avoids the disastrous mistakes of past city transport policy.

9.3.5 Promote and encourage public transport

Cycling, walking and micromobility are suitable for short to medium trips, but there is a need to cater for longer trips within the city. This requires the provision of comfortable and convenient public transport systems, as is the case in many German cities. As Buehler and Pucher (2012, p. 541) explain, an 'integrated package of complementary policies ... explains why public transport in Germany can compete so well with the private car, even among affluent households. Conversely, it is the lack of complementary policies that explains the continuing struggle of public transport in the USA'. Many surveys report that the most appreciated elements of public transport services are frequency and travel time, with station and stop conditions, real-time information, and service reliability also valued (TransitCenter, 2016). Having to consult timetables and organise arrival times at the station is frustrating for passengers, so systems ideally should aim for a 10-minute frequency at worst. Such frequencies support the so-called 'network effect' that 'mimics the flexibility of a road system by interlacing different routes and modes into a multimodal network where transfers between different routes are nearly effortless' (Hyde & Smith, 2017, p. 2).

Whatever the public transport system chosen, success is unlikely unless there are explicit policies to integrate the service with infrastructure for people on foot and bicycle. In many cities (Melbourne, Australia for example), the great majority of public transport passengers arrives and departs on foot (Mees, 2000) so that a bus ride, and even a train ride, can often be considered as the 'sitting down part' between two walk trips. In these circumstances, 'turn up and go' arrangements can be negated if access on foot to the stop or station is unsafe, indirect, unpleasant or uncomfortable. Avoiding this 'means locating all significant stops in the heart of the action, not a block away ... Riders should be able to fall into the bus from a stool at a coffee shop' (Speck, 2012, p. 155). The

FIGURE 9.8 One of the many innovative street maps in Bristol, United Kingdom, on a walking route to public transport. Five-minute walking times are shown by the red circle, indicating that in this case Temple Meads train station (top centre of the main map) is about seven minutes walk away from your current location—critical information for intending passengers. *(Credit: Rodney Tolley)*

contrast between the ease and desirability of using public transport in different cities is illustrated in Figs 9.8 and 9.9.

The importance of high-quality walking routes to public transport has been corroborated by a fascinating piece of research by Hillnhütter (2016). In examining walking distances to public transport, he posited that people would walk further if their senses and emotions were stimulated by their environment and surroundings. He found that people walking react to stimuli only within a radius of 4–6 metres. However, because of the car's need for speed (relative to walking), urban areas that provide sufficient space for convenient car access mostly exceed the abilities of pedestrians' senses to be stimulated, so walking becomes boring and distances appear longer.

He demonstrated the corollary, which he called 'pedestrian propulsion', where attractive conditions increase acceptable walking distances. Additional destinations (such as shops on a route to a public transport stop) increased

FIGURE 9.9 An unappealing bus stop in an unwalkable and dangerous location in suburban Melbourne, Australia. In effect, this sub-standard provision penalises people for trying to use public transport. *(Credit: Rodney Tolley)*

acceptable walking distances by 15–25 per cent and positive sensory (mostly visual) experiences of urban environments by up to 30 per cent. On the other hand, time delays crossing heavily trafficked streets reduced acceptable walking distances by up to 15 per cent and inconvenient street layouts by up to 20 per cent. Hillnhütter concluded that these influences taken together can increase the distance that people will walk to public transport stops by more than 70 per cent, resulting in a tripling of the catchment area and thus of potential public transport users. Public transport operators are sitting up and taking notice, for increasing potential ridership by these amounts would more traditionally involve huge expenditure on the architecture of the network, the vehicles and the signalling, all of which would be much more expensive than improving walking environments.

Following these principles, the public transport operator in Los Angeles has developed its 'First Last Mile Strategic Plan', a menu of street treatments to improve walking and biking conditions near transit, such as: improved signage and wayfinding with time-to-station signage; signal modifications to prioritise pedestrians at crossings; and sidewalk widening, kerb extensions, street furniture, landscaping, lighting and shade. This is a novel approach, contrasting with past subsidies to cars through park and rides, but 'LA Metro understands that while they may not be the lead actor in making street design changes, they need to assume a proactive position if the agency ever hopes to recover lost riders' (TransitCenter, 2017).

Cervero et al. (2017) support these ideas with a very useful discussion of public transport and transit orientated developments (TODs). They provide a comprehensive discussion of the potential and the challenges of TODs, with detailed examples from around the world. TODs involve the coupling of public transport nodes with high-density land use, integrating efficient and environmentally sustainable development with high quality walking and cycling opportunities. The seven Ds are all required, working together in harmony. A good TOD is not simply a place to travel through, it is a place where people want to be, so the P of Placemaking is required too. Thus, an ideal TOD prioritises the 'slow' modes and avoids the place-destroying features of high-speed roads and car parking areas surrounding interchanges. Otherwise, there is the danger that the development turns into a TAD (transit adjacent development), the 'evil twin of TOD' (Cervero et al., 2017, p. 112).

Contrasting examples may be found in Dallas, Texas and Portland, Oregon. In Dallas a multi-billion-dollar public transport system has failed to increase the percentage of people using public transport, a consequence of a lack of sufficient residential density, stations placed next to highways and large parking garages, and no neighbourhood planning. In contrast, the streetcar line in Portland (Oregon) (Fig. 9.10) was built along with a commitment to 'a host of other strategies and policies, including higher density, neighbourhood based

FIGURE 9.10 One of the streetcars in the successful public transport system in Portland, Oregon. *(Credit: 5chw4r7z Portland Streetcar, https://www.flickr.com/photos/5chw4r7z/15266186878)*

urban design, elimination of minimum parking requirements, and ... the whole list of things that add up to walkability' (Speck, 2012). The original $54.5 million outlay has leveraged over $3.5 billion of investment along the line, a multiplier of 64. Population and street life have grown strongly. As Speck (2012, p. 152) puts it, 'you can't just drop in a streetcar'. A streetcar line done well is not just an addition to public transport options, but is a placemaker, fuelling the growth of localism and slow movement in the city.

It is vital that TODs include affordable housing, as otherwise rising prices may force poor residents to live in suburbs that do not have the advantages of the slower environment of TODs. This raises the broader issue of the inability of TODs to slow entire cities. Whilst they may draw people and commerce into nodes, they do little to improve the quality of neighbourhoods in other parts of the city. Thus, in addition to creating places for people in TODs, streets throughout cities need to be transformed into places for people through policies that slow motorised transport or temporarily remove it from streets, as happens with the play streets and school streets described in Chapter 8. The 'slower city' will need land use planning to generate local movement and to support density and diversity, together with investment in facilities for cycling and walking for local needs and for using those modes to access public transport. But as long as extensive road systems and large amounts of parking are provided to make driving cheap and convenient, development conditions would have to be extraordinarily favourable to engineer a growth of public transport ridership at the expense of driving. In other words, the attraction—and indeed feasibility—of cycling, walking and public transport is unlikely to rise unless the space provided in the city for motorised traffic is restricted. The next section will show how this might be achieved.

9.4 Restrictions on road capacity for motorised vehicles

9.4.1 Introduction

Previous discussion in Chapter 3 emphasised that increasing capacity for motorised vehicles generates traffic and that the corollary—traffic degeneration or evaporation by decreasing capacity—also holds true. That raises the question of what road space can be removed and how. We have already discussed parking management, which is fundamental, as few people would set off on a car journey without the confidence that there will be a place to park at the destination. Here we will examine removal of road space used for circulation, beginning with those interventions that specifically encourage more walking and cycling, and moving on to those which de-commission or re-purpose large amounts of road space to enable the 'slower' modes to thrive.

9.4.2 Reclaiming space for walking and cycling

To encourage cycling, providing connected cycle networks is essential, but the space for these should come from re-allocating road space used by motorised traffic. It should never come from appropriating space currently used by people on foot. Paths shared between people on foot and bikes should not normally be used, as they meet the needs of neither group without compromising comfort and safety. Similarly, providing more space for walking can simultaneously reduce space for vehicle circulation or parking. These can be simple interventions, such as the parklets discussed in Chapter 7, but may be more strategic, such as dealing with weak (or absent) links in a walking network. Examples would include mid-block 'build-outs'—sidewalk extensions into the parking lane—to 'increase visibility, reduce the crossing distance, provide extra waiting space, and allow for seating or landscaping' (NACTO, 2016a, p. 89). A variant is sidewalk extensions at all four corners of an intersection that, in addition to the above benefits, allow the removal of slip lanes (which are dangerous for people on foot) and create tight radii for vehicles, which slows motorised traffic. These are sometimes referred to as 'neckdowns' and in snowy countries such as Canada they can be 'sneckdowns' where the portion of road space which is rarely used by vehicles and can be given to people on foot can be identified after snowfall (P. H. (writing for The Economist), 2014).

9.4.3 Creating plazas from street space

An extension of this approach is to develop public plazas, that 'transform underutilised areas of the street into vibrant social spaces for surrounding residents and businesses' (NACTO, 2016a, 212). When more space is provided for people on foot, this often attracts large numbers of people. A striking example of this can be found in in central Santiago, Chile, where a temporary pedestrian promenade installation using colourful urban art was created in one of the city's busiest streets in 2017 (Fig. 9.11). This was so popular with local citizens and the city Mayor that the pedestrianisation was made permanent in the following year. Effective though these schemes have been in showing what is possible, they are relatively easy wins compared to the wholesale conversion of currently active and fully utilised road space that will be necessary in future 'slow cities'.

9.4.4 Redesigning and activating streets to encourage public transport

Re-purposing road space can also be justified to encourage public transport use, by providing dedicated space in the street, which 'helps transit networks to provide reliable, convenient and frequent service to passengers without delays from mixed traffic' (NACTO, 2016a, p. 106). Variations include dedicated transit lanes that are demarcated by signs and markings; transitways that are physically separated by vertical elements such as planted medians or kerbs; or transit streets where private vehicles are excluded, and space is shared with people

FIGURE 9.11 Each day thousands of people walk, stand and sit in Paseo Bandera, central Santiago, Chile, a space formerly dominated by motorised traffic. *(Credit: Carlos Felipe Pardo, Paseo Bandera, https://www.flickr.com/photos/carlosfpardo/31304582747)*

on foot or bicycle. Whatever the street configuration, stations and stops along the route should ideally be activated as well-connected, multi-use destinations, through placemaking techniques, using cafés, markets, art galleries or performance venues, for example. 'In this way, a great station or stop adds value to the surrounding neighborhoods and increases the viability of commercial districts by connecting businesses to commuters and new customers ... Great experiences in great places attract people, more people means more ridership' (Nelson, 2014).

9.4.5 Narrowing motorised travel lanes

Another technique to restrict space for moving vehicles along the roadway is narrowing travel lanes. Many cities have travel lane widths of highway standards, that is 3.5 or 4 m wide, which have been provided to create a more forgiving environment for drivers. The result is that 'Pedestrians are forced to walk further across streets on which cars are moving too fast' (Speck, 2014). Narrowing these lanes substantially would free space for cycle lanes or wider sidewalks and 'would have a positive impact on street safety' (NACTO, 2016a). The potential is very large: for example, in a survey of 49 main streets in Oklahoma, 94 per cent had lanes wider than 10 feet (3m) (Hampton, 2014).

9.4.6 Developing 'complete streets'

When many of the above changes are introduced in concert, the result is what have become known in the United States as 'complete streets'. The term refers to 'roads designed to accommodate diverse modes, users and activities including walking, cycling, public transit, automobile, nearby businesses and residents' (Litman, 2015, p. 1). Such interventions reduce the speed of motorized traffic and smooth its flow, and provide many direct and indirect benefits such as improved accessibility for non-drivers, cost and energy savings, emission reductions, improved liveability and public health, and support for strategic objectives such reduced sprawl (Litman, 2015).

9.4.7 Providing spaces reserved for people on foot

Providing spaces reserved for people on foot may be another valuable technique. However, when space in the city is at a premium and vigorously contested, it is hard to see where these spaces can be created, until we realise that the 'slow city' is both cause and consequence of re-allocating road space away from motorised vehicles and towards the 'slower' modes. The outcome could be the familiar pedestrianised streets, but also new places and squares carved from car-dominated space. Some interventions are temporary and 'can take multiple forms, emphasising active recreation and exercise, commercial activity or food festivals, or celebrating local art and culture' (NACTO, 2016a, p. 304). Varieties include seasonal events, market or play streets, and car-free days, Ciclovías and 'Open Streets'. Some are more regular and frequent than others, but they all are temporary ways to change the purpose of city streets—prioritising people rather than cars travelling at speed—and they all expose residents to new ways of thinking about moving in the city. Moreover, because such programmes are multi-sectoral, they can engender new alliances amongst government agencies, and private and non-profit sectors, which can prepare the ground for future partnerships for action on city transport and space issues.

Temporary closures often are a prelude to permanent conversion to pedestrian-only streets, which are a familiar sight in many countries in cities old and new. In these, vehicular access is restricted, either totally or at certain times of the day, though access arrangements have to be made for emergency vehicles and deliveries. In many cities only one or two streets are involved, perhaps focussed on the shopping heart of the city together with some historic streets. However, where public transport access is good, extensive systems of pedestrianised streets may develop, as seen in Munich. Buenos Aires is also a good example of a city centre currently being converted into (mainly) pedestrianised/slow space (Everett-Green, 2017), with more than 100 blocks reconfigured. The Buenos Aires approach is not to eliminate cars entirely, and a single lane of strictly local traffic is permitted, with motorised speeds restricted to 10 km/h. The higher concentrations of people on foot through the whole area in the last

FIGURE 9.12 Outdoor cafés along Degraves Street, central Melbourne. *(Credit: Paul Tranter)*

few years has increased restaurant and residential development, and parking lots have been rededicated to other purposes (Everett-Green, 2017).

Spaces reserved for people on foot may include retrofitted service laneways and delivery alleys that add to the diversity of the public space network, aid navigation on foot, and open up forgotten spaces and build identity. They also create new front-facing active edges and 'inside-out' intimate al fresco dining opportunities, exemplified by cafés in narrow streets and laneways in Melbourne's CBD, which are a popular tourist attraction (Fig. 9.12).

Typically, city centre pedestrianised areas have strong retail activity and high levels of footfall and, when designed and maintained well, become a destination with opportunities for sitting, people watching, busking and performances. The commercial function has often been the principal criterion for conversion of a street, but we need to note that from an equity perspective there is a need for car-free spaces to be distributed throughout all neighbourhoods of the city, 'offering opportunities for social interaction, active recreation, healthy living and an improved quality of life' (NACTO, 2016a, p. 192). This is important, for it moves the debate from the relatively straightforward issue of removing vehicles from a busy shopping street, to the art of creating great places throughout the city. This is not just about separate squares or parks, which of course are vitally important, but is about the conversion of elements of the existing fast street network into low-speed 'people places'.

9.4.8 Area-wide motorised traffic restrictions

Some cities have had restrictions on access by vehicles to their centres in place for years, such as Singapore with its Area Licensing Scheme and London with its congestion charge. With exemptions for public transport vehicles, deliveries and servicing, the aim has been to keep private cars and through traffic out of city cores to cut congestion and pollution and to allow recovery of public space. Encouraged by increasing concern about competitive advantage with other cities and greenhouse gas reduction targets, many more cities, including Madrid, Paris and Oslo for example, are now moving quickly in this direction.

9.4.9 Filtered permeability

These area-wide traffic restriction interventions are bold and groundbreaking, but as city-centre only schemes, they do not deal with residential areas or suburbs, and road networks across the city. In the 'slow city', space needs to be reallocated in all such areas to allow active travel to flourish. Attempting to achieve this with vehicle bans across the city would be difficult to enforce, expensive and likely to stir political opposition; so alternative methods need to be sought. One set of approaches entails restricting car access whilst making it easier for the active modes.

We have stressed earlier that a grid system with small blocks shortens distances and makes the city more permeable for people on foot or bikes. However, it shortens distances for cars too, so we would still expect the car to be the quickest option. This can be countered by the use of 'filtered permeability', which 'means separating the sustainable modes from private motor traffic in order to give them an advantage in terms of speed, distance and convenience ... Through traffic is channelled onto a limited network of main roads. Suburban developments are often designed as area-wide culs-de-sac for general traffic, while a range of short cuts such as bridges, tunnels, cycle paths and bus gates provide a more permeable network for the sustainable modes' (Melia, 2012, pp. 2–3) (Fig. 9.13). The Dutch city of Groningen employs this principle as a key element of its transport planning strategies. The network is 'coarse-grained' for cars but 'fine grained' for walking and cycling, so that over 60 per cent of all trips are by bicycle.

Freiburg in Germany is one of the best-known examples of consistent, integrated land use and transport planning that prioritises the active modes (Buehler & Pucher, 2011). Of particular interest is the application of filtered permeability in Vauban, its sustainable neighbourhood of 5,000 residents, built over the 1993–2006 period on an edge-of-town brownfield site (Coates, 2013). The neighbourhood is accessible from only one or two directions by car, but from all directions by bicycle and on foot. Car access is on the 'grannies and groceries' principle—cars may access only for setting down and picking up—and must travel at a walking pace. Active travel is supported by liveable-streets design concepts throughout, with a 30 km/h speed limit, bicycle streets and walking paths—and every street is a 'play street', like a Dutch woonerf (Fig. 9.14).

FIGURE 9.13 Filtered permeability in suburban Vancouver, Canada. People on bikes can pass through this intersection in a 30 km/h zone but motor vehicle access is restricted. *(Credit: Paul Tranter)*

FIGURE 9.14 A typical street in Vauban, Freiburg, Germany, featuring a ‘play street’, with a shared surface and filtered permeability, where car use is permitted but is much less convenient than the active modes. *(Credit: Elliot Fishman)*

FIGURE 9.15 School closing time in Houten, the Netherlands. Children cycle along the traffic-safe bicycle spine or walk along the socially-safe footpaths, whilst motorised traffic must detour around the area. *(Credit: Rodney Tolley)*

These infrastructural interventions are supported by innovative community regulations. For example, residents of Vauban must become car-free or otherwise buy a parking space on the edge of the town for €18–22,000. This combination of measures is extremely effective. The bicycle and walking modal split is 64 per cent and car ownership is half that of neighbouring suburbs (Field, 2014). Even amongst the car owners, 61 per cent were reported to choose to cycle to work, and 91 per cent of the non-car householders commute by bicycle (Taylor & Sloman, 2008).

Filtered permeability principles can also be inbuilt from the outset in new free-standing communities. One outstanding example is Houten in the Netherlands (Fig. 9.15) which was developed from the 1970s as an overspill development for 45,000 people, located 9 km from Utrecht. It has a unique structure that facilitates cycling and walking and restricts car use (Foletta, 2014). Each district is only accessible to cars via a peripheral road encircling the town. A network of paths for people on bikes and on foot provides much shorter routes than for cars, including a bicycle backbone that runs through the centre of the town and has absolute right of way over cars. All schools, the railway station and other important buildings are located along this backbone. As a result the modal split is 55 per cent by cycling and walking. Road crash numbers are half that in other new towns, supported by designing out conflict between cars and active modes and ensuring that no residential street is straight for more than 75 metres, in order to keep vehicle speeds down. Bicycles share space with cars in these streets, but speeds are restricted, traffic calming is in place and signs indicate that cars are guests in the street and must give priority to bicycles (Foletta, 2014).

As well as these examples from European cities there are many small-scale examples in cities in other places, including in the US and Australia. For example, the City of Fremantle (near Perth in Western Australia) has been slowing the city by implementing walking and cycling links and cut-throughs, and connecting bicycle lanes through dead-end streets. Berkeley, California provides an example of retrofitting traditional neighbourhoods, dating from the 1990s, where interconnected grid street layouts were permitting excessive traffic and speeds on some local residential streets. In a trial, the grid system was converted into culs-de-sac for cars, by placing barriers to prevent through traffic whilst allowing people walking and cycling to use the interconnected grid (Southworth & Ben-Joseph, 2013, p. 135). Planters were placed in the middle of some intersections to further slow traffic (Cherulnik, 1993). What started as an experiment proved to be so strongly supported by residents that it was later made permanent.

9.4.10 Removing roads

To close this discussion of re-allocation of road capacity, we should return briefly to wholesale removal of roadways for high-speed traffic. Examples of freeway removal were given in Chapter 3 as part of a discussion about congestion and road capacity. Freeway removal is now an urgent consideration for roads built as part of the post-war interstate highway programme in the United States, which was the largest civil engineering project in history and in many cases inserted elevated road structures through cities. Hundreds of those structures are now life-expired and require extremely expensive repair or replacement. The crisis on the one hand is financial, so replacing urban freeways with surface streets, boulevards and avenues is seen by the Congress for the New Urbanism (2019) 'as the most cost-effective, sustainable option for cities grappling with aging grade separated roads'. However, the crisis is also one of an urgent need to repair or replace the once diverse and vibrant neighbourhoods and local economies that were weakened and isolated by freeways. Not surprisingly, replacing freeways with boulevards for people has gained favour as an alternative to repairing expensive road systems. The removal of the Central Freeway in Hayes Valley, San Francisco is an exemplary community-scale intervention. After the freeway was damaged in an earthquake there was pressure to rebuild it, but a long community campaign led to its demolition in 2003 and the conversion of the route into a boulevard and then into a park with playgrounds and pop up markets. The park is named Patricia's Green after Patricia Walkup, a local resident and activist who led the fight to have the Central Freeway removed. Since the change, the formerly polluted and blighted neighbourhood has undergone rapid revitalisation.

9.4.11 Summary

This section has discussed the deliberate contraction of road space capacity for motorised vehicles. It may seem hard to know where to start to put these ideas for street interventions into an integrated approach. However, help is available through NACTO (the National Association of City Transportation Officials) which has published the Global Street Design Guide (NACTO, 2016a), the first-ever worldwide standard for redesigning city streets to prioritise safety, people walking, transit and sustainable mobility. The guide discusses street typologies and provides specific design guidance for many types of streets including pedestrian priority places, shared streets, neighbourhood streets, and avenues and boulevards. To take just one example, Figs 9.16 and 9.17 illustrate the transformation of a 30 metre–wide neighbourhood main street. Before the redesign, this street had a very wide roadbed and unregulated parking and a 60 km/h speed limit. It served primarily as a vehicular thoroughfare and, amongst other issues, was blighted by:

- wide (and potentially fast) turns at the intersection;
- no marked pedestrian crossings;
- angled parking creating dangerous conditions for people on bicycles;
- transit riders having to disembark in the roadway; and
- blocked or interrupted sidewalks by parked cars, poles and furniture.

The design guidance is to 'Redesign the street to better serve the needs of all users. Protected cycle tracks, curb extensions, transit stops and widened sidewalks distribute the space more equitably to encourage walking, cycling, and transit use' (NACTO, 2016a, p. 247). This is achieved by many measures including:

- reducing the roadbed to one travel lane in each direction and making protected cycle tracks;
- converting angled parking to parallel and alternating spaces with other services such as refuge islands, cycle share stations, trees and rain gardens;
- providing island transit stops for fast accessible boarding;
- adding a raised mid-block crossing;
- widening sidewalks to allow multiple activities without obstructing the clear path, and making sidewalks accessible with ramps and tactile strips;
- improving the public realm that supports local businesses; and
- reducing the speed limit to 40 km/h.

The posted speed limit has been lowered in this redesign, but in a way this is irrelevant, because the synergistic set of design changes will slow traffic down naturally. The road now tells the story, that this is a neighbourhood street for multiple (and equal) users.

FIGURE 9.16 A rendering of an archetypal neighbourhood main street before the kind of transformation recommended by the Global Street Design Guide. *(Credit: The National Association of City Transportation Officials (NACTO))*

FIGURE 9.17 The same street after transformation. *(Credit: The National Association of City Transportation Officials (NACTO))*

9.5 The future impact of autonomous vehicles on land use planning and traffic management

Autonomous Vehicles (AVs) have already been discussed in Chapter 8 in terms of road danger, but they are also likely to have very profound impacts on issues that are the focus of this chapter: land use planning and traffic management. In this context, it is useful to reflect on what the 'slow city' would require from the implementation of AV technology. A widely respected set of principles for new mobility options has resulted from a working group of international NGOs (Chase, 2017). In order to achieve a vision in which the future of mobility in cities is multimodal and integrated, the principles deal with broad issues such as planning cities and mobility together, prioritising people over vehicles, and integration and seamless connectivity. However, the tenth principle is very specific to AVs and their adoption: 'We support that AVs in dense urban areas should be operated only in shared fleets'. This is a critical issue for 'slow cities': 'Shared fleets can provide more affordable access to all, maximize public safety and emissions benefits … and actualize the promise of reductions in vehicles, parking, and congestion, in line with broader policy trends to reduce the use of personal cars in dense urban areas' (Chase, 2017).

Future cities may see an expansion of driverless public transport, particularly in smaller vehicles such as mini-buses. Cervero et al. (2017) suggest that public transport may be one of the first areas of city transport in which vehicle automation thrives. Part of the reason for this is the significant proportion of public transport costs devoted to hiring drivers. The lower costs of providing public automated public transport, in addition to door-to-door service capability, mean that the private sector may find this an appealing investment. The shared model is strongly supported by NACTO (2016b) in terms of public transport in their policy statement on AVs: 'Positioning new mobility services to provide access and mobility to all, and to buttress rather than undermine the successful transit lines at the heart of our cities, is vital to realizing the value of fully automated vehicles for mobility'.

Because there are so many uncertainties—technological, political and societal—predicting outcomes of AV implementation is exceptionally difficult. We should note that the outcome will depend on the policies adopted on sharing or private ownership, on streetspace allocated to AVs, and on permitted speeds. Some observers are pessimistic, like Marohn (2018): 'Automated vehicle technology will do nothing to make our streets better places to be and … has the very real chance of setting our cities back another generation'. Others focus on the opportunities that may become available, dependent on the decisions that we take as a society. For example the Project for Public Spaces has argued that 'This could be a once-in-a-century opportunity for reclaiming the street for people … We can simultaneously expand options for limited-mobility populations, provide new combinations of transportation for everyday trips, and develop new alternatives, while also reducing carbon emissions and dramatically decreasing the rate of automobile accidents' (Salama & Kent, 2016). Janette Sadik-Khan, a former Commissioner of the New York City Department of Transportation and the force behind the walking- and cycling-focussed transformation of Times Square and much of midtown Broadway, is in this camp too. She says 'A century ago, the automotive age swept across the nation, and cities responded not by adapting cars and trucks to the varied uses of the street, but with a relentless clearcutting of obstacles from curb to curb—including pedestrians—and all but eliminating street life. Today, as we enter the third decade of the 21st century, and as we anticipate the arrival of self-driving vehicles on city streets, we have a historic opportunity to reclaim the street and correct these mistakes. This course correction starts with a plan … showing how to adapt new mobility technologies to our cities instead of the other way around' (NACTO, 2019a, p. 3).

The choices we make will be political and not determined by technology. Verbeek (2009, p. 245) argues that 'technology is always political'—and this goes to the heart of AV scenarios. Removing the driver from the car does not question fundamental cultural and political assumptions that cars and their speed are an inevitable accompaniment to 'progress and development'. Indeed, rather than changing in any fundamental way how we define transport problems, focussing on the AV serves to re-emphasise the existing speed-orientated transport planning paradigm.

Sadik-Khan emphasises the point, arguing that if we redesign streets to meet the needs of people, 'Curbsides promote commerce and shared mobility and are priced accordingly. Vehicle travel lanes … are not saturated with thousands of single-occupancy vehicles. And a greater proportion of the street space is dedicated to the kinds of mobility that really make our cities move: public transit, walking, biking and shared rides biking and shared rides' (NACTO, 2019a, p. 3). Given that history has provided few examples of cities successfully stemming the onslaught of speed and cars by ownership restrictions, this approach of regulating AVs by reallocating space to the 'slower', sustainable, active modes seems much more likely to be achievable. As Salama and Kent (2016) conclude 'With all this technological change on the horizon, it is useful still to return to one of PPS's favorite adages: *If you plan cities for cars and traffic—self-driving or otherwise—you get cars and traffic. If you plan for people and places, you get people and places*'.

9.6 Conclusion

This chapter began by discussing ways to rearrange land uses in order to shorten trips, which facilitate active travel and would be a major contribution to slowing the city. The seven Ds make this feasible and the P of placemaking augments them by making attractive and welcoming streets for people. The importance of ensuring that zoning ordinances, planning regulations and parking management are fit for this purpose was stressed, not least in the high-speed suburbs that will require particularly careful attention.

Focus then shifted to how the active travel modes can be encouraged through planning and design, recognising their individual needs as well as their synergistic contributions. In the fast city, space for walking and cycling tended to be what was left over after vehicles had been catered for. In contrast, for the active modes to achieve their potential in the 'slow city' of the future, space needs to be won back from motorised vehicles—and a variety of ways to repurpose road capacity were examined and exemplified. However, additional actions are required to reduce the speed of remaining traffic (see Chapter 8) through legal, physical, behavioural and psychological measures, which are increasingly being embedded in holistic approaches such as safe systems and Vision Zero.

To summarise the approach taken in this chapter, whilst the dominant goals of urban planning and traffic management in the 20th century revolved around maximising the speed of motorised traffic, new goals are now gaining favour: creating 'slower cities' where people can live healthy and happy lives and where economies can thrive. Many of the key strategies required to plan such cities have long been understood, and include creating walkable (and more recently cyclable) streets, having good access to local shops and services, and accessible public spaces that best meet the needs of businesses, local governments and residents. These strategies offer more sustainable alternatives to large-scale segregated land uses in sprawling, low-density development, which have resulted in negative economic, health, and environmental impacts.

Whilst this chapter has focussed on the importance of planning and traffic management, it is important to note that the decisions made by other government departments (e.g. education and health) can undermine the work of land use and transport planners. For example, many cities have adopted New Urbanism codes, reduced their rates of greenfield development and built at least a few transit-orientated developments. However, those same cities often have other departments whose goals (e.g. reducing their own costs) can work in direct opposition to the goals of creating healthier and more sustainable cities. For example, education departments building ever-larger schools with wider catchments effectively forces many parents to drive their children to school. Hospitals and university campuses located in outer-suburban locations also discourage accessibility via walking, cycling or public transport. The education issue is particularly egregious. In many north American cities, education departments appear to have no relationship with or understanding of the goals of planning and zoning departments. As (Toderian, 2018) explains: 'achieving better cities requires that we not only start doing the right things, but also stop doing the wrong things – which can often be harder'. In this context, planning schools and hospitals without considering the implications for accessibility is clearly 'doing the wrong thing'.

Having established 'what' we are trying to achieve in the future 'slow city'—improved health and sustainability by conquering our addiction to speed—we need next to examine 'how' these outcomes are to be achieved. The culture of speed is embedded in so many of our daily practices that the 'slow city' can only be delivered through radically changed behaviour by societies, communities and individuals. What are the policies that need to be pursued and the strategies to deliver them? What are the institutional inputs required, such as visions, leadership, co-operation and partnerships? Which communication strategies have most promise and what will be the balance between the carrots of education, promotion and nudging on the one hand, and the sticks of enforcement on the other? The following chapter will seek to shed some light on these issues that are central to the achievement of the slow city norm in the future.

References

Adams, J. (1993). No need for discussion – the policy is now in place! In P. Stonham (Ed.), *Local Transport Today & Tomorrow: A Collection of Essays Published to Celebrate the 100th Issue of Local Transport Today* (pp. 73–85). London: Local Transport Today.

Buczynski, A. (2018). Evolution of cycle superhighways in London. *European Cyclists' Federation*. Available from: https://ecf.com/news-and-events/news/evolution-cycle-superhighways-london.

Buehler, R., & Pucher, J. (2011). Sustainable transport in Freiburg: Lessons from Germany's environmental capital. *International Journal of Sustainable Transportation*, *5*(1), 43–70.

Buehler, R., & Pucher, J. (2012). Demand for public transport in Germany and the USA: An analysis of rider characteristics. *Transport Reviews*, *32*(5), 541–567.

Campoli, J. (2012). Made for walking. Density and neighborhood form. *Lincoln Institute of Land Policy*. Available from: https://www.coliman.org/app/download/755906227/walkingCities.pdf.

Cervero, R., Guerra, E., & Al, S. (2017). *Beyond mobility: Planning cities for people and places*. Washington: Island Press.

Chase, R. (2017). Shared mobility principles for livable cities. Available from: https://www.sharedmobilityprinciples.org.

Cherulnik, P. D. (1993). *Applications of environment-behavior research: Case studies and analysis*. Cambridge: Cambridge University Press.

Coates, G. J. (2013). The sustainable urban district of Vauban in Freiburg, Germany. *International Journal of Design & Nature and Ecodynamics*, *8*(4), 265–286.

Congress for the New Urbanism (2019). *Freeways without futures*. Available from: https://www.cnu.org/our-projects/highways-boulevards/freeways-without-futures.

Cox, C. (2018). The £1.5bn masterplan to create UK's biggest cycling and walking network in Greater Manchester. *Manchester Evening News*. Available from: https://www.manchestereveningnews.co.uk/news/greater-manchester-news/cycling-walking-lanes-greater-manchester-14832995.

CROW. (1993). *Sign up for the bike: Design manual for a cycle-friendly infrastructure*. Ede (Netherlands): Centre for Research and Contract Standardization in Civil and Traffic Engineering.

Davis, A. (2010). *Value for money: An economic assessment of investment in walking and cycling*. Available from: https://bikehub.ca/sites/default/files/valueformoneyaneconomicassessmentof-investmentinw.pdf.

De Nadai, M., Staiano, J., Larcher, R., Sebe, N., Quercia, D., & Lepri, B. (2016). *The death and life of great Italian cities: A mobile phone data perspective*. Paper presented at the Proceedings of the 25th International ACM Conference on World Wide Web.

Everett-Green, R. (2017). Walk this way, In Buenos Aires, pedestrian streets are the way of the future. *The Globe and Mail*. Available from: https://www.theglobeandmail.com/life/home-and-garden/design/walk-this-way-in-buenos-aires-pedestrian-streets-are-the-way-of-the-future/article26108585/.

Ewing, R., & Cervero, R. (2010). Travel and the built environment: A meta-analysis. *Journal of the American Planning Association, 76*(3), 265–294.

Field, S. (2014). *Case study Vauban, Freiburg, Germany*. Available from: https://www.itdp.org/wp-content/uploads/2014/07/26.-092211_ITDP_NED_Vauban.pdf.

Foletta, N. (2014). *Case study Houten, Utrecht, The Netherlands*. Available from: https://www.itdp.org/wp-content/uploads/2014/07/22.-092211_ITDP_NED_Desktop_Houten.pdf.

Form Based Codes Institute. (2018). Form-Based Codes Defined. *FBCI*. Available from: https://formbasedcodes.org/definition/.

Forsyth, A., & Krizek, K. J. (2010). Promoting walking and bicycling: Assessing the evidence to assist planners. *Built Environment, 36*(4), 429–446.

Garrard, J. (2013). *Senior Victorians and walking: Obstacles and opportunities: Summary report*. Available from: http://www.victoriawalks.org.au/Assets/Files/FINALSeniorsSummary.pdf.

Giles-Corti, B., Vernez-Moudon, A., Reis, R., Turrell, G., Dannenberg, A. L., Badland, H., & Stevenson, M. (2016). City planning and population health: A global challenge. *The Lancet, 388*(10062), 2912–2924.

Godefrooij, T. (1997). Segregation or integration for cyclists? The Dutch approach. In R. S. Tolley (Ed.), *The greening of urban transport: Planning for walking and cycling in western cities* (2nd ed., pp. 229–238). Chichester: Wiley.

Gordon, C. (2018). Economic Benefits of Active Transportation. In: R. Larouche (Ed.), *Children's Active Transportation* (pp. 39–52). Oxford: Elsevier.

Graña, A. (2018). How zoning codes reinforce car dependency. *Strong Towns*. Available from: https://www.strongtowns.org/journal/2018/8/23/how-zoning-codes-reinforce-car-dependency.

Grant, J., & Tolley, R. (2005). *A project to improve the quality of pedestrian signage in the South Melbourne Central Activity Centre*. Melbourne: City of Port Phillip.

Greater Manchester District Authority Partners. (2014). *Greater Manchester Cycling Design Guidance and Standards Version 2.0*. Available from: https://www.gmcc.org.uk/wp-content/uploads/2014/03/GM_CDGS_v2-0.pdf.

Guo, Z., & Ren, S. (2013). From minimum to maximum: Impact of the London parking reform on residential parking supply from 2004 to 2010? *Urban Studies, 50*(6), 1183–1200.

Hampton, S. (2014). Jeff Speck Argues for Narrower Lanes. *Institute for Quality Communities*. Available from: http://www.ouiqc.org/2014/10/06/lanewidth/.

Hess, D. B. (2017). New zoning code in Buffalo removes parking requirements. *Strong Towns*. Available from: https://www.strongtowns.org/journal/2017/1/17/new-zoning-code-in-buffalo-removes-parking-requirements.

Hillnhütter, H. (2016). *Pedestrian access to public transport* (PhD Thesis). University of Stavanger, Stavanger.

Hyde, R., & Smith, D. (2017). *Assessing the value of public transport as a network*. Paper presented at the Australasian Transport Research Forum, Auckland.

Kent, J., Thompson, S., & Jalaludin, B. (2011). *Healthy built environments: A review of the literature*. Sydney: Healthy Built Environments Program, City Futures Research Centre, UNSW.

Levine, J., Grengs, J., Shen, Q., & Shen, Q. (2012). Does accessibility require density or speed? A comparison of fast versus close in getting where you want to go in US metropolitan regions. *Journal of the American Planning Association, 78*(2), 157–172.

Litman, T. (2015). *Evaluating complete streets: The value of designing roads for diverse modes, users and activities*. Available from: https://www.ctc-n.org/sites/www.ctc-n.org/files/resources/compstr.pdf.

Litman, T. (2018). *Land use impacts on transport: How land use patterns affect travel behavior*. Available from: https://www.vtpi.org/tdm/tdm20.htm.

London Planning Advisory Committee. (1996). *Putting London back on its feet: A strategy for walking in London*: London Planning Advisory Committee, London.

London Walking Forum. (2000). *Walking: Making it happen:* London Walking Forum: London.

Marohn, C. (2018). Automated Vehicles Will Make Our Streets Worse. *Strong Towns*. Available from: https://www.strongtowns.org/journal/2018/4/2/automated-vehicles-xwkj3.

Matchett, K. (2018). Sexism on the sidewalk: How poor street design keeps women from walking. *America Walks*. Available from: https://americawalks.org/sexism-on-the-sidewalk-how-poor-street-design-keeps-women-from-walking/.

Mees, P. (2000). *A very public solution: Transport in the dispersed city*. Melbourne: Melbourne University Press.

Melia, S. (2012). *Filtered and unfiltered permeability: The European and Anglo-Saxon approaches*. Available from: https://core.ac.uk/download/pdf/5227471.pdf.

Montgomery, C. (2013). *Happy city: Transforming our lives through urban design*. New York: Penguin Random House.

NACTO. (2014). *Urban Bikeway Design Guide*. Available from: https://nacto.org/publication/urban-bikeway-design-guide/cycle-tracks/two-way-cycle-tracks/.

NACTO. (2016a). *Global Street Design Guide*. Available from: https://globaldesigningcities.org/publication/global-street-design-guide/.

NACTO. (2016b). *Policy statement on automated vehicles*. Available from: https://nacto.org/wp-content/uploads/2016/06/NACTO-Policy-Automated-Vehicles-201606.pdf.

NACTO. (2019a). *Blueprint for autonomous urbanism: Second Edition*. Available from: https://nacto.org/publication/bau2/.

NACTO. (2019b). *Guidelines for regulating shared micromobility, Version 2*. Available from: https://nacto.org/wp-content/uploads/2019/09/NACTO_Shared_Micromobility_Guidelines_Web.pdf.

Nelson, D. M. (2014). Thinking beyond the station. *Project for public spaces*. Available from: https://www.pps.org/article/thinking-beyond-the-station.

New York City Department of Transportation. (2017). *Protected bicycle lanes*. Available from: http://www.nyc.gov/html/dot/downloads/pdf/nyc-protected-bike-lanes.pdf.

P. H. (writing for The Economist). (2014). Natural traffic control: Undriven snow. *The Economist*. Available from: https://www.economist.com/babbage/2014/02/13/undriven-snow.

Pharoah, T. (n.d.). The "5 Cs" - criteria for measuring walkability. Available from: http://www.livingtransport.com/results.php?t=asset&search=233.

Project for Public Spaces. (n.d.). What is placemaking? Available from: https://www.pps.org/category/placemaking.

Pucher, J., & Buehler, R. (2008). Making cycling irresistible: Lessons from The Netherlands. Denmark and Germany. *Transport Reviews*, *28*(4), 495–528.

Salama, P., & Kent, E. (2016). Self-driving cars: Futurama 2.0 or cities for people? *Project for Public Spaces*. Available from: https://www.pps.org/article/self-driving-cars-futurama-2-0-cities-people.

Small, A. (2019). Why speed kills cities. *Citylab*. Available from: https://www.citylab.com/transportation/2019/08/low-speed-limit-vehicle-safety-crash-data-traffic-congestion/588412/.

Southworth, M., & Ben-Joseph, E. (2013). *Streets and the shaping of towns and cities*. Washington: Island Press.

Speck, J. (2012). *Walkable city: How downtown can save America, one step at a time*. New York: Macmillan.

Speck, J. (2014). Why 12-foot traffic lanes are disastrous for safety and must be replaced now. *Citylab*. Available from: https://www.citylab.com/design/2014/10/why-12-foot-traffic-lanes-are-disastrous-for-safety-and-must-be-replaced-now/381117/.

Steuteville, R. (2018). 'Urbanizing the suburbs' goes big. *Public Square, a CNU Journal*. Available from: https://www.cnu.org/publicsquare/2018/03/20/'urbanizing-suburbs'-goes-big.

Tachieva, G. (2010a). *Sprawl repair manual*. Washington: Island Press.

Tachieva, G. (2010b). Sprawl Repair: What it is and why we need it. *Planetizen*. Available from: https://www.planetizen.com/node/46481.

Taylor, I., & Sloman, l. (2008). *Towards transport justice: Transport and social justice in an oil-scarce future*. Available from: https://www.transportforqualityoflife.com/u/files/Towards_Transport_Justice_April2008.pdf.

Toderian, B. (2018). 5 steps to making better cities. *Fast company*. Available from: https://www.fastcompany.com/90278237/5-steps-to-making-better-cities.

Tolley, R. (2008). Walking and cycling: Easy wins for a sustainable transport policy. In I. Docherty, & J. Shaw (Eds.), *Traffic Jam: Ten Years of 'Sustainable' Transport in the UK*. Bristol: Policy Press pp 117–137.

Tolley, R., & Turton, B. J. (1995). *Transport systems, policy and planning: A geographical approach*. Longman: Harlow.

TransitCenter. (2016). Who's On Board 2016. Available from: http://transitcenter.org/publications/whos-on-board-2016/.

TransitCenter. (2017). LA Metro Walks the Walk. Available from: https://transitcenter.org/2017/08/30/la-metro-walks-the-walk/.

Transport for London. (2004). *Making London a walkable city: The Walking Plan for London*. Available from: https://fussverkehr.ch/wordpress/wp-content/uploads/2016/09/walking-plan-2004.pdf.

Udell, T., Daley, M., Johnson, B., & Tolley, R. (2014). *Does density matter? The role of density in creating walkable neighbourhoods*. Melbourne: National Heart Foundation of Australia.

Verbeek, P. P. (2009). Moralizing technology: On the morality of technological artifacts and their design. In D. M. Kaplan (Ed.), *Readings in the philosophy of technology* (pp. 226–249). Plymouth: Rowman and Littlefield.

Walk21. (2019). International Charter for Walking. Available from: https://www.walk21.com/chartersignature.

Zarif, R., Pankratz, D. M., & Kelman, B. (2019). Small is beautiful: Making micromobility work for citizens, cities, and service providers. *Deloitte Insights*. Available from: https://www2.deloitte.com/us/en/insights/focus/future-of-mobility/micro-mobility-is-the-future-of-urban-transportation.html.

Chapter 10

A new vision for the city: transforming behaviours, values and cultures

'The world moves fast, but that doesn't mean we have to ... when you slow down, the world slows down with you'.

Haemin Sunim

Abstract

This chapter examines the behaviours, values and cultures that need to be changed to slow city transport. We outline and critique several aspects of transportation demand management (TDM). First, we examine TDM measures based on voluntary change, including nudge theory and social marketing, rather than changes to the transport system. Then we examine TDM approaches that use interventions in the actual transport system to promote changes in the behaviour of individuals. The chapter provides examples of how TDM can be used to either slow motor vehicles or encourage shifts to 'slower' modes. We explain how TDM is most successful when several key aspects are integrated: TDM strategies have cumulative and synergistic impacts. We then examine how a focus on individual behaviour change is unlikely to be sufficient to create 'slow cities'. A shift is needed in the cultural and institutional context of city transport. This is examined under the headings of: leadership; knowledge; professional skills; resources; policies, strategies and community interventions; and cooperation and partnerships. We conclude that creating a 'slower', healthier city requires systemic, holistic changes in culture, not simply changes in local infrastructure or nudges and changes in individual attitudes and behaviour: a fundamental change in the prevailing transport paradigm is required.

10.1 Introduction: demand management as a critical element of policy for 'slow cities'

In the previous chapter we examined how changes in land use and transport supply can help to slow city movement. This chapter examines the complex interplay between physical changes in cities and the behaviours and values of both individuals and key policy makers. Whilst much effort has been devoted to changing the behaviour of individual travellers (sometimes with significant

Slow Cities. http://dx.doi.org/10.1016/B978-0-12-815316-1.00010-1

success), the behaviours, values and assumptions of planners, engineers, politicians and policy makers also need to be reassessed.

A positive development, from the standpoint of 'slowing' the city, is that these values and assumptions are already changing. For example, a 'predict and provide' approach to city transport planning, in which increasing transport supply to meet predicted travel demand (usually for cars), was once the favoured solution to city transport problems. Over the last few decades, this approach has been increasingly questioned. Transportation demand management (TDM) is now accepted as a more realistic approach. Whilst 'predict and provide' might appear to suit a market-led economic growth agenda, the philosophy of TDM recognises that meeting unrestrained demand for travel is neither possible, nor desirable if promoting health (in its broadest sense) is a priority.

The concept of TDM, first introduced in the 1980s, includes any programme or strategy aimed at reducing travel demand and hence mitigating the negative impacts of motor vehicles. TDM can be applied at a range of scales, from nation-wide policies (e.g. fuel taxes) or city scales (e.g. road user charges), to very local site-specific measures (e.g. parking restrictions on a university campus). It includes measures such as physical interventions, education and information to instigate behaviour change, and various incentives (and disincentives) to affect how, where and even whether people travel.

This chapter outlines several of the extensive range of TDM measures that attempt to modify individual travel behaviour. In Section 10.2 we examine voluntary travel behaviour change (VTBC) programmes. Voluntary behaviour change occurs when individuals (or households) make choices of their own accord, without any top–down mechanism to change the city transport system. People are induced to 'voluntarily choose to travel in ways which benefit themselves, the community and the environment' (Philp and Taylor, 2010, p. 3). Then, in Section 10.3 we examine TDM approaches that use interventions in the actual transport system to promote changes in the transport behaviours of individuals.

However, individual transport behaviour is rooted in cultural values such as those held by transport institutions, politicians, planning departments, professional bodies and policy makers. Many of these institutions, particularly during the 20th century, largely accepted speed and mobility as key goals of planning. If we are to create healthy cities, we need to encourage more of these institutions to recognise and conquer their addiction to speed, by valuing accessibility, health and liveability over faster movement. Accordingly, this chapter also discusses how we may create positive institutional frameworks and move prevailing policy paradigms towards acceptance of a lower-speed city in the future.

10.2 Voluntary transportation demand management

10.2.1 Introduction

Space precludes a detailed review of voluntary TDM, so here we focus on the most significant components: VTBC (including nudge theory) and social marketing. Few TDM measures have been designed directly to reduce the speed of motorised vehicles. Nevertheless, if slowing city transport is seen as a goal, voluntary TDM can help achieve this, by encouraging motorists to drive more slowly or to reduce their car use and switch to lower speed, active travel modes. In Section 10.2 we examine TDM approaches that focus specifically on changing individual or household behaviour. Then, in Section 10.3 we examine TDM approaches that involve more substantive changes to cities, involving physical, operational, financial/pricing or organisational measures.

10.2.2 Voluntary travel behaviour change

VTBC programmes are designed to encourage shifts to more sustainable modes of transport by providing motivation or incentives in addition to information. VTBC programmes have been seen by governments as providing cheaper, more politically acceptable and quicker strategies (using so-called 'soft' measures) for reducing the negative impacts of transport than 'hard' measures such as transport system improvements, increasing prices or changes in land use (Brög, Erl, Ker, Ryle, & Wall, 2009). VTBC schemes include personal travel planning, workplace and school travel plans, and car-pooling schemes. These can activate behaviour change, sometimes on the same scale as transport system changes, leading to a reduction in car use, as well as increases in the use of walking, cycling and public transport (Brög et al., 2009; Philp & Taylor, 2010).

One strategy that has become popular in behaviour change is referred to as nudging. This was popularised in the behavioural economics book—*Nudge: Improving decisions about health, wealth, and happiness* (Thaler & Sunstein, 2008), which describes a nudge-intervention as one that changes decision making in a way that steers people's behaviour in a predictable direction. To classify as a nudge an intervention must not prohibit any choices and must allow individuals to choose freely. This appeals to libertarian politicians and policy makers in contexts where corporations and private businesses eschew government interference (Goulden, Ryley, & Dingwall, 2014). Nudges are not linked to financial incentives. They promote or change behaviours without necessarily increasing knowledge or changing attitudes.

Four different types of nudges have been identified (Cooper, 2017):

1. changing the default option;
2. changing social norms and using social comparisons;
3. increasing salience and simplification; and
4. changing the physical environment.

An example of changing the default option could be where free car parking for employees is replaced by incentives such as free bicycle parking and shower facilities, and free public transport passes, all of which would likely nudge employees towards these modes (Litman, 2003b, p. 6). Another example of changing the default would be giving people on bicycles a green signal at intersections a few seconds before the cars, or providing advanced

FIGURE 10.1 An advanced stop line at an intersection in London. Here people on bicycles can enter the junction first, not only increasing their visibility, but also nudging car drivers into reflecting on the advantageous position of cyclists. *(Credit: Carlton Reid, https://www.flickr.com/photos/carltonreid/8008925880)*

stop lines ('bike boxes') providing bicycle riders with a head start at traffic control signals (Fig. 10.1). Providing shorter wait times and longer crossing times for people crossing on foot (and therefore longer waits for car drivers) would also qualify. Such changes provide powerful symbolic messages that the speed of cars is less important than the safety and convenience of walking or cycling. Understanding nudge theory suggests that traffic signal timing should not be left solely to engineers, as it involves values and priorities (drivers versus non-drivers), so ideally it should be the focus of public policy.

An example of the second type of nudge (changing social norms and using social comparisons), involves focussing on the transport options that help slow city transport. For example, instead of advertising that a particular per cent of individuals drive to work, nudging would highlight the percentage who walk, cycle or use public transport, even if this is still a minority. It may also be possible to use the concept of effective speed (see Chapter 4) as part of a nudge towards 'slower' modes (Tranter & May, 2005). This nudge was witnessed amongst some university students, one of whom, after calculating his own car's effective speed as less than eight km/h, decided to sell the car and use the bicycle more.

An example of the third type of nudge (increasing salience and simplification) is locating bicycle parking closer to the front entrance of workplaces or shops or schools, so that bicycles become more obvious (salient) than cars, as employees or shoppers or students leave work, shops or school (Fig. 10.2).

FIGURE 10.2 Increasing salience by placing bicycle parking facilities in highly visible and convenient locations. The Centre for Mathematical Sciences, University of Cambridge, United Kingdom. *(Credit: Christian Mercat—Own work, CC BY-SA 4.0, https://commons.wikimedia.org/w/index.php?curid=6698089)*

Another example of increasing salience involves changes to motor car insurance payments, to make the cost of each car journey evident at the time, which could nudge motorists to drive less. If current fixed vehicle insurance payments were changed to distance-based pricing, motorists would be nudged to drive less and save money. Distance-based car insurance makes insurance costs more fair, and affordable for those who drive less (Litman, 2003b).

The fourth type of nudge, changing the physical environment, could involve the use of lines, textured surfaces and signs, which can be effective in reducing motor car speeds (see Chapter 8). Many villages in Britain have 'gateway' entry points, indicating to drivers that they are entering a slower environment. To help ensure that the driver is nudged to adopt an acceptable response, the gateways are frequently preceded by a series of stripes painted on the road that get progressively closer together as cars approach the gateway, providing a sensation that car speed is increasing, and encouraging drivers to slow down instinctively. Another physical nudge involves signage designed to overcome misperception of distances to local destinations. Strategically located but informal signage, which indicates walking times rather than distances, can encourage people to walk more, especially where the environment is appealing (Fig. 10.3).

FIGURE 10.3 Nudging people to continue to walk to local destinations by locating information about walking times at unexpected places on the sidewalk. City of Port Phillip, Melbourne, Australia. *(Credit: Rodney Tolley)*

10.2.3 Social marketing

Similar to nudging is the approach broadly referred to as community-based social marketing. Social marketing is also 'voluntary' and does not involve the type of physical, financial, operational or organisational changes to be discussed in Section 10.3. Social marketing directs messages to individuals and households, often using personal contact and a toolbox of strategies to encourage changes in social beliefs, attitudes and behaviours, for instance about transport choices. Social marketing first appeared in the 1970s, when it adapted commercial marketing principles to bring about social change. Various techniques are employed, such as 'market segmentation, consumer research, product concept development and testing, directed communication, facilitation, and incentives' (Kotler & Roberto, 1989, p. 26).

Social marketing often focusses on the potential audience that is likely to respond positively to the intervention, so that people who are expected to resist messages and are unlikely to change behaviours are typically ignored. Thus one of the limitations of the approach is that only a subset of the total target group is influenced by the marketing.

Social marketing has been the basis for a number of transport behaviour change initiatives over the last 20 years, including the UK Department of Transport's Smarter Choices programme, and the TravelSmart programmes run by Sustrans in the United Kingdom, and sponsored by state governments in Australia. These were applied mainly at the household level (aiming to switch individual travel from cars to other modes). *TravelSmart* programmes were also implemented for schools and workplaces. Several *TravelSmart* schemes in Australia achieved changes in individual travel behaviour in a cost-effective manner with target populations (James, Burke, & Yen, 2017).

Household *TravelSmart* programmes encouraged household members in a targeted area to reduce their car use using set activities and review materials to help households reflect on their travel. Programmes often involved *TravelSmart* facilitators listening to household members to identify ways in which they might voluntarily change their travel. The programmes provided materials such as pocket timetables for local bus stops and 'free trial public transport tickets, to help "interested" households begin using non-car modes' (James et al., 2017).

Australian state governments invested considerable funds into these interventions between 1986 and 2011. Individualised travel marketing schemes applied across whole neighbourhoods were more widely used in Australia than anywhere else worldwide. The encouraging results in the early years of these schemes were, however, not enough to maintain broad support, and by 2017 these schemes had ceased almost entirely (James et al., 2017).

10.2.4 Critical views of behaviour change and social marketing

Despite many policy makers and researchers showing enthusiasm for travel behaviour change strategies such as social marketing and nudging, the interventions have attracted widespread criticism, regarding: the limited evidence for success; the lack of long-term impact; and ethical issues. Many behaviour change programmes to encourage more use of the 'slower' modes, even if successful at first, are followed by declines in the use of these modes when the behaviour change interventions are withdrawn (Johnston, 2016).

A fundamental issue is that most behaviour change successes involve minor adjustments in a world of increasing consumerism, individualism and quest for increased speed and productivity. Behaviour change programmes do not bring about prolonged social change (Goodwin, 2012), nor do they address the 'wider social and economic structures which also can be seen to frame the uptake and frequency of such behaviours' (Barr & Prillwitz, 2014, p. 5). This is particularly concerning for some researchers who argue that when behaviour change programmes are presented as 'solutions' to issues such as climate disruption, this can divert attention from wider and more radical social changes that are needed. Barr and Prillwitz (2014, p. 15) put this argument forcefully: 'the challenges of promoting sustainable mobility … necessitate political and policy changes that tackle the underlying social and economic contexts for current practices'. Using behaviour change as the main driver for achieving change may simply support the status quo.

From the perspective of the arguments in this book, travel behaviour change programmes are rarely aimed directly at 'slowing' motorised transport. Such programmes do not necessarily question society's addiction to speed. They attempt to move people to other modes without influencing the overall dominance of cars and speed. Indeed, many travel behaviour change programmes have a specific aim to achieve 'free flowing traffic on road networks' (James et al., 2017, p. 2). Even the recent guidelines for promoting mobility behaviour change developed by organisations such as Urban Agenda for the EU and Walk21 provide no mention of 'speed' in their report (Partnership for Urban Mobility, 2019). It appears that the problems of 'speed' are often invisible, even for those committed to improving transport sustainability.

Another important weakness of travel behaviour strategies is the huge challenge they face in competing with forces and messages that help promote speed, rather than slowing city transport. Goulden et al. (2014, p. 144) explain what happens when 'a nudge meets a larger force pushing in the opposite direction. While getting people to switch from cars and to public transport is a central element of the Smarter Choices approach, the car has an established and powerful hold on precisely the same subconscious processes that are targeted by nudge'. Individual travel behaviours are set within a wider cultural context that is influenced by advertising, the media and government and industry. Advertising budgets supporting high-speed transport are large, and advertising images often capitalise on the visceral appeal of speed, as we observed in Chapter 2.

Whilst some critics of travel behaviour change programmes are concerned with the ethical issues involved in manipulating people through 'social engineering', others point out that citizens are all already manipulated, and hence this concern should not be seen as a real issue, particularly in light of the immense challenges surrounding planetary health. 'The "consumer society" is itself a social construct, the socially-engineered creation of post WW-II private enterprise achieved through the help of mass media and the advertising industry. In any case, the urgency of global ecological change clearly requires a redefinition of political practicality' (Rees, 2003).

In recent years there have been many examples of successful changes in societal attitudes with two of the most obvious being smoking and drink driving. Such changes have not happened in the case of the speed of city transport, despite an increased public understanding of the need for changed behaviour. This is apparently perverse. Why is there such a difference between attitudes and behaviour?

One explanation for this lack of change is the way in which people adopt 'coping mechanisms', whereby they continue certain behaviour patterns even though they may actually have come to realise that such behaviour is sub-optimal. Such mechanisms include dogmatism (setting one's mind against a viewpoint, ensuring that the unacceptable facts are simply dismissed); rationalisation ('if the problem is so serious, surely someone more qualified is taking care of it'); fatalism ('It is God's will', even if the problem is clearly man-made!); denial (as with science deniers in the current climate crisis); or simply procrastination ('I have been meaning to change').

Another limitation of behaviour change strategies relates to the concept of 'social traps', where people follow a behavioural path that later turns out to be a mistake, but from which they see no easy way of backing out (Hallsworth, Black, & Tolley, 1995; Tranter, 2006). When caught in a social trap, people feel forced to behave in a certain way (e.g. drive their children to school to protect them from traffic created by other parents driving their children to school), because of uncertainty about how others will behave. Clearly all parents would be better off if the environment was safe enough for every child to be allowed to walk to school, but parents feel unable to influence the behaviour of other parents and so individualistic motivations mean that parents continue to drive. Parents are faced with the choice of either letting their child walk to school and hence being exposed to traffic danger, or alternatively, contributing to this danger for everyone's children by driving their own child to school (Fig. 10.4). The important

FIGURE 10.4 Traffic consisting mainly of cars driving children to a primary school in suburban Canberra, Australia. *(Credit: Paul Tranter)*

point here is that individual behaviour change programmes are unlikely to affect parents' decisions to drive children to school, at least until a social and physical environment is created where children's safety is protected and social traps can be overcome (Tranter, 2006).

Such social traps, with their unintended consequences, encourage people to try to second guess how others will behave so that they can minimise the disbenefit to themselves. This is well seen in the 'tragedy of the commons' scenario (Hardin, 1968), in which the presence of a common pasture encourages all cattle owners to graze as many beasts on the common land as they can, producing a maximum payoff for the owner. Of course, each extra beast reduces the benefits experienced by other cattle owners, but it remains in every individual's interest to keep adding cattle—in the short term. However, in the long term, the common land will become over-grazed, producing maximum disbenefit for all (but of course this may not be experienced until the next generation of owners). As Hardin summarised: 'Ruin is the destination to which all men rush, each pursuing his own best interest in a society that believes in the freedom of the commons. Freedom in a commons brings ruin to all' (Hardin, 1968, p. 1244).

DeRobertis and Lee (2017) draw a parallel between the commons and its free grazing, and the urban arterial on which it is free to drive—and this freedom to drive brings congestion and danger to the commons. Such issues cannot be solved by requesting that people drive less because it is 'better for society', just as the over-grazed common cannot be protected by asking herders to desist from adding cattle. Indeed, DeRobertis & Lee (2017, p. 47) argue that 'those who voluntarily do not abuse urban arterial capacity (bus riders, bicyclists etc.) out of conscience merely make it easier for those who refuse to or cannot give up driving' (see Fig. 3.11, where bus riders queue beside the Beijing Second Ring Road). This creates a situation in which people will only consider changing some behaviour (e.g. driving or speeding) 'when everyone else does the same'.

Hardin's view was that the social trap exemplified by the tragedy of the commons requires 'mutual coercion mutually agreed upon' (Hardin, 1968, p. 1247)—but this collectively-agreed control is particularly difficult to achieve in the case of car use, because as Rees has argued, 'the speed, comfort, and convenience of cars makes them formidable competitors with alternative modes particularly when perceived costs are low' (Rees, 2003, p. 13).

Do all these limitations mean that behaviour change should be seen as irrelevant to the goal of slowing city transport? Whilst it is unlikely that there is potential for large effects from any single intervention, the cumulative impact of multiple behaviour change projects may start to challenge the culture of speed. As Linder, Lindahl, and Borgström (2018, p. 11) suggest, there may even be a growing opportunity for behaviour change programmes to have a positive impact as the world heads towards more densely settled cities 'where small scale changes can reach many people and therefore have large aggregated effects'.

By themselves, the VTBC interventions described earlier will be unlikely to make sufficient difference in slowing city transport to meet the challenges required (e.g. in reducing carbon footprints). There may be much more potential in other types of TDM approaches, which focus not on individuals, but on significant interventions in city transport systems that can be expected to lead to changes in individual transport behaviours. It is these that we will now discuss.

10.3 Physical, operational, financial/pricing and organisational TDM approaches

10.3.1 Introduction

In Section 10.2, we examined TDM approaches that focussed on changing the behaviours of individuals or households, without major changes to the environments in which these behaviours occur. In contrast to nudging and social marketing, another set of TDM approaches aims to influence travel demand by changing the context or the transport environment within which individuals and households operate. In this section we examine such TDM interventions identified by Black and Schreffler (2010) under four headings: physical, operational, financial/pricing, and organisational (or institutional) measures.

10.3.2 Physical TDM interventions

Physical interventions consist of the infrastructure to make TDM work, such as park-and-ride systems, high occupancy vehicle (HOV) lanes, or bus rapid transit (BRT) with bus priority lanes. Transport planners in the Global South, recognising that bus services attract more passengers when they are reliable, convenient and faster, have introduced bus priority lanes in many cities (see Fig. 10.5). In China, for example, by November 2018 bus-only lanes reached 225, 457 and 110 kilometres in Suzhou, Chengdu and Harbin, respectively (The World Bank, 2018).

10.3.3 Operational TDM interventions

Operational measures are practices designed to manage/influence trips through enhanced choices and traveller information about these choices, such as real-time dynamic information and variable highway speed controls. For example, multimodal transport systems use new technology to provide information on a 'combined transport system that stitches each roadway, railway, airway and waterway to produce an integrated travel solution within a smart city' (Smartcity, 2019), that can be used to find the most convenient way to travel for a particular journey. Such systems are developing rapidly in 'smart cities' such as London and Singapore, where unified public transport authorities aim to deliver seamlessly integrated multiple modes, including metro, buses, light rail, and taxis.

Four recent technical innovations in transport operational measures have important implications for any attempt to slow city transport: smart road pricing, performance-based parking pricing, dynamic road management, and mobility as a service (MaaS) (Cohen, 2018). First, smart road pricing allows authorities

FIGURE 10.5 A bus priority lane, with clear separation from the cars in congested traffic in Jakarta, Indonesia. *(Credit: Carlos Felipe Pardo, https://www.flickr.com/photos/carlosfpardo/46509247394)*

to impose charges on motorists (or autonomous vehicles) that vary over space and time, and by type of vehicle. The major obstacle to the implementation of smart road pricing is political, as drivers may object to the collection of data about their movements. However, with the possible advent of autonomous vehicles, opposition to smart road pricing is less likely, as all AVs will have tracking devices. Such pricing has the potential to reduce congestion and improve road safety and air quality, though it might also have a regressive impact if poorer residents pay the same rates as richer residents.

Second, related to smart road pricing is 'performance-based parking pricing', a technique for varying the price of street parking in real time to manage parking demand effectively. When used to achieve an 85 per cent occupancy for parking, this can help reduce the number of cars cruising for parking and hence increase public transport speed and reliability as well as enhance safety for people walking and cycling (Shoup, 2018). This type of parking pricing can be used in conjunction with the removal of minimum parking requirements in zoning ordinances (see Section 9.2.3).

Third, 'dynamic road management' enables transport managers to change road characteristics depending on traffic and environmental factors. This already exists on many city roads, for example, reducing speed limits after a crash or in foggy conditions. The fourth recent technical innovation, MaaS, has significant potential to encourage a switch to the 'slower' modes if implemented with this goal in mind. Advanced versions of MaaS provide travellers with a personally tailored door-to-door journey plan that matches their needs. Payment could be made to a single provider, and any changes in mode would be made seamlessly. Adjustments could be made instantly in response to any variation in circumstance (e.g. equipment failure). Whilst MaaS might encourage a shift to public transport, there is also the risk that it could reduce physical activity if motorised trips replace walking. The impact of MaaS in terms of slowing will depend largely on the availability of non-car options.

10.3.4 Financial/pricing TDM interventions

Black and Schreffler's (2010) third category of TDM intervention comprises financial/pricing measures, which use economics to affect trip choice, with the revenue usually 'ring-fenced'—to be spent on sustainable transport interventions. Financial/pricing measures include workplace parking levies, financial incentives such as free public transport passes, and charging for the right to use vehicles in designated areas (e.g. congestion charges). Whilst such charges will likely result in increased speeds for the motor cars that continue to use the roads, they also significantly increase the average vehicle occupancy rate, as well as reduce the need for expensive transport infrastructure (Shoup, 2005). If the revenue from the tolls is used to support the 'slower' modes, then congestion tolls can provide a powerful form of TDM for 'slowing the city'. Probably the best-known example of this approach is the London congestion charge. Whilst it reduced both congestion and levels of many pollutants, levels of harmful NO_2 increased, likely due to the increased share of diesel cars exempt from the congestion charge (Green, Heywood, & Navarro, 2018). As might be expected, it did not lead to a reduction of existing motor car speeds, but it was a success in slowing city transport in terms of encouraging a mode shift to public transport and cycling from personal cars.

Financial/pricing measures are crucial components of any TDM strategy. As Litman (2003b, p. 7) explains: 'Many transportation problems, including congestion, increasing road and parking costs, excessive accident risk, and a lack of mobility for nondrivers, are virtually unavoidable over the long term until current market distortions that encourage excessive driving are addressed'. An effective TDM strategy to help tackle this weakness is to use 'full-cost accounting' of the environmental/societal/health costs and benefits of any transport proposal. This would involve ensuring that the payback from health improvements (for individuals, businesses and whole city populations) from slowing city transport is included in any decision making, so that the full societal benefits are factored in (C3 Collaborating for Health, 2017). These benefits are rarely considered (if at all) in transport budgets, so a case needs to be made for pooling of resources across sectors of government (such as transport, education and health), so that costs and benefits are considered under one budget. This is possible only by thinking outside traditional silos, where each government department functions independently. It

BOX 10.1 Full-cost accounting: an example from Vancouver, Canada.

To understand full-cost accounting it is necessary to consider the ratio of money paid into the system by users of each mode, to the amount that each mode costs society. Using full-cost accounting in a study of Vancouver's transport, George Poulos asked 'how much does your commute cost (or save) society?' (McLaren, Havlak, & Stewart-Wilson, 2015). Residents who cycle or walk contribute very little (if anything) to the transport system directly, however 'their travel habits result in healthcare savings and improved workplace productivity thanks to the additional exercise they are getting. So their commutes, on average, contribute a net benefit to society' (McLaren et al., 2015). Poulos demonstrated that if walking costs you $1, this 'saves' society 1 cent via savings to the healthcare system and improved productivity resulting from exercise. If cycling cost you $1, this 'saves' society 8 cents. If driving costs you $1, society 'pays' $9.20 (from emissions, the infrastructure for driving, noise pollution, congestion and crash risks).

High levels of subsidy for driving encourage urban citizens to drive further and faster. As Poulos explains, 'Although these costs are easy to overlook, that doesn't make them any less real' (McLaren et al., 2015). An effective stick, a disincentive for using high-speed modes, would involve all transport users paying a fair price for their travel (e.g. via congestion tolls) and their parking.

involves a 'whole of government, whole of society' framework involving 'joined-up thinking' (C3 Collaborating for Health, 2017). The way in which full-cost accounting can demonstrate the huge costs involved in city driving, and the savings to society associated with walking and cycling, are outlined in Box 10.1.

10.3.5 Organisational TDM interventions

The fourth TDM approach identified by Black and Schreffler (2010) involves organisational measures that entail integration with other activities. One example of these organisational TDM measures comes from Lund, Sweden. In 1999 the City of Lund published its LundaMaTs plan (translated as Lund Environmentally Adapted Transport System), updated into its third published strategy in 2015. This plan demonstrates all the TDM categories identified by Black and Schreffler (US Department of Transportation, 2006). Physical measures in LundaMaTs include a ban on road 'improvements' and the reallocation of road space to people on foot and bicycles, as well as motorised speed reductions. Operational measures include a BRT system linking the train station and city centre with the university, hospital and technology centre. This provides high-frequency services on dedicated busways on most of its 10 km corridor, giving priority to buses using signal pre-emption and providing real-time information at the people-centred bus stations (see Fig. 10.6).

Financial/pricing measures in LundaMaTs include using revenue from the land sales along the busway route to develop the system, and providing a free annual pass to entice users for the first year. Organisational measures are

FIGURE 10.6 The Botulfsplatsen bus station in Lund, Sweden, in a square with cafes, restaurants and small shops, making it an attractive place to access public transport. *(Credit: News Oresund, https://www.flickr.com/photos/newsoresund/48488062396)*

arguably the most impressive aspect of LundaMaTs. The City of Lund institutionalised sustainable transport into all of its city's plans, programmes, and policies. 'LundaMaTs implemented a variety of projects all at once, and this has clearly reoriented the way the city approaches transportation and land use decisions' (US Department of Transportation, 2006). The LundaMaTs example is particularly important because its success in reducing the speed and volume of motorised transport occurred during a time of high economic growth (US Department of Transportation, 2012). New travel demand was met through the growth of public transport use and cycling, and after 10 years there was a 2.5 per cent reduction in vehicle miles travelled (Schreffler, 2018).

10.3.6 The need for both carrots and sticks in the integration of TDM strategies

The success of TDM in Lund draws attention to the fundamental importance of integrating a number of key aspects into a successful strategy. TDM strategies have cumulative and synergistic impacts, especially when 'together they provide both positive and negative incentives for motorists to use alternative modes' (Litman, 2003a, pp. 573–574). Black and Schreffler (2010, p. 1) conclude that 'A review of TDM internationally has demonstrated the importance of combining a number of key aspects into an effective strategy. Key to successful policy transfer of sustainable urban transport is integrating the TDM philosophy into urban transport planning, as well as the daily management and operation of transport services and infrastructure' (Black & Schreffler, 2010, p. 1).

Much of the effort involved in behaviour change has focussed on providing incentives, or carrots, to encourage a switch to more sustainable modes. The re-allocation of road space to vulnerable road users has been shown to be an effective enabler of active modes. However, as Piatkowski, Marshall, and Krizek (2019, p. 50) discovered, good planning needs both carrots and sticks: 'interventions that incorporate both enablers and deterrents are most effective at encouraging active transportation'.

Rees (2003) provides a convincing case for the use of both carrots and sticks in planning for sustainable cities. To ensure the carrot component of TDM, policy makers need to convince citizens that slowing city transport is in their personal and collective interests. Citizens first need to see a positive trade-off; to appreciate that better alternatives (e.g. to the speed provided by the car) are available. Rees is optimistic that it is possible to convince people 'that a clean, healthy, safe city, with several transportation modes providing access to increasing numbers of amenities (because of higher densities and the resultant economies of scale) is preferable to a polluted, unhealthy, dangerously congested, auto-dominated city with fewer viable public amenities' (Rees, 2003, p. 12). How this might be done is explored further in Chapter 11. However, it should be noted here that an important component of TDM to slow city transport is the commitment of city governments and planning agencies to develop strong information campaigns to raise awareness of the benefits for health and sustainability of slower transport, and encourage public debate on ways to achieve this.

As well as providing the carrot of the healthy city created by slowing city transport, Rees also argues that the 'economic stick' needs to be brandished. This can be achieved by using full-cost accounting for city transport, through higher registration fees and fuel taxes, road pricing, parking pricing and bridge tolls. Such economic incentives (sticks) are 'effective in changing consumers' behaviour and ultimately their values' (Rees, 2003, p.12).

The key message regarding the integration of TDM methods, supported by a meta-review of active transport studies, is that a combination of different interventions is more effective than using any one tool (Gordon, 2018). Policies that support the slowing of city transport, including the promotion of walking, cycling and public transport, work best when they are combined with economic constraints on high-speed modes: this involves both providing viable alternatives to motorised transport and ensuring that the cost of driving for motorists reflects its real impact (Rees, 2003).

10.4 Transforming cultural values and institutional frameworks

10.4.1 Introduction

The remainder of this chapter outlines further strategies to help transform the values and attitudes surrounding the speed of city transport. Changes in

FIGURE 10.7 The TransMilenio public transport system, an initiative led by Enrique Peñalosa, twice Mayor of Bogotá (Colombia). *(Credit: Felipe Restrepo Acosta—Own work, CC BY-SA 3.0, https://commons.wikimedia.org/w/index.php?curid=24064103)*

attitudes and behaviour are unlikely to take place in isolation, and behaviour change programmes or changes in transport design alone will be insufficient. Changes in the cultural and institutional context will be necessary, and these are examined here under the headings of: leadership; knowledge; professional skills; resources; policies, strategies and community interventions; and cooperation and partnerships.

10.4.2 Vision and leadership at the city level

Many cities across the world have been led to extraordinary changes by the vision of an inspirational leader. One of the best known examples of such leadership is Enrique Peñalosa, twice Mayor of Bogotá (Colombia) who championed Ciclovía and invested in high-quality sidewalks, pedestrian streets, parks, an innovative public transport system—the TransMilenio (Fig. 10.7)—and extensive bicycle paths. Another is Janette Sadik-Khan, a former Commissioner of the New York City Department of Transportation, introduced in Section 9.5. Her philosophy is encapsulated in her observation that 'Once you realize that you can use your streets to improve the quality of life, the

FIGURE 10.8 Rua Quinze de Novembro, one of the many streets in Curitiba, Brazil converted to places for people. *(Credit: enioprado, CC BY-SA 3.0, https://commons.wikimedia.org/w/index.php?curid=59452091)*

economic and environmental health of your city, that is a transformative moment' (Dawid, 2010).

Smaller cities also sometimes have inspiring leaders, though they may not be as well known. Jaime Lerner, three times Mayor of Curitiba, Brazil challenged the status quo by envisioning Curitiba as a city for people, rather than for cars. His achievements include: a bus system that was so effective that car traffic fell by 30 per cent whilst the population almost trebled over a 20-year period; a network of parks to control floods; and the world's largest shopping area for people on foot. Shortly after Lerner became mayor in 1971, he ordered the central city street of Rua Quinze be converted into a pedestrian mall, rather than destroying it with a planned motorway overpass. When he learnt that motorists were planning to protest by driving their cars through the newly pedestrianised mall, he enlisted the support of hundreds of children, armed with boxes of paint and rolls of paper. With encouragement from teachers, the children sat in the mall and drew pictures in the newly traffic-free street, providing an unbreachable defence (Lubow, 2007). The pedestrianised shopping area has since expanded, with more than 20 car-free blocks in the city (Fig. 10.8). Lerner's policies have led to 99 per cent of Curitiba's citizens being happy to live there. In contrast, more than two thirds of São Paolo's citizens would prefer to live in Curitiba (Begg, 2013).

Another smaller city example is found in Oklahoma City, United States, where there were extremely high rates of obesity and very low life expectancies. Mayor Mick Cornett, himself overweight, challenged the city to join him on a slimming journey with the vision that 'This city is going on a diet'. Subsequently, through behaviour change programmes, some 47,000 citizens collectively lost a million pounds in weight. However, Cornett's place as a visionary really comes from his subsequent epiphany that the American healthcare crisis is not so much a care issue as an urban design problem, at which point he raised the sales tax rate to fund city re-design, and oversaw the construction of hundreds of miles of footpaths, bike lanes and a walk-friendly CBD.

By 2018, Oklahoma City—long a victim of out-migration of its young and talented—was attracting well-educated Gen-Ys back to stimulate the future economy. One, Catherine Anadu, reflects how in 2000 she graduated from the University of Oklahoma: 'I literally got my degree, shook the dean's hand, walked off the stage and got on the plane … I never thought I would see the state of Oklahoma again' (Felder, 2015). In 2015 she was back—living in a walkable neighbourhood in downtown.

Another impressive example of leadership in a smaller city comes from Spain. Pontevedra has implemented many of the strategies suggested throughout this book for slowing city transport, and has consequently enhanced several dimensions of health and sustainability. The transformation of this city from a car-dominated 'fast' city to a people-orientated 'slow city' is largely due to the leadership and inspiration from Mayor Miguel Anxo Fernández Lores, who became mayor in 1999, and was re-elected in May 2019, for a sixth term. Previously a medical doctor, Lores explains 'Being mayor is a natural follow-on from my previous career. You can take care of cities in the same way you take care of patients' (Colin, 2019). Box 10.2 outlines the story of how, under Lores' leadership, Pontevedra is now a model for future 'slow cities'.

BOX 10.2 Rescuing a 'fast' city: the transformation of Pontevedra, Spain into a healthier, prosperous, popular and 'slower' city.

Pontevedra, a city of 84,000 people in north-west Spain was, prior to the election of Mayor Lores in 1999, paralysed by motor car traffic. Walking in the city was blighted by noise and air pollution, traffic danger and cars parked on the sidewalks. In his 'New Urban Model', Lores pledged to make the city accessible to everyone, particularly the most vulnerable, including people with disabilities, elderly people and children. He saw walking as not only the most natural means of mobility over short distances, but also 'a means of battling obesity and cardiovascular problems' (Cabiron, 2014).

The dominance of motor cars in Pontevedra is reduced in four major ways. First, their access to central parts of the city is restricted. Second, speed limits

FIGURE 10.9 Whilst cars are permitted in Pontevedra, Spain, they travel slowly and there is plenty of space for walking. *(Credit: Landor LINKS/Transport Xtra)*

throughout the city are set at 20 to 30 km/h, supported by traffic calming. Third, parking is restricted in the city centre, and most cars use parking lots located on the edge of the city, about 10 minutes walk from the city centre. Fourth, in the city centre, streets have been widened and made into shared spaces without sidewalks, so that all users (including people riding bicycles) use the whole space. Benches and street lighting have been installed, and green spaces created. Space for people walking has doubled (Fig. 10.9).

The results of Lores' plans are remarkable. The hierarchy of mobility priorities in Pontevedra is now clearly: walking and wheelchair users first, followed by bicycles, public transport and last, private motor cars. He has slowed the city by effecting a switch to the 'slow' modes: despite having 71 motorised vehicles per hundred residents, 70 per cent of all movements in the city are by walking or bicycle and over 80 per cent of children walk to school. Whilst 30 people were killed in traffic crashes between 1996 and 2006, this fell to three in the subsequent 10 years, and there were none between 2009 and 2019.

Now Pontevedra is a city where the car is unobtrusive. Instead of traffic noise, people hear 'the tweeting of birds in the camellias, the tinkle of coffee spoons and the sound of human voices' (Burgen, 2018). Children play safely in local streets and people walk to gain access to businesses and services. Echoing the point made in Chapter 7 that 'a good walking environment is a good economic environment', whilst other towns in the region are declining in population, Pontevedra is growing, and small businesses there survived Spain's long economic crisis (Burgen, 2018).

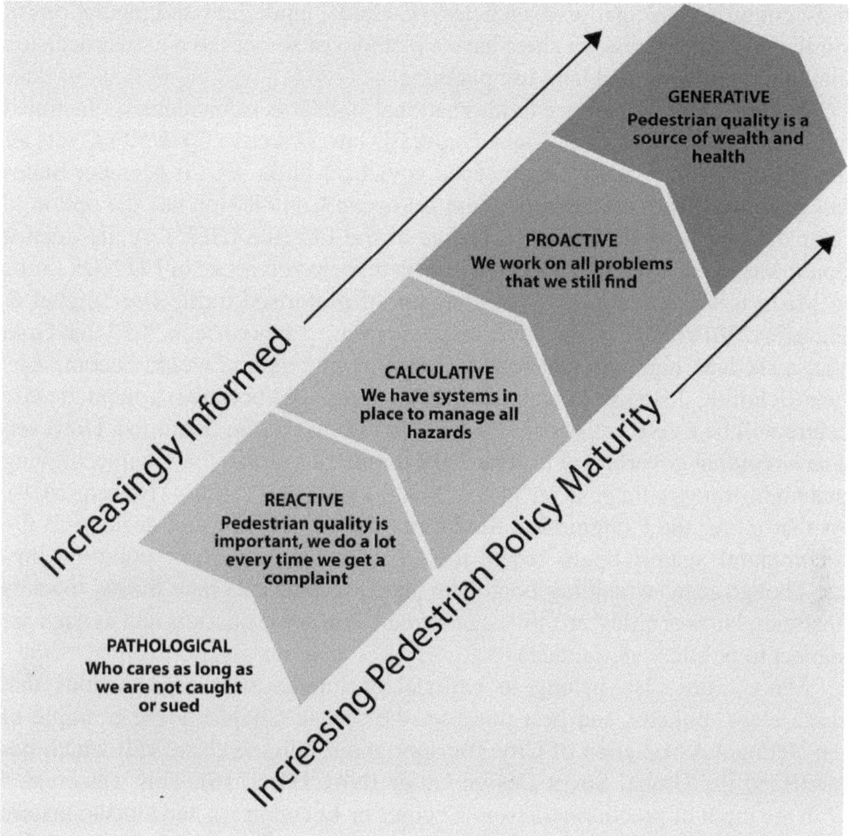

FIGURE 10.10 Pedestrian quality policy maturity. *(Adapted by Jeff Steinacker with permission from Rob Methorst from Methorst (2010))*

Of course, there are other factors in the revival of these cities besides the leadership of Peñalosa, Lerner, Sadik-Khan, Cornett, and Lores but their visions have been key instigators of change. In terms of pedestrian policy maturity (Fig. 10.10), under their guidance, their cities have undoubtedly moved in the direction of 'generative policy', where the increasing quality of the walking environment is seen as a source of wealth and health.

10.4.3 Knowledge

There already exists substantial knowledge about 'how' to slow city transport. There is a myriad of international agencies that set standards and develop exemplar policies in such matters as health, air pollution, climate action, public transport, child-friendliness, road danger reduction and many more. Additionally, most countries have national agencies, standards, guidelines and regulations in similar and other fields, so cities have a plethora of sources to aid their decision making in transport and land use planning.

In some cases, adherence to international standards is mandatory, illustrated by recent events in Madrid, Spain. Under EU law, Directive 2008/50/EC sets air quality limits that cannot be exceeded anywhere in the EU: if Member States fail to comply with the Directive, the European Commission has the option to refer the matter to the Court of Justice of the EU (the CJEU). A file against Spain was opened in 2015 and focussed on repeated breaches of EU NOx limits in Madrid, which were largely a function of motorised traffic (De Miguel & Planelles, 2019). One of the city's responses was to announce in 2017 that Gran Via, a six-lane highway that runs through the city centre, would become car-free (Schmidt, 2018) and that by 2020, 500 acres (202 hectares) around the city centre will be a zero emission zone with no through traffic permitted. However, a new regional government in June 2019 promised to scrap the scheme, arguing that night-time traffic jams are part of Madrid's cultural identity (Neslen, 2019). At that point, the Commission finally ran out of patience and decided to file a complaint against Spain before the CJEU for breach of air pollution limits. Though legal wrangling continues, the case indicates how moves towards healthier, 'slower cities' are still seen as radical in some quarters and as such are subject to political vicissitudes.

Many cities also belong to national or international organisations that share ideas, policies and best practice. We saw in Chapter 9 the example of the National Association of City Transportation Officials (NACTO) which has published the Global Street Design Guide (NACTO, 2016). This was created with the input of practitioners from 72 cities in 42 countries, and aims to inspire leaders, inform practitioners, and empower communities. By 2019 the Guide had been endorsed by more than 50 cities across the world, including capital cities such as Washington, Delhi and London, and had been joined by guidance publications on bikeways, transit, automated transportation and shared micromobility. Cities are encouraged to endorse these guides and to communicate a message to citizens that their city promotes a 'people-' and 'place-' based approach towards street design.

10.4.4 Professional skills

In terms of the needed cultural shift towards sustainable, slow city transport, the influence and actions of traffic engineers are widely seen as problematic. For example, a survey of Australian engineers and elected politicians indicated that pedestrians are seen as 'problems' in a way that other road users are not. The statements made by engineers about pedestrians included: 'they are erratic, unpredictable and stupid' (Daff & Cramphorn, 2006, p. 3).

Other advocates for sustainable transport have similar concerns about the views of engineers. Chapter 3 referred to Charles Marohn's comments on the ideology of the transport engineering profession, whereby many of its core 'truths' are actually 'values' or 'beliefs' (Marohn, 2016). These embedded ideologies have serious implications for the achievement of the 'slower city'. Steuteville (2017) has commented that 'The neighborhood and the five-minute walk have become accepted and understood in planning, but they have yet to become the norm because of traffic engineering'.

An alternative view of the role of engineers sees them as problem solvers, so that outcomes of their skills depend on what problem they are asked to solve. As Litman (2003a, p. 4) observes, 'Transportation planners and engineers receive professional rewards for implementing capacity expansion projects, but are seldom rewarded for finding ways to avoid the need for such projects'. This development of the 'windshield perspective' is rooted in a paradigm of encouraging more speed in urban transport systems, one that creates the norms (ideologies) for educational goals and professional praxis within the transport engineering profession. These ideologies then become systematised and embedded, for example in writing the standards and manuals that, in turn, will guide the approaches of the next generation of professionals. Box 10.3 exemplifies engineers' rigid adherence to a set of 'standards', thereby missing the understanding of the value of streets for people, rather than for prioritising speed.

A further problem in shaping the cultural context for the 'slower city' is the unwitting bias produced by the language that professionals use. For example, we often hear the word 'improvement' to describe an increase in road capacity, yet for active transport users such changes may be the opposite of 'improvement'. Similarly, 'enhance' and 'upgrade' are used to mean to 'expand' and 'widen', and 'efficient' is shorthand for 'faster'. This use of the term 'efficient' assumes that increasing speed increases efficiency, which is questionable on many levels (Litman, 2019). Using language in this biased manner, transport experts normalise vehicular movement and reinforce the status quo of professional practices centered on moving cars quickly through cities, rather than accommodating people.

Indeed, the whole concept of 'automobility' is misleading, and this particular word has been described by Ker and Tranter (2004) as 'bad language'. If 'auto' implies doing something by oneself independently, and 'mobility' means movement, then the motor car does not provide this at all. To move in a motor car requires enormous support from a multitude of groups (e.g. car manufacturers and mechanics, road builders and oil companies), a reality noted by Gorz (1973): 'The apparent independence of the automobile owner was only concealing the actual radical dependency'. The only true automobility is walking.

The point is that in order to achieve the 'slower city' our behaviour must change, yet that transformation is obstructed by the use of language that is often pejorative in relation to the 'slower' modes, and misleading in relation to mobility. We have, for example, already discussed (Chapter 3) the way that 'mobility' has been cast as a legitimate goal of transport policy, when in reality, it is 'accessibility' that we really need.

BOX 10.3 Confessions of a recovering engineer (based on selected quotes from Marohn (2010)).

'A book of standards to an engineer is better than a bible to a priest. All you have to do is to rely on the standards.

'When people would tell me that they did not want a wider street, I would tell them that they had to have it for safety reasons.

'When they answered that a wider street would make people drive faster and that would be less safe, especially in front of their house where their kids were playing, I would confidently tell them that the wider road was more safe, especially when combined with the other safety enhancements the standards called for.

'When people objected to those other "enhancements", like removing all of the trees near the road, I told them that for safety reasons we needed to improve the sight distances and ensure that the recovery zone was free of obstacles.

'When they pointed out that the "recovery zone" was also their "yard" and that their kids played kickball and hopscotch there, I recommended that they put up a fence, so long as the fence was outside of the right-of-way.

'When they objected to the cost of the wider, faster, treeless road that would turn their peaceful, front yard into the viewing area for a drag strip unless they built a concrete barricade along their front property line, I informed them that progress was sometimes expensive, but these standards have been shown to work across the state, the country and the world and I could not compromise with their safety.

'In retrospect I understand that this was utter insanity. Wider, faster, treeless roads not only ruin our public places, they kill people. Taking highway standards and applying them to urban and suburban streets, and even county roads, costs us thousands of lives every year. There is no earthly reason why an engineer would ever design a fourteen foot lane for a city block, yet we do it continuously. Why? The answer is utterly shameful: Because that is the standard' (Marohn, 2010).

The damage done by rigid adherence to standards is humorously further illustrated in a clever cartoon video, 'Conversation with an Engineer', from Strong Towns (2016), featuring a conversation between a mother living on a quiet, liveable street and a project engineer, who wants to 'improve' the street. The distraught resident's view is that by making the street faster, noisier, more polluting, less green and uncrossable, it makes her neighbourhood uninhabitable for her and her children. The engineer in this video displays no understanding of the absurdity of his arguments.

In summarising this section, we may note that for travel behaviour to be changed, skills such as education and marketing need to be applied, but these have not been historically valued in transport engineering agencies. As Litman observes, 'Sustainable planning requires that transportation professionals shift from being traffic engineers concerned only with vehicle flow, into "public space architects" concerned with balancing diverse and often conflicting uses of road environments' (Litman, 2003a, p. 4). It follows that if behaviour is to be shifted to a 'slower', more sustainable ideal, the education of professionals involved in any aspect of city or transport planning—economists, town planners, engineers, urban designers, architects and even doctors—needs to be part of the conversation, for example by integrating courses to find common ground between different professional worlds. One example is a new university programme in Philadelphia that aims to train medical students to think like city planners. The co-director of the course comments of his students that 'These kids are all going to graduate as physicians, and they're going to have a whole new language that nobody who's ever graduated from a med school has had before, so that when they're being tasked to think about how to help to improve this community, they at least know how to have the conversation about the upstream causes of these health outcomes' (Robert Pugliese, quoted in Bradley (2018)).

More communication is needed between disciplines, along with increased coverage of themes such as holistic perspectives and feedback impacts—getting away from reductionist thinking (such as seeking higher speed without thinking about systemic effects on land use and accessibility). Streets are not just conduits for traffic, no matter how 'efficient' or 'improved' they might be. Streets are an integral part of the public realm, where people meet, trade and socialise—indeed, where life happens. For such spaces, it should not be beyond us to provide alternative professional perspectives from those that assume that more speed is the ultimate goal.

10.4.5 Resources

It is unlikely that a reversal of current trajectories of seeking speed in city transport can be achieved without appropriate funding. Insufficient funds for sustainable transport investments may be a consequence of inadequate resourcing of the transport sector in general, but more frequently it is the result of the unbalanced division of transport funding between different modal priorities.

In Chapter 9 we explained that despite clear evidence that investment in walking and cycling projects has high benefit-cost ratios (averaging 13:1), this evidence is not producing the investment needed to fast-track the creation of walking and cycling infrastructure in most cities. Part of the reason for this is the use of cost benefit analyses that value illusory time savings and skew decisions towards road building rather than traffic reduction (Evidence, 2017). Another reason, as we outlined in Chapter 3, is related to politics and 'big-projectitis', where small scale local investments in walking and cycling get overlooked despite their high benefit-cost ratios. The EVIDENCE project report in the EU—a systematic, peer reviewed body of high quality evidence—has noted that measures specifically deployed to achieve sustainable transport objectives have frequently been perceived by funding bodies to be less important than major infrastructure schemes (Shergold & Parkhurst, 2017).

Yet another reason relates to funding structures, where a city's enthusiasm for 'slower' transport may be stymied by grant rules that are institutionally biased towards road building and do not permit funds to be used to support other transport goals. An example is provided by the I-49 Connector inner-city freeway in Shreveport, Louisiana, which Herriges (2019) describes as a 'zombie freeway project' that will accelerate the flight of investment and jobs; bulldoze part of a poor, mostly black neighbourhood; ride roughshod over community opposition; and use 'bogus, voodoo mathematics to claim a positive economic impact'. Continued attempts to build this freeway are driven by State government funding which allows Louisiana officials to leverage federal dollars. Herriges describes this as 'a monstrous disconnect between the needs of Shreveport residents and the priorities of the state legislators and federal bureaucrats who hold the purse strings when it comes to large-scale highway funding'.

To illustrate the advantages of investment in 'slower' modes of transport over highway spending, Box 10.4 presents two hypothetical scenarios: first for spending on highways; and second for investing the same amount of money in walking, cycling and public transport. It uses data supplied by the Center for Appropriate Transport, based on Eugene, Oregon and is closely modelled on research by the International Bicycle Fund (1994), so the costs are in 1994 dollars.

Of course, 'resources' for the 'slower city' include more than funding: resources also refer to those instruments, tools, and information sources required to invest funds wisely, such as the existence of measurement techniques to produce data, from which problems can be identified, benchmarks defined and solutions developed. As far as walking for transport is concerned, until recently almost no city adequately measured it. Systematic treatment of walking in travel surveys and internationally standardised monitoring methods have been lacking, making comparisons difficult or impossible. Not surprisingly, practitioners have long complained that we cannot be taking walking seriously if we do not measure it.

These problems have been addressed in recent years by the development of the International Walking Data Standard (Sauter, Pharaoh, Tight, Martinson, & Wedderburn, 2016), which aimed to develop reliable, valid and yet easy to use travel surveys that include walking in a consistent and appropriate manner. It was hoped that wide adoption by cities and national and international bodies would be achieved—and indeed within the first year the Standard was adopted by Transport for London.

Efforts to level the playing field between the dearth of data on walking (and cycling to a lesser degree) and the abundance of information on faster vehicles are to be welcomed. But there is a caveat: identification of the need for better data is not an excuse to delay the essential immediate action to promote the so-called 'slower' modes. As the urbanist Jan Gehl has exhorted: 'We are realising that if you have people walk and bicycle more, you have a more lively, more liveable, more attractive, more safe, more sustainable and more healthy city. And what are you waiting for?' (Jan Gehl, quoted in Walker (2013)).

BOX 10.4 Play at being Mayor! How would YOU spend a transport budget of US$157 million: the 'fast' or 'slow' transport scenario?

You are the mayor of a small town with a population of 155,000. You must determine the direction of the transportation program for the next seven years. Which scenario would you choose?

Scenario A requires the completion of these three actions:

1. Build five miles of belt-line highway at $7.5 million per mile;
2. Build four miles of parkway at $10 million per mile; and
3. Double the capacity of a one-mile corridor and bridge into the congested central business district at $79.5 million.

Total cost: $157 million

Scenario B requires the completion of these 13 actions:

1. Give every resident over the age of 11 and capable of riding a bicycle (60 per cent of the population), a free commuting bicycle package, complete with baskets, fenders, a lock, lights, rain-gear and a helmet. Bulk purchased $350 bikes are $250 and the accessories are $200;
2. Install 10,000 seven-bike bicycle racks around the city at $350 per rack including installation;
3. Install 10,000 two-bike bicycle lockers for use free of charge around the city at $700 each, including installation;
4. Give away 10,000 car racks for carrying bicycles of people who carpool, $50 each on a bulk purchase;
5. Give away 10,000 $200 bike trailers for carrying kids/cargo;
6. Complete 30 miles of off-street non-motorised paths on the city's Bicycle Master Plan, at $150,000 per mile;
7. Increase the $20,000 annual budget for the ride-share programme tenfold;
8. Completely eliminate the bus fare for all existing regional transit routes. (Fare box revenue is $2.25 million per year.);
9. Provide free bus service to the airport every half hour from 5 a.m. to 1 p.m., seven days a week. (The marginal cost per bus is $32.60 per hour, including capital depreciation, maintenance and labour, and two buses would be needed.);
10. Hire 10 employees at an average of $40,000 per year, plus $25,000 per year in benefits, plus $35,000 per year in support services and supplies to administer the new transportation programmes;
11. Eliminate the projected city budget shortfall from 1994 until the year 2000. ($8 million for FY '94 and $10 million for each remaining year.);
12. Give $100 a month to 1000 homeless people for the period;
13. Use $4.1 million to build a library or lower taxes.

Total cost: $157 million

(Adapted from International Bicycle Fund (1994)).

10.4.6 Policies, strategies and community interventions

Many of the interventions discussed in this book will impact speeds and mode choice over the longer term. To achieve more rapid change, city, organisational, and/or citizen-led approaches to neighbourhood-building have developed, using short-term, low-cost, and scalable interventions to catalyse long-term change (Project for Public Spaces, n.d.). This approach is generally known as tactical urbanism, or 'lighter, quicker, cheaper' interventions, and examples include parklets, guerilla wayfinding, intersection redesign, do-it-yourself bike lanes, hand painted pedestrian crossings and many others. Paradoxically, these fast-paced interventions have slowness as their goal, as many have the effect of reducing speeds and road danger (Fig. 10.11).

Though later stages in the tactical urbanism process are usually sponsored by government in some form, early stages can be led by citizen groups, and are frequently unsanctioned, such as painted intersections to calm traffic in residential areas. Another example is the Kensington Pedestrian Sunday Market in Toronto shown in Fig. 10.12, four years after its launch as an unsanctioned street closure by the community. It is now in its 16th year, officially supported, with its own Business Association and enormous support and affection from

FIGURE 10.11 Tactical urbanism in the form of a pop-up protected bike lane and intersection in Minneapolis, United States. *(Credit: nickfalbo, https://www.flickr.com/photos/83492056@N00/17048572868)*

FIGURE 10.12 Kensington Pedestrian Sunday in Toronto, Canada, seen in 2007 as an unsanctioned community event. *(Credit: Rodney Tolley)*

communities across Toronto (Kensington Market Business Improvement Area, 2019).

A key lesson from the tactical urbanism approach is the necessity of engaging stakeholders from the beginning to generate support for permanent change, for example by organising community workshops, conducting surveys to gauge local opinion, and using chalk, planters and cones to test the geometry of proposed street interventions (Wilson, 2018). 'While it can be time-consuming, this type of engagement makes all the difference in securing the support necessary to move to permanent implementation' (Hanson & Abdulsamad, 2018). A well-known example is the Better Block project, which mobilises resources from the community to convert a city block 'into a walkable, bikeable neighbourhood destination for people of all ages complete with bike lanes, café seating, trees, plants, pop-up businesses, and lighting' (Better Block Foundation, 2019). Such Better Block projects have proliferated, and many have seen their temporary interventions made permanent.

Tactical urbanism interventions have become a powerful instrument for urban planners and 'hacktivists', to improve their cities and gain public and government support for permanent projects. They can inspire citizens and leaders to understand and shape cities in new ways (Lydon & Garcia, 2015). Using tactical urbanism, communities can experiment with projects that allow people to physically experience new options, gather data and test a project before committing to large investments. Importantly, this approach allows for creativity (Wilson, 2018), which is often lacking when large-scale projects, even with the best of intentions, are left to experts such as planners and engineers. In this way pilot projects raise capacity by demonstrating good outcomes and thus alleviate anxiety about change. Tactical urbanism interventions are not the result of a master plan, 'the formal process cities go through to envision change. Instead, these quick and responsive hacks create changes that can actually be experienced—not just imagined—by the people they impact, a way more powerful approach to making change' (Marohn, 2019).

As Marohn observes 'There are a lot of improvements that can be made with paint, straw bales, and a shovel. Working at this scale—using a hacker mindset—allows quick action. There is no need for years of study or deliberation. Little bets can be quickly undone if they don't achieve the desired results, or if they have unanticipated negative consequences ... This is the mechanism that smart, adaptive systems use to assemble themselves' (Marohn, 2019). This pilot project approach was key to the success of the re-design of the Times Square and Herald Square area of Broadway. Blocking off traffic with cones and scattering planters and cheap moveable chairs across the space transformed it not only in reality but also in users' imaginations (Fig. 10.13).

FIGURE 10.13 Herald Square, New York City in 2009 at the pilot stage of transformation, using green paint, moveable chairs and tables, planters and parasols. *(Credit: Rodney Tolley)*

FIGURE 10.14 A sign on the Cattaraugus Native American reservation in New York State. Though it does not specifically mention slowing down, it is clearly an appeal to drivers passing through the reservation to drive with care and consideration for local residents. *(Credit: Rodney Tolley)*

Lastly in this review of community interventions, it is worth referring to those that do not lead to enduring physical change, but seek to shift attitudes and behaviours nonetheless. For example, some communities or neighbourhoods have decided to confront speeding traffic directly, sometimes with home-made signs with images or slogans designed to shock, shame, embarrass, or beguile motorists into slowing down. Fig. 10.14 shows one example—and the cover photograph of this book shows another, a painting of a tortoise on a piece of plywood, tacked to a pole in a suburban neighbourhood in Vancouver, Canada.

10.4.7 Cooperation and partnerships

There is considerable opportunity for partnerships amongst people and agencies concerned with speed, such as in public health, child-friendly cities, local retailers, slow movements, police, public transport unions, psychologists, general practitioners, and road safety organisations. Additionally, practitioners such as traffic engineers and architects, urban planners, urban designers, landscape architects, civil and structural engineers and other members of the design professions all have a role to play. Particularly noticeable is the growth of partnerships involving the health sector. For example, results of a global study of activity levels published in the health journal *The Lancet* identified the most activity-friendly characteristics of neighbourhoods and concluded that there was 'strong justification for public health agencies to work with other constituencies – particularly the urban planning, parks and recreation, and transport sectors – in order to create healthier cities' (Sallis et al., 2016, p. 2208).

Other examples of emerging collaboration can be seen in the development of tools to facilitate evidence-based decision-making towards active transport. The World Health Organization's *Health and Economic Assessment Tool (HEAT)* is an online tool designed to estimate the value of reduced mortality that results from regular walking or cycling. The ARUP *Cities Alive* publication (ARUP, 2016) provides examples of its use, such as by Sustrans in 2011 to estimate the value of existing levels of walking and cycling across the UK's National Cycle Network, calculating the health benefits of walking to be worth £156 million (World Health Organization, 2013).

In other examples, collaboration across sectors has taken place at the development level rather than at the application stage. The Australian Heart Foundation (together with Western Australian Departments of Planning, Transport, Sport and Recreation, Health and more) have produced a Healthy Active by Design website (Heart Foundation, 2014). This brings together evidence, policy alignment, best practice planning principles, guidance, checklists, tools and case studies to facilitate land use, development and design that enable multiple benefits to be realised across health, the economy and the environment.

A final example is one from the private sector. Kaiser Permanente, one of America's largest health care providers and insurance companies, founded the 'Every Body Walk! Campaign' (later a 'Collaborative') in 2010. The initiative may have been partly altruistic in trying to create a healthier population, but it is also sound business, because Kaiser Permanente's clients will be healthier if they walk more, and thus will claim less (and less often) on their policies—but they will still pay their insurance premiums.

By 2016 150 national, state and local organisations belonged to Every Body Walk!, which is the major driving force behind what has been described as 'America's Walking Renaissance' (Walljasper, Simon, & Kraft, 2016). The diversity of members of the Collaborative means that there are many different perspectives on walking, but a unified outcome. This is a classic example of the achievement of 'complementary benefits', in which people from different sectors have diverging missions but converging strategies, which in this case unite to embrace walking as a solution.

10.4.8 Summary

Wherever they are in the world, communities have the right to expect authorities to provide for, support and safeguard their ability to choose safe and health-enhancing modes of movement. They are entitled to ask: are there appropriate policies in place, supported by local action plans, appropriately resourced? Are staff well trained and supported by research? Is there genuine community engagement or ownership? Is success measured and promulgated? And above all, is there a vision? Where a culture of slow movement is in place, the answer to each of these questions will be strongly affirmative.

10.5 Conclusion

Despite the growing awareness of the value of slowing city transport (outlined in the first two parts of this book), and the considerable efforts directed towards reducing speeds and encouraging more use of the 'slower' modes, many of the strategies outlined in Chapters 8, 9 and 10 have limited potential by themselves to have a significant, long-term impact on challenging the addiction to speed in modern societies. Apart from some remarkable success stories (especially in Europe), achievements in slowing city transport have been minor in comparison to the growth of motor car ownership, the increases in the speed potential of cars, the continued investment in road infrastructure to facilitate speed, and the overriding (and we argue misguided) belief in the benefits of speed.

In the way we plan and operate our cities, there is an evident disconnect between the culture of more speed and the futility of attempts to maintain even the existing speed of motor cars in cities. Not surprisingly, there are now calls for futuristic technologies to be deployed in cities, such as unpiloted electric flying vehicles and hyperspeed capsules in underground tubes, 'hyped on the promise of trimming travel time, often for a relatively elite class of users ... available to future riders of their non-existent vehicles' (Small, 2019). Apart from the 'staggering hurdles' to the implementation of such systems, including cost, safety, public acceptance, noise and questions about who will control the infrastructure (Yamanouchi, 2019), such transport technology has the potential to dramatically exacerbate the negative impacts of high-speed transport described in Chapters 2 to 7 of this book. The impact on urban sprawl alone could be massive.

Rather than searching for a technological solution to maintaining speed, we argue for a simpler and proven strategy for promoting health: slowing city transport. As Small (2019) astutely observes '... when the most exciting urban transportation innovation of the decade is a cheap little rented vehicle that struggles to hit 15 mph, perhaps it's time to admit that urban mobility solutions don't necessarily involve flying taxis or Teslas-in-tubes. The tortoise can win this race'.

Values and attitudes that support or glorify speed still pervade many sections of modern societies. The reasons for this include:

- a large public subsidy of the speed provided by cars;
- a legal system that supports cars and speed (e.g. in land use zoning and in laws setting speed limits using the 85th percentile);
- a flawed approach to valuing speed in cost benefit analyses;
- the paucity of data on walking and cycling;

- the powerful promotion of speed (e.g. in car advertisements);
- the (erroneous) belief that the speed of cars provides freedom;
- the neuronic stimulation provided by the sensation of speed;
- the social traps that lead citizens to behave in individualistic ways that have collective impacts that they would like to avoid;
- an over-reliance on modifying transport behaviours of individuals, rather than changing societal values; and
- politicians who lack the courage to challenge the dominance of speed.

Perhaps the most important reason listed here is the subsidy of the speed provided by cars. Removing this so that transport users pay their fair share of the real costs of their transport would, as Rees (2003) suggests, encourage city dwellers to petition governments to improve the 'slower' modes. To achieve the removal of this subsidy, and effectively slow city transport, requires deep political and policy changes that challenge the underlying social and economic environment in which city transport develops. Such changes require strong leadership and broad political and popular backing, along with fundamental cultural shifts in the way we design and build our cities and the way we travel, as well as the way we live, work, shop, learn and play.

We are led to a conclusion that the creation of a 'slower', healthier city requires systemic, holistic change in culture, not just local infrastructure changes, or nudges and changes in individual attitudes and behaviour. Central to achieving any significant change in the transport behaviours of city dwellers is the way in which the perception of problems (and the discussion of them) in transport policy is influenced by the prevailing policy paradigm (Jones, 2009). In many cities this is still dominated by speed, which ensures the free and rapid movement of motor vehicles, as well as the under-funding of public transport and the marginalisation of walking and cycling. Under this paradigm, it is not surprising that policies in many cities still focus on building more roads and parking.

Underlying the dominance of speed in the prevailing policy paradigm is a deception, that this is what the neo-liberal 'free market' wants. However, a careful analysis of the policy framework supporting high-speed transport demonstrates that this speed is produced by a market that is anything but free. As we explained in Chapter 7, speed in urban transport is extensively subsidised, eliminating the free choice of low-speed transport for many people. As Whitelegg (2012, p. 111) explains, the focus on increasing mobility and speed in city transport systems is 'a result of subsidy and political prioritisation ... justified by a false conceptualization of the importance of time savings'.

Given the critical importance of responding to global crises such as the climate emergency, nothing less than 'a radical re-thinking of the policy framework for local governance and development' is required (Rees, 2003, p. 4). However, it will only be possible to achieve 'slow city' objectives if the policies offered are capable of making life better, not worse. Otherwise the chances of receiving enduring political support are slim at best. Fortunately, a promising way to gain this support rests on refocussing policy attention away from 'speed and productivity' and towards the health of people, cities and the environment—and there are strong signs that this is now happening in many creative, prosperous cities, legitimised by the inactivity epidemic and climate breakdown. In this scenario, speed becomes less important than the overall quality of city life and the health of the environment. In the following, concluding chapter, we examine ways in which we might reimagine this healthier and more sustainable future.

References

ARUP (2016). *Cities alive: Towards a walking world*. Available from: https://www.arup.com/-/media/arup/files/publications/c/cities-alive_towards-a-walking-world_lowres.pdf.

Barr, S., & Prillwitz, J. (2014). A smarter choice? Exploring the behaviour change agenda for environmentally sustainable mobility. *Environment and Planning C: Government and Policy*, *32*(1), 1–19.

Begg, D. (2013). World class? London Transport: Progress and future challenges, *Transport Times, London*. Available from: https://www.transporttimes.co.uk/reports.php.

Better Block Foundation. (2019). Better Block. Available from: http://betterblock.org/.

Black, C., & Schreffler, E. (2010). Understanding TDM and its role in the delivery of sustainable urban transport. *Transportation Research Record*, *2163*, 81–88.

Bradley, B. (2018). These future doctors are learning how to influence urban design. *Next City: Inspiring Better Cities*. Available from: https://nextcity.org/features/view/these-future-doctors-are-learning-how-to-influence-urban-design.

Brög, W., Erl, E., Ker, I., Ryle, J., & Wall, R. (2009). Evaluation of voluntary travel behaviour change: Experiences from three continents. *Transport Policy*, *16*(6), 281–292.

Burgen, S. (2018). For me, this is paradise: Life in the Spanish city that banned cars. *The Guardian*. Available from: https://www.theguardian.com/cities/2018/sep/18/paradise-life-spanish-city-banned-cars-pontevedra.

C3 Collaborating for Health. (2017). Why are 'healthy lives' interventions so challenging? *The Health Foundation*. Available from: https://www.c3health.org/wp-content/uploads/2017/07/Why_are_healthy_lives_interventions_so_challenging_2017Jan-1.pdf.

Cabiron, C. (2014). Pontevedra, Spain increases downtown livability by reducing vehicle access. *SmartcitiesDive*. Available from: https://www.smartcitiesdive.com/ex/sustainablecitiescollective/pontevedra-spain-increases-downtown-livability-reducing-vehicle-access/999306/.

Cohen, T. (2018). *Potential impacts of technological and other changes*. Available from: http://nws.eurocities.eu/MediaShell/GetMediaBytes?mediaReference=id173993

Colin, J. (2019). Miguel Anxo Fernández Lores, the traffic doctor. *In Movement: Inventing tomorrow's mobility solutions*. Available from: http://www.inmvt.com/en/success-stories-en/miguel-anxo-fernandez-lores-traffic-doctor/.

Cooper, E. J. (2017). To nudge or not to nudge: Promoting environmentally beneficial behaviors, *Bard Center for Environmental Policy*. Available from: http://digitalcommons.bard.edu/bcep/10.

Daff, M., & Cramphorn, B. (2006). *Signal design for pedestrians as if they were thinking adults*. Paper presented at the 7th International Conference on Walking and Liveable Communities, Melbourne.

Dawid, I. (2010). Ped, Bike, & Bus: Transforming NYC Streets. *Planetizen-Urban Planning News*. Available from: https://www.planetizen.com/node/46405.

De Miguel, B., & Planelles, M. (2019). Brussels takes Spain to justice for pollution in Madrid and Barcelona. *El Pais*. Available from: https://spainsnews.com/brussels-takes-spain-to-justice-for-pollution-in-madrid-and-barcelona-society/.

DeRobertis, M., & Lee, R. W. (2017). The Tragedy of the Commons of the Urban (and Suburban) Arterial. *Institute of Transportation Engineers. ITE Journal*, *87*(6), 44–49.

Evidence. (2017). *Evidence of the proven economic benefits of sustainable transport initiatives to facilitate effective integration in urban mobility plans*. Available from: https://ec.europa.eu/energy/intelligent/projects/en/printpdf/projects/evidence.

Felder, B. (2015). Millennials are changing the city forever. *Oklahoma Gazette*. Available from: https://www.okgazette.com/oklahoma/cover-story-millennials-are-changing-the-city-forever/Content?oid=2960901.

Goodwin, T. (2012). Why we should reject 'nudge'. *Politics*, *32*(2), 85–92.

Gordon, C. (2018). Economic benefits of active transportation. In R. Larouche (Ed.), *Children's active transportation* (pp. 39–52). Oxford: Elsevier.

Gorz, A. (1973). The social ideology of the motor car. Le Sauvage, Sept–Oct. Available from: http://unevenearth.org/2018/08/the-social-ideology-of-the-motorcar/.

Goulden, M., Ryley, T., & Dingwall, R. (2014). Beyond 'predict and provide': UK transport, the growth paradigm and climate change. *Transport Policy*, *32*, 139–147.

Green, C. P., Heywood, J. S., & Navarro, M. (2018). Did the London congestion charge reduce pollution? *Lancaster University Management School, Economics Working Paper*. Available from: https://eprints.lancs.ac.uk/id/eprint/124744/1/LancasterWP2018_007.pdf.

Hallsworth, A. G., Black, C., & Tolley, R. (1995). Psycho-social dimensions of public quiescence towards risks from traffic-generated atmospheric pollution. *Journal of Transport Geography*, *3*(1), 39–51.

Hanson, M., & Abdulsamad, M. (2018). From pop-up to permanent: Five lessons in tactical urbanism. *Global Designing Cities Initiative*. Available from: https://globaldesigningcities.org/2018/04/18/from-pop-up-to-permanent-five-lessons-in-tactical-urbanism/.

Hardin, G. (1968). The tragedy of the commons. *Science*, *162*(3859), 1243–1248.

Heart Foundation. (2014). Healthy active by design. Available from: https://www.heartfoundation.org.au/programs/healthy-active-by-design.

Herriges, D. (2019). The zombie freeway project in Shreveport that won't die. *Strong Towns*. Available from: https://www.strongtowns.org/journal/2019/7/15/the-zombie-freeway-project-in-shreveport-that-wont-die.

International Bicycle Fund. (1994). IBF Math Department. Available from: http://www.ibike.org/engineering/hov.htm.

James, B., Burke, M., & Yen, B. T. (2017). A critical appraisal of individualised marketing and travel blending interventions in Queensland and Western Australia from 1986–2011. *Travel Behaviour and Society, 8*, 1–13.

Johnston, M. (2016). What more can we learn from early learning theory? The contemporary relevance for behaviour change interventions. *British Journal of Health Psychology*, *21*(1), 1–10.

Jones, P. (2009). *The role of an evolving paradigm in shaping international transport research and policy agendas over the last 50 years, Keynote*. Paper presented at the Proceedings of the XII International Association for Travel Behaviour Research Conference. Available from: https://iatbr2009.asu.edu/ocs/custom/resource/Keynote_Jones.pdf.

Kensington Market Business Improvement Area. (2019). Kensington Market. Available from: http://www.kensingtonmarketbia.com/home.htm.

Ker, I., & Tranter, P. J. (2004). A wish called wander: Reclaiming automobility from the motor car. In J. Whitelegg, & G. Haq (Eds.), *Earthscan reader on world transport policy and practice* (pp. 105–113). London: Earthscan.

Kotler, P., & Roberto, E. L. (1989). *Social marketing: Strategies for changing public behaviour*. New York: The Free Press.

Linder, N., Lindahl, T., & Borgström, S. (2018). Using behavioural insights to promote food waste recycling in urban households—Evidence from a longitudinal field experiment. *Frontiers in Psychology*, *9*, 352.

Litman, T. (2003a). Non-motorised transportation demand management. In R. Tolley (Ed.), *Sustainable transport: Planning for walking and cycling in urban environments* (pp. 573–587). Cambridge: Woodhead.

Litman, T. (2003b). *Reinventing transportation: Exploring the paradigm shift needed to reconcile transportation and sustainability objectives*. Available from: https://www.vtpi.org/reinvent.pdf.

Litman, T. (2019). *Evaluating accessibility for transport planning: Measuring people's ability to reach desired goods and activities*. Available from: https://www.vtpi.org/access.pdf.

Lubow, R. (2007). The road to Curitiba. *The New York Times*. Available from: https://www.nytimes.com/2007/05/20/magazine/20Curitiba-t.html.

Lydon, M., & Garcia, A. (2015). *Tactical urbanism: Short-term action for long-term change*. Washington: Island Press.

Marohn, C. (2010). Confessions of a recovering engineer. *Strong Towns*. Available from: https://www.strongtowns.org/journal/2010/11/22/confessions-of-a-recovering-engineer.html.

Marohn, C. (2016). The ideology of traffic. *Strong Towns*. Available from: https://www.strongtowns.org/journal/2016/12/4/the-ideology-of-traffic.

Marohn, C. (2019). Iterating the neighborhood: The big returns of small investments. *Strong Towns*. Available from: https://www.strongtowns.org/journal/2019/9/19/the-strong-towns-approach-to-public-investment-satbook.

McLaren, C., Havlak, C., & Stewart-Wilson, G. (2015). What is the full cost of your commute? *The Discourse*. Available from: https://www.thediscourse.ca/scarborough/full-cost-commute.

Methorst, R. (2010). Systems approach - PQN final report, part A: Introduction and conceptual framework. In R. Methorst, H. Monterde, I. Bort, R. Risser, D. Sauter, M. Tight, & J. Walker (Eds.), *Pedestrian quality needs (PQN) final report of the COST Project* (pp. 1–128). (358). Cheltenham: Walk21.

NACTO. (2016). *Global street design guide. National Association of City Transportation Officials*. Available from: https://globaldesigningcities.org/publication/global-street-design-guide/.

Neslen, A. (2019). Madrid could become first European city to scrap low-emissions zone. *The Guardian*. Available from: https://www.theguardian.com/cities/2019/may/31/madrid-set-to-end-clean-air-project-in-rightwing-power-switch.

Partnership for Urban Mobility. (2019). *Promoting Mobility Behaviour Change: Practical guidance for inspiring more walking, cycling and public transport and minimising car use*. Available from: https://docs.wixstatic.com/ugd/241361_c2a32be0a6284af6a4b528e27544b5b7.pdf.

Philp, M., & Taylor, M. A. P. (2010). *Position Paper 1: Voluntary travel behaviour change and its potential implications for climate change mitigation and adaptation*. Available from: https://www.nccarf.edu.au/sites/www.nccarf.edu.au.settlements-infrastructure/files/file/ACCARNSI_PositionPaper_VTBC.pdf.

Piatkowski, D. P., Marshall, W. E., & Krizek, K. J. (2019). Carrots versus sticks: Assessing intervention effectiveness and implementation challenges for active transport. *Journal of Planning Education and Research*, *39*(1), 50–64.

Project for Public Spaces. (n.d.). The lighter, quicker, cheaper transformation of public spaces. *Public Space Resources*. Available from: https://www.pps.org/article/lighter-quicker-cheaper.

Rees, W. (2003). Ecological footprints and urban transportation. In R. Tolley (Ed.), *Sustainable transport: Planning for walking and cycling in urban environments* (pp. 3–19). Abingdon: Woodhead Publishing.

Sallis, J., Cerin, E., Conway, T. L., Adams, M. A., Frank, L. D., Pratt, M., et al. (2016). Physical activity in relation to urban environments in 14 cities worldwide: A cross-sectional study. *The Lancet*, *387*(10034), 2207–2217.

Sauter, D., Pharoah, T., Tight, M., Martinson, R., & Wedderburn, M. (2016). *International walking data standard: Treatment of walking in travel surveys*. Available from: http://files.designer.hoststar.ch/hoststar10546/file/1-international_walking_data_standard_version_aug_2016.pdf.

Schmidt, A. (2018). Madrid moves to boot car traffic out of its city center. *Streetsblog USA*. Available from: https://usa.streetsblog.org/2018/05/25/madrid-moves-to-boot-car-traffic-out-of-its-city-center/.

Schreffler, E. (2018). Better integrating travel choices into future urban mobility systems: The day the highways stood still. *Journal of Public Transportation*, *21*(1), 82–91.

Shergold, I., & Parkhurst, G. (2017). *Demonstrating economic benefit from sustainable mobility choices - the EVIDENCE project*. Available from: https://www.eltis.org/sites/default/files/evidence_publishable_report_final.pdf.

Shoup, D. C. (2005). *Parking cash out*. Available from: http://shoup.bol.ucla.edu/Parking%20Cash%20Out%20Report.pdf.

Shoup, D. C. (2018). *Parking and the city*. New York: Routledge.

Small, A. (2019). Why speed kills cities. *Citylab*. Available from: https://www.citylab.com/transportation/2019/08/low-speed-limit-vehicle-safety-crash-data-traffic-congestion/588412/.

Smartcity. (2019). Multimodal transport system – enabling efficient access from first to last mile in smart cities. *Smartcity Press*. Available from: https://www.smartcity.press/multimodal-transport-system/.

Steuteville, R. (2017). 25 great ideas of the New Urbanism. *Public Square, a CNU Journal*. Available from: https://www.cnu.org/publicsquare/2017/10/31/25-great-ideas-new-urbanism.

Strong Towns. (2016). Conversation with an engineer. Available from: https://www.strongtowns.org/journal/2016/4/27/conversations-with-an-engineer.

Thaler, R. H., & Sunstein, C. R. (2008). *Nudge: Improving decisions about health, wealth, and happiness*. New Haven, CT: Yale University Press.

The World Bank. (2018). Reducing traffic congestion and emission in Chinese cities. Available from: https://www.worldbank.org/en/news/feature/2018/11/16/reducing-traffic-congestion-and-emission-in-chinese-cities.

Tranter, P. (2006). Overcoming social traps: A key to creating child friendly cities. In B. Gleeson, & N. Sipe (Eds.), *Creating child friendly cities: Reinstating kids in the city* (pp. 121–135). New York: Routledge.

Tranter, P., & May, M. (2005). Using the concept of effective speed as a stimulus for travel behaviour change and policy development. *A Report for the Australian Greenhouse Office, Department of Environment and Heritage, Australia*.

US Department of Transportation. (2006). Managing travel demand: Applying European perspectives to U.S. Practice, Chapter 2: Case studies. *Office of International Programs*. Available from: https://international.fhwa.dot.gov/traveldemand/t1_p08.cfm.

US Department of Transportation. (2012). *Integrating demand management into the transportation planning process: A desk reference*. Available from: https://ops.fhwa.dot.gov/publications/fhwahop12035/fhwahop12035.pdf.

Walker, P. (2013). London: No city for cyclists. Available from: https://www.theguardian.com/environment/bike-blog/2013/dec/03/london-cycling-provisions-laughable-bike-blog.

Walljasper, J., Simon, H., & Kraft, K. (2016). *America's walking renaissance: How cities, suburbs and towns are getting back on their feet*. Available from: https://americawalks.org/americas-walking-renaissance/.

Whitelegg, J. (2012). How much transport can landscape tolerate: new ways of thinking about traffic, landscape and nature? In S. Koerner, H. Holzapfel, & F. Bellin-Harder (Eds.), *Landschaft und Verkeher*. University of Kassel, Germany, Available from: http://www.uni-kassel.de/upress/online/frei/978-3-86219-358-5.volltext.frei.pdf.

Wilson, K. (2018). Our streets are an emergency situation for cyclists. Why should we fix them incrementally? *Strong Towns*. Available from: https://www.strongtowns.org/journal/2018/7/25/our-streets-are-an-emergency-situation-for-cyclists-why-should-we-fix-them-incrementally.

World Health Organization. (2013). Examples of applications of the health economic assessment tool (HEAT) for cycling. Available from: http://www.euro.who.int/en/health-topics/environment-and-health/Transport-and-health/activities/guidance-and-tools/health-economic-assessment-tool-heat-for-cycling-and-walking/examples-of-applications-of-the-health-economic-assessment-tool-heat-for-walking-and-cycling.

Yamanouchi, K. (2019). Are passenger drones the answer to Atlanta's traffic gridlock? *Government Technology, Future Structure*. Available from: https://www.govtech.com/fs/transportation/Are-Passenger-Drones-the-Answer-to-Atlantas-Traffic-Gridlock.html.

Chapter 11

Conclusion: re-imagining the city for a healthier future

'Your future is whatever you make it, so make it a good one'.

Emmet 'Doc' Brown, in the movie Back to the Future Part III (1990)

Abstract

This chapter examines possible low-speed urban futures. It reiterates the importance of 'slow cities' in creating a healthy and sustainable future, and asks whether our obsession with increasing speeds might at least partly explain the inadequate responses to the global challenges facing humanity. Conquering our societal addiction to fast travel in the city represents an enormous challenge, and to help meet this we examine the positive vision of child-friendly cities. A focus on children and their well-being can help build consensus, lifting debates beyond narrow self-interest and encouraging more collective and long-term responses. We show how child-friendly cities must be slower cities, and slower cities are child-friendly cities, and both are healthier for us all. There follows discussion of three opportunities for change in the future: the re-imagining of goals, attitudes and outcomes. Ten key ideas from this book are then presented as the basis for a 'Manifesto for 21st Century Slow Cities'. The chapter concludes with a message from the future written by a 30-year-old in the year 2050, thanking her parents' generation for their efforts in creating slower, healthier, sustainable and child-friendly cities.

11.1 Introduction

'Doc' Brown's advice has not resonated with policy makers who see increasing city transport speeds as a priority. They have used decision-making tools that they claim to be objective and value-free to seek time savings for everyone by increasing the speeds at which we travel. Yet their tools are anything but value-free. Policy makers have fostered a pervasive misrepresentation of the value of speed, so that most people now complain of increasing time pressures, while at the same time being forced to make transport choices that demand ever more time and energy. This almost guarantees that the future of our cities will *not* be 'a good one'. Do we really want a future: where children can no longer walk to school with their friends; where parents have to spend much of their time

Slow Cities. http://dx.doi.org/10.1016/B978-0-12-815316-1.00011-3

transporting children to 'keep them safe'; where physical inactivity levels continue to grow as people increasingly rely on motorised vehicles to move; and where accelerating climate breakdown threatens livelihoods, cities and ecosystems? We argue that a desirable future is one that promotes healthy cities, rather than faster cities. The strategy of slowing city transport may indeed provide a faster route to health.

Throughout this book we have argued that the goal of urban planning should be promoting health for people, economies and the environment. Yet urban planning itself involves addressing 'wicked problems', those that involve multiple stakeholders with diverse views making them seem impossible to solve. Gill (2017a) argues, 'tackling car dependence is perhaps the definitive wicked issue for urban policy makers'. If we are to be successful in slowing the city, car dependence must be reduced. The complexity of urban planning means that achieving a slowing of the city requires more than just technical expertise. Values and attitudes surrounding our addiction to speed must be changed as well. Speed is 'central to the expression of our values about urban life and the public realm. How we choose to balance the freedom of the individual to travel fast, and the well-being of other groups such as children and the elderly, says a great deal about our values and the sort of towns and cities that we desire' (Hamilton-Baillie, 2004, p. 54–55).

To help resolve this dilemma, a useful approach is to engage with child-friendly cities and child-friendly planning. A focus on children and their well-being can provide a potentially fruitful way to navigate complex issues surrounding our addiction to fast modes of transport. It can help build consensus, lifting debates beyond narrow self-interest and encouraging more collective and long-term responses. We saw in Chapter 8 how simply establishing play streets can help change residents' attitudes and inspire them to change their streets, their transport and their city. When citizens are asked to consider the needs of children, this helps them understand the connection between the big issues of pollution and transport planning, and everyday life in local streets (Gill, 2017a).

In this chapter, we provide a good news perspective, examining a child-friendly vision for a future 'slow city'. Slower cities are child-friendly cities and child-friendly cities must be slower cities, and both are healthier for everyone. The chapter assesses whether the pursuit of speed is an obstacle to the provision of healthy, child-friendly and sustainable cities, and asks whether our collective obsession with increasing speed is a central issue in our inadequate responses to the global challenges facing humanity. There follows discussion of three opportunities for change in the future—the re-imagining of goals, attitudes and outcomes. The chapter concludes in the form of a letter from the future: a message from a 30-year-old in the year 2050 thanking her parents for their efforts in creating slower, healthier, more sustainable and child-friendly cities. This letter refers to our 'Manifesto for 21st Century Slow Cities' (Tranter & Tolley, 2020).

11.2 A child-friendly vision for a future 'slow city'

Rather than feeling overwhelmed by growing global challenges, we argue that society needs to focus on positive visions of the future. One such positive vision involves the concept of child-friendly cities, defined as any system of local governance committed to fulfilling children's rights under the Convention on the Rights of the Child (UNICEF, 2009). These rights include their participatory rights to express their opinions and influence decisions that affect them, their rights to be safe and protected from harm and their rights to have environments supporting their needs to learn, play and be social (UNICEF, 2013). In child-friendly cities children should be able to walk safely in the streets, and meet friends and play. Current conditions in cities in many nations do not support these goals (Gilbert, Whitzman, Pieters, & Allan, 2018).

A focus on children provides particular insights into the value of, and strategies for, slowing city transport (Tranter & Sharpe, 2008). For example, children are particularly vulnerable to the dangers created by speed. However, while children's needs and perspectives sometimes overlap with other groups, including the elderly, women and people with disabilities, children exhibit one particular trait more than any other group: their playfulness. They are also far more capable than adults give them credit for, and they may provide important insights, and even leadership to help create slower, healthier and more resilient cities.

While 'slow cities' provide a perfect setting for child-friendly environments, neo-liberalism provides an ideal environment for promoting the addiction to speed. High-speed transport promotes the consumption of resources through the pursuit of the (supposed) 'time saving' that is prized in a capitalist society. Children do not value consumerism, nor speed and productivity, until adults instil these values in them. What matters to children in their everyday travel is their interaction with people and their environments, and living in (enjoying) the moment in playful experiences. 'Slower', non-car travel provides children with opportunities such as playing with friends or siblings, and exploring the world at their own pace. These opportunities are more important to them than 'saving time'. While collectively adults (including economists, planners, politicians and policy makers) have been enculturated into the 'time saving' ethos, left to their own devices children are largely immune to the ideologies of neo-liberalism.

In the following sections we focus on children and child-friendly cities. First, we explain why the slower modes are the child-friendly modes. Then we examine the importance of play and playfulness to children, and how slowing city transport can help promote children's access to opportunities for play. Next we explain how slowing the city can reduce children's vulnerability to many threats and finally, we consider the possibility that children might provide new ideas to help create healthier, 'slower cities'.

11.3 The child-friendly transport modes

As well as recognising the concept of child-friendly cities, it is also possible to identify child-friendly modes of transport. These are the 'slower' active modes of walking, cycling and public transport, as well as other minor modes such as skating and scootering. These modes are child-friendly for four reasons. First, research shows that children (at least those in primary school) prefer to walk or cycle than to be driven (O'Brien & Tranter, 2006). Indeed, children and adolescents in almost every nation have the highest rates of cycling for any age group (Pucher & Buehler, 2008). For children, walking and cycling is fun: they like travelling with friends (see Fig. 11.1). They consider getting to school in cars boring (Fig. 11.2): 'you have to sit still' and 'you don't get any exercise' (Garrard, 2011). As O'Brien (2008, p. 15) explains, 'children's view of transportation (when walking to school) reminds us that transportation is not only about "moving people and goods". It is about wonder, discovery, joy and happiness'. Recent research supports this view, showing that active travel by children to school (walking or cycling) is associated with higher levels of well-being and positive emotions in both children and their parents (Ramanathan, O'Brien, Faulkner, & Stone, 2014).

FIGURE 11.1 Children having fun walking to school together in Marga, Indonesia. *(Credit: Artem Beliaikin, https://www.pexels.com/photo/activity-asian-people-boys-children-1153976/)*

FIGURE 11.2 Children find sitting in cars boring: viewing the world from the back seat of a car isolates them from contact with their environment. *(Credit: Classroom Camera (Cascade Canyon School), https://www.flickr.com/photos/155535822@N07/38592428480/)*

Second, active transport is recognised as being healthy and advantageous for child development (Giles-Corti, Kelty, Zubrick, & Villanueva, 2009). Children who use active modes are less likely to experience obesity, type 2 diabetes, hypertension and depression, and with increased independent mobility, children's mental health is enhanced through contact with their peers and others in local communities (O'Brien, 2003). Physical activity guidelines recognise that children need higher levels of physical activity than adults. In Australia, for example, such guidelines recommend that children need at least 60 minutes (and up to several hours) of moderate to vigorous physical activity every day.

Third, when adults use the slower, active transport modes, whole neighbourhoods become more child-friendly, as there are more 'eyes on the street' to look out for children (see Fig. 11.3). In contrast, the increased speed of motorised transport modes makes cities less child-friendly as streets become more dangerous in terms of traffic, and drivers' attention is focussed on the road ahead, rather than on people in or near the street. Fig. 5.10 illustrates how the driver's cone of vision narrows with increasing speed and in Chapter 10 we showed how in-car phone use has the same effect. Increased speeds reduce children's freedom at the same time as making cities more dangerous for all residents.

Cities where the speed of motorised transport is regarded as the ultimate indicator of success cannot claim to be child-friendly. Speeds above 30 km/h

FIGURE 11.3 Children walking playfully under the watchful eyes of adults in a 'slow' city street in Stockholm, Sweden, which has had 30 km/h speed limits on all residential streets since 2004. *(Credit: Nicola Sap De Mitri, https://www.flickr.com/photos/quatar/28240105242)*

(or 20 mph) are not compatible with a child-friendly (and walking- and cycling-friendly) environment. Such speeds are particularly unsuitable in residential streets, considering the high likelihood of human interaction with motor vehicles, including children playing and people walking, cycling or crossing the street. The importance of reducing speeds in child-friendly cities is now recognised in widely circulated reports such as 'Cities Alive, Designing for Urban Childhoods' (ARUP, 2017).

The fourth reason why slow modes are child-friendly modes is that they provide independent and playful mobility: children can walk, cycle and use public transport without being accompanied by their parents or other supervising adults. This independent mobility is regarded as critical for their mental and emotional development (Kegerreis, 1993). The playful nature of children is an important part of what it means to be human, so to make cities more human and healthier places, they also have to become more playful places for all residents. Thus, there is a case for the special consideration of children's play in the process of slowing city transport.

11.4 Children's playful exploration in a child-friendly city

In a child-friendly city, children have the freedom to explore their neighbourhood and city, safely and playfully, in expanding circles as they mature. In many cities and countries, levels of children's freedoms (their independent mobility)

FIGURE 11.4 Children playing in a New York City street, 1909. *(Reproduced from Library of Congress, Prints & Photographs Division [LC-DIG-ggbain-03232] Original source: https://www.loc.gov/pictures/item/2014683226/)*

have declined markedly over the last few decades (Tranter & Sharpe, 2012). In England the percentage of children allowed to go to school without adult supervision fell from 80 per cent of seven- and eight-year-old English children in 1971, to nine per cent in 1990 (Hillman, Adams, & Whitelegg, 1990). The loss of freedom continued from 1990 to 2010, which saw an increase in the numbers of children being accompanied to school (Shaw et al., 2013).

Data from other nations also show declines in children's freedoms. In Australia, the percentage of 10- to 14-year-old children allowed to walk to school fell from 44 in 1971 to 21 in 2003 (Van Der Ploeg, Merom, Corpuz, & Bauman, 2008). In the United States the number of K-8 children walking or cycling to school fell from 48 per cent in 1969 to 13 per cent in 2009, and there were large increases in the number of children driven to school. By 2009, school travel in the morning peak period accounted for 5–7 per cent of vehicle miles travelled and 10–14 per cent of all private vehicles on the road (McDonald, Brown, Marchetti, & Pedroso, 2011).

One impact of the loss of children's freedom to explore their neighbourhoods and cities independently is that children have fewer opportunities for spontaneous play, opportunities that were once available to children even in inner-city streets (see Fig. 11.4). Even walking to school can be a playful experience. In contrast, children travelling in cars are deprived of 'opportunities to learn from first-hand interaction with the real world and with adults and other children in their neighbourhood' (O'Brien, 2001).

The implications of children's loss of freedom to playfully explore their neighbourhoods are profound, yet poorly understood, even by some who are responsible for children's welfare and education. Play is how children learn to make sense of the world, and to solve problems. When children are deprived of play, they are also deprived of opportunities to take control of their own lives: 'We may think we are protecting them, but in fact we are diminishing their joy … and increasing the odds that they will suffer from anxiety, depression and other disorders' (Gray, 2010).

The playful nature of children can provide insights for adults into what a slower mode of being might be. While time-pressured adults seek ways to 'save time' and often see the next task as more important than the present, children at play have a different perspective: they live in the moment and may have little sense of the passing of time, being completely absorbed in their play. As Carl Honoré (2004, p. 216–217) explains, 'children are not born obsessed with speed and productivity, we make them that way'. Modern societies that emphasise speed, efficiency and saving time have become effective at instilling these values in children. A common phrase that parents use when organising their children is 'hurry up'. Many adults (including some parents and teachers) believe that children playing are wasting their time, and that children should be engaged in stimulating, adult-organised activities. Yet, there is limited evidence that such stimulation is effective: in contrast, unstructured play helps children develop language and social skills, empathy, creativity and their ability to learn (Honoré, 2004).

11.5 Reducing children's vulnerability by slowing the city

The vulnerability of children is also important in terms of understanding the value of slowing city transport. The conceptualisation of children as vulnerable has, in many cases, dominated the ways in which their mobility (and their lifestyle) is provided for by adults, many of whom try to 'protect' their children by driving them everywhere, leading to declining levels of children's freedom to explore their own neighbourhoods and cities (Hillman et al., 1990). In cities dominated by speed, children are vulnerable to several dangers, particularly air pollution, road crashes, lack of physical activity and lack of contact with their local community through restrictions on independent mobility (Edwards & Whitehouse, 2018; Laville, Taylor, Bengtsson, & Zapponi, 2017; O'Brien, 2003; Spycher et al., 2015; Sunyer et al., 2017; Whitzman et al., 2010).

With regard to air pollution, we examined children's particular vulnerability in Chapter 5 (Box 5.1). We stressed that vehicle emissions are the major (and most rapidly growing) source; that health impacts on children are more severe than on adults; that they are much worse than hitherto realised; that children are disproportionately exposed to higher doses of pollution during their journey to school; and that air pollution is more damaging to children *inside* cars than when they are walking or cycling, because emissions are recirculated inside the vehicles. Parents try to protect children from walking and cycling in polluted air by driving them to school. Yet, by doing so, they actually increase the risks to their children, exposing them to higher concentrations of many pollutants including benzene, $PM_{2.5}$ particles and carbon monoxide. For parents this is a classic—and distressing—social trap spawned by the fast city. However, the evidence on in-car pollution is rarely discussed, perhaps because parents either are not aware of the danger or may be rationalising their behaviour through various coping mechanisms such as denial and dogmatism (see Section 10.2.4). The concern that parents have for children's particular vulnerabilities might instead be used to help them embrace the concept of slowing city transport. As Sir David King (former UK government chief scientific adviser) argues: 'If more drivers knew the damage they could be doing to their children [in terms of in-car pollution], I think they'd think twice about getting in the car' (Carrington, 2017).

Low speeds are particularly critical for children's road safety (Herbert, 2017; Li, Alonge, & Hyder, 2016). At the global scale, 186,000 children (aged under 18) die each year from road traffic injury, the fourth leading cause of death among children aged 5–9 years, third among children aged 10–14 years and first among those aged 15–17 years (Li et al., 2016). Children may not pay attention to dangers on the road, they are more likely to sustain fatal injuries when hit by a car, and they have less ability to judge the speeds of approaching cars (Herbert, 2017).

In many developed nations, child pedestrian and cycling injury rates have declined over the last few decades, but this is likely largely due to the removal of children from the street, rather than any significant reduction in the dominance of motorised vehicles or improvements in safety for people on foot or bicycle. For instance in the United States, a 37 per cent decline in the number of children's walking trips was reported between 1977 and 1995 (Henary, Crandall, Bhalla, Mock, & Roudsari, 2003). Recent research indicates that, in the United States at least, this decline is continuing. Buehler, Pucher, and Bauman (2020) found a large drop in the numbers of children walking and cycling there between 2001 and 2017.

Low speed streets largely eliminate the fear of traffic danger, and hence parents are more likely to allow their children to walk or cycle to school and other destinations, and to allow their children to play on or near local streets. Lower speeds also make the streets more attractive for people of all ages to walk and cycle, which means that there are more adults on the streets who can look out for children. In contrast, children living in areas with busy traffic are less likely to have positive perceptions of safety, friendliness and helpfulness of people in their local area (Mullan, 2003).

Many modern societies are in danger of accepting that stranger danger is a real risk, but while stranger danger is a real *fear* for parents, the depth of this fear has no basis in actual risk. Using data from the United Kingdom, Tim Gill (2007, p. 49) argues: 'it can be stated with near certainty that there are no more predatory child killers at large today than there were in 1990 or 1975. These statistics categorically refute the dominant media message that dangerous strangers represent a significant or growing threat to children'. Thus many parents who drive their children to school and other places are 'protecting' children from a risk from strangers that is infinitesimal. Yet in doing so, they place children in situations where other risks are higher, if less obvious or evident only in the long term (e.g. higher pollution levels in cars than outside and reduced levels of physical activity).

The vulnerability of children also means that children are a kind of 'indicator species for cities' (Gill, 2017b). Gill explains that when children are visibly present in neighbourhoods, this is a sign of a healthy human habitat, in much the same way that the presence of salmon indicates the health of rivers. As societies change and streets are perceived as more dangerous, children are the group who are most likely to disappear from public space. In contrast, slowing city transport can reduce the main fears that lead parents to restrict their children's independent mobility: fears of traffic and stranger danger.

In many nations (notably the United States, United Kingdom, Canada, Australia and New Zealand), parents feel strong social pressure to conform to a particular notion of 'a good parent', meaning that they should 'protect' their child by driving or accompanying them to school and to other destinations. In some cases, even parents walking with their children feel obliged to keep their children under tight control (see Fig. 11.5). During the last several decades, during which children's freedoms have been declining, the time spent looking after

FIGURE 11.5 An adult in Ottawa, Canada tries to keep an accompanied child 'safe', consequently restricting the freedom of the child—and herself. *(Credit: Paul Tranter)*

children by parents has been increasing. Research in Britain indicates that the time spent looking after children increased almost four-fold between 1975 and 2000, from 25 minutes a day to 99 minutes a day (Future Foundation, 2006). This huge increase is largely due to the way that parents (and other adults caring for children) make individualistic decisions about the welfare of their children, rather than communities taking a more collective approach to caring for them. This collective approach is more likely to be seen in Japanese cities (or those in Germany, Switzerland and Finland) (Fig. 11.6) where in many cases the

FIGURE 11.6 Primary school children walking to school without adult supervision in Nara, Japan. *(Credit: John Gillespie from New York, United States—School children of Nara, CC BY-SA 2.0, https://commons.wikimedia.org/w/index.php?curid=62144501)*

majority of parents let their children travel unaccompanied to school. In Tokyo, '6-year-olds ride the subway downtown to school alongside the suited businessmen and women. In Switzerland, parents who do not let their kids travel to kindergarten—yes, kindergarten—on their own are looked down on' (Gill, 2017b).

On her first visit to Japan, in 2005, Professor Karen Malone was surprised to see groups of kindergarten children walking to school without an adult. The children were engaged in the playful activities of collecting autumn leaves, balancing on kerbs, skipping, chasing, chatting and laughing. When she asked a Japanese colleague why there were no adults looking after the children, he responded, 'What do you mean, no adults? There are the car drivers, the shopkeepers, the other pedestrians – the city is full of adults who are taking care of them!' (Malone, 2017)

This collective responsibility for all children can be facilitated by slowing motorised traffic, which can help re-create environments that enable children's freedom and playful exploration, as well as their safety. For example, many residential neighbourhoods in Japanese cities have 30 km/h speed limits, and child pedestrian injury rates in Japan are low and have been declining over the last decade (Nakahara, Ichikawa, & Sakamoto, 2016). The high rates of children walking and cycling to school are also supported by Japanese law that requires elementary schools to be located within four km (2.5 miles), and high schools within six km (3.7 miles) of children's homes (Mori, Armada, & Willcox, 2012).

Some likely ways in which slowing the city can benefit both children and parents are outlined in Box 11.1, which considers two contrasting scenarios, both set in middle-class suburbs. The key difference is in the motorised traffic speeds in residential streets.

BOX 11.1 Two scenarios: how high-speed versus low-speed neighbourhoods affect children and adults.

Both children and adults will likely benefit from living in low-speed neighbourhoods, as illustrated in the following two scenarios. In Scenario A, the status quo operates, with speed limits in residential areas of 50 or 60 km/h. Most households have at least two cars, and children are usually driven to school and to other locations. Very little travel is made by active modes.

In this scenario, children do not get the recommended levels of physical activity, nor the playful experiences that occur during walking or cycling to school, so parents feel obliged to drive them to adult-organised activities such as basketball or ballet (Blanchard, 2000, p. 149). Residential streets are regarded as dangerous, not only in terms of traffic danger but also because of stranger danger associated with a lack of eyes on the street. Because children are not allowed to travel independently to visit their friends, parents must organise play-dates and drive their children to these. This may well continue until the children are well into their teens. Parents in Scenario A have committed themselves to spending several hours per week driving their children to school, sport and other activities. Children miss out on opportunities for spontaneous play, which can have significant negative impacts on their development, particularly the development of their creative abilities and their empathy (Whitebread, 2017).

In Scenario B, speed limits have been reduced to 30 km/h for over five years, providing time for residents to adapt to the safer environments provided by the lower speeds. This has led to there being far fewer cars, with most households having one or no cars, and most travel being conducted by walking, cycling or public transport. Local streets are safe enough for most children to walk or cycle to and from school. They visit friends on their own, and parents are confident that children are safe, walking locally where neighbours are often on the streets, keeping an eye out for children. There is a collective responsibility for children, rather than an individualistic approach where parents look after their own children without considering the impact on others. Children get to know the physical and social qualities of their local neighbourhood, and hence develop a strong sense of place. Parents feel less time-pressured: children do not have to be driven to their friends or to sport, as they can play locally, even creating their own sporting games in the local neighbourhood. Children (and adults) are fitter, happier and healthier.

As should be clear from the earlier sections in this chapter, a focus on children and their restricted lifestyles within 'fast city' environments provides an opportunity to reflect on the challenges created by our addiction to speed. If future transport policies use child-friendly principles as a guide, then 'slow', healthy and sustainable cities will develop. However, rather than adults assuming that they know how to create child-friendly environments, they should acknowledge that children themselves have an important role to play in creating 'slower', healthier cities.

11.6 Involving children in the creation of 'slow cities'

The creation of healthier, liveable and slower cities will require creative approaches to the way we design and operate our cities. Encouraging participation by children and young people may facilitate this process as they are more open to new ways of looking at the world, and they may provide innovative strategies for the creation of healthier cities. As Rushkoff (1997, p. 13) argues, 'let's appreciate the natural adaptive skills demonstrated by our kids and look to them for answers to some of our own problems'.

This concept of involving children has been enshrined in international human rights legislation. For example, Article 12 of the United Nations Convention on the Rights of the Child states that 'Children have the right to say what they think should happen when adults are making decisions that affect them and to have their opinions taken into account' (UNICEF, 2006). Unfortunately, such 'participation' rights are the most poorly recognised rights of children (Tranter & Sharpe, 2007). Many governments and organisations recognise and attempt to implement 'protection' and 'provision' rights, but find it difficult to accept that children's views, and hence their 'participation', are important. The dominant view is that children do not have the competence to engage in planning decisions in any meaningful way. However, considerable research has demonstrated that children and young people can make meaningful contributions to their city, if given the chance (Freeman, 2005), and some cities and organisations are making progress in giving children this opportunity.

The participation of children in city planning is now being actively supported by NACTO (the National Association of City Transportation Officials), as part of its Global Designing Cities Initiative. Four cities have been selected in a trial to develop child-friendly streets, with the aim of creating 'safe public space for kids of all ages and abilities to learn, play and move about the city' (Peyton, 2019). Children will be engaged in the design process for developing temporary interventions that transform streets into safer and more playful spaces. An indication of the interest in this initiative is that the four cities were selected from a pool of almost 100 applications from cities around the world.

As the NACTO initiative demonstrates, children's contribution to the planning and design of their cities need not be limited to child-specific settings (homes, schools, playgrounds and skateparks). A recent study involving children in a design process in Auckland demonstrated that children can capably contribute to ideas for redesigning a central city square. In this study children's views were in accord with 'slow city' ideals: 'children approved of the plan to close off access to cars and turn the roadway into pedestrian space … "no cars should be allowed to drive in"'. They also demonstrated an awareness of inclusivity, suggesting that 'Freyberg Square should be a place for people of all ages … even babies' (Witten & Carroll, 2015, p. 17). As well as being able to contribute to specific design challenges, children may even provide leadership in the creation of healthier, slower cities. The School Strikes for Climate (SS4C) are a case in point.

11.7 The role of slowing transport in responding to global challenges

The school strike movement began in 2018, when 15-year-old Greta Thunberg staged a protest in Stockholm to demand that politicians take urgent action to avoid catastrophic ecological breakdown from the climate crisis (see Fig. 11.7). Since the first protest, school strikes have been organised throughout the world, attracting strong support from adults as well as school children (Fig. 11.8), with students from towns and cities in more than 150 nations walking out of lessons. The movement has been described as 'one of the most significant climate movements in history' (Taylor, 2019).

The leadership of Greta Thunberg seems to have threatened the world view of 'a cohort of mostly male, middle-aged, out-of-touch media commentators and journalists' who have dismissed her calls for change as childish and unrealistic (Warren, 2019). In doing so they are in contravention of the UN Convention on

FIGURE 11.7 Greta Thunberg beginning her School Strike for Climate outside the Swedish parliament building in August 2018. *(Credit: Anders Hellberg—Own work, CC BY-SA 4.0, https://commons.wikimedia.org/w/index.php?curid=77270098)*

the Rights of the Child. Thus, while some journalists seem willing to consider 'hyperbolic, factually-incorrect stories' from climate science deniers, they are unwilling to abide by human rights legislation. While still technically a child, 'Greta Thunberg is pissing off all the right people' (Warren, 2019).

In December 2019 Thunberg was named 'TIME Person of the Year', an annual award by the news magazine that profiles a person who has done the most to influence the events of the year. Time Editor-in-Chief Edward Felsenthal explained 'She became the biggest voice on the biggest issue facing the planet this year, coming from essentially nowhere to lead a worldwide movement … She embodies youth activism' (Knowles, 2019). At the World Economic Forum in Davos in 2019, Thunberg made an impassioned plea to world leaders, saying 'I don't want your hope. I don't want you to be hopeful. I want you to panic.

FIGURE 11.8 School students and adults at the Global Climate Strike in September 2019, Melbourne, Australia. *(Credit: Nick Tranter)*

I want you to feel the fear I feel every day. And then I want you to act. I want you to act as you would in a crisis. I want you to act as if our house is on fire. Because it is' (Thunberg, 2019). She followed that by lambasting delegates at the United Nations in New York City, where she accused world leaders of stealing her dreams and childhood with their inaction on the climate crisis. 'This is all wrong. I shouldn't be up here. I should be back in school on the other side of the ocean. Yet you all come to us young people for hope … We are in the beginning of a mass extinction, and all you can talk about is money and fairy tales of eternal economic growth. How dare you! … And if you choose to fail us, I say – we will never forgive you' (NPR Staff, 2019).

During the writing of this book, we became increasingly convinced that speed is not simply an important problem for city transport: the collective societal obsession with increasing speed is also a central issue in our inadequate response to the global challenges currently facing humanity. We are running out of time to deal with major issues surrounding planetary health—the climate emergency and biodiversity loss—and yet current tools and policies that encourage higher transport speeds exacerbate these threats, as Box 6.3 shows. We should also add to the list of global challenges the threat of war, the likelihood of which may be exacerbated by climate disruption and loss of biodiversity. As climate breakdown worsens, large parts of the planet will be unable to support their current populations, likely leading to unprecedented migrations and increased risk of conflict, including nuclear conflict (Helfand, 2019).

However, opportunities for change are emerging amid increasing concern about the acceleration of the climate crisis. There is growing awareness of the imperative of achieving zero carbon emission transport systems in cities, aligned with increasing recognition that electric automated vehicles are not the panacea that the auto industry would have us believe. Globally, transport accounts for about a quarter of global CO_2 emissions, and in the United States transport generates the largest share of greenhouse gases (29 per cent of 2017 emissions). Transport in the world's cities is critical for the response to the climate crisis, because while cities occupy only two per cent of the world's landmass, they generate over 60 per cent of global greenhouse gas emissions (United Nations, 2019a). As Dawson (2017) argues, 'cities are ground zero for climate change, contributing the lion's share of carbon to the atmosphere, while also lying on the frontlines of rising sea levels'.

The need to make city transport systems more sustainable is now more important than ever. There is huge potential to address major challenges through city transport, and solving the climate crisis requires city transport to focus on 'achieving more with less, on reducing land, energy, and material use while increasing the liveability of cities for people' (Rees, 2003, p. 11). A fundamental re-casting of the goals of city mobility and accessibility—towards lower speeds and increased use of sustainable active modes—is absolutely essential to avert climate catastrophe.

It seems that the pursuit of speed may be a central obstacle to the provision of healthy, liveable, sustainable and efficient cities. As Carlos Pardo (2017) asked in his presentation at UN Habitat: 'Why don't we start thinking about speed as a problem rather than as a solution'? Indeed, why don't we? We explore a possible explanation for this puzzle in the following section.

11.8 Cognitive dissonance surrounding the disadvantages of speed

Collectively, as a society, we have come to accept the view that 'speed is good' and 'faster is always better'. As we explained in Chapter 2, speed has a powerful psychological appeal, providing neuronic stimulation that has a narcotic-like effect: 'the thrill of speeding comes from neurochemical changes in the brain as the result of adrenaline' (Griffiths, 2018). Yet the appeal of speed for individuals needs to be seen separately from the impact of speed in city transport.

Speed has had such a powerful influence on our behaviours and attitudes that this appears to have reduced our capacity to appreciate the impacts of speed in the city. We see higher speed as a solution to transport problems, yet we have now reached a stage where the increased speeds have created what John Adams (2000) referred to as 'hypermobility', involving frequent trips over great distances. Adams explains that if individuals were asked in an opinion poll if they would like to live in a 'world in which everyone is richer and more mobile than average', with 'unlimited air-miles, and all the computers and communications facilities enjoyed by Bill Gates'—unsurprisingly they would likely overwhelmingly respond 'yes' (Adams, 1997, p. 96).

However, Adams argues that a more realistic poll would be to ask 'Would you like to live in the sort of world you would get if everyone's wish were granted?' He speculates (with remarkable prescience in 1997) that this world would not only be grossly polluted, noisy, congested and anxious about the security of its energy supplies, but also polarised, sprawling, lacking street life and healthy ecosystems, and with Orwellian law enforcement, remote political authority and disappearing democracy. He comments that 'If, as I suspect, the answer to opinion poll 2 is a resounding NO, our political leaders might consider commissioning a third opinion poll: "Would you like to live in a cleaner, quieter, more convivial world in which you know your neighbours, it is safe to walk and cycle, and children are allowed to play in the street?"' (Adams, 1997, p. 96). In this book, we argue that achieving such a world will only be possible if we make 'slowing the city' a goal.

As we explained in Chapter 4, speed steals our time, our money, and our health. Many people find it difficult to accept this reality: it does not match what they intuitively expect. This creates cognitive dissonance—anxiety resulting from conflict between their beliefs and some more recently acquired information or experience. Specifically, they can struggle to understand three impacts or consequences of 'fast cities'. First, when speeds are increased, this leads to the spreading of the city, which makes it more time consuming to access services, and necessitates ever-increasing speeds to overcome increasing distances. Second, as speeds increase, people (and cities and nations) are obliged to devote a higher proportion of their income to speed. Higher speeds require greater investment in road and parking infrastructure and higher inputs of fossil fuel energy. Users of the 'slower' modes avoid these expenses (see Fig. 11.9). Third, higher speeds exacerbate the negative impacts of transport (e.g. pollution, road crashes and greenhouse gas production). Sometimes these negative impacts trigger even more demand for travel, such as when increased road danger encourages parents to drive their children to school and other locations. All of these impacts are serious and growing. If we consider the costs of addressing these impacts, and the time involved in earning money to cover these costs, then the significant time demands of high-speed transport become evident.

FIGURE 11.9 Biking past the petrol station avoids the significant expense of having to 'pay at the pump'. *(Credit: Richard Masoner/Cyclelicious, https://www.flickr.com/photos/bike/5674626104/)*

The widespread cognitive dissonance over the issue of speed in cities creates a vacuum that can be filled by false narratives propagated by groups whose interests are threatened. A notable example is the 'distracted pedestrian' myth, discussed in Chapter 8. We are now seeing 'distracted pedestrian' laws being enacted that are not evidence-based, but are instead about, as Fraade (2018) has argued, 'maintaining the freedom of motorists to speed in city streets and distracting attention from prioritizing safety over speed'. Instead of distracted pedestrians, a greater concern is drivers being distracted by their phones, and as explained in Chapter 8, distraction levels are the same for hands-free or hand-held phone use (Fig. 11.10).

Shifting the focus away from 'distracted pedestrians' to the much more serious issue of 'distracted drivers' may prove to be very difficult. Although the information concerning the danger of hands-free phone use has been in the public domain for many years, car manufacturers have been conspicuously silent on the issue. They can thus claim the moral high ground by condemning behaviour widely understood to be 'unsafe' (hand-held phone use), but more importantly it allows them to charge higher prices for vehicles with inbuilt (but actually equally unsafe) hands-free technology.

By victim-blaming the 'petextrian', the motoring lobby is trying to invent a new threat and a new scapegoat, just as motordom did a century ago with its 'jay walker' notion. 'The goal, as it has always been, is a transportation system in which people on foot are shamed and regulated into submission for the sake

FIGURE 11.10 Drivers distracted by in-car phone use are a far greater risk for all road users than the 'distracted pedestrians' that are currently being demonised by the motoring lobby. *(Credit: US Air Force photo by Staff Sgt. Keith Ballard, https://www.kirtland.af.mil/News/Photos/igphoto/2000311020/mediaid/465142/)*

of people in cars' (Fraade, 2018). When motordom's myth that 'speed is good' is challenged, it spawns other myths to support it. As we have explained throughout the book, instead of blaming vulnerable road users for road crashes, the strategy should be to reduce the speeds of all motorised vehicles, autonomous or otherwise. However, we should not be surprised if this notion is contested, vigorously: it is, after all, an attempt to fundamentally reverse the path that cities have taken for the past hundred years. In order to achieve such a reversal, society needs to seriously question the assumptions behind 'fast cities' and establish new goals to replace those prioritised by neoliberalism. We can seize on several opportunities for slowing the city, as we explain in the following section.

11.9 Re-imagining opportunities for achieving the 'slow city'

11.9.1 Re-imagining goals

Providing alternative goals for urban residents will be positive for all types of health. Rees has argued that in order to enable people to freely choose slower modes of travel, there is a need to change the values, beliefs, attitudes and behaviours of the consumer society, and to encourage people to value things other than the accumulation of material possessions (Rees, 2003). That of course is a

FIGURE 11.11 The 17 Sustainable Development Goals, adopted by all UN Member States in 2015. *(Credit: UNDP - https://www.undp.org/content/undp/en/home/sustainable-development-goals.html, Public Domain, https://commons.wikimedia.org/w/index.php?curid=52672594)*

laudable statement, but for long it has needed a framework to be implemented. The Sustainable Development Goals (SDGs) adopted by all United Nations Member States in 2015 may now provide such a framework at the global level. These 17 Goals are a blueprint to achieve a better and more sustainable future for all and they address the challenges the world faces, including those related to poverty, inequality, climate action, environmental degradation, peace and justice (United Nations, 2015).

'Reducing city speeds' is not one of the agreed goals, but even a cursory inspection of the SDGs (Fig. 11.11) reveals that many of the specific goals—such as those for gender equality and climate action—are outcomes that could scarcely be achieved without successfully slowing our cities. Crucially, the goals of 'good health and well-being' and 'sustainable cities and communities' are central to the SDGs and of course are at the core of this book, and its title.

At the SDG Summit in September 2019 world leaders called for a decade of action and delivery for sustainable development, and agreed to 'mobilize financing, enhance national implementation and strengthen institutions to achieve the Goals by the target date of 2030, leaving no one behind' (United Nations, 2019b). Action will take place on three levels:

- 'global action to secure greater leadership, more resources and smarter solutions for the Sustainable Development Goals;
- 'local action embedding the needed transitions in the policies, budgets, institutions and regulatory frameworks of governments, cities and local authorities; and

- 'people action, including by youth, civil society, the media, the private sector, unions, academia and other stakeholders, to generate an unstoppable movement pushing for the required transformations' (United Nations, 2019b).

Ensuring success in the goal of 'leaving no-one behind' requires 'mobility justice', addressing the way that high-speed city transport disproportionately affects society and the environment in the Global South (Sheller, 2018). The transport speeds of car-dominated cities require vast inputs of energy (particularly oil) and create huge environmental impacts—and this is acutely felt in the Global South, where cities will also suffer the impacts of global heating far more than the Global North (Dawson, 2017). Yet, these cities are already facing the same issues as cities in the Global North (congestion, pollution, disruption of communities and high economic, environmental and public health costs). Slowing city transport helps address all these issues.

This equity issue is described by the Japanese philosopher Shin'ichi Tsuji: 'Modern society, which has left us with bloated quantities and speed, is as a matter of course not gentle on nature ... Modern society, with its emphasis on getting "more, faster", has also given rise to grotesque disparities between North and South, developed and developing countries. Isn't it time for those who speak of justice, fairness, equality, and democracy, to start seriously considering ways to live with "less, more slowly"?' (Tsuji, 2001).

Though—or perhaps because—time is short, there is now an increasing flow of good news regarding slowing city transport coming from many cities in the Global South. There has been a recent boom in walking-focussed NGOs and while their usual focus is road safety (see discussion of *Amend* in Tanzania in Chapter 8), the end result is a move towards slower city transport. There has been considerable activity in Latin America and South Asia for example, increasingly supported and 'normalised' by the activities of supra-national bodies such as the World Health Organization, the International Transport Forum, the United Nations Environment Programme, SLoCaT (Partnership on Sustainable Low Carbon Transport), the Institute for Transportation and Development Policy and many more. These institutions provide support for and practical action towards the achievement of the SDGs. Though progress is patchy so far, the movement towards 'slow cities' is gathering pace throughout the world.

11.9.2 Re-imagining attitudes

As individuals we can make changes to our lifestyles that, collectively, will make a difference. These may seem insignificant at first, but they add up and they also promote empathy and willingness to support the enormous transitions that will be required in transport, energy, food and other systems to adequately respond to current global crises. To encourage and facilitate these changes, politicians, planners, policy makers and other transport experts need to be courageous and demonstrate a willingness to challenge the cult of speed and consumption. It will not be easy. 'Every initiative that limits the freedom of the car driver runs up against a fierce lobby defending an alleged freedom of movement for motorists' (Diekstra & Kroon, 2003, p. 253). The 'yellow vests' movement that began in Paris in 2018 is a case in point, whereby increases in fuel costs provoked opposition from largely working-class protesters living on the city's periphery, where only basic public transport alternatives to driving were available (McHugh, 2019). In a pessimistic summary Diekstra and Kroon (2003, p. 264) argued that 'Given the mass popularity of the car, the effectiveness with which the values associated with it are protected and the economic and other instruments involved, it would be illusory to expect that in a parliamentary market democracy, decisions will be taken that will have any real impact on these values and interests'.

However, we would contend that in the almost two decades since those observations were made, there has been a transformation amongst city planners, practitioners, researchers and other thought leaders in attitudes towards sustainability and resilience of cities, and by extension, in transport planning and policy. No longer is change in these fields 'illusory'. Beliefs that fast mobility is 'modern' and 'desirable' are changing, even if progress on the ground has to date lagged behind. Now there is a growing realisation that those leaders that prove unwilling to take action to slow their cities will likely find that their own cities:

- will face huge and growing cost outlays for the maintenance of road infrastructure;
- will be less competitive in the global economy;
- will be less able to attract tourists and investment capital;
- will be less attractive to the 'creative class' (college-educated 25 to 34 year-olds) sought by cities across the world to fuel their knowledge economies; and
- will have increasingly unhealthy residents.

In contrast, leaders who are prepared to challenge the culture of speed will be rewarded with cities that are healthier, happier, safer, less unequal, more sustainable and more prosperous. 'Slow cities' will be the most successful cities of the future. Moreover, such attitudinal shifts will be bolstered by the knowledge that positive outcomes are clearly deliverable, as described by Eric Britton in his reference to what he refers to as 'slow mobility' (Britton, 2018). The advantages of slowing city transport include that it is:

- 'a straightforward, non-abstract, easy to remember concept which can be readily understood by all;
- entirely feasible since it has been achieved with success in different cities;
- readily achievable;
- affordable;
- measurable (if you can measure it you can manage it); and
- the results will be immediately and palpably visible and open to public scrutiny' (Britton, 2018).

The strategy of slowing city transport is no longer simply a theory. Many elements of slowing city transport have already been implemented successfully in cities and neighbourhoods throughout the world. While Pontevedra in Spain (see Box 10.2) is one of the most impressive examples of slowing city transport across an entire urban area, with clear positive impacts on human, economic and environmental health, many other examples of elements of slower city transport exist, as we have described throughout this book. Rather than constantly focussing on speed as a solution, based on technical forecasts of increased travel that justify political arguments for faster roads, it is possible to design and retrofit cities so that residents have access to a rich diversity of resources without resorting to high speed transport. The re-imagination of attitudes currently under way will help that vision to be realised.

11.9.3 Re-imagining outcomes

While dealing with global crises may seem to be an overwhelming challenge for many people, there is good news in this book. A critical action to help address the looming crises in planetary health is to slow city transport, and this book has indicated many examples of good practice in Chapters 8, 9 and 10, on speed reduction, planning for slower cities, promoting the slower modes, and changing cultures and behaviours. These may be valuable in particular circumstances, but we have avoided recommending particular actions, because 'good practice' in one city may not be appropriate or achievable in another. 'Cookie-cutter' responses may bring action on slowing cities into disrepute, particularly if applied in cities of different levels of income and resources, as for example between cities of the Global North and South. The examples in this book are therefore tools in a toolbox that may or may not be used in particular situations—and it would be unhelpful to recommend any specific action or combination of actions that should be universally applied to achieve the 'slow city'. But what we can do is focus on outcomes and then select the actions to achieve them, following the advice of Whitelegg (2016) who stressed the importance of 'exploring and defining a desirable future, and then working out how to get there'.

One such outcome is the 20-minute neighbourhood, which was first introduced in Portland, Oregon. There the 1993 Climate Action Plan set an objective for 2030 calling for 'vibrant neighborhoods' in which 90 per cent of Portland residents can easily walk or bicycle to meet all basic daily, non-work needs. Subsequently the description was changed to '20-minute neighborhoods' and became a cornerstone of the 2010 Portland Plan (City of Portland, 2010). The concept has been widely discussed in the past decade, one of the most recent examples being the Plan Melbourne 2017–50 (Department of Environment Land Water and Planning, 2017). This plan seeks to create a city of 20-minute neighbourhoods, which is all about 'living locally', where people can meet most of their daily needs within an 800 metre (10 minute) walk from home to a destination and back again, including access to safe cycling and local transport options

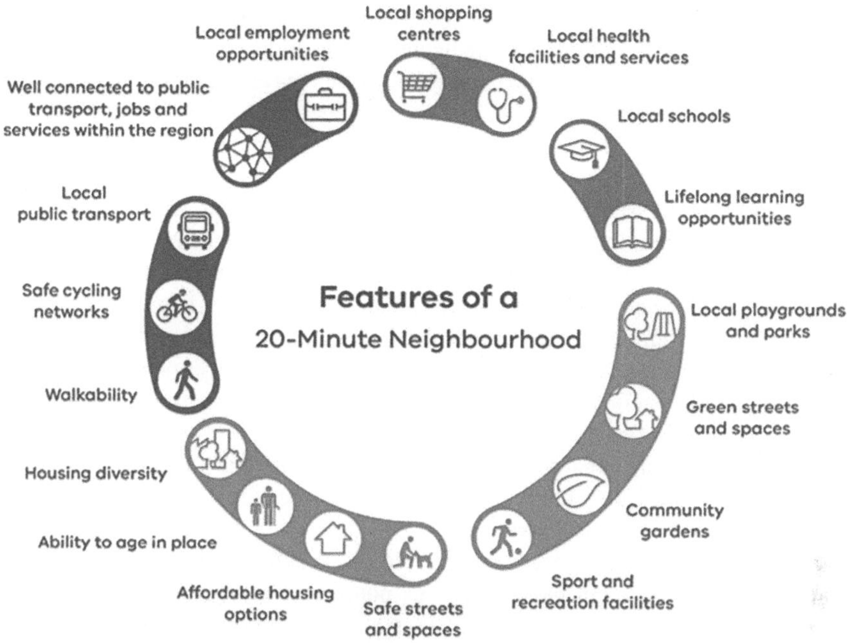

FIGURE 11.12 Features of a 20-minute neighbourhood as seen by planners in Victoria, Australia. *(Credit: Victorian Department of Environment, Land, Water, and Planning)*

(Fig. 11.12). It points out that 'While individually these places may only serve a local community's needs, the network of these places across the city plays a significant role in creating a sustainable and accessible city' (Department of Environment Land Water and Planning, 2019).

The 20-minute neighbourhood is not a specific action or a tool, but is a desired outcome. Many of the detailed interventions discussed in earlier chapters will be applicable of course, but more important is to keep in mind what we are trying to achieve, rather than saying that specific tools are required. The particular methods of achieving 20-minute neighbourhoods will vary from place to place, though density will always be a key component along with the other 'D's' and the P (placemaking) discussed in Chapter 9. Of course, motorised speeds must be lowered and the 'slow' modes encouraged. These 20-minute neighbourhoods offer connected places where people can live, spend their free time and access jobs and higher-order services. They provide a high-quality public realm and open spaces, creating social hubs where connections to neighbours and communities, as well as thriving local economies, can develop. 'These are places where people want to be, where people have the opportunity and choice to live locally' (Department of Environment Land Water and Planning, 2019). We suggest that any city that displays these characteristics is, by definition, a 'slow city'.

The over-arching concept of the 20-minute neighbourhood will face challenges from the introduction of new technologies and over this point we must sound a cautionary note. Technical innovations have increased the energy efficiency of motorised transport, but these gains tend to reduce the cost (and increase the uptake) of transport, rather than reducing carbon emissions. Any increase in motor car speeds, including for AVs (autonomous vehicles), will likely lead to increased distances travelled and the spreading of shops, schools and services. Technology may be marketed on the premise of helping to create 'better' cities, but if 'better' is seen to mean 'faster', strong resistance will be necessary. Faster and/or privately-owned AVs, for example, have the potential to dramatically increase sprawl impacts, whereas applying any new technology in ways that enhance health and resilience rather than simply speed or mobility would be more beneficial to more people. Shared and speed-limited AVs could potentially enable the reclamation of public space for the use of the slower modes on a very large scale—and thus be a powerful force supporting 20-minute neighbourhoods. In other words, new technologies must be applied in ways that support slow and safe movement.

It is important also to recognise the role that can be played by technologies that may not be new, but have enormous potential to help slow city transport in a way that promotes health and sustainability, and a child-friendly environment. The best example is the bicycle, which can be adapted to carry deliveries, cargo and children who are not old enough to ride alone (see Fig. 11.13)

FIGURE 11.13 A mother with her baby on a bicycle in Freiburg, Germany. *(Credit: Elliot Fishman)*

(Schliwa, Armitage, Aziz, Evans, & Rhoades, 2015). These technologies have huge potential in any city, but particularly in cities in the Global South. Yet, as this book has made clear, the solutions we need to create slower, healthier and more sustainable cities are not just technological. Creating 'slow cities' requires a step change in the way we imagine the outcomes—and indeed our future. To help us achieve this transformation, we conclude with a positive vision in the form of a 'Manifesto for 21st Century Slow Cities'.

11.10 Conclusion: a 'Manifesto for 21st Century Slow Cities'

At the start of the 20th century most city residents saw motorised speed as the destroyer of everyday life in their streets. Despite this, largely due to the strategies employed by motordom in the 1920s, politicians, planners and the public all accepted policies to increase the speed of motor cars in cities. By the end of the 1920s faster motorised transport had become a major goal of city policy making. During the 20th century, the term 'slowness' developed negative connotations. Slow transport was seen as being outdated and associated with a hindering of progress, whereas speed was marketed as being part of a 'new age'. However, instead of providing the benefits of a 'new age', policies aimed at promoting speed created inefficient, unhealthy and unsustainable cities.

In the 21st century, the pursuit of speed in cities is increasingly seen as futile and outmoded. In contrast, 'slowing' is seen as a way to achieve the goals of cities we would like to live in, places that are sustainable and that support a high level of well-being. James Howard Kunstler puts it succinctly: 'The 20th Century was about getting around. The 21st Century will be about staying in a place worth staying in' (Kunstler, quoted in Project for Public Spaces, 2008).

How are we to achieve this transformation? So many actions, processes and resources need to come together: better data; new skills, models and tools; different visions; strong leadership; cultural shifts; political commitment; community engagement and buy-in; thoughtful application of new technologies and reaffirmed commitment to old ones; and much, much more besides. This can seem overwhelming when these issues need concurrent attention so quickly—and in the face of pressing catastrophes that demand immediate responses. It is not easy to plan for a better future when you are—literally—firefighting to keep what you have.

Creating 'slow cities' requires a step change in goals and attitudes—and indeed in how we imagine the future. This last point is crucial: as we have already argued, we have to focus on what outcomes we want and then select the actions that will achieve them. To help identify a desirable future, we offer a statement of principles and a declaration of intent in the form of a 'Manifesto for 21st Century Slow Cities' (Tranter & Tolley, 2020) (see Box 11.2).

What will future cities be like if the principles in the Manifesto are adopted? What would be the expected norms for behaviours to 'save time' and 'spend

BOX 11.2 A Manifesto for 21st Century Slow Cities.

Slow is saving time

We must reject measures of efficiency based on the speed of motorised traffic. Higher speeds increase travel distances, trapping people in a spiral of lengthening trips, and lock cities into expensive and futile infrastructure 'fixes'. Slow cities provide enhanced access to goods, services and jobs, saving time for everyone.

Slow is healthy

We must broadcast the evidence that slow travel improves health through reduced pollution, increased physical activity and greater connection with other people and nature.

Slow is safe

We must reduce road danger by lowering the speed of motorised traffic. Serious crashes are minimised by default speed limits of 30 km/h (or less), reinforced by traffic calming and set in a Vision Zero context.

Slow is sustainable

We must acknowledge that slow cities decrease environmental impacts of transport, at all scales from local to global.

Slow is economically successful

We must accept the clear evidence that investment in the slow modes brings enormous economic benefits for individuals, businesses and cities.

Slow is human-scale and equitable

We must cherish the fact that slow cities are child-friendly, human-scale places. Walkable streets, housing and services in close proximity, and plentiful, green, accessible civic spaces benefit everyone, not just the wealthy or tourists.

Slow is smart

We must apply smart city technology to improving health and accessibility using active travel, rather than increasing the speed of motorised traffic. However, if autonomous motorised vehicles are adopted, they must be slow and shared, with the top priority being safety for vulnerable road users.

Slow is achievable

We must learn the lesson from early 20th century urban history that rapid cultural change is possible. Just as society once accepted the illusory benefits of speed, so can it quickly appreciate that a new reality of slowness is achievable.

Slow is quality of life

We must conquer our addiction to speed in order to develop a slow culture that celebrates the health and well-being of all people and communities, cities and environments.

Slow is the future

We must accept that slow cities are essential for a healthy and sustainable world. In the struggle for the liveability of our cities, we invite you to join the winning side.

time'? Will smart technologies be adopted to benefit people rather than motorised traffic? What outcomes might we expect in terms of health, whether human, environmental or economic—in other words in terms of 'quality of life'? And above all, is such a cultural revolution achievable and if so, how will it be reflected in everyday life experiences?

In concluding this book, we anticipate how such questions might be answered. We imagine a message from a 30-year-old mother in 2050, 30 years after the publication of this book, in which she thanks her parents for their generation's efforts to create healthy, sustainable cities, like the one she calls home. She describes life in a truly 'slow city', an everyday experience for her in 2050, but what was, in 2020, still a vision for people striving for a more hopeful future. Having seen the application of many of the ideas expounded in this book and experienced the transition from the old 'fast city', she has found her 'place worth staying in'. With gratitude for the past and hope for the future, she sees what adopting the Manifesto has achieved in the victory of slow over fast in the city.

January 2050
Dear Mum and Dad,

Since I recently turned the big 3-0, I thought I'd write my annual New Year message a little differently this year. Looking back on the past three decades, it's clear that your generation left the world better off than you found it, and I want to thank you for that. I know it wasn't easy—you were left a planet heading towards dire straits. I'm so grateful that you helped change that course.

Creating this better world started with slowing down the city, which your generation worked tirelessly to do over the past 30 years. When you lobbied city councils to adopt the 'Manifesto for 21st Century Slow Cities', did you realise the impact it would have? Where would we be today if you hadn't fought so hard against those who persisted in peddling myths about the 'benefits' of speed in the city?

Thanks to you, Ben and Lulu live in a healthy, happy, safe city, and they play in the street and go to school and friends' houses on their own, just like kids did before cars took over and everything got faster and faster and faster. Lulu laughs when we tell her that children had to be driven everywhere in cars until the '20s!

As one of the first residents of a slow city, I know that we must continue to protect and strengthen healthy and sustainable places, for the sake of your grandkids' generation and those to come. I want you to know that I'll do everything I can to help.

Thank you for everything,
Love you,
Sophia

References

Adams, J. (1997). Can technology save us? In R. Tolley (Ed.), *The greening of urban transport: Planning for walking and cycling in western cities* (pp. 81–97). Chichester: Wiley.

Adams, J. (2000). Hypermobility. *Prospect Magazine*. Available from: https://www.prospectmagazine.co.uk/magazine/hypermobility.

ARUP. (2017). *Cities alive, designing for urban childhoods*. Available from: https://www.arup.com/-/media/arup/files/publications/u/cities_alivedesigning_for_urban_childhoods.pdf.

Blanchard, K. (2000). The anthropology of sport. In J. Coakley, & E. Dunning (Eds.), *Handbook of sports studies* (pp. 144–156). London: Sage.

Britton, E. (2018). Slow mobility advantages: Notes for a thinking exercise. *World Streets Emergency Climate/Mobility Action/Plan*. Available from: https://worldstreets.wordpress.com/2018/12/28/slow-mobility-advantages-notes-for-a-thinking-exercise/.

Buehler, R., Pucher, J., & Bauman, A. (2020). Physical activity from walking and cycling for daily travel in the United States, 2001-2017: Demographic, socioeconomic, and geographic variation. *Journal of Transport & Health, 16*, 100811.

Carrington, D. (2017). Air pollution more harmful to children in cars than outside, warns top scientist. *The Guardian*. Available from: https://www.theguardian.com/environment/2017/jun/12/children-risk-air-pollution-cars-former-uk-chief-scientist-warns.

City of Portland. (2010). *20-minute neighborhood concept analysis*. Available from: https://www.portlandonline.com/portlandplan/index.cfm?a=288098&c=52256.

Dawson, A. (2017). *Extreme cities: The peril and promise of urban life in the age of climate change*. London: Verso Books.

Department of Environment Land Water and Planning. (2017). Plan Melbourne 2017 - 2050. *Victoria State Government, Australia*. Available from: https://www.planning.vic.gov.au/policy-and-strategy/planning-for-melbourne/plan-melbourne.

Department of Environment Land Water and Planning. (2019). 20-minute neighbourhoods. *Victoria State Government, Australia*. Available from: https://www.planning.vic.gov.au/policy-and-strategy/planning-for-melbourne/plan-melbourne/20-minute-neighbourhoods.

Diekstra, R., & Kroon, M. (2003). Cars and behaviour: Psychological barriers to car restraint and sustainable urban transport. In R. Tolley (Ed.), *Sustainable transport: Planning for walking and cycling in urban environments*. Cambridge: Woodhead Publishing.

Edwards, H., & Whitehouse, A. (2018). *The Toxic School Run, Unicef UK research briefing*. Available from: https://downloads.unicef.org.uk/wp-content/uploads/2018/09/UUK-research-briefing-The-toxic-school-run-September-2018.pdf?_ga=2.234006365.298981577.1537257494-289689197.1536231694.

Fraade, J. (2018). Who's Afraid of the "Petextrian"? *Baffler Newsletter*. Available from: https://thebaffler.com/latest/whos-afraid-petextrian-fraade.

Freeman, M. (2005). Children's health and children's rights: An introduction. *The International Journal of Children's Rights, 13*(1–10).

Future Foundation (2006). *The changing face of parenting: Professional parenting, information and healthcare*. London: Future Foundation.

Garrard, J. (2011). Why aren't more kids cycling to school? *The Conversation*. Available from: https://theconversation.com/why-arent-more-kids-cycling-to-school-3531.

Gilbert, H., Whitzman, C., Pieters, J., & Allan, A. (2018). Children's everyday freedoms: Local government policies on children and sustainable mobility in two Australian states. *Journal of Transport Geography, 71*, 116–129.

Giles-Corti, B., Kelty, S. F., Zubrick, S. R., & Villanueva, K. P. (2009). Encouraging walking for transport and physical activity in children and adolescents. *Sports Medicine, 39*(12), 995–1009.

Gill, T. (2007). *No fear: Growing up in a risk-averse society*. London: Calouste Gulbenkian Foundation.

Gill, T. (2017a). Could street play hold the key to creating more sustainable, livable cities? *Rethinking Childhood*. Available from: https://rethinkingchildhood.com/2017/08/02/reports-street-play-key-sustainable-livable-cities/.

Gill, T. (2017b). Crucial indicator for a successful, healthy city: Children. *The Inquirer*. Available from: http://www.philly.com/philly/opinion/20170718_Crucial_indicator_for_a_successful__healthy_city__children.html.

Gray, P. (2010). Freedom to learn: The decline of play and rise in children's mental disorders. *Psychology Today*. Available from: https://www.psychologytoday.com/blog/freedom-learn/201001/the-decline-play-and-rise-in-childrens-mental-disorders.

Griffiths, M.D. (2018). Addicted to speed? (Not the Drug). *Psychology Today*. Available from: https://www.psychologytoday.com/au/blog/in-excess/201811/addicted-speed-not-the-drug.

Hamilton-Baillie, B. (2004). Urban design: Why don't we do it in the road? Modifying traffic behavior through legible urban design. *Journal of Urban Technology, 11*(1), 43–62.

Helfand, I. (2019). Climate change isn't our only existential threat. *CNN International Edition*. Available from: https://edition.cnn.com/2019/07/06/opinions/nuclear-war-climate-change-2020-opinion-helfand/index.html.

Henary, B.Y., Crandall, J., Bhalla, K., Mock, C.N., & Roudsari, B.S. (2003). *Child and adult pedestrian impact: The influence of vehicle type on injury severity*. Paper presented at the Annual Proceedings, Association for the Advancement of Automotive Medicine.

Herbert, W. (2017). Why kids get hit by cars. *Association for Psychological Science*. Available from: https://www.psychologicalscience.org/news/full-frontal-psychology/why-kids-get-hit-by-cars.html.

Hillman, M., Adams, J., & Whitelegg, J. (1990). *One false move: A study of children's independent mobility*. London: Policy Studies Institute.

Honoré, C. (2004). *In praise of slow: How a worldwide movement is challenging the cult of speed*. London: Orion.

Kegerreis, S. (1993). Independent mobility and children's mental and emotional development. In M. Hillman (Ed.), *Children, transport and the quality of life* (pp. 28–34). London: PSI Press.

Knowles, H. (2019). Greta Thunberg is Time's person of the year. *Financial Review*. Available from: https://www.afr.com/policy/energy-and-climate/greta-thunberg-is-time-s-person-of-the-year-20191212-p53j5m.

Laville, S., Taylor, M., Bengtsson, H., & Zapponi, C. (2017). Thousands of British children exposed to illegal levels of air pollution. *The Guardian*. Available from: https://www.theguardian.com/environment/2017/apr/04/thousands-of-british-children-exposed-to-illegal-levels-of-air-pollution.

Li, Q., Alonge, O., & Hyder, A.A. (2016). Children and road traffic injuries: Can't the world do better? *Archives of disease in childhood, 101*(11), 1063–1070.

Malone, K. (2017). Can children be free in a city. *Foreground*. Available from: https://www.foreground.com.au/cities/can-children-be-free-in-a-city/.

McDonald, N. C., Brown, A. L., Marchetti, L. M., & Pedroso, M. S. (2011). US school travel, 2009: An assessment of trends. *American Journal of Preventive Medicine, 41*(2), 146–151.

McHugh, J. (2019). After a violent 'Yellow Vest' anniversary, what's next for the movement? *Fortune*. Available from: https://fortune.com/2019/11/25/yellow-vest-protests-gilets-jaunes-anniversary/.

Mori, N., Armada, F., & Willcox, D. C. (2012). Walking to school in Japan and childhood obesity prevention: New lessons from an old policy. *American Journal of Public Health, 102*(11), 2068–2073.

Mullan, E. (2003). Do you think your local area is a good place for young people to grow up? The effects of traffic and car parking on young people's views. *Health and Place*, *9*(4), 351–360.

Nakahara, S., Ichikawa, M., & Sakamoto, T. (2016). Time trend analyses of child pedestrian morbidity in Japan. *Public Health*, *141*, 74–79.

NPR Staff. (2019). Transcript: Greta Thunberg's speech at the U.N. climate action summit. *NPR*. Available from: https://www.npr.org/2019/09/23/763452863/transcript-greta-thunbergs-speech-at-the-u-n-climate-action-summit.

O'Brien, C. (2001). Children: A critical link for changing driving behaviour. *National Center for Bicycling and Walking (NCBW) Forum (Canada)*, 52, pp. 4–13.

O'Brien, C. (2003). Transportation that's actually good for the soul. *National Center for Bicycling and Walking (NCBW) Forum (Canada)*, 54, pp. 1–13. Available from: http://www.bikewalk.org/pdfs/forumarch0104transportation.pdf.

O'Brien, C., & Tranter, P.J. (2006). *Planning for and with Children and Youth: Insights from children about happiness, well-being and walking*. Paper presented at the Walk 21: Seventh International Conference on Walking and Liveable Communities, Melbourne, October 23–25. Available from: http://citeseerx.ist.psu.edu/viewdoc/download?doi=10.1.1.565.862&rep=rep1&type=pdf.

O'Brien, C. (2008). Sustainable happiness and the trip to school. *World Transport Policy and Practice*, *14*(1), 15–16.

Pardo, C. (2017). Reducing speeds for better mobility and quality of life. *UN Habitat*. Available from: https://new.unhabitat.org/reducing-speeds-for-better-mobility-and-quality-of-life-carlosfelipe-pardo.

Peyton, A. (2019). Press release: Four global cities to receive in-depth training and resources for building child-friendly streets. *Global Designing Cities Initiative*. Available from: https://globaldesigningcities.org/2019/11/20/press-release-four-global-cities-to-receive-in-depth-training-and-resources-for-building-child-friendly-streets/.

Project for Public Spaces. (2008). *James Howard Kunstler*. Available from: https://www.pps.org/article/jhkunstler.

Pucher, J., & Buehler, R. (2008). Making cycling irresistible: Lessons from The Netherlands, Denmark and Germany. *Transport Reviews*, *28*(4), 495–528.

Ramanathan, S., O'Brien, C., Faulkner, G., & Stone, M. (2014). Happiness in motion: Emotions, well-being, and active school travel. *Journal of School Health*, *84*(8), 516–523.

Rees, W. (2003). Ecological footprints and urban transportation. In R. Tolley (Ed.), *Sustainable transport: Planning for walking and cycling in urban environments* (pp. 3–19). Abingdon: Woodhead Publishing.

Rushkoff, D. (1997). *Children of Chaos: Surviving the end of the world as we know it*. London: Flamingo.

Schliwa, G., Armitage, R., Aziz, S., Evans, J., & Rhoades, J. (2015). Sustainable city logistics—Making cargo cycles viable for urban freight transport. *Research in Transportation Business & Management*, *15*, 50–57.

Shaw, B., Watson, B., Frauendienst, B., Redecker, A., Jones, T., & Hillman, M. (2013). *Children's independent mobility: A comparative study in England and Germany (1971-2010)*. Available from: http://www.psi.org.uk/site/publication_detail/852.

Sheller, M. (2018). *Mobility justice: The politics of movement in an age of extremes*. London: Verso Books.

Spycher, B. D., Feller, M., Röösli, M., Ammann, R. A., Diezi, M., Egger, M., et al. (2015). Childhood cancer and residential exposure to highways: A nationwide cohort study. *European Journal of Epidemiology*, *30*(12), 1263–1275.

Sunyer, J., Suades-González, E., García-Esteban, R., Rivas, I., Pujol, J., Alvarez-Pedrerol, M., et al. (2017). Traffic-related air pollution and attention in primary school children: Short-term association. *Epidemiology*, *28*(2), 181.

Taylor, M. (2019). School children go on strike across world over climate crisis. *The Guardian.* Available from: https://www.theguardian.com/environment/2019/may/24/schoolchildren-go-on-strike-across-world-over-climate-crisis.

Thunberg, G. (2019). 'Our house is on fire': Greta Thunberg, 16, urges leaders to act on climate. *The Guardian.* Available from: https://www.theguardian.com/environment/2019/jan/25/our-house-is-on-fire-greta-thunberg16-urges-leaders-to-act-on-climate.

Tranter, P., & Sharpe, S. (2007). Children and peak oil: An opportunity in crisis. *International Journal of Children's Rights*, *15*(1), 181–197.

Tranter, P., & Sharpe, S. (2008). Escaping Monstropolis: Child-friendly cities, peak oil and *Monsters, Inc. Children's Geographies*, *6*(3), 295–308.

Tranter, P., & Sharpe, S. (2012). Disney-Pixar to the rescue: Harnessing positive affect for enhancing children's active mobility. *Journal of Transport Geography*, *20*(1), 34–40.

Tranter, P., & Tolley, R. (2020). Manifesto for 21st Century Slow Cities. Available from: https://slowcitiesmanifesto.com/.

Tsuji, S. (2001). *Four selections from Slow is Beautiful (Surô izu byûtifuru: Ososa toshite no bunka) translated by Andre Haag*. Available from: https://keibooiwa.files.wordpress.com/2008/11/preface-to-slow-is-beautiful-andre-haag-trans1.pdf.

UNICEF. (2006). A simplified version of the United Nations Convention on the Rights of the Child. Available from: https://www.unicef.org.au/Upload/UNICEF/Media/Our%20work/childfriendlycrc.pdf.

UNICEF. (2013). What is a child friendly city. Available from: https://childfriendlycities.org/what-is-a-child-friendly-city/.

UNICEF. (2009). *State of the world's children: celebrating 20 years of the Convention on the Rights of the Child*. UNICEF.

United Nations. (2015). Sustainable development goals. Available from: https://sustainabledevelopment.un.org/?menu=1300.

United Nations. (2019a). Cities and pollution contribute to climate change. Available from: https://www.un.org/en/climatechange/cities-pollution.shtml.

United Nations. (2019b). The sustainable development agenda. *Sustainable Development Goals.* Available from: https://www.un.org/sustainabledevelopment/development-agenda/.

Van Der Ploeg, H., Merom, D., Corpuz, G., & Bauman, A. (2008). Trends in Australian children traveling to school 1971-2003: Burning petrol or carbohydrates? *Preventive Medicine*, *46*(1), 60–62.

Warren, R. (2019). Greta Thunberg's critics just want to be lucrative right-wing talking heads. *GQ Politics*. Available from: https://www.gq-magazine.co.uk/article/greta-thunbergs.

Whitebread, D. (2017). Free play and children's mental health. *The Lancet Child & Adolescent Health*, *1*(3), 167–169.

Whitelegg, J. (2016). *Mobility: A new urban design and transport planning philosophy for a sustainable future*. Shropshire, UK: Straw Barnes Press.

Whitzman, C., Romero, V., Duncan, M., Curtis, C., Tranter, P., & Burke, M. (2010). Links between children's independent mobility, active transport, physical activity and obesity. In E. Waters, B. Swinburn, J. Seidell, & R. Uauy (Eds.), *Preventing childhood obesity: Evidence policy and practice*. Sydney: Wiley-Blackwell.

Witten, K., & Carroll, P. (2015). *Freyberg Square and Pioneer Women's and Ellen Melville Hall upgrade: children's consultation*. Available from: https://kidsinthecity.ac.nz/wp-content/uploads/2015/12/Freyberg-Square-report.pdf.

Afterword

'Slow cities' and the coronavirus pandemic of 2020

Responses to the fundamental issues raised by the 2020 coronavirus pandemic will shape cities for long into the future, and one possibility is the dawn of a 'new age' of healthier and slower cities. 'Slow cities' require accessibility, which necessitates proximity of people and services. But increasing density brings risks such as the sharing of pathogens—so it is understandable that the coronavirus emergency has fuelled a debate over whether fears about these risks will push people back into cars and out to distant suburbs. How realistic are these concerns, and what alternatives might be adopted? From the very uncertain perspective of May 2020, as the virus continues its global spread, we offer some tentative speculation on three potential future scenarios and the implications of a pandemic for the achievement of 'slow cities'.

Scenario 1: stimulating suburbanisation to seek protection through distance
In one possible future the mark of the virus would endure in terms of encouraging people to escape from the city, producing more high-speed roads and more sprawled suburbs of scattered, fenced-off houses, with residents leaving their homes only by car. Such a response would be ineffective in preparing for a future pandemic, because the security that low-density suburbanisation may appear to provide through isolation dissolves when people need to go to work, or to the supermarket or hardware store. Hubs such as these, where people from all over a suburban region concentrate for transactions, encourage the rapid spread of a virus. Indeed, early studies have shown that many low-density, car-orientated neighbourhoods have higher death rates than subway-dependent inner areas.

Although dense cities may face higher exposure to initial transmission, they are also the foci of essential public health and communication infrastructure—both key resources in fighting a pandemic. Moreover, density also engenders resilience, as it is easier to provide services such as elder care and grocery deliveries, and neighbours can support each other in times of uncertainty. Above all, dense places are walkable and cyclable and the resulting slow, active transport improves people's health in general, reduces susceptibility to disease, and increases resistance if infected. As a result of these considerations, in reality the safest place to be during a pandemic is not isolated in a sprawled suburb, but residing in a walk-up building in an urban neighbourhood, with convenient walkable and cyclable access to services and activities, and with social connections that provide support and security.

Pandemic conditions in fact serve to reinforce what this book has constantly stressed—that there are continuing, powerful arguments for denser, vibrant, walkable communities as supportive environments for nurturing health and well-being, environmental responsibility, social connection and prosperity. More disconnected suburban growth would perpetuate all of the negative impacts of sprawl on human, environmental and economic health that this book has laid out, and in particular, it would accelerate climate breakdown, which would likely lead to many more deaths than the coronavirus, and may destroy life for humankind. In short, this scenario would only serve to replace one set of disastrous health consequences with another.

Scenario 2: 'getting back to normal'

Understandably, 'getting back to normal' has been a common refrain through the uncertainty of the crisis. But that 'normal', based on our addiction to speed, has produced environmental destruction, economic and social inequality, huge financial costs, and population ill health through crashes, physical inactivity and polluted air. Indeed, there are indications that the cities experiencing most deaths from the coronavirus (which attacks the lungs) are those where NO_2 and PM2.5 levels (linked to lung disease) were most elevated by motorised traffic in pre-pandemic years. Taken together, these deleterious impacts of speed are hardly a strong recommendation to re-create the old order. Additionally, given that economies throughout the world have been shattered by the coronavirus, it is unlikely that cities will be able to afford to maintain their costly addiction to speed. Low cost solutions that increase space for people walking and cycling are going to be essential.

Scenario 3: the slow city as the preferred urban form

The 2020 pandemic has provoked widespread lockdowns and limitations to motorised movement—and these in turn have produced startling, unforeseen consequences that could point the way towards a more resilient future. For example, during the outbreak the dramatic reduction in city air pollution, much of it from motorised traffic, has saved many lives, arguably more than the fatalities from the virus itself—and maintaining cleaner air will help to reduce future coronavirus deaths. Moreover, in the middle of an unimaginable catastrophe, there is also hope in the flood of heart-warming stories, shared online, of neighbourly acts of kindness, pop-up bike lanes, glittering starry nights and the return of birdsong to city spaces. In many cities, playful activity is creating more child-friendly environments, with children walking in local streets and decorating sidewalks with chalk, and people placing teddy bears and rainbow images in windows and gardens to provide children with an enjoyable and socially distant treasure hunt. For many people around the world, the change to their city is a revelation of a forgotten urbanism and a foretaste of a future they know they need and want. In the space of a few weeks, billions of people have experienced—inadvertently—elements of what a 'slow city' could have to offer. Now that they have seen the transformation with their own eyes, heard it with their own ears and breathed it with their own lungs, they can appreciate more personally what they have been losing, bit-by-bit, from a lifetime's pursuit of speed in the city. No longer can slowness be regarded as some far-fetched theory of what could happen in a future utopia.

Lessons for the future

There will be many lessons to be learned from the global response to the 2020 pandemic. One obvious take-away is our lack of preparedness, despite plentiful warnings that pandemics such as SARS and Ebola were unlikely to be isolated occurrences. That means explicit acceptance that further pandemics are inevitable and, given the reality of accelerating global heating and biodiversity loss, that they may be more frequent too. This requires the preparation of robust plans in every city for rapid, effective action: to shut down the connections and implement social distancing in order to ride out the threat without lasting damage to the city, its population and economy. This implies conceptualising cities as constellations of relatively self-sufficient and independent precincts—such as 20-minute neighbourhoods—that are internally accessible on foot and by bike. In a pandemic, if a flare-up of a virus occurs in one district, the area can be temporarily closed and isolated from other neighbourhoods, while allowing them to function. Such neighbourhoods will need to be able to operate under lock-down conditions, with designed-in social distancing that avoids dense groups of people in elevators or waiting at traffic lights. This will not only make maintaining healthy living easier in the next pandemic, but also create the preconditions for a rapid move to 'slow city' principles.

A second lesson is that the need for physical distancing has exposed the inequitable distribution of public space. Typically, sidewalks and bike lanes in the city are far too narrow to maintain a two-metre personal bubble away from other people's bubbles without deviating into space reserved for motorised traffic. Fortunately, and coincidentally, making increased space for slow mode users has been facilitated by the dramatic decline of city driving during lockdowns and the freeing up of travel and parking lanes. Hundreds of cities and communities around the world have reacted by tactically and rapidly applying many of the road space reallocation techniques described in Chapter 9, including putting filtered permeability in place in residential neighbourhoods, adding new or widened bike lanes and sidewalks, and opening streets for people by restricting or banning motorised traffic.

The future imperative is to ensure that, post pandemic, this bonus of enhanced and expanded space for people is not returned to cars, but is retained and reserved for active travel modes. Among hundreds of examples, the city of Milan—near the epicentre of Italy's coronavirus outbreak—has committed to converting 35 km (22 miles) of its streets with wider sidewalks, cycling lanes and lower speed limits, to make 'slow' modes safer after lockdown is lifted, whilst Paris and the Île-de-France region are rolling out a 650 km network of pop-up 'corona cycleways' in preparation for a post-pandemic world. These tactical interventions are creating huge opportunities for rapid behaviour change, and have the potential to be locked in to future urban planning and design.

Similarly, a third lesson relates to the format for future public transport, which is also likely to be very different from current arrangements. The virus has caused a collapse in ridership, as potential passengers are wary of mixing with strangers in crowded places, and operators deliberately run emptier vehicles to maintain social distancing. Until these conditions ease, revenue streams will be drastically depleted and there will be a considerable call on already crippled economies to financially support public transport systems.

Many former passengers are now working from home, and what proportion of these will resume their former role as commuters is uncertain. The move towards more locally circumscribed lives that the virus has engendered will support the growth of 20-minute districts in the longer term. However, more immediately, continued longer-distance public transport use remains essential to maintain critical urban functions, such as delivering often poorly paid service workers to city jobs from peripheral areas. Any attempt to replace public transport with fast, car-dominated transport would be unaffordable for cities and individuals, even if we ignore the massive cost to public and environmental health. In the meantime, shifting attention and resources towards walking, cycling and micromobility, while promoting measures to make public transport as safe as possible, would be a sensible balance to strike.

The evident inadequacy of prior planning for the coronavirus pandemic points to a fourth lesson, which is our extraordinary capacity to put into place an enormous number of measures, at great speed, when we are faced with a sudden and calamitous threat. What seems overwhelming in 'normal' times becomes manageable when there is no time for indecision—and that has produced almost unprecedented urgency, nimble policy-making and extensive behaviour change. In this book we have cited the example of motordom's successful campaign in the 1920s for more speed in the city as powerful evidence that rapid and widespread change in values and behaviour is achievable. We have argued that, by extension, a swift transformation to 'slow cities' is an equally feasible and realistic goal in the 2020s. The coronavirus crisis has provided an immediate revelation of what a changed world could look like, with lower speeds, far fewer cars and crashes, reduced CO_2 emissions and much cleaner air. Dramatic change is indeed possible.

The terrifying nature of the epidemic has highlighted our vulnerability. However, that concern provides a powerful impetus to ensure that, post-pandemic, we seize the chance for fundamental change, for a paradigm shift in the way that we plan, design and operate our cities. Indeed, it may be the best chance that we will ever get. The coronavirus crisis has shown us what we can do when we make health, rather than speed, a priority. The key is for society to grasp that the speed-induced climate and ecological emergencies are as serious and immediate a threat to life as is the coronavirus pandemic—because they are. As we have argued in this book, it may be no exaggeration to say that if the city itself is to survive, all future cities must be 'slow cities'.

Index

Note: Page numbers followed by "f" indicate figures, "t" indicate tables, and "b" indicate boxes.

I

J

K

L

M

R

T

U

V

W

Z

FSC
www.fsc.org
MIX
Papier | Fördert gute Waldnutzung
FSC® C083411

Kolibri 360 GmbH
Ferdinand-Jühlke-Straße 7
99095 Erfurt, Deutschland
produktsicherheit@kolibri360.de